Law and Force in the New International Order

Published under the auspices of
the American Society of International Law

Law and Force in the New International Order

Published under the auspices of
the American Society of International Law

Law and Force in the New International Order

EDITED BY
Lori Fisler Damrosch
and David J. Scheffer

Routledge
Taylor & Francis Group
LONDON AND NEW YORK

First published 1991 by Westview Press, Inc.

Published 2018 by Routledge
52 Vanderbilt Avenue, New York, NY 10017
2 Park Square, Milton Park, Abingdon, Oxon OX14 4RN

Routledge is an imprint of the Taylor & Francis Group, an informa business

Library of Congress Cataloging-in-Publication Data
Law and force in the new international order / edited by Lori Fisler Damrosch and David J. Scheffer.
p. cm.
Includes index.
ISBN 0-8133-1356-2 — ISBN 0-8133-1357-0 (pbk.)
1. Aggression (International law). 2. Intervention (International law). 3. Self-defense (International law). I. Damrosch, Lori F. (Lori Fisler). II. Scheffer, David J.
JX4471.L39 1991
341.6′2—dc20 91-15229
CIP

ISBN 13: 978-0-367-00438-5 (hbk)
ISBN 13: 978-0-367-15425-7 (pbk)

Contents

Preface

The end of the Cold War has focused new attention on international law, especially in areas that previously seemed to elude legal control. During the long decades when the United States and the Soviet Union were constantly struggling through proxy wars, covert activities, and projections of power around the globe, many questioned whether international law could ever be brought to bear to regulate such behavior. And if the superpowers were acting in many respects as if law had little relevance to their activities, it was hardly surprising that other actors questioned its relevance as well.

Momentous events of recent years have shown the tremendous potential for developing and applying international law, even in the area that has always presented the greatest challenge—the use of force. When the Iraqi army invaded and occupied Kuwait in August of 1990, the United States and the Soviet Union together with other major powers took a united position on the relevance of international law, its normative content, and its enforceability through decisions of the U.N. Security Council. This was the first time since the adoption of the U.N. Charter in 1945 that the five permanent members had acted in concert to enforce the international law governing the use of force against an aggressor state.

The groundwork for many of the recent changes in the outlook for international law was laid by changes in the long-held positions of the Soviet Union with respect to both law and foreign policy. Among the initiatives launched by Mikhail Gorbachev was the idea of the primacy of law over politics, in the international sphere as well as domestically. This idea formed one of the cornerstones of the "new political thinking" that has dominated Soviet foreign policy in recent years.

To American international lawyers, the idea that law should govern foreign relations was not a new one. On the contrary, U.S. leaders had pressed for this idea beginning in the late nineteenth century, though not always consistently. And there were many occasions when the actions of the U.S. government seemed out of compliance with the rules of law that the United States itself had promoted. On such occasions, the claim that law should not bind one superpower alone was frequently heard.

By the end of the 1980s, many American and Soviet international lawyers seemed at least to be speaking the same language about the non-use of force to achieve ideological aims. The Soviet Union had definitively repudiated the Brezhnev Doctrine—the argument that had been put forward in 1968 to justify the invasion of Czechoslovakia in the interests of the preservation of socialism and the promotion of class interests. The Soviet parliament had condemned both that invasion and the 1979 invasion of Afghanistan as violations of international law, thus bringing the Soviet view in line with long-held Western positions. The Reagan Doctrine—which at its core sanctioned U.S. military support for insurgencies against totalitarian governments being supported with arms from the Soviet Union—was not officially repudiated by the Bush administration, but the doctrine became increasingly irrelevant to U.S. foreign policy as Soviet expansionism contracted and the regional conflicts of the 1980s moved toward peaceful resolution. Yet in December of 1989 the United States invaded Panama, putting forth claims that bore at least some similarity to the discredited Brezhnev Doctrine. Could military force be applied for the sake of democracy, when its application for the preservation of socialism was thoroughly rejected? And in the Soviet Union, the central government's use of force to confront independence movements within some of its own republics raised fresh concerns that the Brezhnev Doctrine had risen from the dead to haunt national and sub-national groups struggling to assert sovereignty.

These issues and many more bearing upon the relationship of international law and the use of force following the Cold War were the focus of a joint U.S.-Soviet Conference on International Law and the Non-Use of Force held in Washington, D.C., on October 4-6, 1990. The conference was organized by the American Society of International Law and supported by the Ford Foundation. Approximately 100 international lawyers, scholars, government officials, and practitioners attended the conference. Leading authorities on international law in the United States and the Soviet Union delivered papers and commentaries on a wide spectrum of issues relating to the relationship between international law and the application of armed force to achieve political, military, economic, or humanitarian objectives.

The present volume is based on the conference. It constitutes the first published result of a collaborative effort by U.S. and Soviet experts to rethink international law in light of new political conditions. Special attention is given to the Iraq-Kuwait crisis, which was in progress at the time these papers were in preparation.

Part One focuses on the law of self-defense. Abram Chayes argues that the requirements of collective security can qualify the right of collective self-defense and that the Iraq-Kuwait crisis proved the merit of placing some limitations on the right of self-defense in deference to the primary responsibility of the Security Council when it is taking measures to deal with a situation involving use of force. Rein Mullerson, a Soviet scholar, points out how both the Soviet Union and the United States, as well as many other states, have made exaggerated and unfounded claims of self-defense. He believes that the end of the Cold War offers an opportunity to limit such elastic interpretations, including in situations involving indirect aggression. Michael Reisman believes that the United Nations is not yet an autonomous actor capable of implementing an effective collective security system. In his view, the real challenge facing the new international order is to clarify those policies and contingent events that legitimize unilateral uses of force. Genuine self-determination, Reisman writes, has become the basic postulate of political legitimacy and thus its advancement may justify the unilateral use of force. The commentaries by Richard N. Gardner and David B. Rivkin, Jr., that conclude Part One criticize the Chayes thesis on the relationship between U.N. action and unilateral actions by states; they also address other issues concerning the use of force in self-defense.

Part Two examines collective security through the United Nations, with particular focus again on the Iraq-Kuwait crisis. Oscar Schachter surveys uses of force authorized by the United Nations and regional organizations, including armed force as an enforcement measure taken by the Security Council under Chapter VII of the U.N. Charter or by regional bodies, self-defense measures approved by the United Nations, U.N. peacekeeping forces, and joint action by the five permanent members of the Security Council. Schachter construes Chapter VII as enabling the Security Council to exercise considerable discretion in authorizing military force. Nikolai Krylov of the Soviet Union offers several proposals for strengthening the U.N. collective security system, including the deployment of peacekeeping forces on territory threatened by external aggression. In his commentary, David J. Scheffer examines the relationship between collective security and collective self-defense and argues that various provisions of Chapter VII can be interpreted with flexibility to respond to modern conflicts such as the Iraq-Kuwait crisis.

Part Three addresses four categories of the law of intervention: by invitation, against illegitimate regimes, for humanitarian purposes, and to combat international terrorism and drug trafficking. John Lawrence Hargrove presents a framework of criteria for assessing the legality of intervention by invitation. He argues that international law should permit the use of armed force in cases of internal disorder where consent is obtained from either the host government (provided it is not anti-democratic or repressive) or a dissident group with clearly democratic intentions seeking to replace a clearly anti-democratic and repressive government. Rein Mullerson of the USSR reviews cases where governments have claimed that they were invited by another government to use force on its territory and concludes that the facts relating to the external military threat as well as the character of the invitation itself are often dubious: both the USSR and the United States have made spurious or at least questionable claims of invitation. Mullerson also believes that a government intervening in cases of internal disorder bears a heavy burden of proof that its intervention does not contradict the principles of noninterference, non-use or threat of force, or self-determination of peoples. Commentaries by Ruth Wedgwood and Benjamin Ferencz suggest ways that interventions by invitation can be brought under more meaningful legal control.

Igor I. Lukashuk of the USSR reviews the role of the United Nations in categorizing certain governments as illegitimate and accepting the principle of intervention, under certain circumstances, to change those governments. He examines intervention as a means of combatting illegitimate regimes when there have been mass and gross violations of human rights. Thomas M. Franck discusses the merits of creating a new legal entitlement that would guarantee all citizens of every state the right to participate democratically in the process of governance. Franck believes that the international community needs to create a standard of democratic legitimacy, a system of monitoring and collective enforcement mechanisms, such as denial of access to international and bilateral privileges and facilities. But in Franck's view it is premature to consider military intervention against such illegitimate regimes unless they qualify as threats to international peace and security. Commentaries by Anne-Marie Burley and Ved Nanda draw attention to the root causes of illegitimacy of regimes and to some of the inconsistencies in the practice of states taking sanctions against them.

In his chapter on humanitarian intervention, Tom J. Farer critically examines interventions to combat massive and flagrant violations of human rights. He analyzes the differing jurisprudential approaches of the classical school of international law on the one hand and the realist school on the other, concluding that the former condemns humanitarian intervention as contrary to the U.N. Charter while the latter would legitimize it. Vladimir Kartashkin of the USSR points to the international criminality of mass and flagrant human rights violations and stresses the power of the Security Council to authorize sanctions and military enforcement action to stop such violations. Commentaries by Theodor Meron and Lori Fisler Damrosch consider the possibilities for action under U.N. auspices to terminate human rights violations through military means, as well as some of the objections to such action.

Geoffrey M. Levitt explains that while forcible responses to international terrorism have required re-sculpting the classical self-defense paradigm, the use of force to combat international drug trafficking requires an entirely new legal foundation. Yuri Kolosov of the USSR argues for limitations on the right of self-defense and calls on the U.N. Security Council to undertake collective sanctions against offending states. Commentaries by Jane E. Stromseth and John F. Murphy stress the desirability of combatting terrorism and drug trafficking through cooperative rather than forcible measures.

Part Four examines limitations and safeguards in arms control agreements. John B. Rhinelander provides an overview of existing agreements as well as those that may enter into force in the immediate future. Commentaries by John H. McNeill and Edwin Smith focus on dispute settlement under arms control agreements, as well as on the dynamic rather than static nature of arms control regimes.

In Part Five Richard B. Bilder offers a comprehensive study of judicial procedures relating to the use of force and the advantages and disadvantages of using international tribunals to resolve such cases. Bilder calls for a review of the U.S. policy in current discussions with the USSR to negotiate an exclusion of all use-of-force cases from the jurisdiction of the International Court of Justice. Stephen M. Schwebel, a judge at the Court, explains his dissent in the recent case brought by Nicaragua against the United States, in which he criticized both the Court's fact-finding in respect of the conduct of Nicaragua and its treatment of the international law concerning indirect aggression. The commentary by Gennady Danilenko of the USSR considers trends toward enhancing use of the International Court of Justice, while the commentary by Barry Carter encourages resort to other mechanisms such as arbitration.

It is hoped that the diversity of opinion expressed throughout this book will point toward a manageable synthesis of views between and among U.S. and Soviet legal scholars on how military force can and should be legally regulated in the future. For if the world that emerges from the Cold War is to evolve into a new international order—one that transcends past expectations and realities—then it will be the special responsibility of the United States and the Soviet Union to conduct their foreign relations with an enlightened, mutual understanding of the principles of international law.

Lori Fisler Damrosch
David J. Scheffer

Acknowledgments

This volume has been prepared as a project of the U.S.-Soviet Joint Research Program in International Law, which is sponsored in the United States by the American Society of International Law, and in the Soviet Union by the Soviet Association of International Law and the Institute of State and Law of the Academy of Sciences of the USSR. The Ford Foundation has generously funded the program through a grant to the American Society of International Law.

The editors would like to acknowledge, in particular, the administrative support of the Carnegie Endowment for International Peace and the contributions of the following individuals who assisted in the organization of the conference and the editing of the chapters:

From the Carnegie Endowment for International Peace: interns Michele E. Klubert (Case Western Reserve University, B.A. 1991) and Steven J. Rubick (Texas Christian University, B.A. 1991) for their research assistance; William Keenan for his help with copy editing; Lisa Tepper for her assistance with preparation of the index; and Toula Papanicolas for secretarial support.

From the Columbia University School of Law: Karen Knop (LL.M. 1990); Daryl Mundis (J.D. expected 1992); Jonathan Narins (J.D. 1991); Sarah Osborn (J.D. 1991); Daniel Penn (J.D. expected 1992); and Pranav Trivedi (J.D. 1991). Their Russian language skills were invaluable in the translation of the papers of the Soviet contributors and in numerous research tasks.

L.F.D.
D.J.S.

About the Contributors

Richard B. Bilder is Burrus-Bascom Professor of Law at the University of Wisconsin-Madison. He has served with the Office of the Legal Adviser of the U.S. Department of State and as an arbitrator in international disputes.

Anne-Marie Burley is an assistant professor of law at the University of Chicago.

Barry Carter is a professor of law at Georgetown University and previously served on the staff of the National Security Council.

Abram Chayes is the Felix Frankfurter Professor of Law at Harvard University. He served as Legal Adviser of the U.S. Department of State in the Kennedy administration and as counsel to Nicaragua in the World Court case brought by Nicaragua against the United States.

Lori Fisler Damrosch is a professor of law at Columbia University and has previously served in the Office of the Legal Adviser of the U.S. Department of State.

Gennady Danilenko is a senior research scholar with the Institute of State and Law of the Academy of Sciences of the USSR.

Tom J. Farer is a professor of law and international relations at American University and a former president of the Inter-American Human Rights Commission.

Benjamin Ferencz is an adjunct professor of international law at Pace Law School, a Senior Special Fellow of the U.N. Institute for Training and Research, and a former Nuremberg war crimes prosecutor.

Thomas M. Franck is the Murry and Ida Becker Professor of Law and Director, Center for International Studies at New York University. He is the former director of the U.N. Institute for Training and Research.

Richard N. Gardner is the Henry L. Moses Professor of Law and International Organization at Columbia University. He was Deputy Assistant Secretary of State for International Organization Affairs in the Kennedy administration and Ambassador to Italy in the Carter administration.

John Lawrence Hargrove is the executive director of the American Society of International Law.

Vladimir Kartashkin is a senior research scholar with the Institute of State and Law of the Academy of Sciences of the USSR.

Yuri M. Kolosov is a senior research scholar with the Institute of International Relations of the Academy of Sciences of the USSR.

Nikolai B. Krylov is a senior research scholar with the Institute of State and Law of the Academy of Sciences of the USSR.

Geoffrey M. Levitt is a lawyer in private practice in Washington, D.C. He formerly served in the Office of the Legal Adviser of the U.S. Department of State.

Igor I. Lukashuk is a senior research scholar with the Institute of State and Law of the Academy of Sciences of the USSR.

John H. McNeill is Charles H. Stockton Professor of International Law at the U.S. Naval War College for the 1990-91 academic year. He also serves as Assistant General Counsel for International Affairs and Intelligence, U.S. Department of Defense.

Theodor Meron is a professor of law at New York University and a former representative to the United Nations.

Rein Mullerson is the head of the international law section of the Institute of State and Law of the Academy of Sciences of the USSR and is a member of the U.N. Human Rights Committee.

John F. Murphy is a professor of law at Villanova University.

Ved Nanda is the Thompson G. Marsh Professor of Law at the University of Denver.

W. Michael Reisman is the Wesley Hohfeld Professor of Jurisprudence at Yale University.

John B. Rhinelander is a lawyer in private practice in Washington, D.C. He served as legal adviser to the U.S. delegation in the strategic arms negotiations that led to the SALT I agreements and Anti-Ballistic Missile Treaty of 1972.

David B. Rivkin, Jr., is associate general counsel at the U.S. Department of Energy.

Oscar Schachter is the Hamilton Fish Professor Emeritus of International Law and Diplomacy at Columbia University and served as a United Nations Legal Adviser from 1946 to 1966. He is a member of the Institut de Droit International and past president of the American Society of International Law.

David J. Scheffer is a senior associate in international and national security law at the Carnegie Endowment for International Peace.

Stephen M. Schwebel is a judge of the International Court of Justice. Previously he was Deputy Legal Adviser of the U.S. Department of State.

Edwin Smith is a professor of law and international relations at the University of Southern California.

Jane E. Stromseth is an associate professor of law at Georgetown University. She formerly served in the Office of the Legal Adviser of the U.S. Department of State.

Ruth Wedgwood is an associate professor of law at Yale University.

The views expressed in this volume are those of the contributors in their individual capacities and not of the American Society of International Law or any organization or governmental body with which the contributors are or have been affiliated.

PART ONE

Self-Defense

1

The Use of Force in the Persian Gulf

Abram Chayes

One of the most serious, relevant, and fateful questions concerning the use of force under international law is what actions were open—and under what circumstances—to the forces of the United States and other countries arrayed against Iraq in the Persian Gulf region in 1990. The unspoken assumption of high government officials and certain commentators in the early months of the Iraq-Kuwait crisis was that the United States and its coalition partners, even in the absence of a further attack by Iraq or authorization of the Security Council, remained legally free to take military action upon their own decision. That was the position taken in early August 1990 by the United States on the question of the use of naval force in the Persian Gulf to enforce the U.N. sanctions. The U.S. Secretary of State and others said that such action was permissible as an exercise of the right of collective self-defense of Kuwait under Article 51 of the U.N. Charter, and thus required no further Security Council action.[1]

Cooler heads prevailed. U.S. naval vessels fired shots across the bows of two Iraqi tankers, but took no further action when the ships continued on course.[2] The Security Council was convened to consider the question, and in short order passed Resolution 665, calling on

> ...Member States co-operating with the government of Kuwait which are deploying maritime forces to the area to use such measures commensurate to the specific circumstances as may be necessary under the authority of the Security Council to halt all inward and outward maritime shipping in order to inspect and verify their cargoes and destinations and to ensure strict implementation of the provisions related to such shipping laid down in Resolution 661 (1990) [the sanctions resolution].[3]

Interception and boarding of vessels proceeding to or from Iraq was carried out under the authority of that resolution.

To understand the legal situation, some background on the factual developments of the Iraq-Kuwait crisis and Security Council action is necessary. When Iraq invaded Kuwait on August 2, 1990, the United States and some other nations immediately blocked funds and imposed other economic countermeasures.[4] The Security Council met promptly and condemned the invasion.[5] On August 6, "acting under Chapter VII of the Charter of the United Nations," the Council adopted Resolution 661, imposing comprehensive economic sanctions against Iraq. By virtue of Article 25 of the Charter, these measures are binding on all members of the United Nations. The sanctions later were expanded to include the interruption of air traffic to and from Iraq.[6] U.S. officials and others indicated that compliance with these decisions was satisfactory.[7]

On August 9, Iraq announced that it had annexed Kuwait, and the Security Council promptly declared the annexation null and void.[8] It also adopted resolutions dealing with hostages held by Iraq and the attacks by Iraq against embassies in Kuwait.[9] In all of these resolutions, the Council noted its decision to keep the matter on its agenda for further action as needed.

Also in early August, in the face of widespread reports that Iraqi troops were massing on the southern border of Kuwait, the government of Saudi Arabia invited the deployment of U.S. troops on its territory to deter a possible attack by Iraq.[10] President Bush promptly dispatched ground and air elements, stating that the purpose of the deployment was "to deter further Iraqi aggression." He declared that the mission of the troops "is wholly defensive...They will not initiate hostilities, but they will defend themselves, the Kingdom of Saudi Arabia and other friends in the Gulf."[11] Over the next seven weeks, these initial deployments were increased to about 140,000 troops. Other countries, including a number of Arab states, sent significant contingents to join the U.S. forces.[12]

Some U.S. naval forces were already in the Persian Gulf at the time of the invasion, and these were significantly augmented. On the sea too, the U.S. fleet was joined by ships of other countries.[13] As noted above, for a short time the United States maintained that these forces could be used to blockade Iraq as a means of enforcing the sanctions, but, except for the ineffectual shots across the bow, they took no action until the Security Council authorized it.

By the fall of 1990, there were two situations in which we could expect substantially universal agreement among international lawyers (Iraqi partisans aside, perhaps) that the use of force against Iraq would have been permissible:

First, under the authority of an Article 42 resolution of the Security Council. Article 42 of the U.N. Charter does not require that the Security

Council should direct or order members to use force. An authorizing resolution will do, as in the case of Resolution 665 on the use of naval force to enforce the sanctions against Iraq and a similar action in 1966, authorizing the British to interdict oil tankers bound for Beria in Mozambique in violation of the sanctions that had been ordered against Rhodesia.[14] Furthermore, neither the text of the Charter nor such practice as there is suggests that the Security Council's power is contingent on any prior action by the Military Staff Committee or on the activation of procedures under Article 43 for advance agreement on the numbers and types of forces a member undertakes to put at the disposal of the Security Council.

Second, use of force also would be permitted (subject to limitations as to proportionality) in response to a large-scale armed action by Iraqi forces against Saudi Arabia, the coalition forces deployed there, or the naval contingents in the Persian Gulf.

Beyond these propositions lies a considerable area of disputed terrain. Among the most important of the controverted questions—not because it was necessarily the most probable but because it throws the issues into sharpest relief—was the suggestion noted earlier that the United States was free, even in the absence of further provocation by Iraq or authorization by the Security Council, to use force against Iraq by virtue of some continuing right of collective self-defense emanating from the original attack on Kuwait. In other words, so the argument runs, the original deployments in Saudi Arabia and the Persian Gulf region were made in response to the armed attack on Kuwait and thus could be seen as an exercise of the inherent right of collective self-defense. The Security Council could be said to have acknowledged this position in its reference in Resolution 665 to "Member States co-operating with the government of Kuwait which are deploying maritime forces to the area." It rests with each of those states, perhaps in consultation with Kuwait and others whose forces were also at risk, to decide whether the measures taken in response to the Iraqi aggression were sufficient, and if not, what further action would be needed.

The textual argument against this position, it seems to me, is very strong. Article 51 is not an affirmative grant of a right of self-defense but a statement of the situations in which the exercise of an "inherent right" is not precluded by the Charter. But those situations are subject to a limit of time. They endure only "until the Security Council has taken the measures necessary to maintain international peace and security."

Who is to judge whether measures authorized by the Security Council are sufficient to maintain international peace and security? Again, the text of the Charter argues strongly that the function belongs to the Security Council. Article 39 says the Council shall "decide what measures shall be taken in accordance with Articles 41 and 42 to maintain or restore international peace and security." The same phrase, "measures necessary to maintain international peace and security," is the key to the temporal limitation on the inherent right of self-defense in Article 51. Even more telling is Article 42, the article that empowers the Security Council to adopt measures involving the use of force, which begins: "Should the Security Council consider that measures provided for in Article 41 [i.e., diplomatic and economic sanctions] would be inadequate or have proved to be inadequate...." It seems clear that all of these provisions of Chapter VII—which is entitled "Action with Respect to Threats to the Peace, Breaches of the Peace, and Acts of Aggression"—are interlocking and that the critical phrase, "measures necessary to maintain international peace and security," carries the same meaning in all of them.

In the larger scheme of the Charter, it is the Security Council that has "primary responsibility for the maintenance of international peace and security,"[15] which is recognized as primarily a political rather than a legal task. To carry out that responsibility, the Council, once seized of a matter under Chapter VII, must have the authority to make the political judgments as to the requirements of the situation and the measures necessary to deal with it. Security Council preemption, moreover, reinforces the fundamental objective of Article 2(4) and Article 51 to confine the permissible occasions for the unilateral use of force to the narrowest possible range, where it is immediately and universally apparent that armed response is required.[16]

During the Cold War, when the Security Council was immobilized by reciprocal vetoes, the argument was perhaps available that a state acting in individual or collective self-defense could not be expected to forgo continuing action simply because the Council was debating the situation, with no likelihood of a serious substantive outcome. This also would be the case if the Council's action is plainly incommensurate with the seriousness of the situation. In those instances it would be a plausible argument that the Council was simply not exercising its functions, so that the preemption contemplated by Article 51 when the Council was truly addressing the situation does not come into operation.[17]

From the beginning of the Iraq-Kuwait crisis, as has been widely acknowledged, the Security Council worked "as it was supposed to work" according to the design of its framers.[18] It cannot be argued that the Council failed to address the situation with appropriate gravity or to adopt measures with real impact or to strengthen those measures as the need became apparent. If the United Nations works as intended, judgments as to the ultimate objectives of U.N. action, the sufficiency of the measures to be taken, how long to wait for the sanctions to take effect, and the like are consigned to the Council, which acts by a majority of nine out of fifteen members, including the concurring or abstaining votes of the permanent members. In the process of reaching those decisions the United

States necessarily has a very important voice. Indeed, there is both scope and need for American leadership. The United States can ensure by use of the veto that the Council will not act against its interests. But if the United States cannot induce the necessary number of other Security Council members to agree that additional measures involving the use of force are necessary, the Charter would clearly seem to preclude unilateral action.

"Realists" often portray this kind of analysis as an effort to impose abstract legal constraints on action that is otherwise sound, wise, and effective. And lawyers bearing responsibility for advice to a political leader are understandably reluctant to reduce the available options or otherwise tell him that he cannot do something he wants to do. In the Persian Gulf situation, however, as is true more often than not, the international legal analysis highlights the practical realities of the situation.

Visions of surgical strikes and costless decapitating attacks may dance in the heads of armchair strategists and Pentagon planners, but in real life they almost never come off, except perhaps in the Caribbean. A large-scale attack on Iraq without immediate provocation, even if "successful," entailed very high risks of significant casualties (including many non-combatants in Iraq and elsewhere), destruction of major oil installations, severely negative long-term impacts on the U.S. position with the Arab states, and escalation to a general Middle Eastern war.

As a *practical* matter, in the fall of 1990, it was no longer possible for the United States to use force in the Persian Gulf without the concurrence of those engaged with it. Because these coalition states joined in the U.N. effort, they too became exposed to the military, political, and economic consequences of any military action the United States took. Indeed, the first consequence of such action would have been to shatter the international consensus that gave legitimacy and strength to the enterprise. Among the first to withdraw could well have been the Arab states upon whose request the U.S. presence in the region was based in the first place, and without whose continuing support it could not be sustained.

Between the two poles of a substantial attack by Iraq on the forces deployed against it, and no further aggressive action, lay an almost infinite spectrum of lesser provocations. They included:

- more limited uses of armed force against a variety of targets and with a variety of means;
- assaults against the hostages, again with a broad potential range in terms of extent and brutality;
- terrorist actions, also with a host of potential targets, linkages to the Gulf theater and severity;
- covert or open armed action against a third state such as Israel; and

- preparations, open or secret, to use chemical weapons or other weapons of mass destruction.

In such circumstances as these, opinion, at least among American scholars, has been far from unanimous. The range of factual contingency is so wide and so difficult to specify in advance that it is neither possible nor profitable to try to render judgment on the current state of international law in this or that hypothetical setting.

Is that the limit of what the international lawyer can say in this situation? Are we reduced to throwing up our hands as we contemplate a landscape of bewildering shades of gray? Must we succumb to the kind of enumeration of "yeas" and "nays" of (mostly partisan) publicists that exposes international law and lawyers to the charge of academic abstraction disconnected from reality?

We can venture something more—if not a substantive statement of the law, then a framework of analysis. American lawyers are familiar with Supreme Court Justice Robert Jackson's effort to grapple with the problem of unilateral emergency action by an American president in a case that overturned the seizure of the nation's steel mills at the height of the Korean war.[19] Jackson laid out an approach to the legal evaluation of the exercise of presidential power that has dominated subsequent decision and scholarly comment. He classified presidential action in three categories:

1. When the President acts pursuant to an express or implied authorization of Congress, his authority is at its maximum, for it includes all that he possesses in his own right plus all that Congress can delegate. In these circumstances, and in these only, may he be said (for what it may be worth) to personify the federal sovereignty....

2. When the President acts in the absence of either congressional grant or denial of authority, he can only rely on his own independent powers, but there is a zone of twilight in which he and Congress may have concurrent authority, or in which its distribution is uncertain. Therefore, congressional inertia, indifference or quiescence may sometimes, at least as a practical matter, enable, if not invite, measures on independent presidential responsibility. In this area, any actual test of power is likely to rest on the imperatives of events and contemporary imponderables rather than on abstract theories of law.

3. When the President takes measures incompatible with the express or implied will of Congress, his power is at its lowest ebb... Presidential claims to a power at once so conclusive and preclusive

> must be scrutinized with caution, for what is at stake is the equilibrium established by our constitutional system.[20]

Justice Jackson, of course, was addressing the complex question of separation of powers under the Constitution of the United States, and admittedly his analysis cannot be taken over whole hog into the realm of international law. Yet it seems to me that his approach to the problem of powers shared and divided among many actors is suggestive and can be adapted for our use.

Thus we might say, in parallel with Justice Jackson's Category 1, that if the United States used force in the Gulf with the authorization of the Security Council, its position, both legal and political, would be at the maximum, for then and only then could it claim to be acting with the full authority and in a sense as the delegate of the international community. The analogue to Category 3—action in the teeth of a disabling resolution of the Council—is unlikely, not only formally because of the veto, but also as a matter of the practical politics of the situation.

If, however, as in Category 2, the United States were to have acted when the Security Council remained silent, the legal position would have been much weaker and the political position much more vulnerable. In the fall of 1990, it would have been hard to impute Security Council inaction to "inertia, indifference or quiescence," and it hardly seemed likely that an effectively functioning Security Council would refuse to respond to a truly significant provocation.

If, as Jackson says, in this category "the result of any actual test of power is likely to rest on the imperatives of events and contemporary imponderables," then actors seeking to justify the unilateral use of force must look carefully to the context of the action. What was the degree of provocation? What efforts were made to get Security Council authorization, if not by advance approval then at least by subsequent ratification? What is the nature and quality of the evidence that is put forward to distinguish provocation from pretext? How scrupulously does the action observe the limits of necessity and proportionality? In the end, legal and practical judgment on the action, and even its success, will depend heavily on the weight and configuration of these imperatives and imponderables.

But the Jackson approach amounts to more than just another balancing test. It maps out the lay of the land and shows us which way the presumptions lie. In the Persian Gulf situation it suggests that the presumption against unilateral use of force, always heavy, gains even greater strength. In my view, it could not be overcome except on a showing of the most urgent necessity.

On November 29, 1990, the Security Council took the critical step. It adopted Resolution 678 authorizing "Member States co-operating with the government of Kuwait, unless Iraq on or before 15 January 1991 fully implements the foregoing resolutions [including withdrawal from Kuwait and release of hostages], to use all necessary means to uphold and implement Security Council Resolution 660 and all subsequent relevant resolutions and to restore international peace and security in the area." Further, it requests "all States to provide appropriate support for the actions undertaken in pursuance of Paragraph 2 of this Resolution."[21]

In a sense, the action of the Security Council vindicates the foregoing analysis. Although the United States never formally acknowledged that Resolution 678 was legally required before it could use its ground and air forces in the Gulf region, in both the form of discourse and argumentation in support of the resolution, legal and political elements were so inextricably intertwined that, as is often the case, it is useless to try to attribute proximate causation to either.

At the same time, since Resolution 678 was addressed to "Member States co-operating with the government of Kuwait," it implicitly acknowledged that troops are on the scene in the exercise of the inherent right of collective self-defense. Thus, the elements of Justice Jackson's Category 1 were in place. Subsequent use of force in the Gulf region was grounded on a combination of the collective authority of the Security Council and the right to act "unilaterally" derived from Article 51.

Still, the resolution was an authorization, not a command, under Article 42. It does not follow that the power it granted necessarily must be invoked. Still less does it follow that, because a grace period was provided until a day certain, efforts to resolve the situation and enforce the resolutions without war must be abandoned on that date.

Resolution 678 in effect was a delegation to the President of the United States of the discretion to decide, on the basis of circumstances as he appreciated them and with such consultation of the states associated with him as he deemed necessary, when to use force. Given that the vast bulk of the financial and military costs of the operation were being borne by the United States, it was hard for the Security Council to decline to make such a delegation. The grant, however, did not eliminate but heightened the necessity for judgment in the exercise of discretion. As with all such delegations, not the existence of discretion but the wisdom of the judgment determines the quality of the outcome.

There are wider implications of the decisions and actions in the Iraq-Kuwait crisis for international lawyers, and even for world statesmen. In a sense, we are the beneficiaries of a second chance, something that does not happen often in the inexorable world of international politics. It is almost as if the Security Council had been in suspended animation since 1945, and is now stirring to life new and untouched. The Security Council of the future will be affected decisively by the precedents set in this first case where it has been "working as intended."

That future promises to be no less dangerous than the past, as the crisis in the Persian Gulf amply demonstrated. Indeed, events in the Middle East have confirmed the already conventional wisdom that the disappearance of the inhibiting shadow of potential nuclear war between the superpowers will permit bloodier and more intractable international disputes to emerge.

The United Nations is not the only international instrument for dealing with such disputes, but over the past few years the United Nations, in the person of the U.N. Secretary-General acting in harness with the Security Council and its permanent members, has shown itself to be a powerful catalyst for peacemaking, peacekeeping, and peaceful settlement. And although it can act only through and by the cooperation of its members, it has often been the indispensable instrument for concerting and coordinating the efforts of its members to these ends. In the Iraq-Kuwait crisis, the Security Council accepted its responsibilities under the Charter and exercised them with courage, energy, and wise deliberation.

The most important long-term impact of the crisis, certainly for those concerned with international law (particularly the law governing the use of force) and international institutions, may well be on this new and still fragile growth. If the Security Council is to be preserved and strengthened for the role it was designed to play, it cannot be used simply as a forum for consultation, still less to provide legal cover for unilaterally mandated ends. As the organ of the international community with primary responsibility in situations threatening international peace and security, it must exercise genuine powers of decision. That means that its policies and actions dealing with such situations must be accepted even by states that disagree.

Such a position is the one prescribed by international law. In a world where power is increasingly diffused and mobilization of power on the basis of ideology is increasingly unavailable, it is the position dictated by practical reality as well.

Notes

1. *See Putting Teeth in an Embargo: How U.S. Convinced the U.N.,* N.Y. Times, Aug. 30, 1990, at A1, col. 4; *U.S. Set to Enforce Embargo on Iraq,* Washington Post, Aug. 13, 1990, at A1, col. 5; *see also Transcript of U.S. Statement About Measures Against Iraq,* N.Y. Times, Aug. 13, 1990, at A11, col. 1.

2. *U.S. Warship Fires Warning at Iraqis,* N.Y. Times, August 19, 1990, at A11, col. 1.

3. U.N. Doc. S/RES/665 (1990), adopted 13 votes to 0 with 2 abstentions.

4. *Bush, in Freezing Assets, Bars $30 Billion to Hussein,* N.Y. Times, Aug. 3, 1990, at A9, col. 1; *West Europeans Join U.S. in Condemning Invasion, id.,* at A10, col. 2.

5. U.N. Doc. S/RES/660 (1990), adopted 14 votes to 0; Yemen abstained.

6. U.N. Doc. S/RES/670 (1990), adopted 14 votes to 1.

7. *Weighing the Balance between War and Diplomacy,* N.Y. Times, Oct. 7, 1990, at A20, col. 3; *Can the Sanctions Work? Many Aides Are Doubtful,* N.Y. Times, Nov. 25, 1990, at A12, col. 5; *Sanctions on Iraq Appear Effective as Neighbors Block Trade,* N.Y. Times, Aug. 12, 1990, at A13, col. 1.

8. U.N. Doc. S/RES/662 (1990), adopted unanimously.

9. *E.g.,* U.N. Doc. S/RES/664 (1990) and U.N. Doc. S/RES/667 (1990), adopted unanimously.

10. *Bush Sends U.S. Force to Saudi Arabia as Kingdom Agrees to Confront Iraq,* N.Y. Times, Aug. 8, 1990, at A1, col. 6.

11. *Excerpts From Bush's Statement on U.S. Defense of Saudis,* N.Y. Times, Aug. 9, 1990, at A15, col. 1.

12. *See, e.g., Arabs Vote to Send Troops to Help Saudis,* N.Y. Times, Aug. 11, 1990, at A1, col. 6; *U.S. Says Its Troops in the Gulf Could Reach 100,000 in Months, id.,* at A1, col. 4.

13. *Ships Turn Away from Ports as Iraq Embargo Tightens,* N.Y. Times, Aug. 14, 1990, at A1, col. 6.

14. U.N. Doc. S/RES/221 (1966), adopted 10 votes to 0 with 5 abstentions.

15. U.N. CHARTER art. 24.

16. *See, e.g.,* I. BROWNLIE, INTERNATIONAL LAW AND THE USE OF FORCE BY STATES 255-256 (1963); L. HENKIN, HOW NATIONS BEHAVE 141 (2d ed. 1979).

17. *See, e.g.,* Franck, *Who Killed Article 2(4)? or: Changing Norms Governing the Use of Force by States,* 64 AM. J. INT'L L. 809 (1970).

18. Address Before a Joint Session of the Congress on the Persian Gulf Crisis and the Federal Budget Deficit, 26 WEEKLY COMP. PRES. DOC. 1358, 1360 (Sept. 11, 1990).

19. Youngstown Sheet & Tube Co. v. Sawyer, 343 U.S. 549, 634 (1952) (Jackson, J., concurring).

20. *Id.* at 645.

21. U.N. Doc. S/RES/678 (1990), adopted by 12 votes to 2 with 1 abstention.

2

Self-Defense in the Contemporary World

Rein Mullerson

The new era in Soviet-American relations has brought about a changed international system. This has happened to a great extent because of a complete renewal of the Soviet Union in its domestic as well as international politics. In this new era we can approach questions of use or non-use of force in international relations without any ideological biases. We can evaluate past and current situations in the light of legal norms and not of ideological doctrines, whether they be the Brezhnev or Reagan doctrines. Even if we cannot agree on every point, we will understand each other better and narrow our differences.

Violence is often framed in the context of self-defense. Self-defense was cited by the USSR and East European countries when they introduced troops into Czechoslovakia in 1968, and by the Soviet Union when it invaded Afghanistan in 1979; Iraq and Iran both claimed self-defense as a basis for their positions in 1980; and the United States relied on the principle to justify its actions against Nicaragua in the 1980s and its intervention in Grenada in 1983. More often than not the claim of a right of self-defense is joined with other legal arguments such as the invitation of a lawful government and the defense of one's own citizens. In all of these instances references to self-defense have been disputed by other governments, international organizations, world public opinion, and many authoritative specialists in international law. The overwhelming majority of instances of the use of force in which one of the parties (or even both) referred to the right of self-defense, including all the cases mentioned above except the Iran-Iraq war, occurred in the context of the ideological and political struggle between East and West. That would necessarily inform the juridical evaluation of the behavior of the parties in a conflict, especially by the participants themselves. What was self-defense in the eyes and especially in the words of one party was considered aggression or provocation in the eyes and words of another. One side's self-defense was the other side's aggression.

Concerning self-defense, Professor Oscar Schachter properly notes that in most cases "the differences between states have arisen from divergent perceptions of the facts and motives rather than from conflicting views of the applicable law."[1] Nonetheless, the resolution of the problem is complicated by differences in interpretation of the existing norms regulating the exercise of the right of self-defense.

The clearest ideological approach to self-defense and to the permissibility of the use of force in international relations—one viewed through the prism of the East-West confrontation—appears in the so-called doctrines of Brezhnev and Reagan.

In 1968 the aggression of the USSR and its Warsaw Pact allies against Czechoslovakia was accompanied by—in addition to a reference to the right of self-defense according to Article 51 of the U.N. Charter[2] and an alleged invitation of the Czech authorities—an ideological and essentially anti-legal justification for the actions taken. *Pravda* asserted at the time that those who saw a violation of sovereignty and of the right to self-determination in the introduction of troops of five socialist countries were measuring the events with the aid of bourgeois law, losing sight of the class approach, and forgetting that laws and legal norms are subordinate to the laws of class struggle and social development. Therefore, Communists of the fraternal countries could not allow the socialist governments to refrain from taking action in the name of some abstractly understood concept of sovereignty.[3]

Such an ideological argument undermines and reduces to zero all juridical bases, essentially repeating the approach of E.A. Korovin to intervention: It is forbidden against socialist countries but permitted for the sake of disseminating the idea of socialism.[4]

As justification for the invasion of Afghanistan in December of 1979, the Soviet Union relied on Article 51 of the U.N. Charter, as well as on a bilateral treaty of friendship, good-neighborliness, and cooperation and an invitation by the official authorities in Afghanistan. Reference to the utilization of a right of self-defense in that case, as in the invasion of Czechoslovakia, is all the more incomprehensible since the Soviet Union has always officially supported a narrow interpretation of the term "armed attack" in Article 51 and thus of self-defense.[5] Therefore, even if there had been foreign interference by means of armed bands and aid to the opponents of the Kabul regime, the Soviet Union still should not have relied on Article 51 in the invasion of Afghanistan.

In addition, in objecting to discussion in the Security Council and General Assembly of the introduction of Soviet troops into Afghanistan, the Soviet representative declared that such a discussion would constitute interference by the United Nations in the domestic affairs of Afghanistan in contravention of Article 2(7) of the Charter.[6] In that event it was completely incomprehensible for the Soviet Union to refer to Article 51 of the Charter. Indeed, upon resorting to action in accordance with that article, the USSR should have immediately reported the measures undertaken to the Security Council so that it could adopt measures necessary for the maintenance of international peace and security.

Significantly, the majority of governments and world public opinion did not accept the Soviet Union's legal arguments. The U.N. vote is the most eloquent witness to this fact. In the Security Council the resolution condemning the presence of foreign troops in Afghanistan and calling for their immediate removal received thirteen votes for and two against (USSR and German Democratic Republic); the resolution was not adopted because of the Soviet veto. On a similar resolution in the General Assembly, 104 governments voted for and eighteen against, and eighteen abstained.[7]

As for the United States, in the 1980s the use of armed force against Grenada and Nicaragua occurred if not exclusively then chiefly in the context of the ideological and political rivalry between East and West. If the use of force by the Soviet Union in Czechoslovakia and to a certain degree in Afghanistan was a manifestation of the so-called Brezhnev doctrine, then the action of the United States against Grenada and Nicaragua had its ideological and political foundation in the Reagan doctrine, which was expressed in a series of speeches by Reagan and particularly in the actions of the United States in the 1980s. From the perspective of the right to self-defense, that doctrine stipulates that, "Support for freedom fighters is self-defense and totally consistent with the O.A.S. and U.N. Charters."[8]

Jeane Kirkpatrick and Allan Gerson write:

> Like most American "doctrines," the Reagan Doctrine emerged in response to circumstances: it was developed in response to the Soviets' objective of a global empire and in response to Soviet claims of legitimacy in their imperial venture embodied in the Brezhnev Doctrine and the doctrine of "national liberation wars." More specifically, the Reagan Doctrine was a response to the Soviet Union's efforts to hurriedly establish Marxist-Leninist governments in Third World countries and incorporate these into its "socialist world system."[9]

This is not the place for an explication of how much truth there is in that assertion, although there is undoubtedly some. The Soviet Union, governed by ideological dogma, in fact did attempt to spread both its influence and its ideology. However, in a number of cases the spread of

Communist ideology became possible precisely in those states where the United States supported anti-people's regimes (for example, Cuba, Nicaragua, and several other Latin American countries).

What is important for present purposes is that in the 1990s the factors referred to by Kirkpatrick and Gerson as the basis for the Reagan doctrine no longer exist.

The World Court in the *Nicaragua* case unambiguously condemned doctrines like the Brezhnev and Reagan doctrines as contrary to international law: "The Court cannot contemplate the creation of a new rule opening up a right of intervention by one State against another on the ground that the latter has opted for some particular ideology or political system."[10]

In the new international situation ideological and political doctrines must not take precedence over juridical norms. At the present time a review of fixed views on the question of self-defense is both possible and imperative. It is hardly possible or necessary to create completely new legal norms to regulate the exercise of the right to self-defense. Rather, what is needed in the new conditions is a new view of the norms and mechanisms that already exist, in the light of new political realities.

The Question of Self-Defense in the Case of *Nicaragua v. United States of America*

International legal norms governing the right to self-defense received their most authoritative interpretation in the decision of June 27, 1986, by the International Court of Justice (I.C.J.) in the case of *Nicaragua v. United States of America.* A brief analysis of the problems of self-defense raised in that case allows for an exposition of the basic content of that right.

The U.N. Charter, in speaking of the use of armed force, employs different terms: the use or threat of force, breach of the peace, act of aggression, armed attack. Although their meanings overlap somewhat with one another, they are nevertheless not completely identical. Most importantly, their legal meanings are different and this can lead to very practical consequences. The Court did not neglect this problem, and thus our interest in it is natural.

The basic idea in the Reagan administration's argument was that the United States relied on self-defense against the allegedly secret penetration of international Communism or acts of international terrorism. Thus the U.S. countermemorial asserted that "the United States, pursuant to the inherent right of individual and collective self-defense...has responded to requests from El Salvador, Honduras and Costa Rica, for assistance in their self-defense against aggression by Nicaragua."[11]

The Court rejected the assertion of the American administration that the right to self-defense arises not only in response to an armed attack but also in the case of various subversive or terrorist acts, border incidents, or aid to insurgents in another state. The Legal Adviser of the U.S. Department of State, Abraham Sofaer, wrote that if the principle of non-use of force were to be applied "in such a manner as to preclude any use of force for any purpose, international law would serve to insulate the perpetrators of international violence from any control or punishment for their crimes."[12] Professor John Norton Moore wrote that when the U.S. Senate considered the NATO treaty in 1949, Secretary of State Dean Acheson confirmed that an "armed attack" under Article 5 of the treaty would include a revolution supported by outside force. Asserting that armed aggression has become politically invisible, but that the responsive military measures against such aggression are transformed into an armed attack which is then condemned, Moore defends the thesis that the right to individual and collective self-defense—secured in Article 51 of the U.N. Charter—applies to cases of secret or "indirect" armed attack just as it would in the case of an overt attack.[13] U.S. Secretary of State George Shultz also defended the position that support of terrorist or subversive activities in another state or encouragement of the preparations of terrorists on one's own territory "can amount to an ongoing armed aggression against the other state under international law."[14] In his dissenting opinion Judge Stephen Schwebel indicated that a state "is not necessarily and absolutely confined to responding in self-defence only if it is the object of armed attack."[15] For example, Schwebel considered the seizure of the American embassy in Tehran in late 1979 to be an armed attack and, accordingly, the American rescue mission aimed at extricating the hostages in the spring of 1980 was, as the United States pleaded in the case, "in exercise of its inherent right of self-defence."[16]

The Court rejected such a broad treatment of the concept of "armed attack" and consequently rejected it as a basis for self-defense. For example, aid and support for rebels in another state, according to the Court's holding, although it might violate the principle of non-use of force or non-interference in internal affairs, nevertheless cannot be equated with an armed attack. The Court noted that it is "necessary to distinguish the most grave forms of the use of force (those constituting an armed attack) from other less grave forms."[17]

On a more general level, in response to the accusation put forward by the United States that Nicaragua had invaded Honduras and Costa Rica and had given aid to the rebels in El Salvador, the Court underscored that the activities of which Nicaragua was accused, even if they could be proved and attributed to that government, could justify only proportional retaliatory measures by the state that had been a victim of the alleged action in the particular case—namely El Salvador, Honduras, and Costa Rica. They could not justify retaliatory measures by a third government (the United States) and especially could not serve as a justification for intervention with the use of force.[18]

One ought to agree with the French professor J. Combacau that if it were to be admitted that "armed attack" within the meaning of Article 51 of the U.N. Charter coincides with "aggression" or "use of force" as those terms have been defined in the corresponding resolutions of the U.N. General Assembly, then that would mean a widening of the basis for self-defense since those resolutions address prohibited forms of the use of force which are not embodied in the concept of "armed attack."[19] Commenting on the decision of the World Court, Tom Farer noted that "anything other than a high and conspicuous threshold between an armed attack justifying the exercise of self-defense and lesser forms of intervention...would invite internationalization of essentially civil conflicts."[20]

At the same time, according to the Court, an armed attack includes acts of so-called indirect aggression, in other words, "the sending by or on behalf of a State of armed bands, groups, irregulars or mercenaries, which carry out acts of armed force against another State of such gravity as to amount to" an actual armed attack.[21]

Aggression performed with the aid not of regular troops but by armed bands, irregulars, or mercenaries, that is, so-called indirect aggression, consists of action undertaken by a state equivalent to action by its own organs. Therefore an armed attack may be carried out with the aid of irregular forces, mercenaries, or bands, especially in the case of an attack on a small state. However, here there are many pitfalls that could lead to abuse.

In accordance with the Resolution on the Definition of Aggression,[22] the Security Council can come to the conclusion that the use of armed force by a government itself does not constitute aggression on the basis, in part, that the corresponding acts or their consequences do not have a sufficiently serious character. In other words, acts involving regular armed forces could be determined to constitute not aggression but rather, for example, a border conflict. Consequently, such acts do not qualify as armed attacks within the meaning of Article 51 of the U.N. Charter and do not give rise to a right of self-defense on the part of another state. As regards the use of force with the aid of armed bands, irregular forces, or mercenaries, it would qualify as an act of aggression only in the case of the use of force of such an intensity and seriousness that it amounts to the equivalent of an act of direct use of armed force.

Consequently, in the case of a use of regular military forces by a state, the Security Council can reach the conclusion that this act, because of an insufficiently serious character, does not constitute aggression. Likewise, in the case of a state's utilization of irregular forces, bands, or mercenaries, aggression occurs provided there is a sufficiently serious use of armed force. Qualifying such a use of armed force as aggression falls within the competence of the Security Council.

In the case of the commission of indirect aggression, difficulties also arise in the establishment of the link between the state and the irregular forces, bands, or mercenaries acting at the behest of that state.

All of this bears witness to the difficulties of determining the existence of an armed attack in the case of the use of force with the assistance of irregular forces, armed bands, or mercenaries. To do this it is necessary first to establish that the acts of use of force are sufficiently serious, and second to determine the connection between the irregular forces and the state. As practice and the *Nicaragua* case have shown, this is not easy to do.

Therefore, particular caution is necessary in invoking self-defense in instances of military attack with the assistance of irregular forces or mercenaries. In such a circumstance, military retaliatory measures against the invading band are naturally allowed in order to repel the attack. To carry such military action onto the territory of another state is not precluded but demands particular caution and, of course, may be done only upon notifying the Security Council.

When undertaking actions that constitute self-defense, a state is obliged to report the measures promptly to the Security Council. Therefore the Court underscored that if the actions of the United States against Nicaragua had been measures of self-defense, then in accordance with Article 51 of the U.N. Charter the United States should have made a report to the Security Council. In fact, Nicaragua, accusing Washington of aggression, appealed to the Security Council.

Judge Schwebel offered an entirely unique explanation of this fact. He considered that the United States did not turn to the Security Council because secret defensive measures by their nature cannot be reported to the Security Council.[23] Here is an attempt to introduce into international law a completely new and hitherto unheard-of conception, "*secret self-defense.*"

Professor Richard Falk correctly noted that "[w]e are hardly prepared to endorse a conception of legitimate covert operations that validates state-sponsored terrorism."[24] In reality self-defense is the legitimate use of force, and for the defending state, in contrast to the aggressor, there is no reason to cover up its actions. Moreover, the appeal of the victim of an attack is not only an obligatory demand of the Charter but a completely natural action as well.

The Court considered that collective self-defense, to be legitimate, must satisfy two other conditions. First, the victim of the attack must clearly declare that it has been the victim of an armed attack. A third state does not have the right to invoke collective self-defense on the basis of its own evaluation. Second, for collective self-defense, in addition to the declaration by the victim, there also must be a request for assistance.[25]

The conclusions of the Court cannot be regarded as flawless. The Court understandably desired not to acknowledge the legitimacy of a situation where military aid might have been "imposed" on a government. However, such requirements are derived neither from the U.N. Charter nor from general principles of international law. Besides, it is not difficult to imagine an armed attack, as in the case of a surprise invasion of a small state (for example, Kuwait), when that state's leadership would not have the opportunity either to declare itself under attack or to turn anywhere for assistance.

The development of human civilization is moving along the path of limiting the use of force in international relations, and this development is reflected both in international morality and in international law. From the praise of combat (the most widely known undoubtedly would be poems glorifying the battles of Alexander the Great, Genghis Khan, Tamerlane, Peter the Great, and Napoleon), to the moral condemnation of resort to force in the works of leading thinkers, to the partial legal limitations on the use of force in the Covenant of the League of Nations and the complete prohibition in the U.N. Charter—such is the development of the relationship of humanity to the use of force. Already in the pre-nuclear age international violence became too onerous for humanity. Wolfgang Friedmann was completely correct in noting that "already the first World War clearly showed that the goals of previous wars—territorial expansion, political domination of the victor over the vanquished, economic privileges—are unattainable in the modern era, where states are mutually linked in economics and finance."[26]

The more integrated and interdependent the world becomes, the more destructive for it is any form of violence. One must agree with Friedmann that "the general interest of humans in survival in the nuclear age must have absolute priority over the numerous traditional differences of national, racial, ideological and other regimes."[27]

In our day any kind of broadening of the interpretation of the right to resort to military force is fraught with danger for the survival of human civilization. Therefore, international law must develop along the path of eliminating all loopholes in the legal regulation of the ban on the use of force, which are used by those who still do not understand the necessity of the actual realization of the superiority of general human interests over national or class interests. Unilateral coercive military measures must disappear from international practice in the future. In this regard international law must become maximally clear and unambiguous in not permitting any broad interpretation of the right to rely on force. Obviously, those opposed to such a development in international law assert that their interests cannot be guaranteed without resort to force. Analyzing Washington's argument in justification of the invasion of Grenada, Weiler concludes that the argument is untenable and reaches the correct conclusion:

> The clearer the system's rules for evaluating the legality of use of force and the more sophisticated the legal techniques for applying these rules, the more difficult it will become to maintain this Kantian-like cleavage between action as it really is, and as it is claimed to be. If it were possible to ascertain in every instance precisely and unequivocally the legality or otherwise of action taken, it would not be possible to play the double game. Very simply, governments which wished *to appear to be observing the law* would actually have to observe it.[28]

The analysis of the I.C.J.'s decision in the case of *Nicaragua v. United States of America* leaves no doubt that the Court supports a narrow interpretation of armed attack and, accordingly, of the right of self-defense. Such an approach to self-defense not only is convincing from the perspective of existing norms of international law, but it also accords with the new reality.

If in the years of the Cold War a number of scholars[29] asserted that the limitation of unilateral use of force depends on the effectiveness of U.N. mechanisms, and a broad interpretation of the right to self-defense was put forth in connection with the ineffectiveness of these mechanisms, then the situation already has changed significantly. The aggression of Iraq against Kuwait became, in the words of U.S. Secretary of State James Baker III, a political test of how the world system will work after the Cold War. The Iraq-Kuwait crisis, in Baker's words, represented the first opportunity to strengthen the norms of civilized conduct, as the Charter intended.[30]

The unity of the five permanent members of the Security Council has permitted for the first time not only a condemnation of the aggressor, but also the adoption of collective measures aimed at restraining the aggressor.

One does not need much imagination to envision the development of events in the Persian Gulf if Iraq had attacked Kuwait five or six years ago. Aggression would have occurred in the context of the East-West conflict in the most volatile region on earth: the Middle East. Such an event could have precipitated the third world war.

One of the most important changes in the world associated with the end of the Cold War must be the curtailment of support by superpowers—the USSR and the United States in the first instance—for dictatorial regimes in different regions of the world. It is precisely such regimes that have always presented the threat of use of force, and in supporting or installing them the superpowers have referred, among other things, to Article 51 of the Charter. With the end of the Cold War, it is becoming possible to limit significantly, if not to exclude completely, the different forms of so-called indirect aggression, which has particularly agitated American politicians and jurists. The use of irregular forces or mercenaries, covert or overt delivery of arms to the opposing side in an internal conflict, and the training of revolutionaries or counter-revolutionaries all occurred almost exclusively in the context of the so-called fundamental contradiction of the Cold War—the contradiction between capitalism and socialism.

By virtue of this change in the world situation it is also becoming possible to resolve the question of retaliatory measures against those forms of the use of force that go beyond the narrow understanding of "armed attack:" border incidents, external aid to rebels, terrorist acts supported by states, and threats to the lives of foreign citizens. In the new circumstances, we are convinced, the quantity of such acts will necessarily decline significantly, and the possibility of reaching agreement on the means of combatting these violations of international law will correspondingly increase.

The Iraq-Kuwait Crisis and Collective Self-Defense

The Iraq-Kuwait crisis raised many international law problems linked with the use of force. Not only was the crisis a test of the new political climate, but it also showed how the U.N. mechanism—which was conceived immediately after the Second World War, when the USSR and the United States were close allies—might work under new conditions.

The Security Council took measures necessary to maintain international peace and security; it adopted trade and financial sanctions against Iraq; and it authorized measures to enforce these sanctions.[31] From the moment the Security Council adopted these measures and imposed them on Iraq, the inherent right of self-defense was replaced by these collective measures.

The world was then confronted with a central test: If these measures fail and Iraq continues to occupy Kuwait or continues to hold hostages, what then?

This became an example where requirements of law and politics coincided. It clearly became the interest of the United States to seek Security Council authorization to use military coercion if necessary. Of course, it would have been better for the Iraqi regime to withdraw from Kuwait, but it became apparent to most members of the Security Council that Saddam Hussein would not comply with the requirements of international law, with the demands of world public opinion, or even with pressure from both superpowers.

If the Security Council had not ultimately adopted a "use of force" resolution, as it did on November 29, 1990, what then? In this case the inherent right of self-defense—which was dormant while the Security Council acted and states applied measures authorized by the Council—would have reappeared. If for some reason the Security Council had not ultimately authorized the armed measures necessary to enforce compliance with the Security Council's demands, then in that case states (Kuwait and its allies) could apply armed measures in collective self-defense against Iraq, and they would have had the right under international law to do so.

It is one thing for the resistance in a country to continue to act in self-defense, but it is quite another thing for a superpower that is itself a member of the Security Council to take measures unilaterally, not trying to use other available measures through the Security Council, while that very body is discussing and undertaking measures itself. This interpretation follows from a textual and contextual analysis of Article 51 of the U.N. Charter.

There are dangers inherent in such an approach. For example, Iraq might have attacked the multilateral forces in Saudi Arabia while the Security Council was undertaking measures and while states were seeking authorization to use force under Article 42. But from the legal and political points of view, it was in the interest of the United States and other nations to try to use multilateral diplomacy as far as possible. First, any war is too costly, mainly in human life, both of civilians and of soldiers. Material damages will also be enormous, of course. Thus it is necessary to try all possible peaceful and even coercive measures short of war. Second, it is in the interest of the future of the international system, because if the world community can resolve such important matters with the help of multilateral diplomacy, it would be a much better world.

Notes

1. O. Schachter, *Disputes Involving the Use of Force,* THE INTERNATIONAL COURT OF JUSTICE AT A CROSSROADS 228 (L.F. Damrosch ed. 1987).

2. *See* U.N. Doc. S/PV.1441 at 41 (Provisional Record).

3. *See* Pravda, Sept. 26, 1968; 7 I.L.M. 1323 (1968).

4. From our point of view it is possible to reach a similar result in the application of doctrines that are attractive at first glance, according to which all acts of intervention should be divided into permissible and impermissible ones. Thus, in the words of W.M. Reisman an intervention is permissible if it increases "the possibility of free choice by the people of their government and political structures." *See* 78 AM. J. INT'L L. 643 (1984). As far as such views are concerned, Schachter writes that he does not find support either in the U.N. Charter itself or in the interpretation of Article 2(4) of the Charter which governments have adopted in recent decades. "Such an argument is capable of creating a new normative base for the unlimited use of force by more powerful governments with the goal of ousting

other governments which allegedly have been formed not in accordance with the will of the people." *See* 78 AM. J. INT'L L. 649 (1984). The validity of Schachter's comment has been confirmed by the aggression of Iraq against Kuwait. After all, Saddam Hussein also spoke of, among other things, the overthrow of a corrupt, anti-people's regime in Kuwait.

5. *See, e.g.,* U.N. Doc. A/AC.134 at 16.

6. U.N. Doc. S/PV 2190 at 18. Article 2(7) provides: "Nothing contained in the present Charter shall authorize the United Nations to intervene in matters which are essentially within the domestic jurisdiction of any state or shall require the Members to submit such matters to settlement under the present Charter; but this principle shall not prejudice the application of enforcement measures under Chapter VII."

7. *See* U.N. Doc. A/ES at 67.

8. Address Before a Joint Session of the Congress on the State of the Union, February 6, 1985, I PUB. PAPERS OF THE PRESIDENTS OF THE UNITED STATES: RONALD REAGAN 135 (1988).

9. J. Kirkpatrick & A. Gerson, *The Reagan Doctrine, Human Rights, and International Law,* in RIGHT V. MIGHT: INTERNATIONAL LAW AND THE USE OF FORCE 19, 23 (1989).

10. 1986 I.C.J. 133.

11. 1986 I.C.J. 70.

12. A.D. Sofaer, *Terrorism and the Law,* 64 FOREIGN AFFAIRS 919 (1986).

13. J.N. Moore, *The Secret War in Central America and the Future of World Order*, 80 AM. J. INT'L L. 60 (1986).

14. Sofaer, *supra* note 12, at 920.

15. *Case concerning Military and Paramilitary Activities In and Against Nicaragua (Nicar. v. U.S.), Merits,* 1986 I.C.J. 14, 349 (J. Schwebel, diss. op.).

16. *Quoted in* Schwebel, *id.* at 292.

17. *See Nicar. v. U.S., supra* note 15, at 101.

18. *Id.* at 127.

19. J. Combacau, *The Exception of Self-Defense in U.N. Practice,* in THE CURRENT LEGAL REGULATION OF THE USE OF FORCE 21 (A. Cassese ed. 1986).

20. Farer, *Drawing the Right Line,* 81 AM. J. INT'L L. 112, 113-14 (1987).

21. *Resolution on the Definition of Aggression,* Dec. 14, 1974, G.A. Res. 3314 (xxix), 29 U.N. GAOR, Supp. (No.31) 142, U.N. Doc. A/9631 (1975), at art. 3, para. (g), as quoted by the Court at 1986 I.C.J. 103. The Court regarded this description as reflective of customary international law. *Id.*

22. *See Definition of Aggression, supra* n. 21.

23. *See Nicar. v. U.S., supra* note 15, at 373 (J. Schwebel, diss. op.).

24. Falk, *The World Court's Achievement,* 81 AM. J. INT'L L. 110 (1987).

25. *See Nicar. v. U.S., supra* note 15, at 104-105.

26. W. FRIEDMANN, DE L'EFFICACITE DES INSTITUTIONS INTERNATIONALES 14 (1970).

27. *Id.* at 17.

28. J. Weiler, *Armed Intervention in a Dichotomized World: The Case of Grenada*, in THE CURRENT LEGAL REGULATION OF THE USE OF FORCE 243 (A. Cassese ed. 1986).

29. *See* J. STONE, AGGRESSION AND WORLD ORDER 96 (1958); W.M. Reisman, *The Emperor Has No Clothes: Article 2(4) and the Use of Force in Contemporary International Law,* in UNITED NATIONS FOR A BETTER WORLD 10 (1986).

30. Pravda, Sept. 6, 1990.

31. U.N. Doc. S/RES/665 (1970).

3

Allocating Competences to Use Coercion in the Post-Cold War World: Practices, Conditions, and Prospects[1]

W. Michael Reisman

Law is not the antithesis of force. Legal systems and the political systems of which they are a part and which they seek to regulate are based upon the authoritative use of force. The question for jurists, then, is not "the non-use of force," but the assignment of the competence to use force to appropriate agencies in the community and the determination of the contingencies, purposes, and procedures for the use of authoritative force.

Since Hobbes and Bodin, most scholars in the Western political tradition have assumed that effective political community presupposes centralization and monopolization of the means of coercion in the state apparatus which is thereafter exclusively authorized to use them. However, the international system is a political community that does not fit this model. It is characterized by the absence of centralization of effective control and the distribution of the means of coercion among many different structures. In such a system, actions that would have been assigned exclusively to the state apparatus, if it existed, are perforce taken by individual actors. Though philosophical anarchism would find such an arrangement acceptable, it is not one which has been deemed optimal by most scholars and decision-makers.

The designers of international law have tried to grapple with this problem in two broad and necessarily interrelated ways. First, they tried to limit the contingencies in which actors could unilaterally resort to highly coercive acts by trying to prescribe and limit the so-called *jus ad bellum:* the result was the aggression-self-defense paradigm. And, of course, they tried to maintain a sharp distinction between states of war and states of peace, so that a law of peace could apply without restriction at all times other than those of explicit conflict. When military coercion was used unilaterally, the designers of international law tried to reduce its savagery by regulating the way it would be used through the so-called *jus in bello*. Second, and particularly since 1920, the designers have tried to approximate the centralization of the means of coercion found in advanced municipal systems. But this latter effort has been diluted because the designers were and remain unwilling to abandon the fundamental feature of the contemporary international system, the network of so-called autonomous "sovereign" states. The formation of the state system took many centuries and required great sacrifice and deprivation; we may be in the early stages of its demise and replacement. But, as yet, there has been no incorporation of the various states of the world into a single mega-Leviathan—which might, in any case, create more problems than it would solve—paralleling the incorporation of the various feudal entities into modern nation-states.

None of these efforts has met with spectacular success. But, then again, the objective conditions are daunting. Control of the capability for coercion is distributed among a wide variety of cultures with varying historical views, which have sustained radically different conceptions of when it is appropriate for people to use military force, whether it is Iraq in Kuwait, Argentina in the Falklands, the United States in Grenada or Panama, the Soviet Union in Afghanistan, France in the Central African Republic, Libya in Chad, Tanzania in Uganda, to name only a few examples. The development of modern military technologies with enormous but undiscriminating destructive potential made all but the most basic rules of the *jus in bello* moot.

The constitutive effort to deal with Hobbes' problem, namely the individual use of force and the maintenance of collective security, has tried simultaneously to maintain the state system while assigning essential security functions to the largest and strongest states which are bound by a set of prescribed procedures and which limit the authorized use of force by all other states, except for certain prescribed contingencies. The effort has not been successful. This system, enshrined in the United Nations Charter in 1945, proved unworkable because of profound disagreement between the two superpowers and a competition between them which infected every aspect of international political life. It was further aggravated by deep divisions between wealthy and poorer states, the uneven termination of the colonial and imperial era, the persistence of religious divisions, and the rapidly evolving environment of military technology.

As for the effort to maintain a distinction between war and peace and a corresponding law of war and law of peace, it was all but eclipsed by the Cold War. That long conflict created a system of neither war nor peace, but constant preparation for war, a high expectation of violence on the part of all actors, a tolerance for institutionalized violations of international law, called euphemistically "rules of the game," and the conduct of proxy wars.

Because the Charter's constitutive solution of the collective security problem did not work, operational norms emerged which, not surprisingly, diverged in many details from how the collective security system was supposed to work. This operational code, however, was not oblivious to the Charter's text. It reflected, in some of its parts, basic substantive policies of the Charter, if not all of its black letter textual aspirations. In particular, deference to such textual aspiration led many actors to shape their justifications of the unilateral use of force in terms of self-defense. Even actions traditionally and unquestionably characterized as reprisals or self-help were recast in the mold of self-defense. One of the consequences of this trend has been to render the purported restrictiveness of the doctrine of self-defense more and more elastic. Using the symbols of the Charter paradigm of aggression and self-defense, a much more complex operational code has developed for justifying proactive, reactive, and reprisory unilateral coercions. Trends of decision and studies of incidents also suggest that a very complex calculus for determining lawfulness in particular cases has developed.

I propose to examine, very briefly, past trends and predictions of future trends with regard to two major forms of international coercion: proactive and reactive coercion. I will not consider reprisory and countermeasure coercion. Then I propose to examine possible changes in conditions that may presage different trends in the future. But first, it may be appropriate to interpose a brief note about methodology.

In discussions about legal subjects, jurists are prone to statements on the order of "this is the law," followed by some formulation of legal principle. These characteristic formulations of our science are particularly misleading, for they refer simultaneously and without discrimination to descriptions about flows of decision in the past, predictions about the way decisions may be taken in the future, or statements of preference. Such statements are what McDougal and Lasswell have called "normative ambiguities."[2]

Discussions of the regulation of the use of force in international politics have been particularly hospitable to this intellectual pathology. In order to make relevant the statement "the unilateral use of force is prohibited in international law," it must be made more precise as to the situation or situations in which its use occurs. The statement must also be tested to determine the extent to which its use has shaped a flow of past decisions, the extent to which and under what conditions it is a useful predictor of future decisions, and the extent to which, as formulated, it is an expression of policy likely to contribute to the maintenance of minimum order and the enhancement of those values of human dignity that are central to the contemporary international legal system.

The distinction between past description, future prediction, and policy preference is particularly important at this moment, which could prove to be a point of major and historic change. Many practices and policies which have operated for the past forty years in the Cold War context may terminate or modulate now that that conflict seems to have ended.

Proactive Unilateral Coercion in the Military Instrument

Coercion is not a property unique to the military instrument. If it is understood as the purposive attenuation of the choice options of the target, it is a potential property of all instruments of policy: the economic, the ideological (mass communication to rank-and-file as a way of supporting or undermining elite control), the diplomatic (inter-elite) as well as the military. In a forthcoming book with James Baker, I review trends in each of these modalities. Here I will restrict myself to a brief sketch of trends in the regulation of the use of the military instrument.

Nowhere is the divide between the system of textual myth and aspirational norms, on the one hand, and an operational code, on the other, more apparent and significant for world order than in the continuing international effort to regulate the military instrument. Within five years of the creation of the United Nations, a pattern was established according to which certain unilateral violations of Article 2(4) might be condemned but nothing further would be done. For all intents and purposes the violator could enjoy the benefits of its unlawful act without real costs. Moreover, as the balance of states in the General Assembly shifted, new contingencies for the use of force and intervention emerged which did not just tolerate certain unilateral uses of force but sought to raise them to the level of a lawful duty.

The structural problem caused by the absence of a centralization of authoritative force and an effective monopoly over who can use it had been addressed directly by the League of Nations, and, more boldly and explicitly, by the Charter of the United Nations. The U.N. Charter established a centralized system in which unauthorized uses of force by any state were to be dealt with by the Security Council which was to have, under the Charter conception, access to the military assets necessary to restore peace. The language of the Charter is quite conservative: the contingencies to which the Security Council is to react—"threat to the peace, breach of the peace, or act of aggression"—are all coercive efforts to change the status quo and all are presumptively unlawful.

Under this system, there should no longer have been any need for unilateral resort to military force. Hence the prescription of Article 2(4) of the Charter was not only morally elevated but also politically feasible and responsible:

> All Members shall refrain in their international relations from the threat or use of force against the territorial integrity or political independence of any state, or in any other manner inconsistent with the Purposes of the United Nations.

Some might be inclined to assume that in terms of outcomes, there should have been no difference between Charter law and customary law. Rights which states formerly would have had to protect on their own by military force under customary law now would be protected by the Security Council under the Charter. If the Charter worked, then customary rights to resort to military coercion would have been rendered not only unlawful but also superfluous.

The Charter regime may be compared with customary international law at the time. Even following the Charter's prohibition, customary law permitted the use of force for self-defense, for "self-help," and for the protection and realization of other international rights. Charter law, in contrast, as generally if not necessarily interpreted, prohibited the unilateral use of military force for any reason other than for self-defense. Even then, self-defense depended not on a prior unlawful act or even a concrete territorial incursion but on a prior act of "aggression." Aggression, in this system, became a technical concept whose meaning was not necessarily self-evident.

In short, the Charter sought to establish a new set of words about when and how military force could be used, and the creation of the United Nations endowed a new set of institutions with the competence to interpret and apply those words. A uniquely structured organization, composed of a Security Council and a General Assembly with an intricate and changing relationship between the two, now claimed the authentic and final competence to interpret the words in the Charter. The way in which that competence has been used is of direct relevance to the question we are addressing.

In 1970, the General Assembly provided in its Declaration on Principles of International Law Concerning Friendly Relations and Co-operation Among States in Accordance with the Charter of the United Nations, that

> Every State has a duty to refrain from organizing or encouraging the organization of irregular forces or armed bands, including mercenaries, for incursion into the territory of another State.

and,

> Every State has the duty to refrain from organizing, instigating,

> assisting or participating in acts of civil strife or terrorist acts in another State or acquiescing in organized activities within its territory directed towards the commission of such acts, when the acts referred to in the present paragraph involve a threat or use of force.[3]

Four years later, the Assembly, in its Declaration on Strengthening International Security, made clear that the blanket prohibition on unilateral coercion did not apply when it infringed on the rights of peoples "to determine their own destinies."[4] The Resolution on the Definition of Aggression adopted by the Assembly in 1974 stipulated that nothing in the Definition "could in any way prejudice the right of self-determination, freedom, and independence, as derived from the Charter, of peoples forcibly deprived of that right...or the right of these peoples to struggle to that end and to seek and receive support..."[5] The Declaration on Principles of International Law itself had authorized and mandated support for coercion directed at "self-determination and freedom and independence."[6] In 1981, the Declaration on the Inadmissibility of Intervention and Interference in the Internal Affairs of States again exempted self-determination cases.[7]

Meanwhile, changes in the technical environment and the larger political context occurred which tended to obsolesce many of the key assumptions underlying the basic rules about when and how force was to be used. On the one hand, the nuclear balance reduced the profitability and, to some extent, the likelihood of conventional warfare between the two major antagonists, but it did not reduce the conflict itself. Instead, a variety of non-conventional methods were developed or refined, some conducted by proxies, with careful concealment of the identity and activities of the principal actor. Many of these methods were associated with the independence or changed governments of the new states and were given a mythic nimbus. Developments in communications and transportation enhanced the possibilities of infiltration and subversion, of protracted low-level conflict by well-supplied proxies, of pre-programmed "popular" uprisings followed by "invitations" from local inhabitants, and so on.

International politics has always included many non-state categories of actors. Many of them now seek increasingly to use non-conventional methods of coercion as a way of achieving their political objectives. The ease of communications, the relative miniaturization of weapons of increasing destructiveness, and refinements in methods of pursuing the general objective of mass terror have permitted many groups—some with aspirations to become states, others with anarchist or nihilist objectives—to become involved in military activity.

As these changes in the military and technological environment were taking place, the smaller states—through the United Nations and other international parliamentary arenas—sought to change the international law of military force to make it better reflect their values and objectives. Larger states and the superpowers also behaved in ways, sometimes with elaborate legal justifications, that sought to change Charter law. Some of the resulting new "rules" were never more than aspiration. Others were successful legislative exercises and more closely approximated an operational code. In particular cases, the outcome of their application turned on contextual factors.

A few examples will suffice to demonstrate the point.

Self-Determination

The General Assembly's Declaration on Principles of International Law provides in pertinent part:

> By virtue of the principle of equal rights and self-determination of peoples enshrined in the Charter of the United Nations, all peoples have the right freely to determine, without external interference, their political status and to pursue their economic, social and cultural development, and every State has the duty to respect this right in accordance with the provisions of the Charter.[8]

The operational implications of this right are spelled out three paragraphs later:

> Every State has the duty to refrain from any forcible action which deprives peoples...of their right to self-determination and freedom and independence. *In their actions against and resistance to such forcible action in pursuit of the exercise of self-determination, such peoples are entitled to seek and to receive support in accordance with the purposes and principles of the Charter of the United Nations.*[9]

Note here the beginning of an attempt at inverting customary law. "Peoples" have the right to "self-determination" and "freedom and independence." The state against which these groups are struggling must refrain from any action which impedes the struggle; it must refrain from actions that could otherwise be characterized as self-defense. Third states are obliged to help the struggling groups but cannot be held legally responsible by the targeted state.

This "inversion" is not limited to a few historical atavisms. While "decolonization" may have had a historically specific reference for some drafters and been limited to their perceptions about Portuguese territories, the apartheid government in South Africa, and Palestine, terms such as "self-determination" and, even more, "freedom and independence" are open-ended and can be applied to any group which a majority of the General Assembly wishes.

The International Convention Against the Taking of Hostages, adopted by the U.N. General Assembly in 1979,[10] is even more explicit in setting out the implications of the inversion. Article 1(1) defines the offense prohibited by the Convention as follows:

> Any person who seizes or detains and threatens to kill, to injure or to continue to detain another person (hereinafter referred to as the "hostage") in order to compel a third party, namely a State, an international intergovernmental organization, a natural or juridical person or a group of persons, to do or abstain from doing any act as an explicit or implicit condition for the release of the hostage commits the offense of taking of hostages ("hostage taking") within the meaning of this Convention.

But Article 12 of the same Convention provides in pertinent part:

> [T]he present Convention shall not apply to an act of hostage-taking committed in the course of armed conflicts as defined in the Geneva Conventions of 1949 and the Protocols thereto, including armed conflicts mentioned in article 1, paragraph 4, of Additional Protocol I of 1977, in which peoples are fighting against colonial domination and alien occupation and against racist regimes in the exercise of their right of self-determination, as enshrined in the Charter of the United Nations and the Declaration of Principles of International Law concerning Friendly Relations and Cooperation among States in accordance with the Charter of the United Nations.

These instruments show that a conception of international law as it relates to the use of the military instrument was emerging from the institutions of formal international law-making over a period of time. That conception was straying quite far from customary international law. Indeed, one might say that a type of just war was being created.

A parallel development can be found with regard to the way the new just wars were to be fought: the law of armed conflict or *jus in bello.* Two Protocols additional to the Geneva Conventions, in particular Protocol I, besides establishing new norms of humanitarian conduct for medical assistance and the identification of the missing in action, challenged conventional views as to the norms that govern the conduct of insurgent conflict.[11] Protocol I seeks to internationalize "armed conflicts in which peoples are fighting...in the exercise of their right of self-determination." (Article 1(4)). This facilitates fulfillment of the obligation of states to provide assistance to such peoples embodied in the Declaration on Principles of International Law. Contemporaneous statements by delegates confirm this intention. In addition, Articles 43 and 44 relax the customary and Geneva-based requirements that combatants wear a fixed distinctive sign and carry their arms openly in order to obtain combatant status. These developments favor the irregular soldier, who is often identified with wars of national liberation. They also increase the peril of the non-combatant, the major object of concern of the law of war that was being supplanted.

Brezhnev and Reagan Doctrines

Outside the U.N. structure, some states began to justify proactive unilateral intervention on the grounds of unilaterally characterized claims of self-determination, even if those claims had not received international organizational endorsement, for example, by the U.N. Committee on Colonialism. In this connection, we may note that the so-called Brezhnev and Reagan doctrines contain both defensive prescriptions relating to critical defense zones, which I will treat below, and proactive elements relating to self-styled self-determination, national liberation, or freedom fighters. "Genuine revolutionaries," the Brezhnev doctrine went, "as internationalists, cannot fail to support progressive forces in all countries in their just struggle for national and social liberation."[12] *Mutatis mutandis,* the United States perspective, expressed by President Reagan's Freedom Fighter Corollary, had a parallel structure. In a speech on March 1, 1985, Reagan said, "Freedom movements arise and assert themselves. They're doing so on almost every continent populated by man—in the hills of Afghanistan, in Angola, in Kampuchea, in Central America....They are our brothers, these freedom fighters, and we owe them our help."[13] The Reagan administration, however, was not the first, nor the last, to hear the call and provide different forms of covert support to selected insurgencies against existing governments. The Truman, Eisenhower, Kennedy, Johnson, Nixon, Ford, Carter, and Bush administrations have, at times, been similarly engaged.

Soviet President Mikhail Gorbachev has renounced the Brezhnev doctrine. The United States, to date, has not renounced the Reagan doctrine. It would appear, however, that with the end of the Cold War neither of the erstwhile superpowers will continue to engage in this particular type of action under an open and flaunted doctrine; it is too early to say whether they will try to act covertly.

Humanitarian Intervention

With the paralysis of the U.N. security system, other proactive contingencies for legitimizing the use of unilateral coercion, beyond the scope of self-determination, emerged and reemerged. Thus humanitarian intervention, replacement of an elite in another state, uses of the military within spheres of influence and critical defense zones, treaty-sanctioned interventions and the forceful gathering of evidence for international proceedings have all been cited as legitimizing post-1945 proactive forceful interventions.

At least since Grotius, in theory, and the Greek intervention of 1827, in practice, international practice has uneasily recognized a right of one state to intervene in another in response to violations of human rights which "shock the conscience of mankind." Although the technique is necessarily the same as the forceful implementation of the doctrine of diplomatic protection of nationals, under the doctrine of humanitarian intervention the intervenor need not have a direct link to the persons who are the purported beneficiaries of the protective action.

Critical Defense Zones

The Soviet Union, throughout the Cold War, and the United States, for more than a century, have claimed exclusive prerogatives to "protect" designated geographic perimeters, or critical defense zones. Although often identified as the Brezhnev and Reagan doctrines, these defensive claims are historical in nature and have been exercised under other rubrics. The doctrines purport to be rooted in the right of self-defense, but the two nations also claimed a right to take proactive measures in support of these claims and have done so. Soviet military and diplomatic interventions in Hungary, Czechoslovakia, East Germany, and Poland, for example, even when not explicitly founded on a defensive zone rationale, appear implicitly to have been based on such thinking. A comparable United States claim is witnessed in its frequent military intervention in the 1920s in Latin America, and during the Cold War in Guatemala, Cuba, and the Dominican Republic.

Both doctrines are based in part on security and allegedly defensive strategic considerations. Each expresses the view that the approach by an adversary into its own buffer areas would pose an unacceptable security risk, a risk so great that it would require the threatened state to resort to an anticipatory action that would be unlawful in other circumstances, particularly if it had been taken by other actors. Both are premised on military and geo-strategic theories that may be obsolescing.

The operational code suggests that there was a remarkable degree of tolerance for certain applications of the Brezhnev and Reagan doctrines. The United States and the majority of members of the United Nations essentially accommodated themselves to Soviet "defensive" interventions, except in Afghanistan, although there was considerable protest regarding Soviet covert complicity in the declaration of martial law in Poland.

Whether the tolerance for critical defense zones will continue as the threat of nuclear war decreases is open to question. It is clear that the necessary attenuation of the independence of smaller communities, which is always a consequence of a critical defense zone theory, has been tolerated because avoidance of nuclear war at all costs was viewed as a matter of the most urgent common interest. With the reduction of that threat, there may be a parallel reduction in the tolerance for this particular form of extension of national power abroad. It may, however, be replaced by a resurgence of traditional "spheres of influence," allocated *inter se* by the larger states. Consider Secretary of State Baker's signal to the Soviet Union in the wake of the overthrow of the Ceausescu regime in Romania in December 1989. Asked whether the United States would approve if the Soviet Union sent troops to support pro-democracy forces in Romania, Mr. Baker responded:

> They are attempting to put off the yoke of a very, very oppressive and repressive dictatorship. So I think that we would be inclined probably to follow the example of France, who today has said that if the Warsaw Pact felt it necessary to intervene on behalf of the opposition, that it would support that action....That would be my view, yes.[14]

The Soviet Union refused the invitation, at least at the overt and public level, but the very fact that the invitation was extended is itself significant.

Reactive Unilateral Coercion: Self-Defense

As stated earlier, the development of the Charter scheme required illumination of terms such as "aggression" and the related procedural issue of who could determine, in particular cases, whether an act of aggression had occurred. In its Resolution on the Definition of Aggression,[15] the General Assembly asserted the authority to give meaning to the term and tried to move toward a more precise threshold to determine when the use of force in self-defense would be consistent with Article 51 of the Charter. The Report of the Special Committee on the Question of Defining Aggression and its commentary imply but do not explicitly state that armed attack is "aggression," and that it triggers the right to self-defense under Article 51.[16]

A key part of the regime of Article 51 is unilateral action, which many had thought presupposed a unilateral determination that certain acts, in particular cases, constituted aggression. But the Resolution on the Definition of Aggression decrees that not all uses of force constitute "armed attack" and/or constitute aggression. One objective of this innovation was to reduce substantially the competence of any state which deemed itself under attack to characterize the event as aggression and to respond in self-defense. This was, in effect, an effort to attenuate the right of self-defense.

Gross aggression, like pornography, may not be easy to define, but you know it when you see it. The post-war period was increasingly marked by protracted low-level conflicts whose international legal definition posed more difficulties. The Charter does not make clear whether the prohibition on the use of military force reaches such low-level coercion. In drafting the Definition of Aggression, the so-called Six Powers of the Special Committee moved to include in the definition in Article 1 the proposition that

> ...the term aggression is applicable, without prejudice to a finding of threat to the peace or breach of the peace, to the use of force in international relations, *overt or covert, direct or indirect....*[17]

This proposal was defeated as was an additional amendment which referred to force "however exerted." States feared the language was too broad and would too easily lead to the conclusion that any breach of the peace was an act of aggression.

Article 3(g) of the Definition of Aggression presented interpretive problems in the context of low intensity conflict. Article 3 states *inter alia* that "Any of the following acts...qualify as an act of aggression:"

> (g) The sending by or on behalf of a State of armed bands, groups, irregulars or mercenaries, which carry out acts of armed force against another State of such gravity as to amount to the acts listed above, or its substantial involvement therein.[18]

Following adoption of these earlier resolutions, the General Assembly sought to limit the right of coercive self-defense to "armed attack." As a result, legal attention is focused more on mode and less on where, in the continuum of coercion, the threshold of the term "armed attack" lies. Moreover, merely characterizing certain actors as, for example, "armed bands" or "irregulars" seems to create an assumption that their actions *do not* constitute an "armed attack." Yet even that has changed. As a consequence, from the Definition of Aggression to the merits phase of *Nicaragua,* the threshold for lawful armed response to covert action, as articulated in the language of the United Nations and its organs, has become higher.

The net result of this exercise was to shift the focus of discussions about Article 51 from consequences for the targeted state to the *mode* of attack by the erstwhile aggressor. Henceforth, only specific types of indirect aggression conducted at specified levels of intensity were to be included in the definition. By apparently developing an objective criterion, the drafters here may have thought that they were introducing a degree of international supervision and control to what theretofore had been a matter of unilateral appreciation which might be subject to abuse. At the same time, however, they were closing the safety valve that had made the Charter system acceptable. That would have been a wise move if an international enforcement system could move into the vacuum that resulted and could respond effectively to the sorts of contingencies for which the right of self-defense was designed. Yet the overall paralysis of the international security machinery continued.

One of the consequences of these resolutions was to encourage states to report incidents of covert coercion and actions by limited overt armed force; this was, after all, the remedy that replaced self-defense for these contingencies. Ironically, these same reports, gathered pursuant to agenda items on implementation of the Declaration on the Strengthening of International Security and Good Neighborliness, also make clear that the norms in these resolutions have been ineffective. Whether the complaint entailed initial or reactive force, there has been little condemnation of, or response to, incidents which did not appear to engage Cold War interests, or more recently, self-determination or apartheid. *Faute de mieux*, the target of low intensity armed aggression was itself forced to respond with low intensity options. This regime not only did not appear to deter low intensity adventurism but actually increased the volume of unregulated coercion.

Article 3(g) of the Definition of Aggression, considered briefly above, establishes what initially appears to be a quantitative threshold for the right of self-defense. Thus an armed attack includes acts carried out by irregular forces, if such acts are serious enough to be an actual armed attack conducted by regular forces or with their substantial involvement.

In its affirmative part, this definition reinforces the mode rather than consequence criterion by saying that the mere fact that armed bands emanate from another state and engage in military activities in your state does not constitute "armed attack" or the contingency which would justify your going into the other state's territory after them. Only when this unspecified threshold is exceeded is the victim state entitled to take measures of self-defense. Obviously, this is a formula favorable to low intensity conflict, defined as something that does not reach the level of "armed attack."

The implications of this innovation were made explicit by the

International Court in its judgment on the merits in the *Nicaragua* case (June 27, 1986).[19] There, the Court takes the Charter definition proposed by the General Assembly and transforms it into customary law and vice-versa, thereby excluding, it would seem, the old customary rights.

> However, so far from having constituted a marked departure from a customary international law which still exists unmodified, the Charter gave expression in this field to principles already present in customary international law, and that law has in the subsequent four decades developed under the influence of the Charter, to such an extent that a number of rules contained in the Charter have acquired a status independent of it. The essential consideration is that both the Charter and the customary international law flow from a common fundamental principle outlawing the use of force in international relations.[20]

This merger, as it were, purports to suppress any unilateral right to the use of force which is derived from customary law and to superordinate the Charter regime and the Charter apparatus for the illumination of all putative actions of collective or individual self-defense. In the Court's view, the Charter conception of the contingency for the right of self-defense is even narrower than the General Assembly's view. The Court excludes from "armed attack" and hence from the right of self-defense many of the methods of low-intensity conflict. First, the Court insists that acts of armed bands must "occur on a significant scale."[21] Second, the Court excludes *by definition* from the category of armed attack "assistance to rebels in the form of the provision of weapons or logistical support."[22]

The language of the Court here is instructive. "Such assistance may be regarded as a threat or use of force, or amount to intervention in the internal or external affairs of other states."[23] These are all matters which bring into operation a contingent competence of the United Nations. If the target state thinks it can secure assistance from the United Nations, it can repair there, assuming that the U.N. security machinery is effective and, if it is, that the United Nations has not decided that the group attacking or assisting the military action in the target state is not "struggling for its freedom and independence." But what the attacking group is doing does not amount to armed attack and hence does not warrant any response which can be characterized as self-defense. If a state responds to these low-level activities with its own counter-force, its action itself is apparently a violation of international law.

The legal theory developed by the Court is thus one that is tolerant of different forms of protracted and low-intensity conflict. While such conflict might be internationally unlawful and might give rise to a variety of protests, it does not, according to the theory developed by the Court, permit the victim state to resort to levels of coercion contemplated in the customary right of self-defense. Moreover, the asymmetry established here is one that, *pace* the Court, is identical in both conventional international law (the Charter) and customary international law.

It is no surprise, then, that states which have been the targets of low-level attack emanating from the territory of other states have sought to establish a norm or corollary permitting them to go to the source of the attacks on them, even if that means a physical intervention in the territory and jurisdiction of another state. The claim is substantially the same, whether it is made by Israel with regard to the bases of the Palestinian Liberation Organization in Lebanon or Tunisia, by South Africa with regard to the bases of the African National Congress in Angola, Botswana, Mozambique, Swaziland, or Zimbabwe, by the Soviet Union against Afghan resistance concentrations in Pakistan, by the United States against Nicaragua for its involvement in El Salvador, or by Nicaragua against contra formations in Honduras. The claim has been based either on broader conceptions of the law of the Charter, which I considered above, or on the revival or, as some have contended, the survival of customary international law.

What the content of the new law with regard to reactions to low-level military use will be is as yet unclear. Until 1990 it seemed probable that the theory developed by the General Assembly and the International Court of Justice would be unacceptable, at least to the United States. If one examines the actions of the Security Council in the Iraq-Kuwait crisis, which I will consider below, as the dawn of a new age, it is possible that U.S. attitudes in this regard may change. But the Iraqi case may represent more of a congruence of interests on this particular case than fundamental changes in attitudes about the world constitutive process. In the short term, however, the tolerance for low-intensity conflict implicit in the developments we have recorded will probably lead to a net increase in violence in international politics. If that trend continues, targets of low-intensity warfare will themselves have no choice but to resort to the same techniques. As a result, arena-restricted conflict—a major goal of the law of war and a more urgent one in the modern technical environment—will expand over a wider geographical area as protagonists and antagonists seek to hurt each other in wars of low-intensity conflict around the globe.

The Context of Conditions

I have tried, with the brevity necessary in an enterprise of this sort, to sketch the major trends with regard to the use of force by means of the military instrument in the international community. A description of past trends does not necessarily imply that those trends will be replicated in the future. What occurred in the past was profoundly shaped by a context of conditions, both environmental and predispositional, and changes in those conditioning factors could signal to jurists changes in future trends. It is obvious that the context of many of these trends was characterized by shared expectations in which the likelihood of violence was deemed high and was, accordingly, prepared for. There was a clear delineation of the adversaries, a constant state of preparedness for overt conflict, a common interest in avoiding it, an assignment of some geo-strategic value to every part of the globe, and an implicit "rules of the game" code which included toleration for covert actions below a certain threshold.

In other cases of long-term *bilateral* but suspended conflict, a comparable tolerance and expectation appears to have operated between adversaries. The rest of the international community which, as it were, sat in continuous judgment in both public and private settings, also seems to have viewed these actions differently. Contrast the different appraisals given to actions in the Israel-Arab conflict, the abortive United States action in Iran in 1980, and the French "covert" action in New Zealand.[24]

If this is a key conditioning factor, it may provide some predictive as well as past explanatory value. Assuming that the Cold War does terminate, the threshold of tolerance for unilateral uses of force *inter se* by continuing competitors such as the United States and the Soviet Union will decline. This does not preclude espionage which may continue and even increase but, paradoxically, may contribute to the maintenance of order by keeping each side apprised of its adversary's capacities and intentions.

Neither of the superpowers can be called economically robust, but the plain collapse of the economic base of one of them, the beginning of the disintegration of its inherited empire, and the erosion of the legitimacy of its ideology—all events which have occurred in the past three years—have led to a dramatic increase in cooperation between the two superpowers. For the moment, it appears that the U.N. Charter's solution to the problem of the lack of centralization of coercion in the international political system at last will work. That hope rests on the assumption that the interests of those who dispose of effective power are sufficiently congruent to continue to produce the consensus necessary for the operation of the collective security system. Alternatively, it assumes that the divergence of interests is not so great as to outweigh the common interest of the superpowers in shaping the international system persuasively rather than coercively.

There is some evidence to sustain those assumptions, but the case, while persuasive, is not conclusive. The settlement in Namibia occurred not simply because of superpower agreement, which had largely been accomplished ten years earlier, but because of decisions taken within South Africa and the other states of the region and a redefinition of what "independence" would actually mean for Namibia. The apparent agreement in the Security Council with regard to the future of Cambodia appears too uncertain, at this time, to be presented as a victory for the collective international security system. The international response to the Iraqi invasion of Kuwait may be construed as a major victory for the inclusive security system or, if one believes that action against Iraq forceful enough to reduce its potential threat to the region is necessary, an essentially American enterprise.

One would be mistaken to imagine that the United Nations' response to the Iraqi invasion of Kuwait is, as Professor Abram Chayes believes, a "second chance." I do not think that such opportunities are presented in history. The complex of events that existed in 1945, which propitiously produced the U.N. Charter, have changed radically. It is true that was a moment of relative consensus between the two superpowers of the time. We seem to be at a moment of relative consensus now between the United States and the Soviet Union, although its depth remains to be explored. I do not believe we have a second chance; I think we are facing a radically new situation. And though it may be possible to adapt parts of the structures of the United Nations, we are going to be involved in something new. We cannot simply go back.

The Interpretation of the Charter

It is, in my view, too early to conclude that the system conceived of in the Charter will finally overcome and replace the dynamics of world politics. And even if the United Nations emerges as the world's policeman, it is important to examine the role of the United States and the pressures it brought through its interpretation of the Charter on other more timid or reluctant members. The United States was the major and indispensable actor responding to the Iraqi aggression. Without the clear policy of the United States, its leadership, and its willingness to invest military assets, the Security Council might well have satisfied itself with an anodyne resolution, expressing disapproval, imposing a variety of symbolic and possibly even some material sanctions but essentially yielding to a *fait accompli*. The extraordinary weakness of the Soviet Union at this moment, the dependence of Soviet progressives on Western assistance for *perestroika,* and the absorption of the Soviet elite in internal developments which could presage major rearrangements of relationships between center and periphery there or even the disintegration of the federation may account for Soviet willingness to follow the American lead, to a certain point. There was never any commitment of Soviet forces to join in any U.N.-authorized action to expel Iraq from Kuwait.

These facts are relevant to the construction of the U.N. Charter and, in particular, the determination of whether the right of initiating individual and collective self-defense is reserved by states as a matter of unilateral competence or requires the prior authorization of the Security Council. If the second interpretation prevails, then individual and collective self-defense is henceforth subject to veto by any permanent member of the Council.

It has been United States initiative—leadership, if you like it, pressure if you think it improper—that has moved the Security Council as far as it has gone in the Iraqi case. Should the United States have said that all uses of force in the Persian Gulf (and elsewhere) can only be accomplished through the United Nations, or should it have reserved the right of independent action? The British government said that the first shot was fired and that those states which have responded to the invitation of Kuwait were entitled to act without Security Council authorization. But the Soviet Union took the position that whatever was to be done must be authorized by the Council. Which interpretation should be adopted?

I think it clear from the legislative history of Article 51 of the Charter that the original intention of the framers was to reserve action under Article 51 to the individual state and not to subject it to a requirement of advance Security Council authorization. But after almost half a century of practice and substantial changes in the international political context, legislative history cannot be dispositive. An interpretation based on a conception of the Charter as prohibiting unauthorized unilateral self-defense action when and because the Council is addressing a breach of the peace or act of aggression has a documentary cogency, for large-scale and violent self-help action hardly seems warranted when the sheriff is only a telephone call away. But such a putative interpretation must be examined in terms of real world scenarios to see whether and how it works.

The Charter is not a commercial contract but a constitution. As such, one of its objectives must be the maintenance of community order and the establishment of the institutions indispensable to community decision. Like any communication between human beings, the Charter is susceptible to a range of comparatively plausible interpretations. The constitutional interpreter selects that interpretation which is most likely to achieve these objectives in present and projected factual contexts.

An interpretation of the Charter according to which individual states reserve the right of individual and collective self-defense keeps the pressure on an aggressor nation like Iraq and on the Security Council. An interpretation that says that states no longer have that right bleeds that pressure off. If an aggressor nation should perceive that a United Nations decision is the precondition for the use of force, then it probably will conclude that the pressure is off. Six months of privation caused by a blockade may be an acceptable price for acquiring a new piece of territory and the oil fields appurtenant thereto. More generally, an interpretation that assigns exclusive competence to the Security Council will produce war plans in staff colleges around the planet in which coveted territory is seized and the Security Council is seised, allowing the aggressor to hold and absorb the territory while the Council debates and perhaps orders economic sanctions.

The point is not that one should avoid the United Nations or not try to mobilize it. The point is that the United Nations is not yet an autonomous actor capable of doing the job and that interpreting the Charter as if it were capable of such challenges will undermine the Charter policies which the unorganized system, in its untidy way, has, until now, tried to secure. The most telling indication of the United Nations' continuing weakness may be found in U.N. Secretary-General Pérez de Cuéllar's comments after his mission to Amman, Jordan, on September 2, 1990, to negotiate with Tariq Aziz, the Iraqi Foreign Minister. After two days of unsuccessful talks, the Secretary-General left, saying, with remarkable candor, that the matter was now up to the superpowers![25] Unfortunately, we still do not have a world sheriff.

Nor is it certain that things will get better in the future. A collective security system must have effective power. The security system based on the United Nations was premised on the effective power of the five permanent members of the Council as well as a consensus of views. They may have represented the powers of the world in 1945, but it is far from certain that they still do. It is ironic but hardly surprising that as consensus has at last appeared, the power of the members may be disappearing. A united Germany and a powerful Japan are probably stronger than three if not four permanent members of the Council. Insofar as nuclear weapons prove to be unusable, they may cease to be the membership card in the global elite and many other states may believe that their effective power entitles them to a major role in the security system. The Group of 7 (G-7) appears to have emerged, at the present time, as a major focus of power. Japanese Prime Minister Toshiki Kaifu has already indicated that the G-7 should be undertaking political as well as economic functions. It may become the effective arena in world politics and, even within it, super-superpowers may emerge. As long as the effective power process finds that it is useful to use the apparatus of the United Nations in order to maintain world order, the United Nations structure will remain prominently in view. But even then, it will be essentially epiphenomenal.

Criteria for Appraisal of All Uses of Force

Given the constitutive problem discussed earlier, it should be no surprise that most students of international law concerned with the problem of coercion have focussed on its prohibition. This has led to an odd, oxymoronic quality in international legal discussions about the non-use of force, for all other legal systems are based on and presuppose the use of force and are preeminently concerned with directing its use into avenues that support public order and the major values of the community concerned.

The continuing problem for the international legal system, whether it develops techniques for using force exclusively in a centralized fashion (a development which still seems remote) or continues to tolerate unilateral uses of force of certain types, will be how to determine *which uses* of coercion, at *which levels,* will be appropriate for *which cases* and in *which contexts.*

As one would imagine, the views of jurists on these questions diverge greatly and passionately. For those who reject *any* unilateral use of force that is not self-defensive in the sense of the *Caroline* incident,[26] proactive actions are, by definition, unlawful. If one chooses to base one's understanding of international law exclusively on a strict textual interpretation of the U.N. Charter, it is easy to conclude that the unilateral use of force is prohibited except in self-defense and even that may be suspended if the Security Council is seised of the issue. Only "armed attack" triggers a right of self-defense and its definition in each case may be assigned to the Security Council or the General Assembly. In this particular reading, Article 2(4) would effectively rule out any lawful unilateral proactive use of force, and many self-defensive ones as well.

That approach rests on a rigid and noncontextual reading of Article 2(4), a method of interpretation that is, one might add, inconsistent with international principles found in such documents as the Vienna Convention on the Law of Treaties. As a general matter, one should not seek point-for-point conformity to a rule without constant regard for the policy or principle that animated its prescription. Article 2(4) does not even address the majority of operations which may be politically and ideologically coercive in effect but which do not employ military force. Yet, under any reasonable conception of world order, many such uses of force should be deemed unlawful. Would world order be served by their blanket authorization? The consequence of the textualistic approach does not serve the interests and fundamental objectives of the United Nations nor contribute to the fulfillment of an inclusive or common interest in the maintenance of minimum world order.

The challenge to scholars and students of this area of the law is to clarify, with as much specificity as possible, the policies and the contingent events that will render unilateral uses of force lawful. It is beyond peradventure that the fundamental postulate of political legitimacy of our century has become the right of peoples to shape their own political community and freely to choose governments that are responsive to their wishes and whose actions are consistent with overarching international human rights norms. Those who require textual authority for this proposition may find it in the United Nations Charter, the Universal Declaration of Human Rights, the International Covenants on Civil and Political Rights and on Economic, Social, and Cultural Rights, the Declaration on Principles of International Law Concerning Friendly Relations and Co-operation among States, the Helsinki Accords, and many other texts. International events in the past two years confirm that those documents express the deepest yearnings of most people in this century.

It is equally clear that far too many people about the planet survive in circumstances and under governments that fall far from this international standard. Anyone who is animated by the impulse to help others by mobilizing government support when so-called "autonomous" social or market forces themselves are not likely to remedy serious social pathologies can hardly look across political boundaries at the travail of fellow human beings without demanding some effective remedy. As long as international organizations prove unable to fulfill the promises and achieve the standards required by a public order of human dignity, either individual states (or non-state entities) must act or the promises of basic human rights must be abandoned.

In a decentralized constitutive system, with the black letter of the Charter, the resolutions of the General Assembly, the claims of superpowers and the emergent operational code so often inconsistent with one another, the critical question is not whether coercion has been or should be applied, or by whom, but whether it has been or will be applied in support of or against community order and basic policies, and whether the application will be accomplished in ways whose net consequences include increased congruence with community goals and minimum order. Genuine self-determination is one of these community goals. In my view, as suggested above, it has become the basic postulate of political legitimacy in this century.

I do not minimize the dangers of even a qualified authorization to use force unilaterally, especially in an international political system which lacks the institutions to control potential abuses. Fortunately, the international social process is increasingly integrated, with a system of communications that transmits images of events rapidly to all parts of the planet and retransmits reactions to those initial communications. This system acts as a type of international decision process and may have the potential for being used to make rapid and effective judgments about unilateral uses of force. If there is general agreement on the criteria and method to be applied in such appraisals, the prospect of condemnation may act as some restraint.

This is far from a satisfactory arrangement. But the alternatives seem even less desirable. A blanket prohibition on the unilateral use of coercion in the "right" circumstances and for the "right" reasons simply immunizes evil from remedy. Permitting episodic actions without appraisal, on the theory that there are matters that international law does not regulate or that *inter armes silent leges* appears to incorporate the worst of all the alternatives.

Though all uses of force are lamentable, the fact is that some may serve, in terms of aggregate consequences, to increase the probability of the free choice of peoples about their government and political structure. In some instances, it may be the only possibility. Other uses of force have the manifest objective and consequence of doing exactly the opposite. There is, thus, neither need nor justification for treating in a mechanically equal fashion American actions in Grenada and Panama and Soviet actions in Hungary, Czechoslovakia, and Afghanistan. Such an approach ignores objective and consequence, which is what politics, morals, and law are all about. Governments and their jurists sometimes lapse into just such mechanical applications. The strikingly different appraisals of these various cases by the people of the international system, the source of all legal authority, is often a surer test of lawfulness.

Notes

1. This paper draws on a larger research project with James Baker to be published in 1991 as "Regulating Covert Action."
2. M. McDougal & H. Lasswell, *Legal Education and Public Policy: Professional Training in the Public Interest,* 52 YALE L. J. 203 (1943).
3. *Declaration on Principles of International Law Concerning Friendly Relations and Co-operation Among States in Accordance with the Charter of the United Nations,* G.A. Res. 2625, 25 U.N. GAOR Supp. (No. 28) at 121, U.N. Doc. A/8028 (1971), *reprinted in* 9 I.L.M. 1292 (1970).
4. *Declaration on the Strengthening of International Security,* 25 U.N. GAOR Supp. (No. 28), at 22-23, para. 4.
5. *See* Article 7 of the *Resolution on the Definition of Aggression,* G.A. Res. 3314 (XXIX), 29 U.N. GAOR Supp. (No. 31) 142, U.N. Doc. A/9631 (1975), *reprinted in* 13 I.L.M. 710, 714 (1974).
6. *See supra* note 3.
7. U.N.G.A. 36/103 (1981).
8. *See supra* note 3.
9. *Id.* (italics supplied).
10. G.A. Res. 34/14b (XXXIV), U.N. Doc. A/RES/34/146 (1980), *reprinted in* 18 I.L.M. 1456 (1979).
11. DOCUMENTS ON THE LAWS OF WAR 387-446 (A. Roberts and R. Guelff 2d ed. 1989).

12. *Sovereignty and the International Obligations of Socialist Countries,* Pravda, Sept. 26, 1968, at 4, trans. in 20 CDSP, No. 39, at 12.

13. *Remarks at the Annual Dinner of the Conservative Political Action Conference (March 1, 1985),* I PUBLIC PAPERS OF THE PRESIDENT: RONALD REAGAN 228.

14. *Baker Gives U.S. Approval If Soviets Act on Rumania,* N.Y. Times, Dec. 25, 1989, at A13, col. 5.

15. *See supra* note 5.

16. *Report of the Special Committee on the Question of Defining Aggression,* U.N. Doc. A/8019 (1970).

17. *Id.*

18. *See supra* note 5.

19. 1986 I.C.J. 14.

20. *Id.* at 96-97.

21. *Id.* at 104.

22. *Id.*

23. *Id.*

24. *Greenpeace Attack: Memo in March, Death in July,* N.Y. Times, Sept. 18, 1985, at A12, col. 3.

25. *U.N. Chief Says His Talks Failed and Looks to U.S.-Soviet Effort,* N.Y. Times, Sept. 3, 1990, at A1, col. 6.

26. 2 MOORE, DIGEST OF INTERNATIONAL LAW 412 (1906).

4

Commentary on the Law of Self-Defense

Richard N. Gardner

The address by then Soviet Foreign Minister Eduard Shevardnadze before the U.N. General Assembly on September 25, 1990, was a truly remarkable statement and one of the finest ever made before the United Nations.[1] Among other things, Shevardnadze quoted Immanuel Kant and said that the humane goal formulated by Kant two centuries ago has special relevance today. Kant wrote, "The greatest challenge for the human race, which nature compels it to meet, is to attain a universal civic society based on the rule of law."[2]

In working toward this challenge, the following issues concerning the law of self-defense require further examination:

- preemption of the right of self-defense by the U.N. Security Council;
- anticipatory self-defense;
- whether indirect aggression constitutes armed attack;
- whether defense of nationals overseas can be assimilated to self-defense; and
- fact-finding: how, in a decentralized legal order, can we appraise factual claims to justify self-defense.

Security Council Preemption

On the issue of Security Council preemption, Professor Michael Reisman's philosophical statement is compelling while the textual analysis of the Charter offered by Professor Abram Chayes simply is not correct. Article 51 says: "Nothing in the present Charter shall impair the inherent right of individual or collective self-defense if an armed attack occurs against a Member of the United Nations, until the Security Council has taken measures necessary to maintain international peace and security...." Article 51 does not say, "until the Security Council has taken measures," but rather, until those measures have proved "necessary for the maintenance of international peace and security."

The measures taken by the fall of 1990 against Iraq had not achieved that objective. The aggression against Kuwait continued. The measures might eventually have proven to be necessary and effective, but they had not by that time. If the view were to become accepted that the right of self-defense is suspended simply because some measures have been taken by the Council, it would mean that Kuwait had lost its inherent right of self-defense. If there is some enclave in Kuwait, where some courageous Kuwaiti freedom fighters are holding out against an Iraqi army, they have to be told, "Oh, you can't do that. You're violating international law; you have to lay down your arms; you have no right of self-defense any longer." That cannot possibly be right! Should we inform those Kuwaitis that they have lost their right of self-defense? That would be a very hard sell. And if the Kuwaitis still had their right of individual self-defense against this continuing aggression, so did the rest of the world community, including the United States, have a right of collective self-defense to help these brave people in the face of continuing aggression.

If the right of self-defense were eliminated once the Security Council started adopting resolutions, then the United States and other countries would not make use of the Security Council again in similar situations. It would become very dangerous for a nation to use the Security Council because even if the result is indeterminate, that nation would lose its right of self-defense. This would discourage resort to the collective machinery of the United Nations.

Let us examine a very practical hypothesis. Suppose Saddam Hussein continued to occupy Kuwait in the summer of 1991. His soldiers would still be carrying out their campaign of terror, of rape, and of brutalization of that country. All efforts at peaceful settlement would have been explored, and nothing would have materialized; the sanctions would not have bitten sufficiently to get him out. One year after the Iraqi invasion of Kuwait, let us assume that the United States goes to the Security Council and asks for an explicit authorization to use force. Suppose 13 of the 15 members vote "yes" including the Soviet Union and all the permanent members of the Council except China, which vetoes the resolution. Under the Chayes analysis, because of the Chinese veto, the United States cannot do anything. That just cannot be good law, and it certainly is not good policy.

Chayes' reference to Justice Jackson is surprising. I am a great admirer of Jackson and of the decision he wrote in the *Steel Seizure* case. But what has that got to do with Kuwait? The Jackson opinion is a framework of analysis about the allocation of power in a unitary nation-state as between the legislature and the executive. But we are not talking about a world government in which there is a debate about what is the power of the executive of the world government and the legislature of the world government. Here the question is the allocation of power between a sovereign state and the world organization. By the very words of the Charter, a sovereign state has an inherent right of self-defense. Now, Chayes admits that one cannot take the analysis of Jackson and apply it (in his words) "whole hog" to this situation. With great respect, I would not put any of the "hog" into this; I would throw the "hog" out the window because it really obscures the issue.

Anticipatory Self-Defense

The United States was right in the Cuban Missile crisis not to say that the deployment of missiles in Cuba by the Soviet Union constituted an "armed attack" that would give rise to the right of self-defense. I agree that it would be too dangerous for the world community to allow unilateral uses of force simply because there were some deployments of weapons or modernization of weapons. On the other hand, to say that a nation has to be a sitting duck (to use Professor Myres McDougal's phrase) and wait until the bombs are actually dropping on its soil—that cannot be right either. When attack is initiated and is underway, even though the attacker has not actually arrived in the victim state, measures can be taken. There should be agreement on that principle.

But there are hard cases. Egyptian President Gamal Abdel Nasser announced the blockade of the Gulf of Aqaba in 1967; Israel attacked. I think most people felt that was justified self-defense. But when Israel attacked the nuclear reactor in Iraq in 1981, most people—maybe with the exception of McDougal and one or two others—argued that that went too far. And yet, if anticipatory self-defense cannot cover the Iraqi reactor case (and I have no doubt that nuclear reactor was not for peaceful purposes only), how are we going to deal with a Saddam Hussein who may be preparing to use weapons of mass destruction against his neighbors?

In Shevardnadze's historic speech, he dealt explicitly with this issue. He said, "In our view, there is an urgent need to institute a new norm in international law, which would declare the threat by any individual, for purposes of blackmail, of using weapons of mass destruction, hostage taking or mass terror to be a crime against humanity." He further said, "The world community should also consider the possibility of various unconventional situations arising from the mass taking of hostages, in cases of blackmail, involving particularly dangerous and destructive weapons. The Security Council may find it necessary, upon recommendation of the

Military Staff Committee, to establish a rapid response force, to be formed on a contract basis from units specially designed by different countries, including the five permanent members of the Security Council."[3] If we are not going to stretch anticipatory self-defense to deal with the case where attack is not yet underway, but where a country is preparing weapons of mass destruction for future use, then we have to think of some collective solutions along the lines of what Shevardnadze suggested.

Indirect Aggression

I agree with John Lawrence Hargrove,[4] John Norton Moore,[5] and others who feel that the International Court of Justice (I.C.J.) judgment in the *Nicaragua* case did a great disservice to international law. I cannot understand why the systematic effort of Nicaragua to destroy the sovereignty of its neighbor, by logistical support and arms supplies to an insurrection, would not be an armed attack giving rise to a right to individual and collective self-defense. Why should the victim state be left to its own devices? Can it not call a stronger friend to deal with such indirect aggression, which can be just as devastating to independence and sovereignty as an army marching with flags flying and bugles blowing across its border?

Defense of Nationals

It is very important that the Soviet Union, the United States, and the whole civilized community insist that an attack on one's nationals overseas, or the failure to provide the kind of defense of them that international law requires, is assimilated to the law of self-defense, and that limited action may be taken for the exclusive purpose of removing those nationals from a situation of peril—not of course as a pretext for destroying the sovereignty of the country concerned. The fact is that we live in a world in which threats of terrorism continue. In many countries offenses are committed against foreigners, and there is no other way of protecting them except by the use of force.

Fact-Finding

It is a great weakness of the existing system that nations always say they are acting in self-defense. Almost every use of force, since World War II, has been justified under a claim of self-defense.

We need to develop international processes to find the facts. I do not see the I.C.J. as the best instrument for doing this. I agree with the I.C.J.'s particular judgment in the *Nicaragua* case which found that use of force issues are justiciable. It was wrong for the United States to say that the claim of Nicaragua failed for reasons of inadmissibility. The I.C.J. can pronounce on the legality of a use of force, but how does the Court gather facts in these situations? The Security Council, under Article 33 and subsequent articles, should be used to obtain the facts in disputed situations, where claims of self-defense are made on one side and rebutted by the other. Strengthening the Council's fact-finding capacity should be a major priority for Soviet, American, and other international lawyers, and all persons concerned with collective security.

Finally, I would like to end on a point that reflects my own philosophy: Chapter VII on collective security and Article 51 on self-defense should be regarded as correlative in the U.N. Charter. There is an inverse relationship between them. In other words, the more effective the collective security system becomes in Chapter VII, the more restrictively we should apply the individual and collective self-defense rights under Article 51. The weaker the Chapter VII collective security system—and it has been very weak up till now—the more liberally we should grant the rights of individual and collective self-defense to nations because the international police force is not working. There has to be a relation between the two.

If the Security Council really becomes an effective instrument for international collective security, then we can begin to cut back on our interpretation of what nations are allowed to do to defend themselves. But we are not there yet.

Notes

1. Foreign Broadcast Information Service, Daily Report: Soviet Union 90-187, at 2 (Sept. 26, 1990).

2. *Id.* at 7.

3. *Id.* at 5.

4. *See* Hargrove, *The Nicaragua Judgment and the Future of the Law of Force and Self-Defense,* 81 AM. J. INT'L L. 135 (1987).

5. *See* J.N. Moore, *The Nicaragua Case and the Deterioration of World Order,* 81 AM. J. INT'L L. 151 (1987).

5

Commentary on Aggression and Self-Defense

David B. Rivkin, Jr.

The remarkable degree of global cooperation in standing up to the Iraqi aggression against Kuwait, the assertive and creative U.S. policy that fostered this international consensus, and the heretofore unprecedented boldness displayed by a number of Middle Eastern powers willing to invite large numbers of U.S. troops onto their soil, all combined to make the Iraq-Kuwait crisis a watershed event. The events unfolded amidst dramatically decreased East-West tensions: for the first time in U.N. history, the Security Council, due to harmonized attitudes of its five permanent members, seemed able to take strong actions against an aggressor.

From the very first day of the crisis, President George Bush, convinced that it was important—for a variety of political, diplomatic and military reasons—to organize an international coalition against Saddam Hussein, chose to proceed under the U.N. aegis. Working with a diverse group of traditional allies, Third World countries, China, and the Soviet Union, the United States was able to obtain a number of Security Council resolutions authorizing different types of sanctions against Iraq, all designed to induce the aggressor to withdraw from Kuwait. Since no signs of such an Iraqi withdrawal were imminent by early November, and since in fact the Iraqi grip on Kuwait appeared to be tightening, Bush, in consultation with American allies and other concerned parties, ordered additional troop deployments to the Persian Gulf and began to talk much more explicitly about the possibility of undertaking a military offensive against the aggressor.

The legal debate about the circumstances under which use of force against Iraq was permissible intensified over the fall of 1990. Professor

Abram Chayes emerged as one of the leading proponents of the view that, having brought the Security Council into play, the United States and its allies could not strike at Iraq without an explicit U.N. authorization, granted under Chapter VII of the U.N. Charter.[1]

The official U.S. position on the subject, articulated by Bush, Secretary of State James Baker III, and numerous other government officials, was exactly the reverse—while the U.N. authorization to use military force against Iraq might be sought, it would not be a legal prerequisite to launching military operations.[2] Instead, the fact that Iraq continued to occupy Kuwait enabled the United States and its allies, operating pursuant to Article 51 of the U.N. Charter, to use force to dislodge the aggressor. Irrespective of the Security Council authorization for military operations that was obtained on November 29, 1990, the debate over these legal principles will have important ramifications, both for the future of U.S. foreign policy[3] and for the development of international law.

Given the prominence of various forms of coercion, including the use of military force, in the international system, it is not surprising that international law precepts—bearing upon such issues as when and how force can be used—feature a particularly close nexus between legal and moral norms and the imperatives of statecraft.[4] As John Lawrence Hargrove argues, "the primary rules [governing the use of force], in order to work, must therefore be readily perceivable, by people bearing the actual responsibilities of government, to reflect the practical requirements of the world in which they must survive and conduct their affairs."[5] Indeed, Chayes himself took a pragmatic approach in the past when dispensing legal prescriptions for use-of-force decisions.[6] Clearly, focusing solely on the fact that force is used, without understanding why, is both morally myopic and legally insufficient. International law also has a moral dimension, a fact that is reflected in the common genesis and close connection between such areas of customary international law as *jus in bello* and *jus ad bellum.*[7] Thus, scrutinizing the overall context is highly instructive in thinking about the use of force.

Obviously, no assessment of specific prospects for U.N. cooperation can be divorced from international trends. Yet, in Chayes' assessments of the United Nations, one can detect an unwarranted optimism that the current degree of Security Council harmony is likely to endure. In addition to the Soviets and the Americans, there are three other permanent members of the Security Council, including China, whose future cooperation cannot be taken for granted.

Chayes' "second chance" for the United Nations also is an inappropriate metaphor. To paraphrase a well-known saying, historical ignorance is preferable to drawing erroneous historical lessons.[8] If one assumes that the proper lesson of the past is that we somehow forfeited the first chance to make the United Nations work, then presumably we should be particularly careful not to upset the U.N.'s newly found fragile consensus. If this is not the case, and "we are facing a radically new situation,"[9] then it would be foolhardy to subordinate entire American foreign policy interests to keeping our Security Council colleagues happy.

Even more fundamentally, the implications of the stance that would impose as many constraints on the use of force as possible are extremely disturbing. To paraphrase Henry Kissinger, countries which value peace above all else leave the international system at the mercy of its more ruthless denizens. Moreover, by explicitly ruling out the legitimacy of resort to force against states which sponsor terrorism and insurgent movements, one implicitly sanctions these types of aberrant international conduct. Yet, it is precisely these forms of indirect aggression that undermine stability of many regions, aggravate international tensions, and, left unchecked, often lead to full-fledged wars.

This negative trend is reinforced by the apparent erosion of such heretofore well-accepted principles of international law as anticipatory self-defense,[10] protection of one's nationals from mistreatment or hostage-taking[11] and the universal applicability of the *jus ad bellum* principles.[12] The net result of all these doctrinal innovations is a serious weakening of international legal norms governing the unilateral and collective resort to force, without producing, at the same time, any appreciable enhancement in the quality of the security regime based on Chapter VII of the U.N. Charter. The parties who suffer the most are the law-abiding members of the international community; the beneficiaries of these developments are the most cynical and ruthless international outlaws.

Those who would subordinate U.S. uses of force to U.N. approval imply that the United States cannot be trusted to use armed force responsibly. Accordingly, American warlike proclivities have to be tempered by the need to secure U.N. approval.[13] In many instances, however, if any useful international consensus is to be formed, strong U.S. leadership is required. Professor Michael Reisman's assessment that such leadership was indispensable in getting the United Nations to move in the current crisis is supported by all available evidence. Yet, if the United Nations can only be animated by strong American pressure, then the arguments about the value of securing U.N. blessing for U.S. military action lose even superficial plausibility. Proponents of these arguments are committed to a much stronger notion of world government than is warranted by the existing international realities. In that regard, Reisman's incisive commentary on the contrast between the delegation of authority to use force in the domestic and international contexts is certainly correct.[14] Domestically, the government exercises monopoly on the use of force;[15] the circumstances in which force can be used are prescribed through legally binding legislative and executive decisions; and the validity of judgments in this area is determined by the courts. Internationally, in deciding when, and how, force has been dispensed, one has to use the principles of *jus ad bellum* and *jus in bello* and, while these bodies of law are considered binding, the propriety of judgments to a large extent is tested unilaterally.[16] All in all, we clearly are not at a point when international organizations can control all of the uses of force and are not likely to arrive at that point soon, given the many deformities in the evolving international legal culture. Fortunately, however, our choice is not limited to U.N. monopoly on the use of force or the law of the jungle. There are a lot of possibilities in between, with both customary international law, and what Professor Richard Gardner refers to as working "inside the Charter,"[17] to inform our choices.

Finally, the proper reading of Article 51 would seem to indicate that "the inherent right of individual or collective self-defense" is not impaired and can be freely exercised "until the Security Council has taken measures necessary to maintain international peace and security..." Stated differently, Article 51, properly construed, means that the right of self-defense does not encompass revenge; once the threat to international peace and security has been eliminated, it would be inappropriate for the victim or its friends to engage in further use of force. Article 51 certainly does not proclaim that the right to self-defense ceases while the Security Council is debating the issues, or even after it has passed a set of intermediate measures.

To be sure, the seemingly obvious question that arises in this context is what party has the right to judge whether the measures taken by the Security Council have restored peace and security. In my view, each party to the dispute is entitled to formulate its own opinion. Thus, if the Security Council believes that a given set of measures has adequately restored peace—and even if all the five permanent members of the Security Council agree on this matter—but the victim of the aggression itself concludes differently, nothing in the U.N. Charter precludes it from engaging in self-defense and summoning its friends for help.[18]

One can certainly imagine a situation where a country has been invaded by a hostile neighbor and the Security Council, whether or not acting unanimously, decided to impose some set of sanctions on the aggressor. Let us further assume that the application of these sanctions has resulted in the cessation of the hostilities by the aggressor, or even its partial withdrawal. Let us also stipulate that the Security Council, faced with these favorable developments, has concluded that enough progress has been made and that no further sanctions are warranted, either because peace should be given a chance and remaining problems resolved through negotiations, or even because it concluded that a return to the pre-aggression *status quo ante* was not a goal worth fighting for. Irrespective of the wisdom of these policy judgments by the Security Council, it would be ludicrous to argue that the victim of the aggression does not have the legal right to mount military operations against the aggressor, for the purpose of restoring sovereignty over its territory. To argue otherwise would imply that the U.N. Charter effectively transferred all the key attributes of national sovereignty from member states to the Security Council.

Moreover, Chayes' interpretation of Article 51 could lead to a number of undesirable consequences. To begin with, if the resort to the Article 51 procedures results in the impairment of the right to self-defense, victims of aggression and their allies would be less likely to invoke this process. Thus, paradoxically, Chayes' attempt to aggrandize the power of the Security Council would most likely lead to its underutilization. Moreover, if the right of self-defense is viewed as dissipating quickly once active military operations by an aggressor cease, then the parties exercising that right would be tempted to act precipitously instead of opting to explore the path of negotiations and compromise first.

Overall, given the emerging international trends and evolving international legal patterns, retaining a full panoply of Article 51 rights is of utmost importance to the protection of American national interests and preservation of world order.

Notes

1. *See* Abram Chayes, *supra* ch. 1. Chayes carefully caveats his views on the role of the Security Council, noting that, if the United Nations did not function as "intended"—meaning, presumably, that the Security Council, because of a veto by one of five permanent members, failed to take any steps against Iraq—he would have been much more hospitable to the notion of a unilateral or multilateral military action against Saddam Hussein. This reservation explains why Chayes does not condemn all of the Cold War uses of force by the United States (when the Security Council was deadlocked), although he has been harshly critical of such American ventures as the war in Vietnam, and military operations in Grenada and Panama. *See, e.g.,* Hammarskjöld Forum, Expansion of the Vietnam War into Cambodia—The Legal Issues, 45 N.Y.U. L. REV. 664 (1970) (comments of A. Chayes); *Grenada Was Illegally Invaded,* N.Y. Times, Nov. 15, 1983, at A35, col. 1.

2. According to newspaper accounts, this view was shared by both the United States and Britain, while France, the Soviet Union, and China preferred to obtain U.N. authorization. It appears, however, that the difference was largely attributable to the political and diplomatic considerations, rather than to a different reading of the U.N. Charter. To the best of my knowledge, no permanent member of the U.N. Security Council has embraced the legal position advocated by Chayes.

3. The international law quandary has an important domestic counterpart—the constitutional law debate about whether or not President Bush could launch military operations against Saddam Hussein without first securing a declaration of war from Congress, or at least a congressional resolution authorizing such an action. Arguably, there is a close connection between these two debates. To the extent one believes that the President possesses inherent authority to use force to defend the United States, its nationals, and allies from aggression, then if the U.S. operations against

Iraq are construed as being undertaken pursuant to Article 51 of the U.N. Charter, the case for congressional involvement is less credible. In contrast, if military operations against Iraq are treated as an offensive use of force, albeit authorized by the Security Council, the case for congressional involvement becomes stronger. For an excellent discussion of the respective war powers of the President and Congress, *see, e.g., Going to War Over War Powers,* Washington Post, Nov. 18, 1990, at C1, col. 1. In general, making a persuasive argument regarding the legality of our actions in the Persian Gulf is an important prerequisite to sustaining the domestic legitimacy of this venture. This is all the more important given the residual ambivalence displayed by large segments of the American electorate about the desirability of interventionist foreign policies.

4. Clearly, while international law deals with a multitude of subjects, "[i]n its grandest (or most grandiose) form, international law is about the use or support of armed force against another nation." Bork, *The Limits of "International Law,"* 7 NATIONAL INTEREST 3 (Winter 1989/90).

5. Hargrove, *The Nicaragua Judgment and The Future of the Law of Force and Self-Defense,* 81 AM. J. INT'L L. 137 (1987), *quoted in* Sofaer, *International Law and the Use of Force,* NATIONAL INTEREST 54 (Fall 1988). The difficulty of reconciling the imperatives of statecraft and international legal norms pertaining to use of force has been largely fostered by the inherent tension between the hortatory view of international relations, espoused by many a legal scholar, and much less attractive realities of international life. Some scholars, including Robert H. Bork, find this tension so disquieting that they are moved to deny the very existence of international law—"whatever reality this wraith called international law possesses is not visible to the non-expert." Bork, *supra* note 4, at 5.

6. *See* Chayes, *A Common Lawyer Looks at International Law*, 78 HARV. L. REV. 1396 (1965).

7. *Jus in bello* governs the actual use of military force and contains a number of proscriptive and prescriptive themes, for example, proportionality, discrimination, impermissibility of direct attack on noncombatants, etc. In contrast, *jus ad bellum* provides normative principles for permissible recourse to military force. Both of these bodies of law are rooted in Judeo-Christian tradition, to wit, the Just War theory. Significantly, while the laws of war—*jus in bello*—have to be obeyed irrespective of the virtues of the underlying cause, the entire enterprise is illegitimate unless one's original resort to force—governed by *jus ad bellum* principles—was just. To be sure, as part of the recent international law "reforms," the U.N. General Assembly has held, on a number of occasions, that parties waging wars of national liberation or fighting for other "progressive causes" apparently do not have to comport with traditional *jus in bello* norms.

8. E.R. MAY, "LESSONS" OF THE PAST: THE USE AND MISUSE OF HISTORY IN AMERICAN FOREIGN POLICY (1973).

9. Reisman, *supra* ch. 2, at 42.

10. "[I]nternational law before the U.N. Charter did recognize the right of anticipatory self-defense when the 'necessity of that self-defense is instant,

overwhelming, and leaving no choice of means, and no moment for deliberation.'" Gardner, *Sovereignty and Intervention: The Just Use of Force,* 10 FREEDOM AT ISSUE 19 (March/April 1985), (quoting Daniel Webster's famous missive to the British government in the *Caroline* case, August 6, 1842).

11. "It is increasingly accepted that a state may take steps to rescue victims or potential victims in an action strictly limited to that purpose and not likely to involve disproportional destruction of life and property in the state where the rescue takes place." RESTATEMENT (THIRD) OF THE FOREIGN RELATIONS LAW OF THE UNITED STATES § 177 (1987). *Cf.* J. Crown and J. Fried, *A Legal Disaster,* THE NATION, May 24, 1980; *Rescue Mission Violated the U.N. Charter,* N.Y. Times, May 5, 1980 (letter to the editor), *all cited* in Sofaer, *supra* note 5, at 63 nn. 10-11.

12. This value-neutral applicability of legal principles is the bedrock of any legal system. In the *jus ad bellum* context, this means that a state may legitimately use force to repel an armed attack irrespective of how "unprogressive" its ideology may be or how noble the aspirations and motives of the attackers might be. In contrast, numerous General Assembly resolutions have held that when people are exercising their "legitimate self-determination" rights, the affected states have no right to defend themselves against these actions, and other members of the international community may not render them help. Reisman, *supra* ch. 2; Bork, *supra* note 4, at 10. *See supra* note 7 for discussion of a similar double standard influencing *jus in bello.*

13. One is struck by an interesting parallel between this argument and the claim that, domestically, an imperial presidency is prone to using the force rashly, and accordingly, has to share responsibility for making foreign policy decisions with an allegedly more responsible and peace-loving Congress. This oft-invoked assertion is, however, entirely incorrect. For an excellent discussion of this issue, *see, e.g.,* ROBERT F. TURNER, RESTORING THE RULE OF LAW IN NATIONAL SECURITY AFFAIRS: A CRITICAL LOOK AT THE WAR POWERS RESOLUTION (1991). The notion that legislative bodies are able to conduct a more successful foreign policy than the President is both historically wrong, and, in the U.S. domestic context, contrary to the Framers' design.

14. *See* Reisman, *supra* ch. 2.

15. To be sure, even domestically, citizens are allowed to use deadly force in a very narrow range of circumstances, primarily when they have a justifiable fear of physical assault.

16. When the parties to the dispute agree, there is, of course, the possibility of international adjudication. Theoretically, the International Court of Justice (I.C.J.) should be able to render judgments about whether or not the parties to a given conflict used force in violation of the U.N. Charter and other relevant international norms. However, as the discord surrounding the I.C.J. decision in the *Nicaragua* case demonstrates, given the continuing divisions in the world community, the I.C.J. and other international legal tribunals are ill-equipped to handle such cases. *See Military and Paramilitary Activities In and Against Nicaragua (Nicar. v. U.S.),* 1986 I.C.J. 14.

For an excellent discussion of this issue, *see, e.g.,* J.N. Moore, *The Nicaragua Case and the Deterioration of World Order,* 81 AM. J. INT'L L. 151 (1987).

17. Gardner, *supra* note 10, at 24.

18. Gardner makes a similar argument. Gardner, *supra* note 10, at 2.

PART TWO

Collective Security

6

Authorized Uses of Force by the United Nations and Regional Organizations

Oscar Schachter

I am faced here with a choice between a fox and a hedgehog. The fox, it is said, knows many things, the hedgehog one big thing.[1] My subject is wide and many-sided; it calls for a fox. Yet at this time, our attention is focused on one big thing—the collective use of force to repel the Iraqi aggression against Kuwait. A hedgehog seems to be needed or at least a fox with a good sense of priorities.

A lawyer's view of the U.N. Charter and practice reveals as many as six legal categories for the use of force. In brief, they are:

1) Armed force as an enforcement measure taken by the Security Council under Chapter VII, particularly Article 42;

2) Collective self-defense in accordance with Article 51;

3) Individual self-defense under Article 51;

4) Enforcement measures under regional arrangements or by regional agencies under Article 53;

5) Peacekeeping forces of the United Nations authorized by the Security Council or General Assembly and deployed in agreement with the states concerned; and

6) Joint action by the five permanent members pursuant to Article 106 of the Charter.

With the exception of this last provision, all of the foregoing categories have been applied, at one time or another, to characterize military action as legitimate under the U.N. Charter. I shall comment on each of them, but give more detailed treatment to collective enforcement measures.

The Use of Force Under Chapter VII

U.N. enforcement action against an aggressor is presently the center of world attention. It is often referred to as collective security, an expression not used in the Charter but widely regarded as the principal goal of the United Nations. The Charter does list at the very beginning (Article 1(1)) among the purposes of the United Nations "to take effective collective measures...for the suppression of acts of aggression or other breaches of the peace...." The legal framework for such collective measures is found mainly in Chapter VII, a part of the Charter that received more attention during the drafting and ratification stages than all the rest of the Charter. The idea of an international "police" force to deter and suppress aggressors seemed to be the giant step to world order that had long been advocated by idealists. On the other hand, skepticism was also prevalent and a fear that the "great powers" could not be trusted to act justly or wisely, even if unanimously. The veto offered assurance to the permanent members and to some others that rash action would be unlikely.

The experience over 45 years has amply revealed the gap between the plan of Chapter VII and its implementation. Plainly, many acts of aggression and breaches of peace have occurred since 1945 without any recourse to the enforcement measures of Chapter VII. In only one prior case—the response to the North Korean invasion of 1950—were armed forces mobilized and deployed in response to Security Council resolutions.[2] That action did not fit into the pattern of Chapter VII as originally envisaged. Its legality has been questioned because it did not have the required "concurring vote" of the USSR. It did, however, succeed in repelling the aggression, and it showed that enforcement action could be taken in response to a recommendation.

We are now in the middle of the second major enforcement action involving armed force, the Iraq-Kuwait crisis. Here, unlike the Korean case, the Security Council has not faced challenges to the legality of its decisions. Its resolutions have been in accord with the graduated measures laid down in Chapter VII. They have not, however, established a United Nations force or command. Instead, the Council adopted a number of mandatory decisions under Article 41 which impose sanctions against Iraq falling short of use of armed force.[3] The use of armed force has been authorized in two resolutions. The first, adopted in August 1990, calls on members "cooperating with the Government of Kuwait" with maritime forces in the area to use measures "as may be necessary" to halt maritime shipping that would be in contravention of the economic embargo against Iraq.[4] The second and more far-reaching resolution authorized the members cooperating with Kuwait to use "all necessary means" to uphold and implement the Council resolutions mandating Iraq's withdrawal from Kuwait and related measures.[5] Thus, the Council has authorized—not mandated—"all necessary means," a phrase plainly intended to include the use of armed force.

It may seem strange, at first blush, that the Security Council resolutions in the Iraq case, as well as those 40 years earlier relating to Korea, contain no reference to Article 42, the key article on the use of force by the United Nations. It is, in fact, the only article of the Charter that expressly empowers a U.N. organ—the Security Council—to take action "by air, sea or land forces" as may be necessary for international peace and security. This does not mean that the United Nations has no other legal basis to use military force. In 1962 the International Court of Justice rejected the contention that "peacekeeping forces" deployed in the Middle East and in the Congo had to be based on Article 42.[6] It declared: "The Court cannot accept so limited a view of the powers of the Security Council under the Charter."[7] However, a decisive point in that case was that the military force for peacekeeping was not coercive, not used against a state but with its consent. The situation is different in actions against an aggressor government. In such cases, there is good reason to conclude that the use of force by the Council should meet the requirements of Article 42, even if the Council chooses not to refer to the article. Those requirements are important safeguards against hasty or arbitrary decisions that could have devastating effects. To begin with, the Council should make a finding of a threat to the peace or breach of the peace or act of aggression in the particular case, thus applying Article 39. An explicit determination of this kind indicates that the matter is considered appropriate for measures under Chapter VII.

A second condition would seem to be called for—though not mandated—by Article 40. Under that Article, the Council may call on the parties concerned to comply with "provisional measures" without prejudice to their claims or rights. Typically, a cease-fire or withdrawal is a provisional measure. The Security Council requested such action initially in both the Korean and Iraqi invasions.

A third condition is expressly required by Article 42. It prescribes that the Council "consider" that the non-forcible measures of Article 41 (for example, an economic embargo) would be inadequate or have proved inadequate before it takes military action. This provision underlines the necessity of employing non-violent sanctions before force is authorized. It is left to the Council to determine whether Article 41 "sanctions" will prove to be adequate to bring about compliance with the Council's decisions.

Article 42 has been construed, particularly in the early years, as requiring "action" in the special sense of an obligatory enforcement measure. One reason for this has been the conflating of "enforcement" with "mandatory effect." It was assumed that an enforcement measure must be peremptory. This point is reinforced because "action" by the Security

Council when used elsewhere in the Charter (for example, Article 11(2)) means more than "recommendation."[8] Since "action" is used in Article 42 the conclusion drawn is that a Security Council recommendation or authorization would not come within Article 42 and need not meet its conditions.

Though these arguments merit consideration, I find no compelling reason to accept them as imposing a limit on the Council's recommendatory power. Inasmuch as the Council is empowered to adopt a mandatory action under Article 42, it should have the lesser power to recommend or authorize such action. It does not make sense to require a binding decision where a request or authorization would suffice. As the Korean experience showed, a Council recommendation is adequate where member states are ready and willing to act. This is also the premise of the Security Council's resolutions in the Iraq-Kuwait case which authorize (but do not require) member states cooperating with the government of Kuwait to use all "necessary means" to implement the earlier decisions of the Council.

The Special Agreements Under Article 43

One of the legal questions concerning the present applicability of Article 42 arises from the requirement of Article 43 that the Security Council conclude special agreements with member states for the provision of armed forces and facilities to be on call for Security Council action. During the early years of the United Nations, and even recently, it was thought that such agreements were a condition precedent to collective military measures undertaken by the Security Council. This view may have been held by the governments in the San Francisco Conference.[9] It was often expressed by commentators on the Charter.[10] On the other hand, no explicit language in Article 42 or in Articles 43, 44, and 45 (which refer to the special agreements) precludes states from voluntarily making armed forces available to carry out the resolutions of the Council adopted under Chapter VII.[11] As we observed above, the response to the resolutions in the Korean action is a clear precedent. In that case, sixteen states provided armed forces and military facilities to assist South Korea in repelling the North Korean aggression. They did so in response to a recommendation[12] and no legal argument was made that a mandatory decision was necessary.

Article 43, though drafted in obligatory language, has never been applied. The Security Council has not taken the initiative to negotiate such special agreements though Article 43 requires that this be done "as soon as possible." It does not appear that any member state requested such negotiation. In effect, Article 43 has become a dead letter. Even when a majority of U.N. members (including the United States) emphasized the need for states to make armed forces available for service under U.N.

aegis, they did not urge recourse to Article 43 agreements. Thus, the General Assembly adopted resolutions during the Korean War that recommended that "each Member maintain within its national forces elements so trained, organized and equipped that they could promptly be made available in accordance with its constitutional processes for services as a U.N. unit or units upon recommendation by the Security Council or the General Assembly."[13] It is not surprising, of course, that at that time no consideration was given to agreements negotiated by the Security Council, which was then hopelessly split by the Korean action and more generally by the Cold War. The Collective Measures Committee set up by the General Assembly to consider means of strengthening collective military action reported on various proposals but did not suggest any use of Article 43.[14] Whatever measures were considered (including stand-by forces or even a "reserve" of individual volunteers) were not linked to the agreements under Article 43. The underlying premise was that if member states supported use of armed force under the United Nations, they would be expected to provide the means without legal compulsion.

The fact that Article 43 agreements have not been concluded and have not been found necessary for military measures does not mean that the Article is devoid of present interest. One implication of the Article is important. It makes it clear that member states cannot be legally bound to provide armed forces unless they have agreed to do so. It thus affirms a limitation on the authority given to the Council by Article 42 and by Articles 48 and 49. True, this important point rests on an inference, not express language. However, there is added support in the legislative history of the Charter and in the process of ratification for concluding that the Security Council may not impose an obligation on a member state to make armed forces available unless that state agreed to do so through a special agreement with the Council.[15]

Implications for National Constitutional Requirements

This conclusion has interesting implications for national constitutional requirements. Article 43 requires that the special agreements be subject to ratification by the signatory states in accordance with their respective constitutional processes. Such express reference to national constitutional requirements is rare in the Charter. It is found elsewhere only as a condition for ratification of the Charter itself (Article 110) and for amendments (Article 108). There are several provisions of the Charter that contemplate agreements between the Organization and individual member states but none of them refer to national constitutional requirements (see Articles 26, 35, and 77). The fact that such reference is contained in Article 43 reflects an understanding that an agreement to provide armed forces for enforcement action under Article 42 may involve constitutional requirements of member states. We can be almost certain that this point was made by the United States during the San Francisco Conference.

When the Charter was before the U.S. Senate for its consent to ratification, the Senators concerned placed emphasis on the Article 43 agreements as a necessary condition for an obligation by the United States to make armed forces available for enforcement action under Chapter VII. This position was affirmed in the 1945 law authorizing U.S. participation in the United Nations.[16] The President was authorized therein to negotiate a special agreement under Article 43 which would be subject to the approval of the Congress. It was specified that such agreement would enable the President to make forces available to the Security Council when it acted under Article 42.[17] The statute indicated that this did not apply to "support of U.N. activities" not involving armed forces contemplated under Chapter VII.

The Security Council resolutions after the North Korean invasion contained no explicit reference to the Charter. They were recommendations and they requested the United States to act as the command of the multilateral forces under the U.N. flag.[18] President Truman referred to the U.N. measures as a "police" action and concluded that no special agreement was necessary for the United States to commit its armed forces. In his view it was not necessary to obtain a declaration of war by the Congress, despite the extensive scale of hostilities.[19] In support of this position, it was argued by the Department of State that the U.S. military action was authorized by the Charter which as a treaty had the status of a law in the United States and consequently fell within the constitutional power of the President to "take care that the laws be faithfully executed."[20] The implication is that the Charter requires "faithful execution" and that even a recommendation for a police action must be carried out as if it were a law.

These arguments were revived in 1990 with regard to U.S. military action against Iraq. In respect of United Nations law, an argument has been made that a Security Council resolution authorizing a police action "becomes an obligation which none can shirk."[21] The Korean case is cited as a precedent, as a Charter interpretation that "does not leave room for each state, once the Council has acted, to defer compliance until it has authority from its own legislature."[22]

There is more than one reason to reject this argument. A recommendation by a U.N. organ, when clear and explicit, cannot be converted into an obligation without further agreement by the states concerned. Nothing in the U.N. proceedings during the Korean War suggests that the Council recommendations for military force were considered to be mandatory. Nor is there any indication that the authorizing resolutions in the Iraq-Kuwait case obliged the cooperating states to employ armed force. The distinction between an obligation and an authorization remains important in the U.N. legal system and to member states. The fact that the Charter has the force of a treaty under national law cannot alter the effect of the Security Council resolutions which recommend or authorize rather than command and require.

But even if the Security Council adopted obligatory resolutions under Chapter VII, it could not require member states to provide forces and facilities unless that state had agreed to do so under Article 43. As indicated above, the legislative history of the Charter shows a clear intent to distinguish the provision of armed forces from other obligations that the Council may impose under Articles 42, 48, and 49. Hence it cannot plausibly be maintained that member states by their adherence to the Charter have given up their own constitutional controls on the provision of armed forces. This was expressly recognized in the United States by both the executive and legislative branches at the time of ratification. No U.N. "precedent" has altered this.

It might be considered desirable, in view of the constitutional controls that many countries have in regard to the use of troops abroad or in waging war, to seek to revive Article 43 so that armed forces could be provided promptly when the Security Council requests or requires such action. Such agreements would require approval by constitutional processes of the respective states as the Charter notes. It should be expected that the agreements would contain limitations considered necessary by the governments. The limitations would be especially important for all the states that lack the veto since they might be subject to U.N. mandatory decisions requiring armed forces under the terms of the special agreements whether or not they agreed. The five permanent members, protected by the veto, should have less reason to fear military action imposed on them. However, some of them, notably the United States, would face the historic problems of executive versus legislative authority. This would complicate reaching an agreement that might render a legislative decision unnecessary. It would be excessively optimistic to expect that such special agreements could be negotiated in the near future but the hoped-for strengthening of collective security through the United Nations may in time make it politically feasible to seek such agreements. Perhaps it is not too soon to study and reflect on the possibilities.

Authority and Command

Chapter VII contemplates that armed forces will be placed "at the disposal of the Security Council" (Article 47). A Military Staff Committee is established to advise and assist the Council on "all questions relating to the Security Council's military requirements [and] the employment and command of forces placed at its disposal" (Article 47). The Committee is also to be responsible under the Council for "the strategic direction of any armed forces placed at the disposal of the Security Council" (Article 47). The Charter establishes the composition of the Military Staff Committee, which consists of the Chiefs of Staff (or their representatives) of the permanent members of the Council. The Military Staff Committee may invite other member states to be associated with it when required for the efficient discharge of its work.

Chapter VII envisages but does not expressly require combined military action by national forces placed at the disposal of the Council. It declares that questions relating to the command of such forces shall be worked out subsequently. A report prepared by the Military Staff Committee in 1947[23] had recommended that a "supreme" or "overall" commander be appointed by the Council for all the forces made available to it.[24] The national contingents would retain their identity, serve under their respective commands and be subject to their own military discipline. Although these recommendations were unanimous, the Committee could not agree on the size and relative contributions of the armed forces or on their location.[25]

The United States had favored a much larger force than had the Soviet Union and France. The United States also favored stationing the troops in bases around the world and requiring all states to provide rights of passage. These proposals were not acceptable to the Soviet Union; hence the report lacked unanimity. It was not adopted by the Council and the Military Staff Committee ceased to be active. It obviously could not be involved in the Korean War in view of the Soviet position that the U.N. action was illegal.

In that action, as we noted, the Council requested the United States to designate the commander of the forces made available to assist South Korea to repel the aggressor. The United States named General Douglas MacArthur as the commander. He was not responsible to the United Nations but to the U.S. Joint Chiefs of Staff and the chain of command up to the President. In testimony, MacArthur said his connection with the United Nations was "purely nominal."[26] The U.S. government described itself as the "Executive Agent of the United Nations" in its agreements with other participating states for troop contributions.[27] MacArthur used the title of United Nations Commander-in-Chief and the U.S. reports consistently referred to the "United Nations forces."

Although the U.S. government considered itself an "agent" of the United Nations, it did not consider the United Nations as a principal entitled to exercise authority over the forces or strategic goals. The bi-weekly reports routinely sent to the United Nations by the United States were purely factual summaries of past activities; they were not meant to be a basis for discussion, let alone direction. An early proposal by the U.N. Secretary-General for a committee of governments to coordinate assistance was rejected by the United States.[28] Later on the United States held regular meetings in Washington with an advisory committee of representatives of the participating states.

The basic question of the authority of the United Nations over the objectives and strategy of the U.N. forces arose fairly early when those forces pursued the North Korean forces into their territory. This raised the issue whether the U.N. aim was to restore the status quo or to destroy the aggressor forces and bring about the unification of Korea by use of force. Differences between the United States and many other members emerged on this issue.[29] They were emphasized by MacArthur's plans to carry the war up to the border of China and for hot pursuit into China. The entry of large numbers of Chinese Communist troops and reversals for the U.N. forces brought about an increased demand in the United Nations to bring about an end to the conflict on the basis of the status quo before the invasion. Eventually, the United States accepted the status quo ante but significant differences arose in the protracted armistice and truce negotiations with regard to the role of the United Nations.[30] The armistice negotiations were carried out by the U.N. Command (in other words, the United States) and after the armistice entered into effect, the U.N. General Assembly approved its terms.[31] The Assembly resolution noted that a political conference had been agreed upon, and it then recommended that the member states contributing forces would be the participants, thereby in effect removing the United Nations from further negotiations.

Obviously, the Korean War situation will not be repeated but the problems of authority and control are almost certain to complicate any future large-scale enforcement action. In fact, these problems also came up in the major peacekeeping actions such as in the Congo and Cyprus where the Council's mandate to the Secretary-General and the forces left ample room for different interpretations.

In the Iraq-Kuwait crisis, the Security Council defined the main objective as the complete withdrawal of Iraq from Kuwait and the restoration of the legitimate government of Kuwait.[32] A number of subsidiary aims and demands were included in the twelve resolutions adopted from August through November 1990. Armed forces were sent to the area by the United States and several European and Arab states as collective self-defense measures in accordance with Article 51. The Council expressly affirmed that right as applied in this case.[33] It also adopted mandatory non-forcible sanctions under Article 41 and later it called on members deploying maritime forces to use such measures "as may be necessary under the authority of the Security Council" to halt maritime shipping so as to ensure compliance with the economic embargo.[34] A more general authorization to use force was contained in the November 29 resolution, authorizing member states cooperating with the government of Kuwait in the event that Iraq did not withdraw by January 15, 1991, to use "all necessary means" to implement the Council resolutions and to restore peace and security in "the area."[35]

This resolution did not expressly raise issues of command or control. It did not call for combined action although coordination by the participating states was envisaged. Some states, particularly the Soviet Union, asked that the Military Staff Committee advise and assist the Council, as contemplated in the Charter. The Council resolution that authorized the cooperating states to use naval forces to enforce the economic sanctions (Resolution 665) requested coordination of such actions "using as appropriate mechanisms of the Military Staff Committee." The Military Staff Committee has had some meetings to discuss military problems raised by the Council resolutions on Iraq but its "advice," if any, has not been disclosed.

The combined military action against Iraq begun in January 1991 was characterized by the participating states as an operation undertaken pursuant to the authorization of the Security Council. However, the Council was not asked or expected to exercise strategic direction or responsibility for the military operation. Unlike Korea, the Council did not designate a commander and it did not authorize the U.N. flag. The Secretary-General was given no role by the Council in this connection. It was left to the military forces of the states taking action to coordinate and combine their operations.

Legal Limits on Ends and Means

One question raised in public debates on the Iraqi invasion was whether the participating states should go beyond the stated objectives of the Council resolutions in order to eliminate the military capability of Iraq and remove its leadership. This raised legal as well as political issues. Could the states deriving legal authority to use force from the Council's resolution go beyond the Council's stated aims? This was an issue, as we saw, in the Korean case. With respect to the Iraqi case, the resolution was clear as to the immediate objective: withdrawal of Iraq from Kuwait and restoration of the legitimate government of Kuwait. However, it also included a little-noticed but pregnant additional aim—namely, "to restore international peace and security to the area."

The question becomes more complicated if the legal basis for the use of force is collective self-defense under Article 51. We will discuss collective self-defense below in some detail but at this point, it is appropriate to note that self-defense (individual or collective) is not limited under all circumstances to securing withdrawal by the aggressor. It may extend to temporary occupation of the aggressor's territory and the imposition of full or partial demilitarization. With regard to the Iraqi case, the Security Council may itself authorize or order such measures as necessary for the restoration of peace and security in the area.

An important question concerns the principles of the Charter and their effect as a limit on Council action and on collective self-defense. The Council's power to take measures to maintain and restore international peace and security may, on its face, appear to be virtually unlimited. It is limited, however, by the basic declaration in Article 24(2), that in discharging its duties, the Council shall act in accordance with the purposes and principles of the United Nations. One may infer from this that the Council is under an obligation to respect "sovereign equality" and the right of states to political independence and territorial integrity. These principles and the major Charter purposes—including respect for human rights and self-determination—have a bearing on the legal authority of the Council to impose coercive measures on a defeated aggressor state.[36] On the other hand, maintenance of peace and security may necessitate measures of control that would limit states in their military capabilities. No pat answer can fit all circumstances. The analogy of the U.N. forces as police and the aggressor as a criminal does not provide a solution but it enables us to see that measures of protection may have to go beyond restoring the status quo ante. At the same time, certain basic rights of the people in a country cannot be ignored or arbitrarily overridden because of a prior aggressor regime. A criminal regime may have to be ousted and its leaders punished but the people would still be entitled to self-rule and basic human rights.

Application of the Law of Armed Conflict to U.N. Forces

The analogy of police versus criminal has also added complications to the question of whether forces acting under U.N. aegis are fully bound by the law of war—the *jus in bello.* Should an aggressor, branded as criminal, have the full protection of rights under the customary law of armed conflict?

In the Nuremberg trial, arguments presented by the prosecution maintained that the criminal motive of the acts of the aggressor destroyed their legal character as acts of war.[37] Therefore the responsible leaders could no longer claim privileges under the law nor could the aggressor forces benefit from rights bestowed by the law they had violated. During the Korean War, a committee of leading international lawyers in the American Society of International Law noted that the use of force by United Nations against an aggressor is legally different from war by a state and that the "purposes for which the laws of war were instituted are not entirely the same as the purposes of regulating the use of force by the United Nations."[38] The Committee finally concluded that "for the time being" the United Nations should not feel bound by all the laws of war but should select those laws that "fit its purposes" such as the rules on prisoners of war and on belligerent occupation.[39]

This conclusion is mistaken, in my opinion, as is the argument that the aggressor should be denied the rights of a belligerent under customary law and the Hague and Geneva Conventions. To abandon the principles of equality and reciprocity in this regard would weaken the basis for any observance of the humanitarian rules of armed conflict. Individual soldiers on both sides would find themselves at risk, subject to cruelties long outlawed. It is true that a widely supported U.N. decision designating the aggressor may be regarded as definitive and as excluding the subjectivity that might otherwise characterize such condemnation. However, the practical necessity of equality to ensure observance remains the compelling reason for requiring that U.N. forces comply fully with the humanitarian rules of the law of armed conflict. The Institut de Droit International reached this conclusion after some years of study and discussion. Its resolution adopted in 1971 declared that the humanitarian rules of the law of armed conflict applied to the United Nations and that they must be complied with in all circumstances by U.N. forces engaged in hostilities.[40] The resolution construed humanitarian rules broadly. It included rules concerning weapons and those aimed at protecting civilian persons and property.[41] The resolution also prescribed a number of actions to be taken by the United Nations and by the governments of the national contingents to secure effective compliance.[42]

In a subsequent resolution adopted in 1975 the Institut concluded that the rules of armed conflict are applicable to hostilities in which U.N. forces are engaged, even if those rules are not specifically humanitarian in character.[43] That resolution included an exception to the law of neutrality, declaring that member states may not take advantage of the general rules of neutrality to evade obligations laid upon them by a decision of the Security Council. States may still be neutral (subject to the Council decision). Moreover, they may not depart from rules of neutrality for the benefit of a party opposing the U.N. forces.

The foregoing comments relating to the obligations of U.N. forces under the law of armed conflict would obviously apply also to national forces operating under the aegis of the United Nations, such as is authorized by the Security Council resolutions on the Iraqi invasion of Kuwait. The states participating in accordance with the U.N. decisions remain bound by the Hague and Geneva Conventions and the relevant customary law. They are therefore directly accountable for compliance, irrespective of U.N. authorization. They would also be subject to Security Council decisions that imposed limits on their operations, as for example, restricting the use of weapons of mass destruction. Such decisions would have to be concurred in by the permanent members and by the required majority of the Council.

Self-Defense and U.N. Authority

The right of states to use armed force in self-defense is recognized both by customary law and explicitly in Article 51 of the Charter. In almost every case where a state has used force since 1945, it has claimed that it did so as legitimate self-defense in response to an unlawful armed attack (or to a threat of imminent attack) upon it or upon another state. In the latter case, collective self-defense, expressly referred to in Article 51, was the stated legal ground. Legitimate self-defense, individual or collective, provides an exception to the prohibition against armed force in Article 2(4) of the Charter.

Article 51 describes self-defense as an "inherent right." The I.C.J. has construed this expression as referring to self-defense under customary law and as indicating that the customary law rules exist alongside the Charter law. The Court observed that the customary and Charter rules on self-defense are not identical in content but it added that the customary law has developed during the last four decades under the influence of the Charter.[44] Whatever the difference, it is generally accepted that self-defense permits an attacked state to use armed force provided such force is necessary and proportionate. The same conditions apply to collective self-defense by third states coming to the assistance of an attacked state. This is not the place to enter into a further discussion of the law on self-defense, which is dealt with elsewhere in this volume. My particular aim here is to consider self-defense as an aspect of the role of the United Nations in authorizing the use of force.

Unlike other uses of force under Chapter VII, the use of force under Article 51 does not require the prior authorization of the Security Council or any other body of the United Nations. A state is entitled to use force as long as the requirements of self-defense are satisfied. It is free to decide for itself in the first instance whether those requirements have been met and to use force necessary and proportionate to repel an unlawful attack. As the conditions of self-defense are imposed by law, the state claiming self-defense cannot be the final arbiter of its legality.[45] The international community, acting through the competent U.N. organs or the decentralized responses of states, may pass judgment on the legality of the self-defense claim. Many situations involving such claims have been discussed in the Security Council and the General Assembly; resolutions were adopted in a number of cases. In nearly all such cases, the majority of states rejected the claim of self-defense.[46] The I.C.J. did so in the one case where the issue was squarely raised, the *Nicaragua v. United States of America* case.

What is interesting for our present discussion are the rare cases in which the Security Council and the General Assembly have affirmed and endorsed the application of self-defense by a state victim of an attack and by other states coming to its assistance with armed force. This possibility provides in effect an alternative to enforcement measures under Chapter VII.

Some of the legal commentary at the time of the Korean War brought this out. Scholars such as Hans Kelsen and Julius Stone, who regarded the Security Council resolutions of June 1950 as invalid because they did not receive the concurring votes of all the permanent members, concluded, nonetheless, that the use of force to defend South Korea was a legal collective self-defense action under Article 51.[47] The U.N. Commission's findings considered by the Security Council and the General Assembly were regarded as convincing evidence of the North Korean aggression and of the necessity for collective self-defense to repel that aggression. There was no reference to self-defense in U.N. decisions on Korea but there is a plausible case for its applicability.

In the Iraqi case, an explicit recognition of the right of collective self-defense was included in an early resolution of the Security Council after the Iraqi invasion. That resolution included a preambular paragraph "affirming the inherent right of collective self-defense, in response to the armed attack of Iraq against Kuwait..." (Resolution 661, August 6, 1990). The United States and other governments that sent armed forces to the Gulf region prior to the authorization to use force declared that their actions were based on the collective self-defense provision of Article 51.

This position became somewhat controversial when questions arose as to whether the states in question such as those "co-operating with Kuwait" could use armed force against Iraq without further authorization by the Council under Article 42. The main legal point centered on the phrase in Article 51 that said nothing shall impair the right of self-defense "until the Council has taken measures necessary to maintain international peace and security." It was argued by some that the phrase quoted had to mean that the right of self-defense no longer applied when the Security Council adopted measures it considered necessary. The United Kingdom and the United States maintained that the right of self-defense, individual and collective, still applied; other governments, including some permanent members, suggested that the Council's decisions on non-forcible sanctions were intended to preclude the use of armed force in the absence of further authorization. The controversy was stilled when the Council decided in Resolution 678 to authorize the members "co-operating with the Government of Kuwait," to "use all necessary means" to implement the resolutions calling on Iraq to withdraw from Kuwait if Iraq did not do so by January 15, 1991. This resolution clearly was intended to authorize the use of force under the conditions stated.

The resolution, it will be noted, did not indicate that it was intended to replace collective self-defense by enforcement measures under the authority of the Security Council. Clearly, the Council would have the right to do so under Article 51. The claim sometimes advanced that self-defense as an inherent right cannot be taken away is not consistent with Article 51. That Article not only requires states claiming self-defense measures to report immediately to the Council; it says such measures shall not "in any way affect the authority and responsibility of the Security Council" to take such action as it deems necessary. The Council has in fact never doubted its right to reject a self-defense claim and call on states making such claims to cease hostilities. It would be absurd to maintain that the use of force under a claim of self-defense cannot be denied and overridden by the Council when it determines that such action is necessary.

However, the Council's right to replace self-defense with other measures requires evidence of the Council's intent. There is no reason why the Council has to be explicit on this point as long as its intention is clear. A resolution ordering a "cease-fire" for all parties would be adequate to preclude the use of force in self-defense. But a resolution for economic sanctions would not in itself preempt armed self-defense unless that intention was expressed or clearly implied in the resolution or in statements by the Council members. The resolution authorizing "all necessary means" to compel Iraqi withdrawal was consistent with collective self-defense, even though no reference was made to Article 51. Significantly, it did not provide that the armed forces to be deployed were to be placed at the disposal or under the control of the Security Council. It was an authorization to use force that under the Charter was compatible both with collective self-defense under Article 51 and "action" under Article 42. Under either article, the Council retains the authority and responsibility to adopt other measures that would be binding on the states deploying armed force. It could impose conditions relating to the objectives to be attained or the means that may be used. To be sure, its legal authority is limited, as we indicated, by the purposes and principles of the Charter. Pragmatically, a crucial factor is the voting requirement—in particular, the necessity for unanimity of the permanent members and for the qualified majority of nine members of the Council as a whole. A decision that would limit the right of self-defense cannot be made without meeting these requirements. In effect, a veto by a permanent member would bar such a decision and leave intact the right of self-defense in response to the prior armed attack. This falls short of the ideal of collective security but it provides a legal ground to attack the aggressor.

The Use of Armed Force in United Nations Peacekeeping

"Peacekeeping" has come to be a term of art in U.N. usage. It refers to the use of military personnel under United Nations authority and direction for purposes other than enforcement measures in the sense of Chapter VII. Eighteen distinct peacekeeping operations have been carried out by the United Nations between 1948 and 1990.[48] Ten of these operations have been primarily observational, involving on-the-spot monitoring and verification. They are carried out mainly by unarmed (or lightly armed) military officers made available by member states. The remaining eight peacekeeping operations have been carried out by contingents of armed forces, equipped with light defensive weapons which they are authorized to use only in self-defense. These forces have varied: that in the former Belgian Congo (now Zaire) reached nearly 20,000; most of the other forces have had about 6,000 to 7,000 troops.

In functional terms, the peacekeeping operations have been used for various purposes (usually described as "missions"). They fall into the following eight categories:

1. Monitoring and supervision of cease-fire, truce and armistice agreements. This involves observation posts, on-the-spot reporting and communication with the parties concerning violations. The first example was the Truce Supervision Organization to supervise implementation of the armistice agreement between Israel and her Arab neighbors; it still functions.
2. Frontier control and border patrol, such as manning entry points and checking documents.
3. Interposition, that is, the U.N. force is deployed as a buffer between hostile forces. The U.N. force in Cyprus is an example. Its functions also involve border patrol and manning posts in sensitive border areas.
4. Maintaining law and order in a country at the request of its government where the breakdown of internal order and stability has resulted in a threat to international peace. The Congo operation is the main example.
5. Assisting in the defense and security of an area placed under U.N. control. The temporary U.N. administration in West Irian had a U.N. security force as a part of its administration of the territory.
6. Maintaining security in an area in which plebiscites or elections are being conducted, as in Namibia. This may also involve supervising the dismantling of local armed forces.
7. Assistance in the demobilization of local forces and their disarmament. This was done by U.N. military personnel in Nicaragua and Honduras.
8. Protection of U.N. operations and personnel engaged in relief and assistance in troubled areas or after natural disasters. This role has been proposed but not yet carried out.

The legal authority to establish peacekeeping operations and the competent organ to do so have been subjects of controversy throughout their history. The first controversy centered on the claim that the Charter provided for the use of military units by the Organization only under the terms of Chapter VII, particularly Article 42. Related to this was the claim that Article 43 agreements were a necessary condition for such forces. The opposing positions were based essentially on the proposition that the proposed use of military units did not involve "enforcement," or the coercive use of force against a state. Hence the provisions of Article 42 and the related Articles were not applicable. Several other Charter provisions were suggested as applicable.

The first official suggestion for a type of U.N. force that would not have enforcement functions came from the Secretary-General in 1948.[49] He proposed a U.N. guard to protect U.N. missions, a proposal made a few days after the assassination of the U.N. mediator, Count Bernadotte, in Palestine. Several other cases of attacks on U.N. field missions had also occurred. The Secretary-General referred to his powers under the Charter (Articles 97, 98, and 100) to provide the staff required to carry out decisions of the Organization.[50] The proposed guard would not function in any territory without the consent of "the territorial sovereign." The proposal was strongly opposed by the Soviet Union and its allies as *ultra vires,* and as a violation of the Charter provisions in Chapter VII. A much modified scheme emerged from the General Assembly, providing for a U.N. Field Service to assist field missions and, if necessary, to provide limited protection.[51] However, the ideas and discussions entered into the institutional memory and influenced the later proposals for peacekeeping forces.

The resolutions establishing the "observational" peacekeeping activities, such as truce supervision, did not raise problems of constitutional authority. They were all authorized by the Security Council and it was implicitly understood that they fell within the Council's general authority under Article 24 as well as under Article 36 (which authorizes recommendations of "appropriate procedures" for resolving disputes). The question of Charter authority became a matter of controversy only in regard to the two large peacekeeping forces that had functions beyond the observational tasks of truce supervision. The first of these forces was the U.N. Emergency Force (UNEF) established in 1956 by the General Assembly following the Suez invasion of Egypt by British, French, and Israeli forces.[52] The second was the U.N. Force for the Congo (ONUC) established in 1960 by the Secretary-General pursuant to a decision of the Security Council.[53] The disputes over the Charter basis for these actions came to a head when several member states (notably the USSR and France) refused to pay the financial assessments for expenses of these forces.

The I.C.J. was asked for an advisory opinion on the obligation of members to pay the assessments. While the Court did not consider that it was necessary to decide the constitutional issue (the Charter basis), it did comment *obiter* on some of the legal points. It expressly rejected the argument that such forces required agreements under Article 43, pointing out that these forces were not used for "enforcement" in the sense of Chapter VII.[54] The key point was that they were not authorized to take military action against a state. The Court noted that the Charter empowered both principal organs to establish subsidiary organs as deemed necessary and also that they could under Article 98 require the Secretary-General to carry out their decisions. With regard to the General Assembly's authority to establish UNEF, the Court referred to Article 14 authorizing the Assembly "to recommend measures for the peaceful adjustment of any situation likely to impair the general welfare or friendly relations among nations...."[55] With regard to the Security Council, the Court observed that "it must lie within the power of the Security Council to police a situation even though it does not resort to enforcement action against a state."[56] It is consistent with the Court's opinion to conclude that the Security Council may establish a peacekeeping force under Chapter VII (as well as under Chapter VI). In the Congo case, Chapter VII was the basis for decisions that were mandatory, even though they were not enforcement action under Article 42.

At the present time, it seems safe to say that there is no longer any serious question as to the authority under the Charter for the Security Council to establish and deploy a U.N. armed force for peacekeeping missions as summarized above. The former opponents of this position, particularly the Soviet Union, have reversed their stand. There also appears to be general agreement that financial assessments for such authorized peacekeeping operations may be obligatory, if so decided by the General Assembly under Article 17. But the fact that the United States and some other countries are still in default casts some doubt as to the actual acceptance of the principle of mandatory assessment.

Other important questions of legal character may still be somewhat controversial. One relates to the power of the Security Council to impose obligations on member states in carrying out decisions that do not involve enforcement measures under Articles 41 and 42. More precisely, the question is whether Articles 48 and 49 apply to such decisions. An answer was given by the Security Council in one of its early resolutions in the Congo operation. It referred to Articles 25 and 49 when it called on all states to accept and carry out decisions of the Council.[57] This had particular reference to the Council's demand that Belgium withdraw its troops from the Congo. A plausible inference was that the Council's decisions came under Article 40 which provides that the Council may call upon members to comply with such provisional measures as it deems necessary or desirable.[58] Withdrawal of Belgian forces was one such measure as was the more general demand that all states refrain from action to impede the restoration of law and order. That these resolutions were applications of Article 40 was recognized in a Secretary-General's report to the Council.[59]

Limits on Peacekeeping

A more complicated legal aspect concerns limits of peacekeeping, particularly as it is required to be non-coercive—that is, not used against a state. That principle calls for restraint on the part of the United Nations in cases where the operation applies to relations between two or more states and in situations involving internal order and security. With regard to the first category, inter-state relations, the general principle has been that the peacekeepers—whether observers or buffer forces—should maintain strict neutrality and impartiality. The "guiding principles" for UNEF proposed by the Secretary-General and approved by the General Assembly declared that the force shall not influence the military or political "balance" between the parties in the conflict.[60] It is not too difficult to sustain this principle in situations where the parties have undertaken to desist from active hostilities and violations are of a minor character. However, where the situation involves continued or sporadic fighting, particularly when infiltration and guerrilla units are active, the activities of the force in detecting or interfering with hostile acts are bound to influence, in one way or another, the military and political balance. This is likely to be significant where the force is relatively small and the hostilities continuous. The utility of the force in such cases tends to diminish greatly so that its role is little more than a symbolic affirmation of the international concern. The experience of the U.N. force for Lebanon is an example.[61]

Where the force is used for internal security and related functions, the guiding principle is non-intervention in internal affairs and impartiality as between competing political factions or as between communities. Experience shows that impartiality has been generally maintained in the situations involving elections and disarming of local troops. It is likely to be more severely tested in situations involving large-scale internal conflicts approaching civil war. The Congo operation showed how difficult it was for a force to avoid action that favored one side such as the central government when competing factions resorted to violence for political ends.[62] Current unrest in many countries indicates that there may well be other cases in which U.N. forces would be requested by a government to help in restoring order when opposition elements seeking separation or autonomy have challenged the central government. The United Nations would have no authority to employ armed force in such a case unless international peace was imminently threatened by the internal conflict. This may occur and an international force may be authorized. However, it is highly problematic whether a U.N. peacekeeping operation would or should be used to enforce "law and order" at the request of the *de jure* government, in order to repress a movement for self-determination or autonomy. An exceptional case may arise where the United Nations has had a role in bringing about a settlement between conflicting parties in an internal conflict that also involved foreign intervention. As in West Irian, it may be called upon for temporary administration and assistance in maintaining internal order and protection against external military intervention.[63] A current example is suggested by the consultations concerning Cambodia. In a case of this kind, it would have to be within the mandate of a U.N. force to act against factions that use violent means to overturn the agreed settlement. While this may be necessary to carry out a U.N. decision supporting a settlement, the use of U.N. forces against "local" insurgents will severely strain the principle of non-intervention and political neutrality.[64] The parties to the settlement agreement and the Security Council would have to foresee this kind of contingency and provide guiding rules and appropriate procedures.

Use of Force in Peacekeeping

U.N. official doctrine has emphasized that peacekeeping as distinct from enforcement is based on consent and cooperation; it is not meant to achieve its aims by force of arms.[65] The symbolic significance of the Blue Helmets as an instrument of the world community would render a fighting force unnecessary. Why then arm the peacekeepers? The answer from the outset was that weapons were to be used solely for self-defense. This limitation created no serious difficulties for the peacekeeping of an observational character such as truce supervision and border patrol. However, when peacekeeping forces were used on a fairly large scale to "maintain quiet," or to act as a buffer force, or especially, to assist in maintaining law and order within a country, the practical necessities placed considerable strain on the limit of self-defense. But there was great reluctance in the United Nations to go beyond self-defense as the touchstone of the right to use force. The Secretary-General and members considered it essential from a political and legal standpoint to distinguish peacekeeping from enforcement by restricting the use of force to self-defense as well as requiring consent of the parties to a conflict.

The unsurprising result was that the self-defense principle was stretched far beyond its usual legal meaning. This occurred particularly in regard to the Congo operation where the mandate required the force to assist the central government in maintaining law and order and in securing the withdrawal of foreign troops. The early mandate of the Congo force and the instructions of the Secretary-General prohibited the force to take the initiative in the use of arms and only to respond with armed force when attacked.[66] It was made clear, however, that attempts to compel the units of the force to give up their "positions" such as guard-points or blockades could be resisted by force as self-defense.[67] This interpretation of self-defense had also been adopted in regard to UNEF in 1956.[68] A significant extension of self-defense resulted from granting the ONUC freedom of movement throughout the country. Such freedom of movement was considered essential for the U.N. force to assist in keeping order in various parts of the country beset by tribal conflicts, armed political factions opposed to the central government, and undisciplined troops engaged in pillage and assaults. In effect, according the force freedom of movement together with the right to use arms in defense of positions occupied allowed the U.N. contingents to use force to occupy and control key points in the country.[69] It was in effect a license to use force beyond self-defense. Force had been expressly authorized by the Security Council when civil war threatened to occur on a large scale in the Congo. The Council resolution of February 1961 urged the U.N. force to take appropriate measures to prevent a civil war, including the halting of all military operations, the prevention of clashes, and the use of force, if necessary, as a last resort.[70] Hammarskjöld, then Secretary-General, considered this authorization to extend only to interposition. In his view it did not allow an attack on an organized army group since such attack would make the U.N. force "a party to the conflict," a result contrary to the Charter's prohibition against intervention in essentially domestic affairs.[71] However, a later Council resolution (November 1961) authorized the U.N. force to use force to capture and expel all foreign military personnel and political advisers who were not under the control of the U.N. Command.[72] The force was also authorized to prevent the entry or return of such foreign personnel and of arms that would support their activities.

These authorized functions clearly involved use of force by U.N. troops beyond self-defense. A more significant use of force by the U.N. occurred when it moved its troops into areas occupied by Congolese opposition armies (Katanga provincial forces) as an exercise of the right to freedom of movement. In overcoming the armed resistance of the Katanga forces, the U.N. force brought an end to an internal political conflict and led to the collapse of the secession movement.[73] It is difficult to consider the use of force by the United Nations in this connection as self-defense. It was, however, an action that contributed to a political objective that had the support of the majority of the Security Council—namely, the preservation of the unity and territorial integrity of the newly independent Congo (now Zaire).

The Congo experience indicates that future peacekeeping operations, though based on the consent of the territorial sovereign and on agreement of other parties to a conflict, may require the use of force beyond self-defense of the force itself. Current negotiations for a settlement of the conflict regarding Cambodia suggest this possibility. Other situations may plausibly be envisaged in which U.N. forces (in one form or another) would be established by the Security Council or by the international agreement to provide internal security. This would probably require the force to protect groups and individuals against violence and to police and control movements of persons across borders or inside of the country. In fact, a case of this kind arose in the aftermath of the 1991 Gulf conflict when displaced Kurds in Iraq were attacked by Iraqi troops. At first, protection of the Kurds was given by units of the coalition forces that had defeated Iraq and subsequently by United Nations "guards" with Iraq's implied acquiescence. A U.N. force in these situations is likely to require the right to resort to arms in a forceful manner against organized units or individuals that have resorted to violence. Such use of force should be clearly limited to what is necessary and proportionate, but if faced with a large-scale resistance or insurgent army, the U.N. force would be taking sides in a civil war. Dag Hammarskjold had warned members of the United Nations against using U.N. forces "to influence the outcome of any internal conflict, constitutional or otherwise," and this postion was affirmed by the Security Council in its resolution of August 1960. Subsequent political pressures influenced a change in position so that U.N. force was employed to put down an insurgent movement that sought autonomy for a part of the country. Most members of the United Nations supported that solution and it may have been politically desirable to do so in the particular case in view of the covert foreign intervention and the threat to international peace. But the basic issue of principle and of Charter law is likely to arise again. Clearly, the Charter does not contemplate that U.N. armed force should be used in order to put down internal rebellion, even if the government invites such force and even if a foreign state supports the rebellion by economic or political means short of actual armed intervention. A prudent and legally correct position would avoid the use of U.N. armed force in such cases, in recognition that collective force should be used only where clearly necessary to maitain and restore international peace and security.

Force Authorized by Regional Organization

The U.N. Charter recognizes in its Chapter VIII that regional arrangements and agencies are appropriate means for maintaining peace and security, provided that their activities are consistent with the purposes and principles of the Charter. Indeed, Article 52 of the Charter requires states to make every effort to achieve peaceful settlement of "local disputes" through regional arrangements or agencies before referring such disputes to the U.N. Security Council. The idea that disputes and threats to the peace involving states within a region should preferably be dealt with primarily by regional bodies has been an early and persistent influence. At San Francisco the Security Council was perceived as a forum of last resort when states were unable to resolve conflicts between them through the peaceful means listed in Chapter VI or through regional instrumentalities.[74]

U.N. experience has revealed difficulties in applying this conception in some situations. The main difficulty arises when one of the parties to a dispute perceives itself as likely to be accorded prejudicial treatment by the regional body. It sees itself as an "outsider" for political or other reasons.[75] It may then look to the global body for support from states with which it has political affinities or ethnic and religious ties. Such linkages of an extra-regional character have become increasingly important. Hence the priority for regional procedures of settlement, while still expressed as a general ideal, has been subject to exceptions in many disputes. As might be expected, the tension between U.N. authority and regional organizations has been more acute when armed force is in issue.

The Charter in Article 53 expressly directs the Security Council to utilize the regional arrangements or agencies covered by Chapter VIII for enforcement action where appropriate. The regional bodies are indirectly authorized to undertake enforcement action inasmuch as Article 53 states that they may not do so without the authorization of the Security Council. Thus the failure of the Council to grant permission for enforcement action would bar such action. A permanent member could therefore prevent enforcement action by a regional organization. Cases have come before the Security Council involving decisions of the Organization of American States (O.A.S.) to apply diplomatic and economic measures that were in the nature of sanctions as envisaged in Article 41 of the U.N. Charter.[76] In these cases, the Council did not decide that those measures were covered by Article 53. The majority of members maintained that such non-forcible coercive measures were within the competence of individual states. Since states were free to sever trade or diplomatic relations, they could do so by concerted action under the aegis of a regional organization.[77] The reasoning is not wholly compelling since concerted action by a regional body to impose sanctions of the kind contemplated in Chapter VII (Article 41) would appear to be within the meaning of enforcement action in Article 53.

It is, of course, more likely to be considered enforcement when the regional body approves the use of armed force by member states. This legal issue emerged in 1962 when the O.A.S. "recommended" that its members take measures including the use of armed force which they deemed necessary to prevent Cuba from receiving military material from the "Sino-Soviet powers" that may threaten peace and security of the continent and to prevent missiles in Cuba from ever becoming a threat.[78] The U.N. Security Council did not authorize this action; in fact it was not requested to grant such authorization. The legal reason, expressed by the U.S. government lawyers, was that the O.A.S. resolution was a recommendation and consequently, it was not "enforcement action" under Article 53.[79] However, this legal position was not adopted by the U.N. Security Council at the time and it has not been raised in later cases.

The issue may be complicated, moreover, by the legal contention that the legitimate use of force in response to an armed attack (or threat of an armed attack) falls under collective self-defense. While the Security Council may still order an end to the hostilities, that order would need a Council decision by the required majority, including the concurring votes of the permanent members. Hence it is unlikely as long as at least one permanent member supports the action of the regional organization. However, the debate in the Security Council and perhaps in the General Assembly may have political influence if significant majority views emerge.

Apart from collective self-defense, regional organizations may institute peacekeeping operations that do not involve coercive measures against a state. This has been done in a number of cases. However, it has not always been agreed that the regional peacekeeping operation has actually received the consent of the territorial sovereign. Questions of this kind have come up where it was uncertain who, if anyone, may legitimately grant such consent in the absence of effective and recognized governmental authority. This emerged as a problem when U.S. forces together with troops from several Caribbean countries intervened in Grenada, claiming *inter alia* that they had been authorized to do so by a regional body (the Organization of Eastern Caribbean States) to bring peace and order to a country in a condition of anarchy.[80] The General Assembly condemned the intervention as a violation of the Charter.[81] However, there was no international criticism of a regional peacekeeping force of West African states that sought to bring an end to a bloody internal conflict in Liberia in 1990. This was clearly not an enforcement action or collective defense, nor was there an invitation from a government enjoying international recognition. A case of this kind would suggest an interpretation of peacekeeping by regional bodies that allows for a collective military intervention to help end an internal conflict when a government has been deposed or no longer has effective authority.

It is probable that peacekeeping actions and perhaps limited enforcement will be employed by regional organizations more frequently in the future. They are likely to be used to assist in monitoring and border patrol and perhaps to help to provide order to a country in internal conflict or near-anarchy. All such actions and any contemplated are required to be reported to the Security Council under Article 54. The Council may find it necessary to take decisions in these cases to avoid threats or breaches of international peace and security. It may also have to consider whether the regional body's activities are consistent with the purposes and principles of the U.N. Charter, as required by Article 52. In exercising this responsibility, the Council may have to exert its authority to ensure that the basic Charter principles of sovereign equality, political independence, self-determination, and human rights are upheld by the regional bodies and the states concerned. Experience suggests that this will not always be easy to achieve.

This survey of the authorized uses of force by the United Nations and regional bodies reveals the range of options open to governments in acting against aggression or in taking preventive measures when peace is threatened. The principal focus in this paper has been on issues of authority and legitimacy under the U.N. Charter and related international law, and not on the factors of power and interest that influence government action within and outside of international bodies. Of course, governmental decisions are not made on legal grounds alone and international organizations are not expected to behave like judicial bodies. But this truism does not exclude the influence of the Charter and related legal rules. Experience shows that governments, acting collectively, are helped by a shared conception of permissible ends and means. That need is met, in large part, by the accepted body of principles and procedures embodied in the Charter and other international instruments. This paper has sought to show how those principles and processes have been applied when states have chosen to use force in collective action. It is fair to conclude that while the ideal of collective security has not been attained, the United Nations and regional organizations can be useful instruments for combatting aggression and preventing wars through judicious use of collective military force.

Notes

1. I. BERLIN, THE HEDGEHOG AND THE FOX: AN ESSAY ON TOLSTOY'S VIEW OF HISTORY 1 (1953). The source is an ancient Greek poem.

2. *See* L. GOODRICH, KOREA (1956); R. HIGGINS, 2 UNITED NATIONS PEACEKEEPING 153-312 (1970).

3. U.N. Doc. S/RES/661 (1990); U.N. Doc. S/RES/670 (1990).

4. U.N. Doc. S/RES/665 (1990).

5. U.N. Doc. S/RES/678 (1990).

6. *Certain Expenses of the United Nations,* 1962 I.C.J. 151 (Advisory Opinion of July 20).

7. *Id.* at 167.

8. *Id.* at 164-65.

9. *See* R. RUSSELL, A HISTORY OF THE UNITED NATIONS 1052 (1958). Article 106 of the Charter supports that interpretation. It reads: "Pending the coming into force of such special agreements referred to in Article 43 as in the opinion of the Security Council enable it to begin the exercise of its responsibilities under Article 42...."

10. *See* L. GOODRICH & A. SIMONS, THE UNITED NATIONS AND THE MAINTENANCE OF INTERNATIONAL PEACE AND SECURITY 398-405 (1955); H. KELSEN, THE LAW OF THE UNITED NATIONS 756 (1950); K.P. SAKSENA, THE UNITED NATIONS AND COLLECTIVE SECURITY 93 (1975). In 1948 U.N. Secretary-General Lie also stated that action under Article 42 required the agreements under Article 43. *See* 3 U.N. GAOR (Part 2), U.N. Doc. A/656 (1948).

11. *See* D. BOWETT, UNITED NATIONS FORCES 277 (1964); L. Sohn, *The Authority of the United Nations to Establish and Maintain a Permanent Force*, 52 AM. J. INT'L L. 230 (1958).

12. U.N. Doc. S/RES/83 (1950).

13. G.A. Res. 377 (V)(Para. 8) (1950); G.A. Res. 503 (VI)(Para. 2) (1952).

14. 7 U.N. GAOR Supp. (No. 17, 1952).

15. KELSEN, *supra* note 10, at 756. *See* references *infra* note 17.

16. Pub. L. 79-264; 59 Stat. 619; 22 U.S.C. 287 (1945).

17. The Congressional Committee reports noted that the statutory authorization did not extend to forces beyond the terms of the agreements. *See* H.R. REP. NO. 1383, 79th Cong., 1st Sess. at 8 (1945); S. REP. NO. 717, 79th Cong. 1st Sess. at 7 (1945). *See also* M. Glennon, *The Constitution and Chapter VII of the United Nations Charter,* 85 AM. J. INT'L. 74 (1991); *Note, Congress, the President and the Power to Commit Forces to Combat*, 81 HARV. L. REV. 1771, 1800 (1968).

18. U.N. Doc. S/RES 82, 83, 84 (1950).

19. Some Republican Senators, particularly Senator Robert Taft, urged that Congressional authorization be sought. Taft said he would support the authorization but without it the President's commitment was of doubtful constitutionality. The President disagreed, moved by a conviction that the Presidency was a "sacred trust...which he [Truman] was determined to pass on unimpaired by the slightest loss of power or prestige." D. ACHESON, PRESENT AT THE CREATION 415 (1969). *See also* 96 CONG. REC. 9320 (1950).

20. 23 DEP'T. ST. BULL. 173-7 (1950).

21. Franck, *Declare War? Congress Can't*, N.Y. Times, Dec. 11, 1990, at A27, col. 2.

22. *Id.*

23. 2 U.N. SCOR Supp. (No. 1) at 1, U.N. Doc. S/336 (1947).

24. A combined U.S., USSR, and Chinese text referred to an "overall commander" whereas a British-French text provided for a Supreme Commander and Commanders-in-Chief of land, sea and air forces all to be appointed by the Security Council. *See* BOWETT, *supra* note 11, at 17.

25. *Id.* at 15-17. *See also* W. FRYE, A UNITED NATIONS PEACE FORCE 53 (1957).

26. *Military Situation in the Far East: Hearings Before the Senate Comm. on Armed Services and Foreign Relations,* 82d Cong., 1st Sess. 10 (1951) (Part 1).

27. *See* BOWETT, *supra* note 11, at 37.

28. *Id.* at 41.

29. GOODRICH, *supra* note 2, at 133-34, 142-43.

30. BOWETT, *supra* note 11, at 47-53. *See also* G. WEISSBERG, INTERNATIONAL STATUS OF THE UNITED NATIONS 94-103 (1961).

31. G.A. Res. 711, 7 U.N. GAOR Supp. (No.20B), U.N. Doc. A/2361/Ad.2 (1953).

32. U.N. Doc. S/RES/660 (1990).

33. U.N. Doc. S/RES/661 (1990).

34. U.N. Doc. S/RES/665 (1990).

35. U.N. Doc. S/RES/678 (1990).

36. *See* M. MCDOUGAL & F. FELICIANO, LAW AND MINIMUM WORLD PUBLIC ORDER 254-255 (1961).

37. *See* B. Meltzer, *A Note on Some Aspects of the Nuremberg Debate,* 14 U. CHI. L. REV. 455, 461 (1946-47).

38. Report of Committee on Study of Legal Problems of the United Nations, *Should the Laws of War Apply to United Nations Enforcement Action?,* 46 PROC. AM. SOC. INT'L L. 216, 220 (1952).

39. *Id.*

40. 54 ANNUAIRE, INST. DE DROIT INTERNATIONAL 465-470 (1971).

41. *Id.* art. 2 at 466.

42. *Id.* arts. 4, 5, 6 at 467-8.

43. 56 ANNUAIRE, INST. DE DROIT INTERNATIONAL 541-545 (1975).

44. Military and Paramilitary Activities In and Against Nicaragua (Nicar. v. U.S.), 1986 I.C.J. 95-97.

45. *See* O. Schachter, *Self-Defense and The Rule of Law*, 83 AM. J. INT'L L. 259, 261-63 (1989); H. LAUTERPACHT, THE FUNCTION OF LAW IN THE INTERNATIONAL COMMUNITY 179-80 (1933).

46. Schachter, *supra* note 45, at 263-64. *See also* J. Combacau, *The Exception of Self-Defense in U.N. Practice*, in THE CURRENT LEGAL REGULATION OF THE USE OF FORCE 9-38 (A. Cassese ed. 1986).

47. *See* H. KELSEN, RECENT TRENDS IN THE LAW OF THE UNITED NATIONS 936-37 (1951); J. STONE, LEGAL CONTROLS OF INTERNATIONAL CONFLICT 232-235 (1954).

48. UNITED NATIONS, THE BLUE HELMETS: A REVIEW OF UNITED NATIONS PEACE-KEEPING (2d ed. 1990). A valuable documentary history is R. HIGGINS, UNITED NATIONS PEACEKEEPING, 4 volumes, 1969-1981.

49. *Report of the Secretary-General to the General Assembly*, U.N. Doc. A/656 (1948).

50. *Id.* Appendix A (Memorandum of the Legal Department).

51. *See* BOWETT, *supra* note 11, at 18-21.

52. G.A. Res. 998 and 999 (ES-1) (1956).

53. U.N. Doc. S/RES/143 (1960). Resolution 143 authorized the Secretary-General "to take the necessary steps in consultation with the Government of the Republic of the Congo to provide the Government with such military assistance as might be necessary."

54. Certain Expenses of the United Nations, 1962 I.C.J. 151, 166 (Advisory Opinion of July 20).

55. *Id.* at 163-65.

56. *Id.* at 167.

57. The Security Council expressly referred to articles 25 and 49 of the Charter in its resolution of August 9, 1960, calling on all member states to carry out the decisions of the Council. These references had the effect, according to the Secretary-General, of legally requiring compliance by members with the resolutions. *See* G. ABI-SAAB, THE UNITED NATIONS OPERATION IN THE CONGO 29, 34, 109 (1978).

58. *See* ABI-SAAB, *supra* note 57, at 103; BOWETT, *supra* note 11 at 175-180; E.M. Miller (pseudonym for O. Schachter), *Legal Aspects of the United Nations Action in the Congo*, 55 AM. J. INT'L L. 1 (1961).

59. *Statement at Security Council,* 920th Mtg., 13 Dec. 1960, para. 75.

60. GAOR U.N. Doc. A/3302 (Nov. 6, 1956). *See also* THE BLUE HELMETS, *supra* note 48, at 48.

61. *Id.* at 111-152.

62. *See* ABI-SAAB, *supra* note 57, passim.

63. The U.N. Security Force in West New Guinea (West Irian) was established in 1962 by the Secretary-General pursuant to an agreement between Netherlands and Indonesia and an authorizing resolution of the General Assembly (G.A. Res. 1752 (XVII) (1962)). The Security Force was a part of the U.N. Temporary Administration for the area of West Irian that was in the process of transfer from Netherlands to Indonesia. *See* THE BLUE HELMETS, *supra* note 48, 263-277.

64. On the role of law in U.N. decision-making for the Congo Operation, *see* ABI-SAAB, *supra* note 57, at 48-53, 193-200.

65. *See* THE BLUE HELMETS, *supra* note 48, at 4-7. On problems of consent and withdrawal of consent *see* BOWETT, *supra* note 11 at 412-436. For a detailed account of the circumstances surrounding the controversial withdrawal of UNEF from Egypt, see I.J. RIKHYE, THE SINAI BLUNDER (1978). In that connection it was argued that while the territorial sovereign was free to withdraw its consent, it may waive that right by agreeing in advance not to exercise it unilaterally.

66. *Report of the Secretary-General to the Security Council,* July 18, 1960, paras. 7-15.

67. *Id.*

68. This right was more extensive than accorded to UNEF which had the right to use roads, airfields, canals, etc. within the area of operations. For analysis of the Congo provision, *see* BOWETT, *supra* note 11, at 435.

69. *See* BOWETT, *supra* note 11, at 432-454.

70. U.N. Doc. S/4741 (Feb. 21, 1961).

71. *See* ABI-SAAB, *supra* note 57, at 104-106.

72. U.N. Doc. S/5002 (Nov. 24, 1961).

73. *See* ABI-SAAB, *supra* note 57, at 174-191.

74. *See* E. JIMÉNEZ DE ARÉCHAGA, *La Coordination des Systèmes de l'ONU et de l'Organisation des États Américains Pour Le Règlement Pacifique des Différends et la Sécurité Collective*, 111 HAGUE ACAD. REC. DES COURS 423, 431-436 (1964).

75. *See* A.L. LEVIN, THE ORGANIZATION OF AMERICAN STATES AND

THE UNITED NATIONS (1974), *partly reprinted in* REGIONALISM AND THE UNITED NATIONS 147-224 (B. Andemicael ed. 1979). The author observes:

> It is well to remember that the OAS and other regional organizations as well have tended to ostracize States within their respective area regarded as a threat to regional values and solidarity and have made them a target of punitive measures.

Id. at 190.

76. *Id.* at 165-66, 168.

77. *Id.* at 208, nn. 91-92.

78. *Id.* at 171.

79. *See* A. Chayes, *The Legal Case for U.S. Action on Cuba*, 47 DEP'T ST. BULL. 763-65 (1962); *Defensive Quarantine and the Law*, 57 AM. J. INT'L L. 515-24 (1963); *contra* E. Jiménez de Aréchaga, *International Law in the Past Third of a Century*, 159 HAGUE ACAD. REC. DES COURS 141-42 (1978).

80. *See* J.N. Moore, *Grenada and the International Double Standard*, 78 AM. J. INT'L L. 145, 154-59 (1984); *contra* C. Joyner, *Reflections on the Lawfulness of Invasion*, 78 AM. J. INT'L L. 131, 135-37 (1984); O. Schachter, *The Right of States to Use Armed Force*, 82 MICH. L. REV. 1620, 1641 (1984); L. Doswald-Beck, *The Legality of the U.S. Intervention in Grenada*, 31 NETHERLANDS INT'L L. REV. 362-366 (1984).

81. G.A. Res. 38/7, 38 U.N. GAOR Supp. (No.47), U.N. Doc. A/38/L.8 (1983).

7

International Peacekeeping and Enforcement Actions After the Cold War

Nikolai B. Krylov

There have been more than 140 major armed conflicts since 1945. Only a few of them have been settled through the efforts of the United Nations. Although in several cases the aggression has been prevented by pressure from the United Nations, there is no single case in which the United Nations was absolutely instrumental in the prevention of the armed conflict.[1] At the same time the effectiveness of U.N. actions cannot be weighed on any simple scale. Historically when members of the United Nations renounced narrow national interests in the interest of universal common needs, international peace and security were strengthened. In such cases the United Nations functioned as an effective mechanism of international cooperation.

Until recently an ideological confrontation dominated the work of the United Nations. Now favorable conditions exist for the international organization to perform its historical purpose, namely "to save succeeding generations from the scourge of war, which twice in our lifetime has brought untold sorrow to mankind." This reflects a growing recognition of the U.N.'s role in international relations in an era of increasing interdependence and is highly connected with the general improvement of the international climate. The politics of consensus are emerging step-by-step at the United Nations in such events as the transformation of Soviet-U.S. relations, the strengthening of a dialogue on the European continent, and the settlement of several regional trouble spots.

At the same time international peace and security remain distant goals. In 1990 a real threat to the welfare of the world community appeared. With its invasion and occupation of Kuwait, Iraq flagrantly violated the U.N. Charter, customary principles of international law, universally-recognized principles of morality, and standards of civilized behavior. This act of international terrorism was perpetrated against the emerging new world order. It was a major affront to mankind and a new test for the peacemaking skills of the United Nations. If it passes the test, the United Nations will immeasurably enhance its prestige and gain new experience and capabilities.

We are, however, at another of those moments in history when, as Winston Churchill wrote of the days before World War I, every man had only to do his duty to wreck the world.[2]

The United Nations was created in 1945 as an instrument of law and order, to preserve international peace and security. For that purpose Article 2(4) of the Charter prohibits the threat or use of force. The Security Council was entrusted with the task of ordering collective action in case of a threat to the peace, a breach of the peace, or an act of aggression.

However, one of the early international casualties[3] of the Charter era was the procedure for organizing the U.N. security forces in accordance with Article 43, which provides:

> All Members of the United Nations, in order to contribute to the maintenance of international peace and security, undertake to make available to the Security Council, on its call and in accordance with a special agreement or agreements, armed forces, assistance, and facilities, including rights of passage, necessary for the purpose of maintaining international peace and security.

That means that the capacity of the Security Council to take military action on its own initiative was dependent on the subsequent negotiation of special agreements with member states to make standby military forces and facilities available "on call" to the Security Council. When they adopted the Charter, member states made only a moral commitment to support U.N. military sanctions and postponed to a later date any limitation on the right to control their own military forces.[4]

The initial perception of the founders of the U.N. Charter was that an Article 43 use of force would be an enforcement action where the Security Council found "a threat to the peace, breach of the peace, or act of aggression." But this initial conception was soon set aside when it proved impossible to reach agreement on the terms of Article 43 arrangements or to solve several regional problems.

Because of the failure to reach agreement on creating Article 43 forces, the emphasis shifted from enforcement to peacekeeping. Collective security thus was never realized, but the United Nations found another way to remain relevant in the control of international violence.

It is evident that U.N. peacekeeping operations have become a very different sort of activity from that which was planned in 1945 as the U.N.'s main contribution to the maintenance of international peace and security. The United Nations intended to enforce peace when the necessity arose. Peacekeeping, however, requires that all parties be willing to refrain from battle. The essence of peacekeeping is the use of soldiers as the catalyst for peace rather than the instrument of war. It is, in fact, the exact opposite of the military enforcement action against aggression foreseen in Chapter VII of the Charter. Thus the relationship of peacekeeping to peace is of a secondary order, whereas collective security serves as a primary buttress of peace.

The second major element of peacekeeping is the complete prohibition of the use of force except for purposes of self-defense. Peacekeeping forces must separate the enemies but cannot be involved in the battle.

Apart from the non-combat characteristic of U.N. peacekeeping operations, there are several other characteristics. In particular, consent by the parties concerned is the main prerequisite of U.N. peacekeeping. Whenever the Secretary-General has submitted a report to the Security Council at the end of the mandate period of a particular peacekeeping force, he has recommended that the mandate of that force be renewed. But the Secretary-General has always confirmed that he sought and obtained the agreement of the host states with regard to such an extension.[5]

U.N. peacekeeping forces for any particular mission are established for a limited period of time either by the Security Council or, in some cases, by the General Assembly under the Uniting for Peace Resolution. At the end of any such period it is necessary for the authorizing U.N. body to grant an extension of the deployment. The Security Council in particular often has approved extensions to peacekeeping mandates.

Nonetheless, it is not so easy to discover peacekeeping in the framework of the U.N. Charter. One can argue that U.N. peacekeeping operations are between Chapter VI and Chapter VII of the Charter, that they occupy a distinctive place between the pacific settlement of disputes and collective security. Peacekeeping represents "an effort, not directly to promote the settlement of disputes, but to arrest or prevent their degeneration into violent conflicts, thus to restore or to maintain the possibility that peaceful solution may be found."[6]

Without any doubt peacekeeping operations are an essential and important element of preventive diplomacy, which in the words of former Secretary-General Dag Hammarskjöld,

> ...aim at filling the vacuum so that it will not provoke action from any of the major parties, the initiative from which might be taken for preventive purposes but might in turn lead to counter action from the other side. The ways in which a vacuum can be filled by the United Nations so as to forestall such initiatives differ from

> case to case, but they have this in common: Temporarily, and pending the filling of the vacuum by normal means, the United Nations enters the picture on the basis of its non-commitment to any power bloc, so as to provide to the extent possible a guarantee in relation to all parties against initiatives from others.[7]

In recent years a number of longstanding conflicts have yielded to common sense, negotiations, and U.N. arrangements of which peacekeeping operations are an important part. Successful operations have shown what is required for peacekeeping to succeed:[8]

1. There must be a strong and supportive international consensus. Without any doubt this is the main prerequisite for successful U.N. peacekeeping. The comparatively low results of earlier peacekeeping operations were influenced by the great Cold War confrontation among the permanent members of the Security Council.
2. A peacekeeping operation must have a workable and realistic mandate which is supported in a practical manner by the international community.
3. A peacekeeping operation must be well-disciplined, capable, manned by contingents from several member states, and assisted by an effective, integrated command.

If these prerequisites are fulfilled, then U.N. peacekeeping forces can be successfully deployed. It is equally evident, however, that U.N. operations of interminable duration, with indefinite objectives, and costing hundreds of millions of dollars a year, are unlikely to command the necessary support within the Security Council and among other nations over the long term. Despite the obstacles erected by the Cold War, U.N. peacekeeping forces were often successful in their missions.

With the end of the Cold War the superpowers have drawn closer to each other in their understanding of both international law and politics. Andrew Carnegie, speaking at the Hague Peace Palace in 1913 of an *entente* of three or four principal civilized nations, stressed that they should act in concert against the disturbers of world peace. This task appears more urgent now than at the beginning of the century. Only the collaboration of the permanent members of the Security Council can transform the United Nations into an effective institution and lead the world organization from the era of preventive diplomacy into the era of collective coercive measures.

This does not mean that the world community is ready at this time for full implementation of Chapter VII of the U.N. Charter. Notwithstanding numerous appeals, members of the United Nations remain reluctant to permit the use of their armed forces in strict accordance with the original intent of the framers of the United Nations. Nevertheless, it is more or less evident that member states are now prepared to consider making collective decisions in the field of international peace and security. That is why so many new proposals not only develop the institution of U.N. peacekeeping but also draw the United Nations nearer to the provisions of Chapter VII of the Charter.

U.N. peacekeeping operations will be more effective and the possibilities for the prevention of aggression will be greater when any member of the United Nations is entitled to request the deployment of a peacekeeping force to its territory in order to prevent a potential aggressive attack from outside its borders. Of course such military or para-military activity will cost hundreds of millions of dollars each year but such financial burdens should be borne by the host state.

U.N. peacekeeping missions in recent years have shown their own continued potential. Further, the activities of the Secretary-General should be taken into consideration. Past experience argues in favor of initiatives by the Secretary-General to settle regional conflicts.

In periods of confrontation the Secretary-General must encourage any efforts towards a peaceful solution. It is evident that "*refuser d'agir et ne pas se préocccuper de l'issue d'une question ou d'un différend serait totalement inadmissable de la part du Secrétaire général. Il faut qu'il soit impartial mais pas indifférent.*"[9]

There are two possible ways. First, permanent military forces should be organized on the basis of small contingents of troops (5,000 or 10,000 troops) from each permanent member of the Security Council. If the permanent members of the Security Council agree to allot the necessary troops to the United Nations, then these military forces will be the major factor in the success of any future coercive measures. Each permanent member of the Security Council would be obligated to allot and make available a certain number of trained forces to the United Nations. Such troops would need to be in permanent readiness and be able to be deployed immediately, at the decision of the Security Council, to any part of the world.

If, however, the permanent members of the Security Council are not ready to supply troops to a U.N. military force, then that seriously complicates the settlement of future conflicts. An alternative would be for members of the United Nations voluntarily to supply national troops for a U.N. military force. But the ultimate success of the use of force by the United Nations will depend on the ability of the organization to establish a permanent U.N. military force capable of implementing coercive measures in order to prevent the aggravation of potentially hostile situations and to maintain or restore international peace and security.

There is also the question of effective command of a U.N. military force. Unfortunately, this problem remains unsolved. The Military Staff Committee provided for under the Charter was practically idle for more than four decades. This body was intended to advise and render assistance in all the questions pertaining to the military needs of the Security Council in the sphere of supporting international peace and security, including preparation of plans for using military forces, exercising command responsibility, and undertaking strategic direction of the military forces available to the Security Council.[10]

One of the evident defects in the work of the Military Staff Committee has been the participation of relatively low-ranking military officials in its meetings. The Committee is supposed to consist of the Chiefs of General Staffs of the Security Council permanent members in order to hold high-level talks on substantive matters. Holding sessions on the level of the Chiefs of General Staffs could improve the functioning of this body of the Security Council. In order to manage the U.N. military forces more effectively, each member of the Military Staff Committee could take command of the forces for rotating periods of not more than three months each.

In addition, certain regional organizations might establish military operations which could be defined as peacekeeping operations in accordance with U.N. practice. The consent of all parties concerned would need to be obtained and prohibitions on the use of such peacekeeping operations would need to be conducted effectively by the regional organizations. The establishment of a strictly defensive, non-combative policy for regional peacekeeping forces not subject to the discipline of U.N. administration and regulations may prove quite difficult. The practice of the regional organizations, such as the Arab League, shows that obstacles to their peacekeeping operations are political rather than technical and legal.[11]

The problems which are so often the roots of the conflicts are so complicated that decentralizing the machinery for the maintenance of peace might produce the best results.[12] That is why regional organizations must enjoy freedom of action in resolving conflicts provided that they not use coercive measures without the consent and the guidance of the Security Council. Otherwise the deep political confrontation between some developing countries could lead not to the settlement of disputes but to the unreasonable use of force.

There is another complicated question which relates to the regional organizations. Recognized regional organizations are prone to being manipulated to justify otherwise questionable uses of military force. The U.S. reliance on the "request" of the Organization of Eastern Caribbean States to legitimize its invasion of Grenada in 1983 is a case in point. There is no ready answer in the Charter, so this problem can continue seriously to complicate interstate relations.

In conclusion, several tasks can be accomplished during the transition period of the United Nations from the era of preventive diplomacy to one of collective security:

1. Deploy U.N. peacekeeping forces at the invitation of a member state in case of a threat of force against such state;
2. Grant power to the Secretary-General to dispatch U.N. forces to patrol national borders with the prior approval of the Security Council;
3. Organize permanent and properly trained U.N. military forces; and
4. Ensure the effective management of such U.N. forces.

Notes

1. Berkhof, *Maintaining International Peace and Security: The Military Dimension*, 35 NETHERLANDS INT'L L. REV. 297 (1988).

2. W. CHURCHILL, THE WORLD CRISIS (1931), *quoted in* C. COOTE, A CHURCHILL READER: THE WIT AND WISDOM OF SIR WINSTON CHURCHILL 210 (1954) ("Nothing in human power could break the fatal chain, once it had begun to unroll. A situation had been created in which hundreds of officials had only to do their prescribed duty in their respective countries to wreck the world. They did their duty.")

3. R. RIGGS & J. PLANO, THE UNITED NATIONS, INTERNATIONAL ORGANIZATION AND WORLD POLITICS 128 (1988).

4. *Id.*

5. E. SUY, PEACE-KEEPING OPERATIONS/MANUEL SUR LES ORGANISATIONS INTERNATIONALES 387 (1988).

6. I. Claude, Jr., *The Peace-keeping Role of the United Nations,* THE UNITED NATIONS IN PERSPECTIVE 52 (E. Berkeley Tompkins ed. 1972).

7. *Introduction, Annual Report of the Secretary-General on the Work of the Organization, June 16, 1959-June 15, 1960* 15 U.N. GAOR Supp. (No. 1A) at 4.

8. Urquhart, *The Future of Peace-keeping,* 36 NETHERLANDS INT'L L. REV. 54-55 (1989).

9. Pérez de Cuéllar, J. Le Rôle du Secrétaire Général des Nations Unies, LXXXIX REVUE GENERALE DE DROIT INTERNATIONAL PUBLIC 235 (1985).

10. L. GOODRICH, THE UNITED NATIONS 162, 164 (1959).

11. I. Pogany, *The Arab League and Regional Peacekeeping,* 34 THE NETHERLANDS INT'L L. REV. 74 (1987).

12. UNITED NATIONS PEACE-KEEPING: LEGAL ESSAYS 119-121 (A. Cassese ed. 1978).

8

Commentary on Collective Security

David J. Scheffer

Elihu Root, who represented New York in the U.S. Senate and who was one of the great international lawyers of the twentieth century, once wryly noted that, "The people of the State of New York are in favor of prohibition, but against the application of it."[1] When one considers Chapter VII ("Action with Respect to Threats to the Peace, Breaches of the Peace, and Acts of Aggression") of the U.N. Charter and the debate over its application during the Iraq-Kuwait crisis, a similar observation would be warranted. Governments are quick to favor the principles of Chapter VII but have a harder time supporting the application of them.

Collective Self-Defense and Collective Security

Much of the debate has centered on how to harmonize collective self-defense with collective security. Professor Oscar Schachter points out that the Security Council did not deny the relevant parties in the Iraq-Kuwait dispute the inherent right of self-defense. Significantly, Resolution 661 affirmed the inherent right of individual or collective self-defense "in accordance with Article 51 of the Charter."[2] Subsequent resolutions reaffirmed the provisions of Resolution 661. They reflected a consensus about the continued existence of an inherent right of self-defense that nonetheless was to be exercised in accordance with the procedures set forth in Article 51, which Schachter interprets with precision and common sense. The question with regard to the Iraq-Kuwait crisis was whether the inherent right of individual or collective self-defense could be implemented at any time without the participation of the Security Council. The twelve resolutions of the Security Council established the basis for collective security to reverse Iraq's aggression without denying the continued existence of a right of self-defense. But a unilateral exercise of collective self-defense under such circumstances would have been inconsistent with the Security Council's work. With unprecedented speed and determination, the Security Council put the collective security train in motion immediately following the Iraqi invasion of Kuwait in early August 1990. Thereafter, as long as the Security Council remained actively seised with the issue, the principle of collective self-defense had to be harmonized with collective security in the implementation of these particular resolutions.[3]

An effective collective security system determines how the principle of self-defense will be implemented. If the system of collective security proves incapable—as it so often has since World War II—of responding to an act of aggression, then there has been a failure to implement the principle of self-defense on the kind of collective basis envisaged by the framers of the U.N. Charter. If and when collective security fails, then there certainly arises, or more likely reappears, a legitimate basis for relying upon the inherent right of collective self-defense affirmed in Article 51 of the Charter. In the Iraq-Kuwait crisis the United States was confronted, for all intents and purposes, with a no-lose legal proposition: If it obtained the approval of the Security Council to use force against the Iraqi army, then collective security was working. If, however, the Security Council had balked at a proposed resolution of authorization and drifted into a state of perpetual indecision while Iraq's aggression against and occupation of Kuwait remained unchallenged, then the United States and its allies could have fallen back on Article 51 and employed armed force in collective self-defense of Kuwait. When that point would have been reached would have been a speculative and subjective determination. It would be futile to define the point where sole reliance upon collective security can be legally abandoned in favor of sole reliance upon the right of collective self-defense. But this imprecision in international law does not deny the legitimacy of the distinction. The Iraq-Kuwait crisis at least established the important precedent that collective security can be implemented within a reasonable period of time.

A collective security action taken with the authorization of the Security Council arguably may permit the use of armed force in a manner that exceeds some of the traditional parameters of self-defense actions. The law of collective self-defense labors under certain constraints—necessity, proportionality, and the request of the victim state. But if the Security Council authorizes military action to enforce its resolutions—as was the case in the Iraq-Kuwait crisis—then the need and right may arise to employ disproportionate force not only to repel an aggressor but to defeat it in a definitive manner so that the aggressor no longer can be a threat to international peace and security. In Resolution 678 of November 29, 1990, the Security Council authorized "all necessary means" to require the withdrawal of the Iraqi army from Kuwait as well as to "restore international peace and security in the area." The latter objective can encompass actions, such as attacks to destroy or weaken Iraqi military assets far from the Iraq-Kuwait border, that normally might not be considered legitimate for purposes of self-defense.[4] Further, whether a U.N.-authorized military action must comply with all of the laws of war in order to achieve the Security Council's objective, remains a debatable proposition. One could argue that the higher moral objective of a collective security action—for example, to restore international peace and security and eliminate the threat of the aggressive use of nuclear, chemical, or biological weapons or other threats of future aggression—might permit a larger degree of collateral civilian casualties and property damage and use of certain highly destructive weaponry that otherwise would be prohibited by the laws of war, particularly in a limited self-defense action.[5]

The Charter as a Flexible Document

Chapter VII establishes a step-by-step procedure partly designed to compel performance by member states. The escalating steps include condemnation, provisional measures, economic sanctions and other non-military actions, the Security Council's authorization to use military force, and finally the use of military forces made available "on call" to the Security Council pursuant to special agreements which member states would have entered into with the Security Council and ratified "in accordance with their respective constitutional processes." This elaborate scheme anticipates the hard case, namely one where a member state not only can be directed to participate in an enforcement action, but would be obligated to provide a pre-determined number of military forces at the request of the Security Council. In many respects, however, the Iraq-Kuwait crisis represented the easy case.

The multinational army that was deployed to the Persian Gulf region at the request of Kuwait and Saudi Arabia obviated the need for the special agreements contemplated by Article 43 of the Charter and the U.N. military command structure described elsewhere in Chapter VII. The technical arguments about whether the Security Council can authorize any military action in the absence of Article 43 forces[6] were overshadowed by the larger realities that the permanent members acted in unison on the Security Council (notwithstanding China's abstention on Resolution 678), and that three of them committed troops to the defense of Saudi Arabia and other Gulf states. The fact that the coalition troops were transformed into a potential enforcement army with the adoption of Resolution 678, and finally a fighting armed force on January 16, 1991, represents an extraordinary development in the history of the U.N. Charter and, for that matter, the history of warfare.

The Iraq-Kuwait crisis served to remind us that the Charter is a flexible document and can be interpreted as such. Narrow, rigid interpretations of the Charter by U.N. enthusiasts may have the unintended result of creating unnecessary obstacles to the effective implementation of critical Charter provisions. For example, there was some discussion during the early months of the Iraq-Kuwait crisis that trade sanctions must be proven to have failed before the Security Council could authorize use of force under Article 42 of the Charter. However, the text of Article 42 offers more latitude. It states, "Should the Security Council consider that measures provided for in Article 41 *would be inadequate* or have proved to be inadequate, it may take such action by air, sea, or land forces as may be necessary to maintain or restore international peace and security." (emphasis added) The Security Council could make a determination at any time that trade sanctions "would be inadequate" and move on to Article 42 and the use of force. Iraq, for example, was not driven to economic collapse (which could have taken years) before the Council, by adopting Resolution 678, concluded that economic sanctions were not achieving the objective of forcing Iraq to withdraw from Kuwait. The Security Council decision reflected a judgment by the governments of some of its members—particularly by the Bush administration—both that the economic sanctions had proved to be inadequate up to the date of the Council action and would be inadequate, at least in the event Iraq continued its policy of non-compliance following the deadline of January 15, 1991, established in Resolution 678.

Authorizing the Use of Force Under Chapter VII

Another question raised during the early months of the Iraq-Kuwait crisis was whether the special agreements called for by Article 43 of the Charter must be ratified, and forces made available "on call" to the Security Council, before that body could take military action. First, pursuant to Article 39 the Security Council can recommend military actions to maintain or restore international peace and security.[7] Second, Article 42 does not condition an authorization to use military force on the existence of any special agreements. Nothing in the Charter language prevents the Security Council from authorizing a member state to use its national armed forces to enforce Council resolutions. The legislative history of the Charter suggests that the intention of the framers was to create a U.N. rapid deployment force which the Council could call upon at any time to dissuade would-be aggressors or to respond quickly to acts of aggression.[8] With Article 43 special agreements in place, the Council could direct or command member states to participate in a military action and contribute certain numbers of armed forces to the collective effort. In the absence of those agreements, the Council certainly can authorize a member state to use its armed forces in an enforcement action if that member so chooses. Whether the Council could legally compel a member state to use armed force without the foundation of an Article 43 special agreement lingers as an intriguing question even though, as Schachter explains, a strong case can be made for the requirement of a special agreement.[9]

Professor Hans Kelsen explained that the Security Council can take enforcement actions even in the absence of Article 43 agreements:

> It seems that according to the intention of the framers of the Charter the Security Council is authorized to take enforcement action involving the use of armed force only through the armed forces made available to it by the special agreements concluded in conformity with Article 43. But the wording of Articles 39, 42, 47 and 48 does not exclude the possibility of a decision of the Security Council to the effect that Members which have not concluded a special agreement under Article 43 shall have a definite enforcement action, or that Members which have concluded special agreements shall provide armed forces in excess of those which they have placed at the disposal of the Council in their special agreements. The wording of Articles 39 and 42 does not even exclude the possibility of the establishment of an armed force of the Organization different from and independent of the armed forces placed at the disposal of the Security Council by the Members. Article 42 refers to "air, sea or land forces" without providing that these forces must be armed forces placed at the disposal of the Security Council by the Members.[10]

It certainly was not inconceivable during the Iraq-Kuwait crisis that the Security Council could invoke Article 42, acknowledge the presence of the multinational force that had gathered in the Persian Gulf region, and authorize the various contingents of that force to enforce the Security Council resolutions. Of course, the Security Council action would be an authorization, not a legal command. Therefore, it would remain in the hands of each participating government in the multinational force to decide whether its troops would be committed to an offensive campaign. And that is precisely what happened in January 1991 when the Gulf War commenced.

Significantly, however, the Security Council did not explicitly invoke Article 42 when it adopted Resolution 678. Rather, the Council referred generally to its authority under Chapter VII to authorize the military enforcement action against Iraq. This was not unusual, for the Security Council had acted under Chapter VII in many of its prior resolutions on the Iraq-Kuwait crisis and had acted (sometimes without referring even to Chapter VII) in other situations which required enforcement action in earlier years.[11]

The Military Staff Committee

Nikolai Krylov may be too optimistic in what he proposes for the Military Staff Committee. The Military Staff Committee need not necessarily command any U.N.-authorized military action. The Charter makes clear that the Committee—comprising the military chiefs of staff of China, France, the Soviet Union, the United Kingdom, and the United States—serves at the pleasure of the Security Council. In the three relevant articles—45, 46, and 47—the operative word is "assistance." The Military Staff Committee is empowered to assist the Security Council with the Council's determination of how national air-force contingents will be used for international enforcement action, with plans for the application of armed force, and "on all questions relating to the Council's military requirements for the maintenance of international peace and security, the employment and command of forces placed at its disposal, the regulation of armaments, and possible disarmament." Article 47(3) states that the Military Staff Committee "shall be responsible *under the Security Council* for the strategic direction of any armed forces placed at the disposal of the Security Council." (emphasis added) But in the following sentence the Charter clarifies that, "Questions relating to the command of such forces shall be worked out subsequently." The Charter thus does not stipulate that the military command of a U.N.-authorized enforcement action must be created within the Military Staff Committee. The Charter leaves the issue of operational command open for treatment on a case-by-case basis by the Security Council. In these respects, then, the Military Staff Committee need not be viewed as an obstacle to the efficient implementation of Chapter VII enforcement actions. Further, Article 47(2) requires the Military Staff Committee to invite any member state not permanently represented on the Committee "to be associated with it when the efficient discharge of the Committee's responsibilities require the participation of that Member in its work." So there is a considerable degree of flexibility that can be accommodated in the operation of the Military Staff Committee.

At Dumbarton Oaks, where the U.N. Charter was initially drafted in 1944, the command issue was left purposely vague. The delegations did not advance their work beyond the general idea that the command of a U.N. enforcement action should be exercised in some way by the Military Staff Committee.[12] That indecision reinforces the flexible character of the Charter provisions.

Ad Hoc Forces

The drafters of the U.N. Charter opposed creation of a standing U.N. police force or U.N. army. First, it was argued that it is easier to control an *ad hoc* army than a standing army because the former minimizes the danger that a U.N. police force might itself become a threat to world security. Second, an *ad hoc* force dissuaded notions that the United Nations would become a superstate with a large standing army that could intimidate member states at will. Third, the *ad hoc* force was more acceptable to the great powers—China, France, the Soviet Union, the United Kingdom, and the United States—that convened at Dumbarton Oaks because each wanted to keep its own armed forces under national control except in the kind of emergency situations that they all would agree would require concerted action under Article 42.[13] Kelsen explained the arrangement in this way:

> [W]hether the Charter establishes an armed force of the United Nations distinct from armed forces of the Members through their own armed forces, cannot be answered simply in one or in the other way. The Charter has created a type which is in the midst between two extremes . . . [T]here is no armed force of the United Nations distinct from the armed forces of the Members. However, the armed forces of the Members are unified by being placed at the disposal and under the command and strategic direction of a single body, the Security Council, assisted by a Military Staff Committee.[14]

There also is the unique arrangement provided for in Article 45 that would require that national air force contingents be "immediately available" to the Security Council, but still separate from the Council's formal organization. In 1942 U.S. Vice President Henry Wallace said of a U.N. air corps: "When this war comes to an end, the U.N. will have such an overwhelming superiority in air power that we shall be able to enforce any mandate."[15] He later said the method would be to "bomb the aggressor nations mercilessly" until they ceased fighting.[16] The unprecedented bombing campaign waged by the coalition air force during the Gulf War reflects, perhaps unwittingly, the original concept underpinning Article 45. In fact, at Dumbarton Oaks the Soviet delegation was the strongest advocate of a U.N. air force.[17] But what evolved was only the less formal arrangement described in Article 45.

Regional Arrangements

Chapter VIII of the Charter (Articles 52-54) refers to enforcement action that may be taken by "regional arrangements or agencies." Although such regional arrangements typically would be established by treaty among its members (for example, the North Atlantic Treaty Organization and the Organization of American States), Chapter VIII is open to a more flexible interpretation encompassing arrangements which could fall short of formal treaty-based defense organizations. If it had exhibited more explicit organizational trappings, the multinational force that was created in 1990 to confront Iraqi aggression might have qualified for a Chapter VIII "arrangement" and therefore have been authorized by the Security Council to use military force pursuant to that chapter rather than Chapter VII. The fact that the principal participants (the United States, the United Kingdom, and France) of the multinational force arrayed against Iraq were from outside the Middle East might have appeared awkward in any such arrangement, but Chapter VIII does not necessarily limit the composition of regional arrangements to member states of the geographical region in question.

The Continued Relevance of Article 106

Article 106 of the Charter was drafted to deal with the very kind of situation the United Nations continues to confront in the absence of the special agreements called for under Article 43. Article 106 authorizes the five powers which became the permanent members of the Security Council to take "joint action on behalf of the Organization as may be necessary for the purpose of maintaining international peace and security." This special authorization remains available until "the coming into force of such special agreements referred to in Article 43 as in the opinion of the Security Council enable it to begin the exercise of its responsibilities under Article 42...." There is no requirement that the decision to take joint action under Article 106 must be made within or outside the Security Council. On the one hand, Article 106 may be interpreted to authorize the five powers to take joint action involving the use of force only after the Security Council has determined the existence of a threat to, or a breach of, the peace, and decided that enforcement action involving the use of armed force is necessary. But on the other hand, Article 106 provides a rather convenient method by which a multinational force of the character which was deployed during the Iraq-Kuwait crisis could take enforcement action under the direction of the great powers, which could have reached a decision outside of the Security Council to use force against Iraq in conformity with the U.N. Charter and on behalf of the United Nations.

Proposals for U.N. Forces

Krylov's proposal to deploy U.N. peacekeeping forces at the invitation of a member state in case of a threat of force against such a state has admirable intentions but presumably would require Security Council authorization in each case. His second proposal empowering the Secretary-General to dispatch U.N. forces to patrol national borders with the prior approval of the Security Council should be understood to require the

Council's authorization in every instance. But the functional character of the proposal—to patrol national borders under threat—would constitute a major step forward for U.N. peacekeeping and would be well within the Charter norms.

A permanent U.N. military force, even if properly trained and effectively managed, is not the answer for the near term. There remains little likelihood that the major powers or even other governments want to cut the umbilical cord to those national forces that would be contributed to the permanent U.N. force. The framers of the Charter had the right idea when they drafted Article 43 with its requirement for special agreements between each member state and the United Nations. Even though negotiations among the major powers broke down in 1947 over the obligations that would be imposed by special agreements,[18] the end of the Cold War offers a realistic prospect that these negotiations can be resumed. It is more pragmatic at this precarious stage in the development of collective security to require of nations that they make certain, limited forces available "on call" to the Security Council rather than to place them permanently in the service and under the command of the United Nations. A permanent standby U.N. force might be a vision worth pursuing for the twenty-first century, but the Organization will have taken a major step if it can implement the Charter's original design in the coming years.

Notes

1. *Quoted in* H. KELSEN, THE LAW OF THE UNITED NATIONS 769 n. 1 (1950, 4th printing 1964).

2. U.N. Doc. S/RES/661 (1990), *reprinted in* 29 I.L.M. 1325-1327 (1990).

3. *See also* the author's writings: *The United Nations in the Gulf Crisis and Options for U.S. Policy*, Occasional Paper No. 1, United Nations Association of the USA, at 6-11 (October 1990), *reprinted in* 136 CONG. REC. S18032 (daily ed. Oct. 24, 1990); *United Nations and International Law Are Flying High, but Real Test Is to Come*, L.A. Times, Sept. 2, 1990, at M2, col. 3; *In the UN Charter, Room for an Assault on the Iraqis*, Int'l Herald Tribune, Oct. 20-21, 1990, at 4, col. 3; *Go-It-Alone Policy Is Dangerous in Gulf*, Wall St. J., Nov. 29, 1990, at A13, col. 1.

4. *Compare with* Scheffer, *Bush Wins the Right to Look for Trouble*, L.A. Times, Nov. 30, 1990, at B5, col. 4.

5. For an early but comprehensive discussion of this issue, see D.W. BOWETT, UNITED NATIONS FORCES Ch. 15 (1958). Schachter argues that the laws of war must be complied with in connection with a U.N.-authorized action. *See* Schachter, *supra* ch. 6, at 75-76.

6. *See* Schachter, *supra* ch. 6, at 68-69.

7. Hans Kelsen examined how Article 39 was employed in 1950 at the outbreak of the Korean war in KELSEN, *supra* note 1, at 931-940.

8. *See* KELSEN, *supra* note 1, at 748-756; R. RUSSELL, A HISTORY OF THE UNITED NATIONS CHARTER 467-472 (1958). The requirements of the Charter with respect to the use of force were explored at great length during the U.S. Senate's consideration of the resolution of ratification for the U.N. Charter in July 1945 and during floor debate on the U.N. Participation Act in late 1945. For the author's analysis of these deliberations, *see War Powers and the U.N. Charter: Constitutional Roles of Congress and the President in Declaring and Waging War: Hearings Before the Senate Committee on the Judiciary,* 102nd Cong., 1st Sess. Appendix (statement of David J. Scheffer, Senior Associate, Carnegie Endowment for International Peace)(scheduled for publication in 1991). *See also* Glennon, *The Constitution and Chapter VII of the United Nations Charter*, 85 AM. J. INT'L L. 74 (1991). *Contra* Franck & Patel, *UN Police Action in Lieu of War: "The Old Order Changeth,"* 85 AM. J. INT'L L. 63 (1991).

9. *See* Schachter, *supra* ch. 6, at 68-70.

10. KELSEN, *supra* note 1, at 756.

11. Examples include action taken by the Security Council regarding the Korean conflict (U.N. Doc. S/RES/83 (1950) and U.N. Doc. S/RES/84 (1950)), regarding Southern Rhodesia (U.N. Doc. S/RES/221 (1966) and U.N. Doc. S/RES/235 (1968)), and regarding South Africa (U.N. Doc. S/RES/418 (1977)).

12. *See* HILDERBRAND, DUMBARTON OAKS 156-158 (1990); RUSSELL, *supra* note 8, at 472.

13. *See* HILDERBRAND, *supra* note 12, at 140-141.

14. KELSEN, *supra* note 1, at 767-768.

15. *Quoted in* HILDERBRAND, *supra* note 12, at 142.

16. *Id.*

17. *See* RUSSELL, *supra* note 8, at 470-471; HILDERBRAND, *supra* note 12, at 142-156.

18. *See* BOWETT, *supra* note 5, at 13-18; Schachter, *supra* ch. 6, at 72.

PART THREE

Intervention

9

Intervention by Invitation and the Politics of the New World Order

John Lawrence Hargrove

In the contemporary international system, the principles of non-use of force and peaceful settlement of disputes serve as the architectural features of a "regime of restraint," to use George Will's phrase, on the arbitrary exercise of power by public authority. This regime is embedded in the U.N. Charter. Characteristically we think of international law, in this role, as concerned with the exercise of force *between* states, and as having the mandate to hold violence within the community on that plane to the minimum consistent with other legitimate policy concerns of governance. This is in fact the primary role of these two principles, both in the sense of relative importance, and in the sense that the law gives this role a dominant place in its hierarchy of fundamental principles. International law protects against the use of force even those states that may not be in full compliance with their international legal obligations, including obligations about individual rights. But contemporary international law also is concerned with restraining the exercise of power *within* the domain of a state's own jurisdiction. For international law now encompasses a dynamic and extensively developed law of human rights. At this moment we are witnessing a great burgeoning of the notion—now well-buttressed in the international law of human rights—that constitutional democracy is a *sine qua non* for lawful restraint on the internal exercise of arbitrary power, and that for this purpose constitutional democracy must also embody legal protections of *other* fundamental civil and political rights than those having to do directly with political governance (for example, rights of free expression and association, freedom from arbitrary detention, and others).

The sometimes antagonistic relationship between these two roles of international law as a part of the "regime of restraint" has troubled international law scholars for decades. The reason is that one of the most perplexing questions in this area has to do with the limits on intervention by an outside power, in support of one party or the other, in a conflict which includes some element of armed contention between a purported government and dissident groups. Assuming there are some such lawful limits, in what way if any are they affected by the probable impact of such intervention on the future internal state of affairs, as regards restraint on the exercise of arbitrary power by those who end up in control? How can international law, with its bias (for good and sound reasons) in favor of limits on the unlawful exercise of force *between* states, cope with the problem that this bias may in some cases be pursued only by sacrificing restraints on arbitrary public power *within* the state? Is it capable of developing principles, if they now do not exist, that will cope with the twin problems of democratic and anti-democratic revolution (and for that matter the problem of entrenched tyranny in a presently peaceful domestic order)? Can it find ways to do so that will be at least as effective as the means by which it seeks to cope with the problem of arbitrary violence between states—namely through the instruments of self-defense and of collective security under the U.N. Charter?

Assumptions

A main burden of this chapter is to put forward some suggestions as to the possible progressive development of principles relating to forcible intervention by invitation, particularly as to the class of situations just mentioned. In so doing, however, it proceeds on a number of assumptions. These cannot be elaborated or argued here, but only summarized, as follows:

1. There is a need for a kind of reform in international law *as a legal system,* and the realistic prospects for developments in specific areas such as those explored in this chapter depend heavily on the prospects for such reform in the system as a whole.
2. A major characteristic of the system that demonstrates this need is the notorious ineffectuality of its processes of appraisal, decision, and compliance in particular cases. In some major areas, they are weak and sometimes spurious, lacking the integrity

required for an effectively working system, and foster chronic if misplaced doubts about the genuineness of the international legal system overall. Predominant among these areas are those touching on the most fundamental interests of the states that comprise the system's participants—the control of violence among states, and, more broadly, restraint on the arbitrary exercise of power both among and within states: such as problems of human rights and the illicit use of international force.

3. What principally accounts for this weakness is the fact that the implementation processes have not frequently or consistently engaged in adequately broad support among the international community's major sources of political, economic, and military power, and of moral authority. It was precisely these conditions that were made unachievable in the Cold War. That protracted political condition made it impossible for these processes to reflect a broad and sustained commitment to certain shared values, and to a coherent system of procedures and institutions along with the substantive principles articulating those values. Such a system would be one which survives over a considerable period of time, and in the survival of which every participant shares an interest, despite the fact that, of necessity, its outcome in particular cases will not always serve the immediate interests of each participant. Both the conduct of major powers (not to mention lesser ones), and their official utterances in justifying their conduct, have so often been so inconsistent and even contradictory from one case to another as not only to render the law's implementation processes ineffectual, but to be of little utility as a body of practice from which the content and evolution of its substantive principles can be ascertained.
4. The Cold War has of itself been enough to keep international law, in important respects, in this state of arrested adolescence for some decades. Its disappearance, and replacement by a stable, non-confrontational, and cooperative set of political, economic, and security relations among the major powers of North America, Europe, and Asia—still far from an accomplished fact—is a necessary condition for appreciable change in this legal state of affairs and would be a powerful stimulus for such change. But while necessary, it would not of itself be sufficient, even though wise management of major seminal episodes such as the Iraq-Kuwait crisis can have a very large effect in a relatively short period of time. Such basic changes in the way international law works as a legal system must engage the whole international community, and with or without the Cold War both the major and the lesser powers of course will continue to conduct themselves as

states with their various divergent as well as convergent interests.

Consent

Intervention by invitation[1] concerns *consent* as a justification for a threat or use of force by a state which would be unlawful in the absence of that consent, unless some other legal justification (for example, self-defense, or authorization by the United Nations) can be shown.

The paradigm case is the introduction of the military forces of one state onto the territory of a consenting state, where these forces are actually engaging—or clearly expected by both states to engage—in some form of military conflict while there. Kuwait was alleged to have given such consent, by invitation of a newly-installed government, to the invasion by Iraq in August 1990.

But the mere presence of armed forces, without any such activity or expectation, is also one in which consent is a sufficient and (in the absence of any other legal justification) necessary condition for lawfulness. This may be the case where military forces are present for training purposes, or pursuant to a defense treaty, or to facilitate their lawful use wholly or partly on the territory of a third state (for example to oust an aggressor from the territory of a neighboring state).

And consent is a sufficient and likewise possibly necessary condition for the lawfulness of an exercise of force other than on the territory of the consenting state, in collective self-defense with that state on the high seas or on the territory of a third state. This was the well-founded position of the United States in 1990 vis-à-vis Kuwait in the interdiction of Iraqi maritime traffic on the high seas or, potentially, in action against Iraqi territory. This was also the position put forward by the United States—El Salvador being the inviting state—in justification of U.S. support for "contra" rebel actions in Nicaragua against the Nicaraguan government.

A Framework of Principles

What follows is a simple framework of principles for addressing the matter of forcible intervention by invitation, which is defensible if not always uncontroversial as an accurate rendition of existing international law. It will provide a basis for moving in due course to examine what implications the possible new opportunities for systemic reform in international law might have for this special area.

1. *In general, conduct involving the threat or use of force by one state, in derogation of the sovereign prerogatives of another, is unlawful. Such conduct may, however, be made lawful by the consent of the latter state—provided it does not entail activities which would have*

been unlawful by the latter state if acting alone. (The last point has nothing peculiarly to do with forcible intervention, but follows from the fact that states, being sovereign, have the capacity to consent to restrictions on their sovereign rights if they find it useful to do so, and that moreover, they can lawfully do together what—but only what—one of them might lawfully do alone.) Such lawful conduct would include, for example:

(a) the introduction and maintenance of armed forces on the territory of another state for various non-combat purposes, such as training or mere stationing. This might include the extension of the stay of such forces beyond the time of the expiration of a formal indication of consent—for example, a treaty—where consent by less formal means can be shown.
(b) collective self-defense actions either (1) on the territory of another state, to deter a threatened aggression or expel an aggressor that has already entered that territory or (2) outside that territory.
(c) some range of activities involving the actual deployment of force for the purpose of maintaining or restoring internal order.

2. *The consent given, however, must be valid, in two respects:*

(a) in respect of the standing of the entity from which it emanates to exercise sovereign prerogatives of statehood for this purpose for the territory in question (normally, the entity is a state); and
(b) in respect of the capacity of the agent purporting to give consent to do so (normally, it must be a government, and the government of the consenting state).

3. *Further, the consent must be genuine, in two respects:*

(a) its freely-given character, and
(b) the effectiveness of the mode of indicating consent actually to communicate it.

In this regard, an advance and explicit invitation is not a necessary condition in all cases, inasmuch as in some classes of situations, at least, such an invitation is properly regarded as only an evidentiary factor, rather than as required as a matter of law. By the same token, mere acceptance or acquiescence may be sufficient in some cases to indicate consent.

Evidentiary Factors

A variety of evidentiary factors are among those to be taken into account in applying any of the foregoing criteria:

(i) Where is the activity consented to going to take place—on the territory of the consenting state, or elsewhere? In the case of a collective defense action participated in by troops previously lawfully present for other purposes on the territory of a state that becomes the object of an actual or threatened aggression, mere acquiescence or acceptance, by a government that appears to be functioning normally, might well be sufficient. But as indicated earlier, collective self-defense activities outside the territory of the victim state, for example, on the high seas or on the territory of a third state, presumably would be subject to a stringent test in which the evidentiary value of an explicit invitation or request would be more important. In such cases it might plausibly be argued that an explicit invitation is required as a matter of law.
(ii) When was public knowledge of an explicit invitation or other formal indication of consent first available—after the action purportedly consented to, or before? from what source?
(iii) Were there any unusual or irregular aspects of the functioning of governmental institutions approximately contemporaneous with the purported communication of consent? For example: Has anyone experienced an overnight meteoric rise from the ranks to the top? Have any key actors in the conduct of governmental affairs been forcibly removed? Has any key actor just recently arrived back from exile in (say) the capital of the intervening state? The list could be multiplied.
(iv) In cases of collective self-defense, was there a report to the Security Council? At what stage, and by whom? A report to the Security Council is not a legally necessary condition in order to show consent, just as a timely report would not in itself legally establish it. But such a report, promptly rendered by all states participating in a collective self-defense action, would be of strong evidentiary value.

Special Perplexities Posed by Intervention by Invitation

What are we to make of the three principles for consent, as regards the special perplexities which the notion of intervention by invitation presents, and the implications for this notion of any possible systemic reforms in international law?

First, given the generally more favorable political environment that an emerging new order might bring, the question of the genuineness of the invitation or other modes of indicating consent seems not of the greatest importance in either respect. This is true notwithstanding that this question has been the focus of public attention in some of the more important cases, including the Soviet interventions in Hungary, Czechoslovakia, and Afghanistan, as well as the U.S. interventions in the Dominican Republic and Grenada. It seems largely a question of fact, and hence likely to turn in most cases on heavily evidentiary considerations that draw on common sense and the concepts of ordinary discourse that one uses in distinguishing the real from the spurious. Its attendant legal issues are resolvable on the basis of familiar concepts drawn straightforwardly from other areas of the law than those having to do directly with restraints on the exercise of force—for example, the law of treaties.

This is the way it should be. It is perhaps a fair question whether lawyers should not turn their attention to devising some more formal rules or procedures designed to ensure that such invitations are not spurious. The International Court of Justice (I.C.J.) tended in this direction in its treatment of the question of notice to the Security Council in the case of the U.S. intervention in Nicaragua. This, however, would be a misconceived effort, unlikely to produce any very useful result, and perhaps even pernicious. One need only remember the slogan that was incorrectly invoked regarding the quite different enterprise of developing a definition of "aggression," which was warned against as a "trap for the unwary and a guide to the transgressor." As regards distinguishing phony invitations from real ones, the best position for international law to be in may well be to make clear that the fate of nations and peoples should not hang on technicalities. Indeed it will not be permitted to, in the real world, and for the legal system to pretend that it will, may only invite consignment of the law to irrelevancy in decisions affecting really fundamental interests.

Second, of the three classes of cases cited as examples of situations in which consent may justify conduct that would otherwise be an unlawful use of force, only the third seems to me to pose especially difficult problems of legal policy, again assuming the more favorable general political environment that could emerge with a new order.[2] That is to say, the most perplexing and serious policy issue in the law governing the legitimacy of intervention by invitation would be the extent to which the consent of a state may be sufficient to legitimize the use of force by an intervening state for the purposes of maintaining or restoring internal order.

The problem, touched upon at the very outset of this chapter, is how to accommodate legitimate demands for effective vindication or preservation of certain fundamental human rights in cases of either democratic or anti-democratic revolution, without unacceptably diminishing the basic restraint on the use of force. It arises from the asymmetry between the remedies provided by contemporary international law to deal respectively with two kinds of injurious conduct that are equally violative of fundamental rights: the use of force by one state against another, and the deprivation of the fundamental human rights necessary for democratic governance. In the one case, all else failing, armed force in the exercise of the right of self-defense may be invoked. In the other, even in those situations where as a practical matter armed assistance might be clearly called for as the only effective means of avoiding immediately irreparable or indefinitely protracted injury, those aggrieved appear to have been left to rely on the various means of marshalling public stigma against the offending government, which only possibly might lead to more concrete remedial measures and ordinarily have not done so. When they *have* done so, as in the case of sanctions imposed by the Security Council under Chapter VII of the Charter against South Africa and against the Smith regime in Rhodesia, the sanctions have not included authorization of armed force. In any event, any such measures would be based on concepts of the Charter (such as "threat to the peace") rather than on general law. It is the latter that is under consideration here.

Methods of Analysis

These are perplexities over which scholars have long agonized, with a persistent devotion not always matched by governments. Is there now any greater likelihood of a more promising resolution?

1. It is a fair question why this should be a problem at all. Given the new coalescence of governmental attitudes on such matters, why should not the basic restraint of Article 2(4) simply be adjusted, to add, alongside the self-defense exceptions, exceptions directly legitimizing, among other things, armed force by outside powers to assist both governments and dissident groups struggling to protect democratic rights against anti-democratic alternatives? It is profoundly unwise to think that such problems can be solved by whittling away directly at the great stabilizing concepts of the international legal order, among which the non-use of force has a prominent place. The idea that when this fundamental principle is found to have an inconvenient consequence one simply carves out a corresponding additional exception, is pernicious because it invites an open-ended succession of such diminutions.

For the same reasons it would be no more wise, and even less plausible, to propose simply making specific exceptions to the criteria by which being a "state" or a "government" is determined to the effect that a state or government has to be and remain properly democratic or else pass out of legal existence.

Any effort to introduce the appraisals that are involved in certifying the democratic credentials of a government or group, as a basis for determining whether the use of force is lawful, is a risky enough enterprise as it is. It must be more carefully hedged about as a matter of legal craftsmanship, so as to minimize damage done to the fundamental concepts of the legal order.

2. One can turn more hopefully to the consent principle, namely, that conduct by a state in respect of another state that otherwise would amount to an unlawful use of force against the latter state, may be rendered lawful by the consent of the latter—provided that it does not entail activities which would have been unlawful by the latter state if acting alone. A direct appeal to the underlying requirement of the lawfulness of the action in which the participation is invited, if undertaken by the inviting state alone, is sufficient to rule out intervention by invitation in certain classes of cases, and to authorize it in one.

Specifically:

(a) The consent principle would rule out forcible assistance in quelling internal disorder when it is provided to an existing and clearly anti-democratic and repressive regime, whether or not it invites such help, at least where it is equally clear that what is involved is an effort to replace that regime with one of reasonably democratic credentials and promise.

(b) The consent principle would authorize providing forcible assistance invited by a clearly democratic government in an effort to resist being replaced by a dissident group of equally clear anti-democratic and repressive intentions.

(c) By the same token the consent principle would rule out assistance to a dissident group of clearly anti-democratic and repressive intentions, that has sought help in its effort to replace a clearly democratic government and constitutional system. (In this connection it should be noted that an issue would arise as to the standing of any group not constituting a government to give consent to and thus make legal any action in derogation of the prerogatives of a state, whether such action involves the use of force or otherwise. Here, however, that issue would not need to be addressed since—however this issue of standing might be resolved—the action being undertaken could not be made internationally lawful because it would be in violation of the substantive law of human rights.)

3. Finally, there is the most difficult case: a forcible intervention at the request of a dissident group which has clearly democratic intentions and

promise, seeking to replace a clearly anti-democratic and repressive existing government. It can be plausibly argued that, by the same reasoning, an intervention may be authorized by the dissident group's request for such assistance where no reasonable alternative appears as a means of avoiding irreparable or indefinitely prolonged injury. In this case the government will already have forfeited the right to seek assistance on its side of the conflict, by reason of the fundamental unlawfulness of the purposes to which this assistance would be turned. Beyond this, however, the law would have to recognize that in the most egregious of circumstances that government has further forfeited its prerogative to invoke the protection of Article 2(4) of the Charter, if so doing would have the direct result of greatly exacerbating or indefinitely protracting its unlawful conduct against its own people. That strictly limited but fundamental prerogative would thereupon necessarily devolve upon the people, to be exercised by whatever is the most reasonable agency available.

The latter step is more plausible than might initially appear, particularly to those who are rightly concerned with the stability of concepts—such as "statehood"—that are basic to the contemporary legal order. It is instructive in this connection to reflect on the history of the issue of the legitimacy of third-party support for "wars of national liberation" and other allegedly pro-democracy dissident groups—which incidentally provides a case study of the difficulties of trying to deal reasonably with legal and policy problems of this sort in the confrontational political environment of the Cold War, particularly as reinforced by the understandable anti-Western bias of the decolonization period.

Support for Wars of National Liberation

The matter begins with the treatment of colonial or other cases of non-self-governing territories falling under Chapters XI and XII of the U.N. Charter. At the outset of the Charter era there was no question as to the status of the colonial power as a state or that, for a time at least, it was entitled in international law to exercise sovereign prerogatives vis-à-vis the non-self-governing territory, including Article 2(4) prerogatives. It was reasonable to think, however, that in due course this state of affairs would gradually change, to the extent that the colonial power continued to fail to comply with Charter obligations to move toward self-determination. Its intransigence would become progressively less excusable with the gradual development of U.N. institutions and principles for facilitating self-determination, and for certifying its successful conclusion, ordinarily by emergence into full statehood and admission to the United Nations.

It was difficult to argue that at *no* time in this period of increasingly unreasonable clinging to power could the prerogatives of statehood ever have passed willy-nilly from the colonial power even in the absence of U.N. "certification", and devolved upon some group reasonably competent to speak for the people of the aspiring new state. Ordinarily some entity had established itself which was a reasonable candidate for such a role, at least to the extent of being entitled to invite and receive third-party support for an armed struggle of liberation against an illegal occupant. This analysis provided a theoretical underpinning for the increasing insistence of Third World and Communist Bloc powers in the United Nations on such a right on the part of "national liberation" groups. The United States and others in the West continued to insist on regarding such support as contrary to Article 2(4) in the dwindling number of clearly colonial cases that remained, avoiding the need to address the question of whether that legal state of affairs might *ever* change in advance of U.N. certification of completion of the self-determination process.

Meanwhile supporters of "national liberation" groups came to insist on passing out similar prerogatives to such groups in a select number of non-colonial cases—for example, those struggling on behalf of Palestinian self-determination or against apartheid in South Africa. The United States for its part, while shunning the language of "national liberation" (which it had long regarded, often accurately, as implicated in efforts to extend Soviet influence and Communist local control), came increasingly to insist on analogous prerogatives for dissident groups in a select number of African cases where less-than-democratic, professedly Marxist governments had emerged in the post-colonial era, and later in Afghanistan during the Soviet intervention in support of the Afghan government. (The United States did not, however, rely on such a theory in its legal argumentation in the *Nicaragua* case during the 1980s.) Both sides seemed to have limited their favors largely to the Third World or selected sectors thereof.[3]

Sadly, for various geo-political reasons, it seems never to have occurred to either side to assert that anyone, anywhere, suffering under a genuinely repressive regime, colonial or otherwise—at least if they genuinely seek a democratic alternative with decent protection of other basic rights—ought to share on an equal footing in whatever benefits the international legal system might be able to eke out for any single group of them. The whole historical episode is a stark example of the distortions of the international legal system imposed in considerable measure by the Cold War, abetted in this case by the attitudes of the stressful period of active de-colonization.

The simple assumption that seems to underlie the positions taken on all sides is that there must be some conceivable point at which a government's violations of the fundamental civil and political rights of its people becomes so egregiously severe or protracted that it must give up at least that particular sovereign prerogative that in fact shields its continued repression, which then can only return to the people from whom it springs. It does not necessarily forfeit all, and simply pass out of existence as a government in relation to the territory in question, nor would there be any practical need for its doing so. The practical result is that it can no longer abuse its people under protection of Article 2(4) of the U.N. Charter. The U.N. General Assembly was putting into effect an analogous but broader proposition in the case of South West Africa/Namibia, when it declared in its 1966 resolution[4] that South Africa had forfeited its sovereign prerogative as to South West Africa, which thereupon became the "direct responsibility" of the United Nations. Of course the Assembly was acting not just under the law of the Charter but also was exercising its legal responsibilities under the Mandate Territory regime.

The question of consent—by invitation or request—by those in a position to give consent is of the same relevance in this case as it is in others in determining the lawfulness of the ensuing intervention. Here, as in other classes of cases discussed above, international law issues no general license to any volunteer intervenor—whether well-intentioned or self-serving—to move in unilaterally with armed force. (This is true notwithstanding the fact that the consent issue does not figure prominently in scholarly discussion of the broader questions of "humanitarian intervention" or intervention to oust illegitimate regimes or, uniformly, in the actual practice of governments in this limited body of cases.)

It is an open question (as always) whether such intervention is wise policy from the point of view either of the intervenor or those whom it is intended to assist; the latter may well not want it, since for example it may burden them with a political stigma they hope to avoid as long as possible.

Legal Criteria for Intervention by Invitation

In sum, situations of internal disorder suggest the following: First, it is just and salutary that international law move in the direction of permitting the application of armed force in cases of internal disorder to correct the problem of governments that are in egregious violation of human rights regarding democratic governance. This must be done, if at all, with care and judiciousness, and certainly not simply by purporting to add *ad hoc* exceptions to the principle of non-use of force, or to make the use of force available to remedy human rights violations across the board. Rather, it should be accomplished within the confines of an existing exception to that principle—consent. Hence the best approach seems to be one by which (a) consent—through invitation or otherwise—is required, and (b) the lawfulness of the conduct in which an outsider's assistance is sought, when judged by certain international human rights standards, must be demonstrated. The human rights standards in question would cover only the right to democratic governance and the basic civic freedoms and personal protections which comprise the constitutional environment necessary for democratic government to flourish.

This is probably the most promising way to deal with what as a practical matter has been a very large aspect of the problem of intervention in episodes of internal disorder—although by and large it would not deal with all those aspects of the problem that what is called "humanitarian intervention" seeks to deal with. It seems the most prudent approach, and the one least damaging to the law's fundamental principles and concepts. At any rate it is about the best that can be offered by way of a guide to the future development of international law for the purposes at hand.

The difficulty is that there is no way to do this without introducing into the legal appraisals that must be made concepts such as "democratic governance" which are even more subject to abuse than the relatively more concrete concept of self-defense as an exception to the prohibition on the use of force. The notion of self-defense does, after all, turn in part more directly on considerations involving physically describable and measurable phenomena. But at bottom the problem is not one just of clever or even of wise legal craftsmanship. It is a problem of developing and maintaining the political environment in which international law can function as a genuine legal system, and then setting about in good faith as a community of states to make it work. This is why it has not been possible to think realistically of the possibility of such developments in the prevailing environment of the Cold War.

Developing legal principles relating to intervention by invitation along the lines described above would require: (1) limiting intervention to the clearest of cases—the most egregious of violators, the most obviously genuinely democratic of victims, the most compellingly desperate of circumstances; (2) careful political calculation in each situation as to the likelihood of eliciting a broad supporting consensus in the international community (for example, through seeking Security Council authorization grounded on the concept of "threat to the peace"); (3) seeking to multilateralize the judgments involved as early as possible; (4) diligence in exhausting non-forcible alternatives; and (5) moving vigorously to strengthen both the substantive principles of human rights law relating to democracy and its supporting cluster of other human rights concepts, and (as Professor Thomas M. Franck argues[5]) the full range of methods of monitoring and appraising individual situations on the basis of these principles—methods that would routinely function even in the absence of any conflict situation. There is much that has been done in this latter respect in recent years, particularly as to methods of appraisal, and there are large opportunities for further development.

But whether the newly emerging political order will make this kind of enterprise sustainable in the legal order is, in the end, a political calculation and a challenge to politicians and lawyers alike. In these promising but uncertain times, a cautious optimism is warranted.

Notes

1. Any international lawyer concerned with this subject owes a large debt to Louise Doswald-Beck for her long article, *The Legal Validity of Military Intervention By Invitation of the Government,* 56 BRIT. YB. INT'L L. 189 (1985). This study exhaustively catalogues cases since 1945 and provides a thoughtful and careful analysis of their possible international legal implications.

2. I have chosen not to deal in this chapter with the question of a purported break-away new state in a secessionist conflict—not because it is not relevant, but because it requires some extended treatment. While it has not frequently figured in post-World War II cases, this may change in the political circumstances now developing.

3. A good number of the interventions during the Cold War period that were undertaken by the United States in particular were of such a scale and character as to cross the threshold of the actual use of force. They have been done covertly, and it is to be presumed that this has also been the case not only for the Soviet Union but for a variety of other powers. This has the convenient consequence of making it unnecessary to engage in any international legal argumentation about it—so long, of course, as it stays covert. A problem for U.S. policymakers in this respect has been that, in general, covertness has been an increasingly ephemeral quality for any U.S. policy, even the most sensitive. Americans thus have been presented for years with the curious spectacle of extended public debate on the national and international legal, and other, aspects of overt "covert" activities, with the implicit recognition that there must remain a class of non-overt, *really* covert activities of the sort that we were accustomed to, but did not speak of, in the good old days.

4. U.N. Doc. A/RES/2145 (XXI), *reprinted in* 5 I.L.M. 1190 (1966).

5. *See* Franck, *infra* ch. 14.

10

Intervention by Invitation

Rein Mullerson

Intervention by invitation of a legitimate government is frequently among the arguments invoked to justify the use of armed force, although it is almost never the main or exclusive argument.

In the analysis of the lawfulness of intervention entailing the use of armed force, intervention by invitation must be distinguished from collective self-defense in response to an armed attack by one state against another. Such help to the victim of an armed attack not only is lawful, but generally does not constitute intervention, even though one state's troops may be present and operating in the territory of another state. Also outside the scope of the problem of intervention by invitation is the furnishing of assistance by one government to another in the case of uses of force directed against the latter that do not constitute armed attack (for example, border incidents), without expanding the armed activities onto the territory of a third state. In such a case it is appropriate for one state to seek the assistance of another state in the exercise of a legitimate right of self-help. These appeals for assistance in coping with the use of force by a third party or parties, made by a government whose legitimacy is not open to doubt either *de jure* or *de facto*, serve as the foundation for rendering such help. Thus there is no question of intervention in the sense of armed interference of one state on the territory of another, albeit by the invitation of the government of the latter: there is simply no interference.

The application of this position, which is perfectly clear from the juridical point of view, is in practice nonetheless fraught with dangers from misapplication, just as the analysis of problems connected with self-defense has shown that states often had no basis for their reliance on Article 51 of the U.N. Charter as the grounds for their actions connected with the use of armed force.[1]

Thus the Soviet Union when using force in Hungary (1956), Czechoslovakia (1968), and Afghanistan (1979) invoked as a legal basis the necessity to repel aggression or external interference, and also claimed that it had been invited by the lawful governments.[2] In the discussion of these cases in the U.N. Security Council—which in any event could not adopt resolutions condemning the Soviet invasions and demanding the withdrawal of foreign troops because of the Soviet Union's exercise of the right of veto—the main attention of the Security Council members was focused not on the problem of invitation, but rather on the presence or absence of foreign interference or aggression against which the Soviet invasion was allegedly aimed.

The Soviet force in Hungary and in Czechoslovakia (acting in the latter case together with the forces of four other members of the Warsaw Pact) suppressed popular revolutions and the processes of democratization of these societies. In Afghanistan Soviet troops interfered in civil war and participated in the palace coup.

The United States also has relied upon the justification of an invitation from a lawful government as the basis for intervention (along with self-defense, rescue of citizens, and decisions of a regional organization), for example when intervening in the Dominican Republic in 1965 and in Grenada in 1983. The discussions in the Security Council again concentrated not so much on the question of invitation as on whether there existed in general a justification for the intervention. The majority of states, both within the framework of the United Nations and outside it, did not accept the arguments of the United States government regarding the invasion of the Dominican Republic but instead judged it to be interference in internal affairs.[3] The U.N. General Assembly by an overwhelming majority (108 for, 9 against, and 27 abstentions) characterized the U.S. armed intervention in Grenada as a gross violation of international law and of the independence, sovereignty, and territorial integrity of that state.[4]

The unsubstantiated legal claims put forward by both the Soviet Union and the United States in these cases as justifications for the interventions included unsubstantiated assertions concerning the invitations as well. There is ground for doubt both as to the fact of the invitation in general, as well as whether it came from a competent organ.

Thus, in the case of the armed intervention of Soviet forces in Hungary in 1956, there is no doubt that the invitation could not have come from the lawful government headed by Imre Nagy. On November 1, 1956, the government of Hungary informed the U.N. Secretary-General that it had demanded of the Soviet government that it immediately *remove* the Soviet troops from Hungary, and on November 4 a corresponding radio broadcast by Imre Nagy took place.[5] Although the question of the fact or legitimacy of the invitation was not uppermost in the discussions in the Security Council the representative of France, for example, expressed doubts about the existence of any invitation.[6]

The situation in 1968 was similar. Late in the evening of August 20, the troops of five socialist countries began the invasion of Czechoslovakia, alleging that there had been an invitation from the government of Czechslovakia. On August 21, however, the Presidium of the Central Committee of the Communist Party and the Presidium of the National Assembly of Czechoslovakia registered a decisive protest against the invasion. According to the declaration of the Presidium of the Central Committee of the Communist Party of Czechoslovakia, the invasion took place "without the knowledge of the President of the Republic, the Chairman of the National Assembly, the Prime Minister, the First Secretary of the Central Committee of Czechoslovakia, or those organs."[7]

Thus in both the Hungarian and Czech cases, if an invitation even occurred, it could only have come from persons who came to power as a result of the foreign intervention.

Also unsubstantiated was the assertion of the Soviet Union that the invasion of Afghanistan of December 1979 was undertaken at the request of the Afghan government. The Soviet version at the time alleged that such requests came both from Noor Mohammed Taraki and Hafizullah Amin, as well as from Babrak Karmal.[8] But today it has become known even from Soviet sources that things did not happen that way. Amin was not sentenced by a revolutionary court and executed, as Pravda asserted on December 29, 1979, but was killed by Soviet commandos in their raid on the palace of the President of Afghanistan;[9] and Babrak Karmal, who turned to the Soviet Union for assistance, was not at the head of the Afghan government but on Soviet territory.[10] The declaration of Babrak Karmal was made on December 27, but according to Anatoly Gromyko, the son of the former Foreign Minister of the USSR Andrei Gromyko, who learned of it from his father, the decision on Afghanistan was apparently taken in November or the beginning of December of 1979.[11] Thus there could have been no invitation from the legitimate government of the country in this case either.

In the case of the American intervention in 1965 in the Dominican Republic, doubts arise not only about the existence of any legal bases for the invasion but also about the invitation of a legitimate government. President Lyndon Johnson's televised broadcast to the nation on May 2, 1965 announced the existence of a telegram from the U.S. embassy in Santo Domingo according to which certain officials from the law enforcement agencies and the armed forces had informed the U.S. embassy that the situation had gotten completely out of control and that the police and the government could no longer guarantee the safety of Americans and other foreigners.[12] What is dubious is not so much the existence of the communication as its character. First, can information given to the U.S. embassy in the Dominican Republic constitute an invitation? Second, did the Dominican police and military have the right to invite foreign troops? The answers to these two questions must be in the negative. In the text of the telegram cited by the President, there is no mention at all of an invitation to foreign forces; the information only concerns the circumstances prevailing in the country. The information did not come from the parliament, from the head of the state, from the government, or from the foreign ministry, which would represent the state in its international relations.

The American intervention in Grenada in 1983 also gives rise to questions not only about the existence of the circumstances to which the U.S. government referred (a threat to the lives of American citizens; collective self-defense), but also to the legitimacy of the invitation. The doubts concern both the timing of the invitation (before or after the invasion?)[13] and the competence of Governor-General Sir Paul Scoon to take an action of this sort. The Constitution of Grenada reserved to the Governor-General merely ceremonial functions. All his actions must be taken upon the advice of the members of the cabinet.[14] As W.C. Gilmore writes concerning the intervention in Grenada, the proffered justifications are unconvincing both individually and collectively.[15]

All the cases of intervention by invitation considered here occurred in the context of global confrontation between East and West. In reality they were based not on international legal principles and norms, but on the respective doctrines of Johnson, Brezhnev, and Reagan, that were premised on an ideological and political division of the world. It is not surprising that in these cases doubts arise either about the very fact of an invitation or about its genuineness and legitimacy; it would be strange if this were not the case. Indeed, armed force in each of these instances was applied not against foreign troops invading the country, but against the peoples of the countries themselves.

Some instances of intervention by invitation have been based on a real invitation issued by the legitimate government of the inviting state. Thus in 1958 Great Britain sent 2000 troops to Jordan at the request of King Hussein, in reliance both on Article 51 of the U.N. Charter and on the fact that according to King Hussein there had been a transborder incursion and supply of weapons into Jordan from Syria.[16]

In the same year American troops landed in Lebanon at the request of Lebanese President Chamoun, who also referred to an external threat. However, while there is no doubt in that case about the existence of an invitation and about the fact that it came from a competent authority, there are great doubts about whether an external threat existed. The U.N. observer group did not detect any intrusion by armed personnel or any supply of weapons across the borders of Lebanon.[17] Therefore this action seems rather to have been an interference in an internal conflict in Lebanon at the request of the head of government.

The views of members of the Security Council diverged on the evaluation of the intervention of Belgium in the Congo in 1964 at the request of the head of government, Tshombe. The goal of the intervention was the rescue of foreigners who were citizens of Belgium. The evaluation of this intervention was complicated by the fact that a significant part of the territory of the state was controlled by forces hostile to the Tshombe government. While many African governments agreed with the statement of the representative of Mali and perceived an attempt on the part of Belgium to "consolidate imperialistic hegemony over the Congo under the cover of their puppets,"[18] other African countries and the Western governments considered this a lawful action aimed at saving human lives.[19]

The interference of France in the armed conflict in Chad in the 1980s took place upon the invitation of the government of Chad. Although a war between different internal factions was in progress in this country, France justified its interference by reference to the intervention of Libya on the side of one of the contending forces.[20]

This brief review of the above cases shows that although there may be no doubt from the juridical point of view about the right to introduce forces into another state at the invitation of its lawful government with the goal of using them to repel acts of armed force committed against that state, the facts relating to an external military threat are often dubious, as is the character of the invitation.

The case becomes more complex when the inviting state has not been the object of an armed attack but when it is involved, for example, in internal disorders, armed insurrection, or civil war. Can another state, at the request of the government, introduce its troops with the objective of supporting the efforts of that government to stabilize conditions in the country?

In international law there are no norms directly prohibiting these activities, just as there are no norms directly permitting them. But it is worth noting that the situation is quite distinct from that of internal law, where one of the principles of a law-based state should be the rule that whatever is not prohibited by legal norms is permitted; in any event, this rule should relate to the rights and freedoms of citizens, but not to the scope of review of officials or organs of government. In contrast, in international law it is by no means the case that everything is permitted that is not explicitly prohibited.

Notwithstanding the absence of concrete norms regulating the various spheres of international relations or activity, the fundamental principles of international law influence all areas of international life.

In the case of *Nicaragua v. United States* the International Court of Justice (I.C.J.) indirectly recognized the right to intervene on the side of a legitimate government, declaring: "[I]t is difficult to say what would remain of the principle of non-intervention in international law if intervention, which is already permitted at the request of the government of a State, were also to be allowed at the request of the opposition."[21] However, this passage cannot support the conclusion that the I.C.J. would sanction any interference under any circumstances, provided that there had been an invitation from the legitimate government. John Perkins correctly points out that "[o]ne should not read the Court's words as sanctioning aid to the government in circumstances where that support would transgresss the people's right of self-determination or the political independence of the state."[22]

International legal scholarship reflects doubts concerning an unconditional right of intervention upon the invitation of a government. Thus the research undertaken by the Institut de Droit International in 1975 concerning the principle of nonintervention in civil wars expressed the conclusion that "[t]hird States shall refrain from giving assistance to parties to a civil war which is being fought in the territory of another State." The majority of Western authors consider that international law does not forbid the rendering of military assistance at the request of a legitimate government with the aim of restoring order in the case of internal disorders, but that it is nonetheless impermissible to interfere in a civil war, no matter which side makes the request.[23]

One must agree that armed interference on either side of a civil war is impermissible, as such interference infringes the principle of self-determination and the freedom of peoples to choose their own paths of social and political development. It is immaterial whether such interference takes place at the request of the government or of the opposition.

Is there nonetheless an unconditional right of armed intervention upon the invitation of the government with the aim of helping to restore civil order in the case of internal disorders? From our point of view this is hardly the case.

The Legal Adviser of the U.S. Department of State declared with respect to the 1983 intervention in Grenada: "[T]he lawful governmental authorities of a State may invite the assistance in the territory of military forces of other states or collective organizations in dealing with internal disorder as well as external threats."[24]

International practice reveals the dangers of such an approach. On the one hand, frequently in times of internal disorders and struggles for control within a state it is not clear who will emerge as the legitimate rulers of the country. On the other hand, the very necessity of a government's appeal to a foreign state for military assistance places the legitimacy of such a government in doubt. As early as the 1920s W. Hall wrote:

> Supposing the intervention to be directed against the existing government, independence is violated by an attempt to prevent the regular organ of the state from managing the state affairs in its own way. Supposing it on the other hand to be directed against rebels, the fact that it has been necessary to call in foreign help is enough to show that the issue of the conflict would without it be uncertain and consequently that there is a doubt as to which side would ultimately establish itself as the legal representative of the state.[25]

Thus, in conclusion, although international law does not prohibit rendering assistance even by means of the dispatch of armed forces to the legitimate government upon its request in cases of internal disorders within a state, the rendering government bears a heavy burden of proof that such an intervention does not contradict the principles of noninterference, non-use of force or the threat of force, and self-determination of peoples. In such a case it must be entirely clear that the invitation emanates from a government that is in power both *de jure* and *de facto*. Such an intervention should not be directed against a popular uprising, or else there would be a violation of the right of peoples to self-determination.

The principal danger of "intervention by invitation" is that it is fraught with the possibility of violating the principle of self-determination of peoples and infringing the right of peoples to choose their own paths of development.

Accordingly, an invitation or a request from the legitimate government of another state may be a necessary prerequisite for the lawfulness of both the introduction of armed forces onto the territory of that state and their participation in military activities there; but by itself an invitation or request does not legitimize an intervention that would violate the fundamental principles of international law.

Notes

1. *See* Mullerson, *supra* ch. 2.
2. *See* 746th Meeting of the Security Council, Oct. 28, 1956, Security Council Official Records, 11th year, vol. 47; U.N. Doc. S/PV 1443, at 163-65 (Provisional Record); Pravda, Dec. 28, 1979; Security Council debate, Jan. 6, 1980, U.N. Doc. S/PV 2187.
3. *See, e.g.,* Security Council Official Records, 20th year, vol. 12, p. 228.
4. G.A. Res. 38/7 of Nov. 2, 1983.
5. *See* L. Doswald-Beck, *The Legal Validity of Military Intervention by Invitation of the Government,* 1985 BRIT. YB. INT'L L. 225 (1986).
6. *Id.* at 223.
7. 1968 I.L.M. 1285-86.
8. Pravda, Dec. 31, 1979.

9. S. Kondrashov, *From the Darkness of the Unknown*, 8 NOVY MIR 191 (1989).

10. D. Gai, *Afghanistan: What Happened,* VECHERNYAYA MOSKVA, Sept. 12-13, 1989.

11. *How We Went Into Afghanistan*, 38 LITERATURNAYA GAZETA 14 (1989).

12. 52 DEP'T ST. BULL. 144-48 (1965).

13. *See* Doswald-Beck, *supra* note 5, at 236.

14. *See* W.C. GILMORE, THE GRENADA INTERVENTION: ANALYSIS AND DOCUMENTATION 65-67 (1984).

15. *Id.* at 74.

16. *See* Doswald-Beck, *supra* note 5, at 214.

17. First Report of U.N.G.I.L. of July 3, 1958, U.N. Doc. S/4040; Second Report of U.N.G.I.L. of July 30, 1958, U.N. Doc. S/4069.

18. *See* Doswald-Beck, *supra* note 5, at 217.

19. *Id.* at 218.

20. *Id.* at 221.

21. 1986 I.C.J. 126.

22. Perkins, *The Right of Counterintervention*, 17 GA. J. INT'L & COMP. L. 195 (1987).

23. *See, e.g.,* O. Schachter, *International Law in Theory and Practice,* 178 RECUEIL DES COURS 160-66 (1982-V).

24. *See International Law and the United States Action in Grenada: A Report,* 18 INT'L LAW. 331 (1984), *quoted in* Perkins, *supra* note 22, at 183.

25. W. HALL, A TREATISE ON INTERNATIONAL LAW 346-47 (1924).

11

Commentary on Intervention by Invitation

Ruth Wedgwood

Do we need to amend the normative standards governing the international use of force in those situations where intervention has been invited by one party to a conflict?

In an international conflict, invitation may be seen as an *ad hoc* form of collective security. Aggression is less likely to succeed, or to be prosecuted vigorously, when the aggressor knows that its weaker neighbor is entitled to seek aid from countries that may refrain from permanent alliance, but offer assistance in particular disputes. In an international order that seeks to assure that force is not used by any entity in the pursuit of unjust ends, and that the resort to force will be minimized because of war's unpredictable destruction, several questions present themselves.

Immediate Referral to the Security Council

Individual intervention carries the danger that the conflict will spread. An adversary's invitation is likely to precipitate invitations from the opposing side, seeking to return the balance of military force to its initial weighting. The limits on the use of force in the U.N. Charter are not sufficient to prevent this; claims of self-defense are often made on both sides; permitting intervention to aid "self-defense" carries the danger of a conflict engulfing other nations and regions. As a safeguard against the expansion of armed conflict, one is bound to propose that before intervening, an invited power should report the matter to the Security Council of the United Nations and ask for collective assistance from the United Nations. Article 51 of the Charter permits the exercise of the inherent right of self-defense where the Security Council has not taken measures necessary to maintain peace. Security Council referral is not suggested as a mandatory prerequisite to intervention, but as a desirable first step. Mobilization of national forces often takes time; hence pressing first for Security Council action need not interfere with the effective defense of the threatened nation. Other countries are less likely to enter the fray on the opposing side when the United Nations has condemned the aggressor's action.

Independent Duty to Verify the External Threat or Attack

A country asked to intervene in a dispute should have the same burden as the requesting party to demonstrate that its use of armed force is defensive. It is not sufficient simply to receive an invitation; otherwise, an unscrupulous government could overawe its neighbors by fabricating a claim of unprovoked attack and inviting external assistance. Independent verification of the threat also provides a useful check on the partiality that may keep one country from recognizing the danger it seems to pose to its own neighbors.

Addressing the Merits of the Dispute

The notion of what constitutes the defensive use of force is not always an easy matter. The U.N. Charter forbids violating the territorial integrity or political independence of another country, and ordinarily forbids firing the first shot. Yet under one allowable reading of *Corfu Channel*,[1] a state actor does not have to refrain from the physical exercise of rights merely because it is anticipated that another country may resist by force. In *Corfu Channel* the United Kingdom was found to have a right to traverse that international waterway. But what of cases where, prospectively, one cannot be certain that the claim of right will be upheld? One country may believe it is merely engaging in the physical exercise of rights, while the other believes it is merely resisting physical invasion of its own rights. With this ambiguity, should an intervening power not have the burden of ascertaining that the initial exercise of rights was well-founded? One does not want to reward any aggressive use of force, to be sure, but it is not in all cases simple to tell what was the aggression. There is also the awkward fact that, despite the prohibitions of the U.N. Charter, willingness to reach accord on the merits of a dispute is sometimes influenced by the implicit threat of force. By joining one side, the intervening power may come to underwrite its ally's unwillingness to compromise on disputes where it may be partly wrong on the merits. The desirable goal of avoiding armed conflict may interfere with the desirable goal of assuring a just settlement of claims. As part of the justification for its intervention, does a major power have any obligation to attempt to refer the merits of the underlying dispute to some form of peaceful settlement?

Maintaining the Balance of Power

The U.N. Charter does not speak articulately about the problem of balance of power, because of the immediate post-war optimism that collective security could meet any threats to the peace. But in less halcyon days, when the Charter's optimism was stymied by ideological and bloc competition, the classical problem of balance of power reasserted itself, regionally and strategically. The effect of intervention on regional and strategic balances must be seen as part of the responsibility of an invited intervenor. If intervention could significantly destabilize a region, an intervenor has a moral if not legal responsibility to structure assistance so that it has the least effect possible on the balance of power. This may be accomplished by asking for assistance from less dominant parties, by using a collective form of decisionmaking, by limiting the introduction of particular weapons systems into regional conflicts, and by announcing and abiding by a limited set of war aims.

The Scope of Invitation

An intervenor may be asked to give assistance, and be willing to do so not only to repel aggression but also to advance independent aims in the region. This is not illegitimate, but the method of fighting a war may be different depending on long term goals. Some methods may involve greater risk to the population and infrastructure of the inviting power, or to its long-term political situation. Invitation should be regarded as a continuing check; it is not a simple assignment of a claim of self-defense. Though the intervening power will want to minimize casualties to its own forces, as a condition of its continued involvement, it is also obliged to respect the concerns of the host country in minimizing the destructive impact of the fighting on the host's population and on long-term political relations. The settlement of the conflict may serve as a test of this obligation. Where the host country is willing to end the fighting, could an invited intervenor properly continue the fighting? Is the intervenor not limited to the war aims of the inviting power, and if not, why not?

A number of equally serious problems arise in the case of non-international armed conflicts.

The Legitimacy of the Regime

The premise of America's eighteenth century revolution was that sovereignty resides in the people, and can be reassumed when government becomes grossly abusive and other remedies are unavailable. With this inheritance, the United States could hardly take the position that every existing government has a right to be protected against internal upheaval, much as we may prefer nonviolent methods of resistance. Where an existing regime asks for assistance against internal rebellion, it is difficult to escape the obligation to evaluate whether the regime is legitimate. This is not a simple question. It involves questions of political democracy, the availability of civil liberties, even economic fairness. It also requires, as any legist of the tradition of the law of nature and nations would teach, evaluating whether the rebel force promises a better or worse regime than those presently in power. Claiming to act in the name of the people does not guarantee that the actor will be a more faithful agent. The conservation of human life and preservation of public amity promised by evolutionary change, rather than violent revolution, also demands weight. The problem of outside intervention masquerading as indigenous rebellion is equally difficult. But, whether called self-determination or a Lockean right of revolution, it is hard to evade our inheritance that there is an ultimate right of revolution against unjust regimes. A democratic power asked to intervene is obliged to assay the character of the regime making the request.

Constitutional Competence

Ordinarily, in international agreements, one country is not responsible for monitoring the internal constitutional processes of the other. An agreement is binding so long as the agent acting on behalf of the state had apparent authority. But in the case of intervention within domestic armed conflicts, we may wish to impose a stronger obligation to evaluate the internal constitutional competence of the requesting organ. Otherwise, the effect of intervention may in fact be to displace constitutional processes, rather than to vindicate them.

Showing a Bona Fide Invitation

Even when made by a legitimate regime, an invitation to intervene raises concern about the conditions of the invitation. Voluntary consent surely requires that the intervening power ask for consent in advance, and that it be made clear force will not be interjected if consent is not given. A domestic government faced with the Hobson's choice of suffering intervention against its will, or of giving *pro forma* consent, may well have to take the second course to avoid the confession of impotence. Consent should be given openly, if at all possible. Secret "deniable" consent challenges the ability of the international legal community to monitor and sanction the use of force, and so should be disfavored. The argument that a request for intervention cannot be made openly because it would raise nationalist sentiment, may reflect real political problems, but raises serious questions concerning the legitimacy of a regime. Should an outside power be free to act upon the request of a government that is disfavored by a majority of its country's population?

Notes

1. 1949 I.C.J. 4.

12

Commentary on What International Law Demands and How States Respond

Benjamin Ferencz

All wars of aggression are fought in "self-defense." And all unlawful interventions are based on "lawful invitation." That's the society in which we live. It is a phony business, and that is a pretty sad commentary on the world.

We live in a state of "arrested adolescence." The truth is that states do not want to give up their power or to restrict their use of force. They want to retain the use of force despite what is written in the U.N. Charter and despite all of their protestations to the contrary. No one could read the minutes for the last ten years of the U.N. Special Committee on Enhancing the Effectiveness of the Principle of Non-Use of Force in International Relations, and be left with any doubts on this subject.[1] After ten years of debate by qualified international lawyers representing all nations, the Committee concluded that nations should not use force unless they are interested in "self-determination" or in fighting against "colonial or racist regimes" or "other forms of alien domination." Those words are found in the Special Committee's Declaration,[2] as well as a host of other declarations such as the Definition of Aggression[3] and the Convention against Terrorism.[4] All of these documents reflect the language of the Declaration on the Enhancement of the Effectiveness of the Principle of Refraining from the Threat or Use of Force: "Nothing in the present Declaration could in any way prejudice the right to self-determination, freedom and independence, as derived from the Charter, of peoples forcibly deprived of that right..., particularly peoples under colonial and racist regimes or other forms of alien domination,"—whatever that is—"...nor the right of these peoples to struggle to that end and to seek and receive support..." Then they add more malarkey about, "in conformity with the principles of the Charter," as the justification for saying that everything they want to do is legal. That is the result of ten years of effort!

I would like to suggest another system. Professor Abram Chayes has made reference to Justice Robert Jackson, a very able jurist, who was our representative in the creation of the International Military Tribunal established after World War II. Together with the other Allied Powers, Jackson drew up a charter which said that aggression is a crime against peace.[5] The Allies did not define aggression in detail at that point, but they declared it to be an international crime, for which people would be hanged.[6] They also said there is such a thing as crimes against humanity, where the offenses are so great as to shock the conscience of mankind. An international court was a pretty rational approach. No one seemed to object at the time; indeed we thought it was a very good idea. Jackson, and many of us who were involved, thought we were laying down rational principles for a future world order under law.

In the new order of relations among states, what is required is a clearer codification of what is permissible and what is not permissible. We also must have courts to determine whether these standards have been violated.

The Iraq-Kuwait crisis offers a good example. When Iraq first invaded Iran, did we make a fuss or demand that the Security Council invoke sanctions? When the Iraqis used poison gas against their Kurdish minority, or when they used poison gas against Iran, did we make a fuss? Even though aggression was a crime, the use of poison gas was a crime, and offenses against humanity were crimes, did we support an international court? Did we even suggest an international court? We did not! On the contrary, we *opposed* an international court. And we still do today. That kind of hypocrisy does not sit very well when, in international fora, one attempts to say, "Look, let's rearrange our international legal structure." So we suffer from the fact that we are not all really sincere.

What we are trying to do is to impose our own perception of what is right and what is wrong, and to use our own power in order to put it into play if necessary. That makes for a very dangerous world. It is also an unlawful world—and that is the challenge. People have consistently said that force is the last resort, and we must try all other methods first. Yet some are prepared to say that if there is a regime which is "terribly undemocratic" (that means we do not like it at all), then we are authorized to intervene to save the people. Who decides? If every nation can decide for itself when it can intervene with the use of force, either with an invitation or with a phony invitation (and they are all phony, whether the Russians do it or the Americans do it or anybody else does it), then we will pay for it in blood. We may pay for it in blood very soon unless we shape up and find a better way.

The challenge to the international legal community is to cut out the phony invitations and phony declarations by governments, and use common sense and reason.[7] A rational world of law and order requires restraint. It requires laws that are clear. It requires courts to determine if the laws have been violated. If we could create an unbiased Security Council to be the equivalent of courts, that would be fine, too. But we must have third-party determination in place of self-help, and we must have a system of effective enforcement. We also must have conditions in the world which make compliance with law tolerable. This means improved social justice to help eliminate the discontents and demands for self-determination and other rights which give rise to lawbreaking.

Until we begin to think globally, in planetary terms,[8] all of these debates (which are very entertaining and sometimes not so entertaining) will continue to be absolutely meaningless and will not alter the real world in which we live.

Notes

1. *See* U.N.G.A. Res. 32/150 (1977); 42 U.N. GAOR Supp. (No. 41), U.N. Doc. A/42/41 (1987).

2. *Draft Declaration on the Enhancement of the Effectiveness of the Principle of Refraining from the Threat or Use of Force*, 42 GAOR Supp. (No. 41) at 25, U.N. Doc. A/42/41 (1987).

3. *Report of the Special Committee on the Question of Defining Aggression*, 29 U.N. GAOR Supp. (No. 19), U.N. Doc. A/9619 (1974); *See also International Convention Against the Taking of Hostages (Art. 12)*, 34 U.N. GAOR Supp. (No. 39), U.N. Doc. A/34/39 (1979).

4. *Reprinted in* B. FERENCZ, AN INTERNATIONAL CRIMINAL COURT (1980).

5. Report of Robert H. Jackson, Dept. of State Publ. 308, Int. Org. and Conf. Series II (1949) at 43. *See also* 1 The Trial of German Major War Criminals. Proceedings of the IMT Sitting at Nuremberg, Germany (1946).

6. *See* B. FERENCZ, 2 DEFINING INTERNATIONAL AGGRESSION (1975).

7. *See* B. FERENCZ, A COMMON SENSE GUIDE TO WORLD PEACE (1985).

8. *See* B. FERENCZ, PLANETHOOD (1991).

INTERVENTION AGAINST ILLEGITIMATE REGIMES

13

The United Nations and Illegitimate Regimes: When to Intervene to Protect Human Rights

Igor I. Lukashuk

The problem of the legitimacy of political regimes has a long history. We shall not dwell on this history, nor shall we recall how the problem was formerly settled by the Pope or the Emperor. In recent times the idea of legitimacy was embodied in the Holy Alliance of 1815, which all the monarchs of continental Europe eventually joined. The members resolved to allow neither revolution nor even liberal reforms initiated by the government within a continental monarchy. They appropriated the right to intervene in the internal affairs of independent states in cases where they considered the established regime to be a threat to peace in Europe.

The establishment of revolutionary regimes in Spain, Portugal, Naples, and Sardinia provoked the intervention of the powers of the Holy Alliance. Even intervention in America was contemplated, which, as is well-known, was one of the reasons for the Monroe Doctrine. In the final analysis, the attempt to base legitimacy on the monarchy failed because it ran counter to progressive historical development.

The conflict with Soviet Russia was another major case of intervention by the Great Powers against a regime that they considered illegitimate. All available means, including full-scale military intervention, were used in the course of this conflict. The new regime was declared illegitimate.[1] In a letter dated August 5, 1918, to the American Consul, the RSFSR People's Commissar for Foreign Affairs wrote, "Neither laws nor justice are observed in relation to us....Bare-faced robbery of us is considered possible."[2]

The documents of the Allied Powers are of great interest for the problem under consideration. From them, it can be seen that war was being waged not only against the state that initiated the aggression, but also against the Nazi regime, whose existence was incompatible with the aim of securing peace. Thus the Report of the Crimea Conference (Yalta) read: "It is our inflexible purpose to destroy German militarism and Nazism and to ensure that Germany will never again be able to disturb the peace of the world."[3] The goal was to wipe the Nazi party and Nazi laws, organizations, and institutions from the face of the earth. The Potsdam Declaration included as one of the aims of occupying Germany to prepare "for the eventual reconstruction of German political life on a democratic basis."[4]

Intervention by the Allied Powers extended to liberated states as well as former German allies. The Declaration on Liberated Europe (Yalta) stated:

> [T]he three governments will jointly assist the people in any European liberated state or former Axis satellite state in Europe where in their judgment conditions require (a) to establish conditions of internal peace; (b) to carry out emergency measures for the relief of distressed peoples; (c) to form interim governmental authorities broadly representative of all democratic elements in the population and pledged to the earliest possible establishment through free elections of governments responsive to the will of the people; and (d) to facilitate where necessary the holding of such elections.[5]

We note that this provision contains what is perhaps the most important criterion for the legitimacy of a political regime: a freely-elected government responsive to the will of the people. An international criterion for the legitimacy of a regime also runs through the Allied documents: a policy that poses a threat to world peace should not be inherent to the regime.

It is clear from the foregoing that the Allies quite actively resorted to intervention in the interests of peace, democracy, and building a world order on legal principles devoted to peace, security, freedom, and the general well-being of mankind.[6] To a significant extent, this was no doubt due to the special circumstances of a world war. The fact that the corresponding measures were taken by decision of the Allies, rather than of a single state, also played a sizable part. Nevertheless, all this was exceptionally important for elaborating the criteria for legal intervention.

Another important aspect of legitimating intervention deserves attention. This is moral legitimation on an international, rather than a national, scale. The intervention of the Allies was supported by world public opinion. This factor has acquired particular significance today in connection with the increased significance of world public opinion for foreign policy. For example, it is well-known that the American invasion of Panama was supported by the American public but met with a negative reaction in other countries. When the danger of civil war arose in Romania, not only public opinion, but also a number of governments, reacted positively to the possibility of humanitarian intervention. When France offered to send troops if the Romanian Army had difficulty overcoming the security forces loyal to the old regime, U.S. Secretary of State James Baker III declared that the United States would support a move by the Soviet Union to intervene militarily. After pointing this out, the American journalist Stan Sesser referred to another case where humanitarian intervention would have met with understanding. He posed the question as follows: "Would it have been morally wrong for France, or the United States, or the Soviet Union, to intervene in Pol Pot's Cambodia and thereby to have saved at least one million Cambodian lives?"[7] To this legitimate question, I would add that such intervention would have been morally justified had it been based on a collective decision. There is yet another fundamental aspect. Only the significant increase in mutual trust between the USSR and the United States has made it possible for the United States to look favorably on potential humanitarian intervention by the USSR. This element is of prime importance in understanding the possibilities for humanitarian intervention. Moral and political factors play a particularly important role here.

Let us return to the period of the Second World War. The following statement from the Potsdam Declaration, relating to former German allies in Europe, has particular significance for the question at hand. "The conclusion of peace treaties with recognized democratic governments in these States will also enable the three governments to support applications from them for membership of the United Nations."[8] This introduces additional criteria for legitimacy, besides that of a democratic government. They are, namely, international recognition and the legal settlement of issues arising from responsibility for their part in the aggression. In the given case, recognition followed from the constitutive theory of recognition.

Finally, the position which the participants in the Berlin Conference (Potsdam) took with respect to the Spanish government is worthy of attention. They explained that they would not support the application for

U.N. membership made by the Franco government which, "having been founded with the support of the Axis powers, does not, in view of its origins, its nature, its close association with the aggressor States, possess the qualifications necessary to justify such membership."[9] In this case, we encounter such criteria for the legitimacy of a regime as its origin, nature, actions, and association with the aggressors.

The foregoing facts indicate that on the eve of the founding of the United Nations, a new concept of the legitimacy of existing state regimes was beginning to form, to wit, their conformity with the U.N. members' requirements. Subsequent U.N. practice contributed to the concretization and development of this concept. This concerned first of all those regimes which had already been called into question during the war years.

The problem of the Franco regime in Spain was repeatedly discussed. To illustrate the positions taken by governments on this problem, we may cite the record of the Security Council meeting of June 13, 1946. At the meeting the proposals of the Subcommittee on the Spanish Question were discussed. The Subcommittee recommended that the Security Council submit to the General Assembly the evidence and reports of the Subcommittee

> together with the recommendation that, unless the Franco regime is withdrawn and the other conditions of political freedom set out in the declaration are, in the opinion of the General Assembly, fully satisfied, a resolution be passed by the General Assembly recommending that diplomatic relations with the Franco regime be terminated forthwith by each Member of the United Nations or alternatively such other action be taken as the General Assembly deems appropriate and effective under the circumstances prevailing at the time.[10]

The American, Egyptian, and Dutch representatives stated that they supported the proposed resolution with the reservation that they retained the right to adopt a different position in the General Assembly. The Soviet representative Andrei Gromyko expressed the opinion that the Franco regime constituted an international problem. To prove his point, he cited the establishment of the regime by foreign interference and its association with Hitler's Germany. The international aspects of the regime were thus cited as grounds. This position may be explained by the USSR's general position on the principle of non-intervention, which was understood as absolutely prohibiting intervention for domestic reasons. Moreover, the U.N. Charter provides for the possibility of taking measures against a state only in the case of a threat to the peace or breach of the peace (Article 39). Nevertheless, Gromyko could not completely ignore the domestic aspects, as his following statement shows: "The situation in Spain is such that it not only demands moral condemnation of the Franco regime but also calls for practical action in conformity with the U.N. Charter." In conclusion, the Soviet representative, referring to Articles 39 and 41 of the Charter, stated: "The Security Council, as the organ appointed to safeguard the maintenance of peace and security, ought not to shirk taking a decision on practical and speedy measures in respect of the Franco regime."[11]

These facts show that from the very beginning, the United Nations has accepted, in the main, the concept of an illegitimate regime reflected in the acts of the Allies and also the possibility of intervention against such a regime in certain circumstances. Since the U.N. Charter provided for the use of force only in the case of a threat to the peace or a breach of the peace, this provision came to be broadly interpreted. The gist of this interpretation is roughly that the existence of a regime whose origin, nature, and policies are incompatible with the main purposes and principles of the United Nations may be characterized as a threat to the peace.

There is little doubt that in 1946 the Franco regime did not represent a real threat to the peace. This was verified by the Subcommittee on the Spanish Question, whose proposals stated that the situation in Spain did not at the time constitute a threat to the peace and that therefore it did not fall within Article 39 of the Charter. To circumvent this, the Subcommittee proposed characterizing the situation in Spain as a potential threat to the peace, thereby enabling states to take measures to influence it by way of a General Assembly recommendation, rather than a Security Council decision.

These proposals were subsequently approved and developed by U.N. actions. U.N. measures with respect to the Republic of South Africa and Southern Rhodesia are of particular interest in this regard. Both cases bear witness to a new trend in the development of the concept of an illegitimate regime which henceforth included colonialism in all its forms. The 1960 Declaration on the Granting of Independence to Colonial Countries and Peoples,[12] adopted by the United Nations on the initiative of the USSR, served as the moral and political normative basis for the development of this new trend. Discussion of the issues of the Republic of South Africa and Southern Rhodesia, and the adoption of the corresponding General Assembly and Security Council resolutions,[13] were based on the Declaration. The main provisions of the Declaration were reaffirmed in other U.N. declarations, were widely recognized, and may now be considered norms of general international law.

International acts show that a colonial regime constitutes a mass violation of the rights of the individual, as well as peoples and nations, and a threat to the peace. In other words, its illegitimacy is based not only on the phenomenon of colonialism itself, but also on the other criteria for an illegitimate regime previously established. While all this is of course interrelated, the colonial regime is nevertheless a particular type of illegitimate regime.

Its relation to human rights violations deserves particular attention. Neither doctrine nor state practice provides broad support for the legality of humanitarian intervention in response to individual instances of human rights violations. The following provision of the U.N. Declaration on Non-intervention deals with this subject:

> No State may use or encourage the use of economic, political, or any other type of measures to coerce another State in order to obtain from it the subordination of the exercise of its sovereign rights or to secure from it advantages of any kind. Also, no State shall organize, assist, foment, finance, incite, or tolerate subversive, terrorist, or armed activities directed to the violent overthrow of the regime of another State, or interfere in civil strife in another State.[14]

The quoted provision categorically prohibits humanitarian intervention by a state or group of states in order to protect human rights. At the same time, this provision may be interpreted differently—as prohibiting only abuse of this type of intervention, in other words, those cases where it is used "as a means of interference in the internal affairs of States, of exerting pressure on other States or creating distrust and disorder within and among States or groups of States."[15]

It appears that the spirit of the Declaration strictly prohibits this sort of intervention. This is also confirmed by the provision of the Declaration which includes in the principle of non-intervention

> the right of self-determination and independence of peoples and nations, to be freely exercised without any foreign pressure, and with the absolute respect for human rights and fundamental freedoms. Consequently, all states shall contribute to the complete elimination of racial discrimination and colonialism in all its forms and manifestations.[16]

This provision may be treated as one which refers the protection of human rights on the territory of a state to the internal competence of that state. Mass and gross violations of the rights of nations and peoples are a separate category. The foregoing relates not only to states, but also to the United Nations which in my opinion should not interfere in a state's affairs in individual cases of human rights violations.

Human rights are connected with other elements of social and political systems. According to the principle of sovereign equality, every state and every people may freely choose its economic, political, and other system, but it must be organized in such a way as not to go against the principles of the U.N. Charter. As President Bush noted concerning Iraq, there had been a history of outrageous disregard for basic human rights, including execution on political and religious grounds and use of poison gas against Kurdish villages. Totalitarian, antidemocratic regimes threaten our common peace. Thus in a very recent treaty between the Soviet Union and Germany (1990), the parties pledge that they will "secure priority of universally recognized rules" not only in their foreign policy, but in their internal politics as well. It is a very interesting legal development.

Turning to U.N. practice, we shall see that cases where violations of the rights of individuals or groups were condemned are quite numerous. Thus on March 14, 1968, the Security Council unanimously adopted a resolution requiring the Republic of South Africa to immediately release all South West African patriots sentenced by a court and to return them to their native land. It further called on U.N. member states to assist in carrying out the decision.[17]

Other U.N. bodies also adopted resolutions on the protection of individuals. Thus in March 1968 the Special Committee on the Implementation of the Declaration on the Granting of Independence to Colonial Countries and Peoples adopted a resolution which expressed its deep concern for the situation in Southern Rhodesia concerning the punishment of three convicted African freedom fighters. The Committee called on the United Kingdom to take urgent and effective measures to prevent repetition of such crimes.[18]

The cases cited undoubtedly concern the international protection of individual human rights. However, it is clear from the circumstances that they were perceived as the most outrageous concrete manifestations of an illegitimate regime, rather than as discrete cases.

On the whole, humanitarian intervention as a means of combatting illegitimate colonial regimes in no small way changes the meaning of the principle of non-intervention,[19] but the principle's importance is increased and not diminished. Not coincidentally the same Declaration on the Granting of Independence to Colonial Countries and Peoples indicates that it must be implemented on the basis of the principle of non-intervention. This point is extremely important. As the practice and international acts of the U.N. show, very powerful means, including force, are considered acceptable in the fight against colonial regimes.

The case of Southern Rhodesia shows how this can give rise to complex new legal problems.[20] In the early 1960s the white minority in Southern Rhodesia, which constituted less than five percent of the population, seized power in that British colony. The world community actively opposed this action.[21] Nothing of the sort occurred when the apartheid regime was established in South Africa. I refer to this only to emphasize how much the world community's position with respect to illegitimate regimes has changed.

In November 1965 the British Prime Minister declared in Parliament that the establishment of the illegal Smith regime in Southern Rhodesia was an act of rebellion and that the British government would refrain from "dealings of any kind with the rebel government."[22]

The Soviet government's statement maintained that the purpose of proclaiming "independence" in Southern Rhodesia was to perpetuate the colonial order in the country and that this created a threat to the peace. The government "decisively condemns the new crime against the African peoples and declares that it does not recognize the racist regime that has usurped power in Southern Rhodesia. The Soviet Union fully supports the decisions of the U.N. Security Council and General Assembly concerning the situation in Southern Rhodesia and will strictly abide by them."[23] It further stated that the USSR would cooperate with the African countries in rendering all possible support to the people of Zimbabwe "in their just and legal fight for freedom and true national independence."[24]

It is very important that not one state recognized the Smith government.[25] The African states took the most extreme position. At an extraordinary session of the Organization of African Unity (O.A.U.) in December 1965, the Council of Ministers adopted a resolution requiring all members to break off diplomatic relations with the United Kingdom if it did not bring about the downfall of the racist regime. It was decided that the African states would impose a complete economic embargo on Southern Rhodesia and would sever all ties with it.[26]

After Southern Rhodesia had been proclaimed a sovereign republic, the O.A.U. Council of Ministers passed a resolution which called upon African states to appeal to the Security Council to require that the United Kingdom use force to free the people of Zimbabwe from the illegal power of the white minority. Should the United Kingdom refuse, the Security Council was to take the measures specified in Article 42 of the U.N. Charter. Any recognition of the illegal regime would be considered an act hostile to Africa as a whole. Independent Africa resolved to provide immediate assistance to the people of Zimbabwe in their fight for the restoration of their legal rights.[27]

What is particularly significant in the case of Southern Rhodesia is that the United Nations throughout played the main role in bringing the illegal regime to an end. This proves that the Organization had sufficient moral and political authority, legal foundation, and practical resources to fight illegitimate regimes. This should not, however, lead to a simplification of the problem. This victory cost the United Nations greatly: much time and effort was spent and the resolutions adopted in this case are so numerous as to be difficult to count.

These acts characterized the events in Southern Rhodesia as a rebellion and a usurpation of power and the racist regime as illegal. In the beginning, the General Assembly invited and called upon the United Kingdom to take the measures necessary to quell the rebellion and bring an end to the illegal regime.[28] When these appeals failed, it condemned the government of the United Kingdom for its unwillingness to overthrow the illegal regime.[29] The Security Council adopted several decisions on sanctions and saw to it that they were carried out by U.N. member states. Resolution 253 of the Security Council established a committee to control the implementation of sanctions.

The aforementioned resolutions and decisions posed anew a number of legal problems, including the problem of the correlation of international and municipal law. Thus the General Assembly, in its resolution on "The Question of Southern Rhodesia" adopted at its sixteenth session, considered the constitution of Southern Rhodesia as non-existent in so far as it was rejected by the "vast majority of the population." The General Assembly on this basis requested the Administering Authority to undertake to convene a constitutional conference for the purpose of formulating a new constitution for the country. It further indicated not only the procedure for representation at the conference, but also the basic principles of the future constitution. The rights of the majority of the population were to be guaranteed in conformity with the principles of the U.N. Charter and the Declaration on the Granting of Independence to Colonial Countries and Peoples. All restraints and restrictions on the exercise of freedom of political activity, including all laws, ordinances, and rules which sanctioned practices based on racial discrimination, were to be removed.[30]

The General Assembly resolution of November 17, 1971, on the "Question of Southern Rhodesia" is important for an understanding of the new tendencies in the issue of the correlation of acts of municipal law and resolutions of international bodies. Having cited the decision of the U.S. Congress permitting the importation of chrome from Southern Rhodesia, the General Assembly called upon the U.S. government, "in compliance with the relevant provisions of Security Council resolutions 253 (1968), 277 (1970), and 288 (1970) and bearing in mind its obligations under Article 25 of the Charter of the United Nations, to prevent the importation of chrome...."[31] In this way, the case of Southern Rhodesia shows the considerable development of U.N. humanitarian intervention in cases where the regime's illegitimacy derives from its colonial racist nature.

The case of South Africa proves that the Rhodesian question was not an exception. The role of the United Nations in forming the state of Namibia and determining its constitutional basis is of special interest. The success of the United Nations in such cases lays the groundwork for increasing the possibilities for humanitarian intervention by the United Nations against other illegitimate regimes. The decisive role, particularly at first, will be played not so much by legal factors as by moral and political factors, and by the extent to which states and public opinion support the United Nations. This is typical of the formation of complex new international legal institutions.

The problem of intervention against illegitimate regimes is fundamentally associated with the institution of international recognition.[32] For centuries, states, particularly major states, adhered to the constitutive theory of recognition, either officially or actually. According to this theory, a newly formed state becomes a subject of international law only as a result of its recognition by other states. A government that has come to power unconstitutionally is able to represent the state after being recognized. The constitutive theory enabled the Great Powers to pressure newly-formed states. One need only think of the practice of the Holy Alliance. Almost all the Great Powers succumbed to the temptation to use the institution of recognition to pressure other countries.[33] The struggle to democratize international relations was therefore linked to the establishment of an alternative theory, namely the declaratory theory. According to the declaratory theory, recognition is declaratory only and establishes the fact that a new state has been formed or a new government has come to power.[34]

The Soviet government, which had itself experienced the negative consequences of mass nonrecognition, took part in the fight against the constitutive theory. Supporting on the whole the declarative theory, the Soviet government proceeded from the view that recognition does not resolve the issue of the legitimacy of the new regime, and does not signify recognition and approval of its social and political nature.[35] One point of view saw non-recognition as a hostile act.[36] Nevertheless, both before and after World War II there were cases in Soviet practice of non-recognition on the ground that the regime was illegitimate. Examples include the non-recognition of the regimes of Franco and South Korea.[37]

After the adoption of the U.N. Charter, it became evident that the constitutive theory was incompatible with the basic principles of international law, above all principles such as sovereign equality, non-intervention, and self-determination. The point was often made, in state practice as well as doctrine, that the only basis for recognizing a regime is effective control of territory.[38]

The declaratory theory has found concrete expression in international law. In our view it was not coincidental that it was embodied in the Charter of the Organization of American States (O.A.S.), as the problem of recognition has always been extremely critical for those states. Article 9 of the Charter states: "The political existence of the State is independent of recognition by other States."[39]

Some authors have gone even further, believing that the principle of cooperation creates a legal duty to recognize newly formed governments and states.[40] Less radical authors regard such a duty as extending only to states that are U.N. members.[41]

It would seem that the issue of recognition as a means of determining the legitimacy of a regime has finally been settled in the negative sense. However both the practical and the theoretical issues proved more complex. Despite the international legal norms, the Great Powers did not renounce interventionist doctrines regarding the legitimacy of regimes. Among the Warsaw Pact countries, the approach which came to be known in the West as the "Brezhnev doctrine" met with a certain recognition. In essence, this was a doctrine of "socialist legitimism." It provided that only socialist regimes could be legitimate in Eastern Europe. Only the restructuring (*perestroika*) of Soviet foreign policy on the basis of the new political thinking put an end to the "Brezhnev doctrine".

We note that this doctrine was not unique in global politics. The North Atlantic Treaty Organization (NATO), whose aim was to prevent the establishment of communist regimes in Western Europe, was founded on an analogous basis, albeit one with a different social and political content. We also note that the question of providing assistance to the *perestroika* regime, associated with Soviet President Mikhail Gorbachev, is currently being discussed within the NATO framework. The U.S. administration has the greatest difficulty in giving up the "right" to determine the legality of regimes in other countries. Both the "Reagan doctrine," to which allusion has already been made, and the policies concerning Nicaragua and Panama prove this point. It is rare that the International Court of Justice condemns a Great Power for intervention in the internal affairs of another country.

It is submitted that the above-noted aspects of the Great Powers' policy were, to a significant extent, brought about by the special conditions of the Cold War. With the end of the Cold War they can no longer be endured. However, this in no way means that the problem of the legality of regimes has been taken off the agenda. Moreover, to the extent that the interdependence of states has intensified, it has assumed additional importance. In our view, the main point is that a state whose regime conflicts with the fundamental goals and principles of the world community and with its standards cannot realistically be a member of that community. This problem must therefore be resolved, but not as it was in the past.

The institution of recognition of new regimes by states will, to a certain extent, continue to be important. Experience shows that this institution, even when based on the declarative theory, may serve as a fairly powerful instrument. We do not have in mind those very widespread cases where an illegal regime practically stands outside international law.[42] Even within the framework of international law, appreciable pressure may be brought to bear on a new regime. While the latter may have the full range of rights in the international sphere, the possibility to make use of them will be limited to the utmost. In practice, rights can only be enjoyed with the cooperation of other states. Even breaking off diplomatic relations impairs considerably the functioning of the legal mechanism.[43] It should be noted that recognition is fundamentally a political institution, not a legal one. The question of recognition of a regime is within the discretion of each state. It would therefore be advisable to reach a certain level of legal regulation of this institution. The opinion has been expressed in doctrinal work that this goal can be met under current conditions.[44] This is even more important as the constitutive theory has not yet disappeared either from theory or practice.[45]

Even though the legal significance of recognition by individual states is not growing, the same cannot be said of collective recognition by regional and universal international organizations. The role of the United Nations and regional organizations in the recognition of the legitimacy or illegitimacy of regimes already has been discussed. As regards the O.A.S., it is sufficient to refer to that body's expulsion of Cuba. The Arab League and the O.A.U. also use collective recognition very actively. The United Nations takes into consideration the results of recognition by these organisations.

Guided by the practice of the African states, the Ugandan professor A. Mazrui sets out the concept of the recognition of states and the legitimacy of their regimes in the following form. He writes that diplomatic recognition rests on the principle of continental jurisdiction. The regime of an African country may lay claim to full recognition as a member of the African community only if it meets certain requirements. In the process, the author stipulates that the requirements need not all be satisfied at the same time. He numbers among the requirements a) *de facto* control over the relevant territory; b) racial representativeness; c) legitimate assumption of power; and d) legitimacy in the sense of conformity to the relevant constitutional principles.[46]

The world community is becoming an increasingly important and unified social and political system. No state is in a position to exist outside this system and every state must therefore be a member. One of the community's chief sanctions is to limit relations with a state that has broken the law. Complete exclusion from the community is hardly possible. States have an interest in the normal functioning of the community and the community in the well-being of its members. This poses afresh the problem of the correlation between national and international interests as well as of the mechanisms for their protection. The course of history itself requires recognition of the primacy of common human interests. In this regard, the appearance of a complex of fundamental international legal principles which reflect the interests of the entire world community and which can be changed only by the community as a whole is extremely typical. They are endowed with higher moral, political, and legal force for all states. Community control over states' activities, above all in the person of the United Nations, is expanding. This includes control over their internal activities to the extent that the latter concern the interests of other countries and the community as a whole.

This sort of development substantially strengthens the basis of international law and international organizations and necessitates broadening their competence. This requirement can only be met on a democratic basis. It is necessary to guarantee, on the one hand, the active participation of every country in solving general international problems and, on the other hand, the proper control by the community over its members.

The world community will be characterized by the co-existence of a wide variety of national systems and regimes, but at the same time the interaction between them will intensify, their unity will be strengthened, and many parameters will be unified. In the long run, the gradual rapprochement of national systems will lead to convergence. The fate of the human race depends in no small measure on the normal development of these processes. International law is called upon to play a considerable role in all this. We must therefore be guided by these tendencies in determining ways to improve international law.

The United Nations, in its capacity as the center of the system of regional and specialized international organisations, will play a greater role in the functioning of international law. Naturally, new conditions will necessitate some changes in the United Nations. In our view, the "socio-representative" nature of the United Nations must be enhanced. At present it represents governments. The creation of a parliamentary assembly within the U.N. system would greatly increase its representativeness. This assembly would be formed by states' parliaments which would take into account their population and a number of other factors. Acts adopted by such a body would have to be morally and politically binding and to be considered by all U.N. bodies and member states.

As has already been noted, moral and political factors and world public opinion play an exceptionally important role in the politically significant changes in international law as well as in its implementing acts. This also relates to the institutions under consideration. The creation of a parliamentary assembly would thus be of paramount importance for developing the principle of non-intervention and ensuring lawful humanitarian intervention under new conditions.

Notes

1. The mass media mentioned this fact time and again.
2. DOKUMENTY VNESHNEI POLITIKI SSSR (Foreign Policy Documents of the USSR) 418 (1957).

3. VNESHNIAIA POLITIKA SOVETSKOGO SOIUZA V PERIOD OTECHESTVENNOI VOINY (Foreign Policy of the Soviet Union in the Period of the Patriotic War) 103 (1957). An English version of the Report on the Crimea Conference (Feb. 11, 1945) is found in THE YALTA AGREEMENTS (Z.C. Szkopiak ed. 1986).

4. *Id.* at 341.

5. *Id.* at 105. An English version of the Protocol of the Proceedings of the Crimea Conference (Feb. 11, 1945) is found in THE YALTA AGREEMENTS, *supra* note 3.

6. *See* Declaration on Liberated Europe, *id.* at 106.

7. Sesser, *Are Invasions Sometimes O.K.?*, N.Y. Times, Jan. 17, 1990, at A25, col.1.

8. *See* Part X of the Potsdam Declaration (Aug. 2, 1945), *supra* note 3.

9. *Id.* at 353.

10. Izvestiia, June 15, 1946. This quotation is the recommendation of the Sub-Committee as modified by the Security Council. 2 U.N. SCOR (45th mtg.) at 326 (1946).

11. *Id.*

12. G.A. Res. 1514 (XV) (1960), 1 RESOLUTSII, PRINIATYE GENERAL'NOI ASSAMBLEEI NA PIATNADTSATOI SESSII (Resolutions adopted by the General Assembly at the Fifteenth Session) 74-75 (1961).

13. *See, e.g.*, *Question of Southern Rhodesia*, G.A. Res. 2765/XXVI, U.N. Doc. A/Res/2765/XXVI (1971).

14. G.A. RES. 2131/XX (Dec. 21, 1965); *See* OSMANCZYK, ENCYCLOPEDIA OF UNITED NATIONS AND INTERNATIONAL RELATIONS 631-32 (1990).

15. *Declaration on the Inadmissibility of Intervention and Interference in the Internal Affairs of States*, G.A. RES 36/103 (Dec. 9, 1981).

16. G.A. RES. 2131/XX (1965), *supra* note 14.

17. Pravda, Mar. 16, 1968.

18. The Soviet government's position on this issue was expressed in the TASS statement: "The Soviet Union condemns absolutely the Rhodesian regime's policy of bloody terror. The Soviet Union proceeded and continues to proceed from the position that all states must take effective measures to stop the racist terror in Southern Rhodesia and to protect African lives. It is the duty of the UN to take immediate steps in this regard." Pravda, Mar. 9, 1968.

19. *See* Starushenko, *Printsip ravnopraviia i prava narodov rasporiazhat'sia svoei sud'boi*, in 2 KURS MEZHDUNARODNOGO PRAVA (Course on International Law) (1989); McDougal & Reisman, *Rhodesia and the United Nations: The Lawfulness of International Concern*, 62 AM. J. INT'L L. 1 (1968).

20. *See* Fawcett, *Security Council Resolutions on Rhodesia*, 41 BRIT. Y.B. INT'L L. 103 (1965-1966); Cervenka, *Legal Effects of Non-recogntion of Southern Rhodesia's Unilateral Declaration of Independence in International Law*, 1967 CASOPIS PRO MEZINARODNI PRAVO, No. 2.

21. *See* E. WINDRICH, THE RHODESIAN PROBLEM: A DOCUMENTARY RECORD 1923-1973 (1975).

22. Pravda, Dec. 7, 1968.

23. Statement of the Soviet government in connection with the situation in Southern Rhodesia, Pravda, Nov. 16, 1965.

24. TASS statement, Izvestiia, Oct. 26, 1965.

25. On the problem of recognition with regard to South Rhodesia, see H. Blix, *Contemporary Aspects of Recognition*, 1970 REC. DES COURS vol. II, at 672.

26. Izvestiia, Dec. 5, 1965.

27. Pravda, Mar. 5, 1970.

28. *See, e.g., Concerning Rhodesia*, G.A. Res. 2024 (XX) (1965).

29. *See, e.g., Resolution on the Elimination of All Forms of Discrimination*, G.A. Res. 2646 (XXV) (1970).

30. *The Question of Southern Rhodesia*, G.A. Res. 1747 (XVI) (1962).

31. G.A. Res. 2765 (XXVI) (1971).

32. *See* D.I. FELDMAN, PRIZNANIE GOSUDARSTV V SOVREMENNOM MEZHDUNARODNOM PRAVE (The Recognition of States in Modern International Law) (1965); P.L. BOBROV, SHAG, PRODIKTOVANNYI ISTORIEI (A Step Dictated by History) (1974); K. MISRA, INDIA'S POLICY OF RECOGNITION OF STATES AND GOVERNMENTS (1966); Antonowicz, *On the Nature of Recognition of States in International Law,* 8 POLISH Y.B. INT'L L. (1976).

33. A 1927 Memorandum of the U.S. State Department stated: "We do control the destinies of Central America and we do so for the simple reason that the national interest absolutely dictates such a course...Until now Central America has always understood that governments which we recognize and support stay in power, while those we do not recognize and support fall." *Quoted by* R. ARMSTRONG & J. SHENK, EL SALVADOR 225-226 (1982). *See also* T. GALLOWAY, RECOGNIZING FOREIGN GOVERNMENTS: THE PRACTICE OF THE UNITED STATES (1978).

34. *See* G. Mencer, *Zasada nevmesovani a instituce uznani*, 2 CASOPIS PRO MEZINARODNI PRAVO (1968).

35. Thus a Note of the Soviet ambassador to China to the Japanese envoy stated that "if the USSR recognizes the government of Japan and Japan recognizes the government of the USSR, then it will not be interpreted in the sense that the Soviet government has recognized the bourgeois capitalist regime of Japan, just as it will not mean the recognition of the socialist regime by Japan..." Izvestiia, Aug. 28, 1924.

36. *See* M. LITVINOV, VNESHNIAIA POLITIKA SSSR (Foreign Policy of the USSR) 224 (1937).

37. During the debates at the U.N. General Assembly session in February 1949, the U.S. representative stated that the Assembly had approved the elections in South Korea which were the basis for the establishment of the government. It was thus as if its legitimacy had been recognized. The Soviet representative responded that such approval was insufficient as it was the result of the Anglo-American bloc vote. It was necessary that the elections be approved by the people of Korea and reflect their will. Pravda, Feb. 17, 1949.

This case is of interest in understanding the U.N.'s evolving role in the determination of a regime's legitimacy. When the United States and its allies controlled the majority of votes in the United Nations, they were prepared to recognize the corresponding right of the Organization, while the USSR was not prepared to do so. The Soviet Union viewed recognition by the people as the decisive criterion and reduced the importance of recognition by the United Nations to a minimum. With the changes in the United Nations, the positions of states on the U.N.'s role in this question are also changing.

38. Thus in 1949 the British representative stated in the United Nations: "If the government effectively controls the entire country or the greater part of it, then this is sufficient grounds for recognition. The English government does not consider recognition to be approval of the recognized government." Pravda, Dec. 5, 1949.

"...According to a binding norm of international law, an effective state and government are thus the same as the legitimate state and government." J. SYMONIDES, ZASADA EFFECTYWNOSTI W PRAWIE MIEDZYNARODOWYM 169 (1967).

39. OAS CHARTER, in BASIC DOCUMENTS, SUPPLEMENT TO INTERNATIONAL LAW, CASES AND MATERIALS 143 (1987).

40. *See* P.L. BOBROV, OSNOVNYE PROBLEMY TEORII MEZHDUNARODNOGO PRAVA (Fundamental Problems of the Theory of International Law) 258 (1968); I.P. BLISHCHENKO, PRETSEDENTY V MEZHDUNARODNOM PRAVE (Precedents in International Law) 57 (1977).

41. *See* J. DUGARD, RECOGNITION AND THE UNITED NATIONS 80 (1987).

42. This feature has long been taken into account in diplomatic practice. Thus a February 2, 1929, letter from the USSR Deputy People's Commissar for Foreign Affairs to the plenipotentiary representative of the Soviet government in Germany stated: "One of the basic features of our policy concerning Yemen is that we will assist Yemen by broadening international legal recognition of the independent state of Yemen. At present Yemen as well as Hejas are seriously inconvenienced by fact that the circle of states that recognize them is extraordinarily limited. As a result, their direct antagonists violate all norms of international law completely uncontrollably and without fear of publicity." 12 DOKUMENTY VNESHNEY POLITIKI SSSR (Foreign Policy Documents of the USSR) 61 (1967).

43. We draw attention to the opinion of the International Court of Justice on this issue. Regarding the Treaty of Amity, Economic Relations and Consular Rights between the United States of America and Iran, the Court noted that "[t]he machinery for the effective operation of the 1955 Treaty has, no doubt, now been impaired by reason of diplomatic relations between the two countries having been broken off by the United States" although "its provisions remain part of the corpus of law applicable between the United States and Iran." *United States Diplomatic and Consular Staff in Tehran (United States of America v. Iran),* 1980 I.C.J. 3, at 29 (Judgment).

44. *See* Bundy, *Recognition of Revolutionary Authorities,* 27 INT'L & COMP. L. Q. 45 (1978).

45. *See* Devine, *Recognition, Newly Independent States and General International Law*, 10 S. AFR. Y.B. INT'L L. 26 (1984).

46. A. A. MAZRUI, TOWARDS A PAX AFRICANA 122 (1967).

14

Intervention Against Illegitimate Regimes[1]

Thomas M. Franck

The Cold War is over, but Americans seem puzzled over the implications of this development. We wonder whether we can have a foreign policy without enemies.[2] We exult in smug satisfaction at "the end of history."[3] We write learned dissertations on "Why We Will Miss the Cold War"[4] that exude premonitions of nostalgia about the good old days when lesser nationalisms were kept in line by the confrontational superpowers and fears of a nuclear holocaust. What we seem not to be doing is seizing the moment to rethink the basic structures and processes of the international system.

For this, future generations may not readily forgive us. The late Judge Richard Baxter of the International Court of Justice collected phrase books. One of these, an English phrase book for Japanese executives published in Tokyo, illustrated the use of the phrase "missed the boat" in the sentence: "Japan certainly missed the boat when it failed to attack Russia in 1919." A more felicitous usage might be: "The world will certainly miss the boat if it does not use the end of the Cold War to create a global system for the new millennium, one which preserves the peace, fosters economic growth, and prevents the deterioration of the human physical, socio-cultural, and environmental condition."

The Moment for Seizing

Professor George L. Sherry, the former U.N. Assistant General for Special Political Affairs (peacekeeping), recently has written that the U.N. system "is being rapidly transformed by the radical shifts affecting the Soviet Union, Eastern Europe, and the Soviet-American relationship. Multilateralism, which only three years ago seemed obsolescent, is rapidly acquiring new and important functions in maintaining security in the transformed world order towards which we are heading."[5] This is true, but while the system is busier than it used to be, it is not necessarily also getting better in the sense of using these unusually good times to prepare to withstand the strains and disequilibrium of future adversity.

History affords few moments so ripe as the present ones with opportunity for institutional and philosophical reevaluation; and most of the earlier ones were missed or diminished through pathetic failures of human will and imagination. The Congress of Vienna is one of many examples. Occasionally, however, the moment is seized, as it was in Philadelphia in 1787, where the success of the American Revolution, together with the evident failure of confederation among the former colonies, brought about a deliberate systemic transformation that has survived two centuries of good times and severe strain. The constitutionalism of confederation, despite its political, and some economic, success did not prevent "a sense of collective crisis in the 1780s in part because the utopian expectations of the American Revolution were discredited by apparent failures in constitutional design...." which had failed to take adequate advantage in the "challenge and opportunity of constitutional construction of the fortunate circumstances...."[6] The authors of the new American Constitution knew they were capable of better. They were imaginative, historically-aware philosophers who seized that unique opportunity to transform social structure. In the words of Professor David Richards, "That sense of challenge and opportunity fired the founders to initiate with the American people a great collective democratic deliberation on constitutionalism...."[7]

Such a great, collective, democratic deliberation should now be going on in the world. A rare opportunity has been created by the transformation of the global ethos. People have been liberated from the obsessive constraints of the Cold War; but they have also realized—as the Iraqi attack on Kuwait reminds us—that future global security and well-being cannot be achieved with nineteenth century methods and institutions. It should be understood that future generations will judge our leaders and thinkers by how they responded to the challenge of 1990, just as surely as we judge those who gathered in Vienna from 1814 to 1815, or in Philadelphia in 1787.

This paper is one of a series in which the author has adduced his own and examined others' proposals for a new global order in which security, economic development, and fundamental entitlements of individuals should be defined and advanced through collective action. Specifically, this paper addresses the question of multilateral action to promote the legitimacy of regimes.

Democracy as the Ultimate Global Entitlement

The defining characteristic of the systemic transformation which has been underway during these past five years has been the nearly global move towards democracy, characterized by free, secret, multiparty elections. While this achievement cannot be credited to the efforts of the international system,[8] it nevertheless has at least a potential for dynamic impact on that system and its institutional and normative structures. In short, the United Nations has not reinvented democracy, but democracy may reinvent the United Nations.

This is likely to be helpful to the cause of world peace. Opinions vary as to whether there is a correlation between the openness of national governance and the degree to which states are likely to be peaceful. It is at least arguable—and was argued by Immanuel Kant—that democratic states are more inclined to be peaceful than totalitarian ones.[9] Although the argument is not conclusive, it is worth noting the historian's finding that, in the past 150 years, "no liberal democracies have ever fought against each other."[10] Or as Professor Tony Smith has recently observed, it "could be argued...that a democratic society operating under a market economy has a strong predisposition toward peace."[11] This, he thinks, is because only in a democracy is the decision to go to war truly in the hands of those who must pay the real price of such a policy.

Whatever the significance of that correlation, it is becoming quite clear that the desire for multiparty electoral democracy in a social context of free expression is becoming a basic, unquenchable drive of almost all societies. It is not, as elitists in the West once argued, a luxury item enjoyed by a small number of prosperous nations of the developed world, societies which had evolved over long, historic periods towards a parliamentary system. Also, democracy is not a system inapplicable to states composed of different nationalities or religions; although homogeneity may make the system easier to operate, disparity creates an even greater need for the sort of consensus-building which democracy alone can promote. If homogeneity, or prosperity, were its prerequisites, then democracy indeed would have little relevance for much of humanity. Sadly, however, the elitist theory of the irrelevance of democracy to Third World nations has been fully tested. The Napoleonic cycle from populist-modernizing authoritarian to emperor has been replayed there with no regard for the lessons of history. "Mobilizational" authoritarian regimes, so ardently popularized by some Western academic admirers of populist dictators like Ghana's Dr. Kwame Nkrumah, ultimately culminated in the disastrous excesses of Field Marshal Idi Amin and Emperor Bokassa. As after the defeat of Napoleon at Waterloo, the promise of African, Asian, and Latin American "mobilizational" dictatorships quickly dissipated after they had led their nations to economic and political calamity.

But was it all necessary? Are we doomed continually to repeat the same costly mistakes? When Amin was deposed at last, his successor, Godfrey L. Binaisa, went to the General Assembly to chide its delegates for their indifference to the plight of his country. "In light of the clear commitment set out in...provisions of the Charter, our people naturally looked to the United Nations for solidarity and support in their struggle against the fascist dictatorship," he said. "For eight years they cried out in the wilderness for help; unfortunately, their cries seemed to have fallen on deaf ears." Thus the Amin regime "continued with impunity to commit genocide against our people." Binaisa complained that "somehow, it is thought to be in bad taste or contrary to diplomatic etiquette to raise matters of violations of human rights by member states within the forums of the United Nations."[12] Perhaps that taboo, this time around, is beginning to lose much of its force.

Binaisa might also have added that the fora of the United Nations had been particularly inhospitable to any suggestion that there might be a connection between the wretched excesses of regimes like those of Idi Amin, Emperor Bokassa of the Central African Empire, or General Ne Win of Burma, and the denial of the people's right to choose their own governors. To have made that fairly elementary connection between anti-pluralist autocrats and human rights violations, at least during the period up to the mid-1980s, would have rallied a legion of dictatorships of Eastern Europe, Latin America, Africa, and Asia against intervention in their domestic affairs. During this period, it was still widely perceived as legitimate for governments to oppress their own people in the name of African socialism, anti-tribalism, and anti-colonialism. These shibboleths have now been exposed. At best, they were the honest delusion of an elite that their people were not to be trusted. At worst, they were a smokescreen of lies behind which greedy elites, for too long, were licensed by a political fraud to monopolize the scarce resources of their societies.

Whether "the people" *can* govern themselves is always an open question in democracies. What became apparent during the mid-1980s was that they—the people everywhere—were determined to try. The overthrow of the Marcos regime in the Philippines was the first democratic revolution to be televised globally. It spawned passionate imitators. Soon popular uprisings were being staged in South Korea, Pakistan, Burma, and all over Eastern Europe. With the disintegration of the myth of the dictatorship of the proletariat on the streets of Leipzig, Prague, and Moscow, most one-party regimes—in Africa, Asia, and Latin America—lost their legitimacy. African socialism, as the philosophical underpinning of one-party regimes, was exposed as a fig leaf pretending to disguise personal dictatorship. The new rulers, far from being socialist, empowered themselves as heirs of the colonial raj. It did not take long for this to dawn on people, but only in the late 1980s, thanks to Soviet *glasnost* and *perestroika,* did the magnitude of the failure of totalitarianism fuse with a reasonable political belief that something could be done to alter the systematic underpinnings of calamity. In East Berlin, Dakar, Maputo, Karachi, Phnom Penh, and many other capitals, regimes began to seek the validation of democratic elections in the context of a more open society. In Moscow, at the Twenty-eighth Communist Party Congress, President Mikhail S. Gorbachev said,

> When somebody says this is the "collapse of socialism," we counter it with the question, "What 'socialism'"? That which had been, in point of fact, a variation of Stalin's authoritarian bureaucratic system that we have ourselves discarded?...
> Of course, [where] these countries will go in their social and economic development is an open question. But that is up to the peoples concerned. We on the other hand have acted and we will act in strict compliance with the principle of the freedom of choice, which has become an imperative for the progress and a condition for the survival of all modern civilization.[13]

What the President of the Soviet Union enunciated in 1990 is but the latest manifestation of the enlightenment as it was manifest in Western Europe and the American colonies in the eighteenth century. This has always been a philosophy—in that sense like others with which it has competed—which cherishes global aspirations. Unlike others, however, it was a philosophy of the emancipation of the individual. John Adams, in Massachusetts, identified it as a "great struggle" proceeding from "a love of universal liberty"[14] and its objective was "government of the state more agreeable to the dignity of human nature."[15] What had long been a love of universal liberty, at the end of the twentieth century, became at last a universal love of liberty.

Making Democracy a Normative Entitlement

The above-quoted statement by Soviet President Mikhail Gorbachev, the twentieth century's most remarkable leader, suggests that we may be at the threshold of a new global system in which the rights of member states' citizens to participate in their national governance will be guaranteed by the global community as a new legal entitlement. Rights to political participation may be on the verge of becoming the new generation of human entitlements.

While this appears to be a radical departure from strict notions of state equality, which have tended to emphasize equal sovereignty and entitlement to noninterference in all nations' domestic affairs, there has been a trend in the direction of a global conscience capable of interfering with injustice. Interference against gross "domestic" human rights abuses already has become relatively normative in the system. What is new is the idea that the system would include among those gross abuses triggering international concern those instances where governments deny their own populations the right to participate democratically in the process of governance.

In effect, this would merely bring the U.N. Charter's proclaimed norm of self-determination into the twenty-first century.[16] The way to do this is with two related moves. The *first* is to establish a recognized, institutionalized process for determining whether a government has crossed the line from democracy to totalitarianism. The *second* is to create in law a significant range of penalties—a withholding of various bilateral and multilateral entitlements—if a government crosses the line. The implementing of penalties, moreover, must be the prerogative not of individual states but of legitimate, credible, international machinery charged with finding facts and determining the appropriate penalties.

Monitoring compliance and imposing penalties for noncompliance could be criticized as undermining the U.N. Charter provisions, especially Article 2(7), against intervention in the domestic affairs of member states. Some small third world nations have already expressed such concern and, acting on that fear, at first opposed U.N. monitoring of Haiti's elections in 1990.[17] Such concern, however, has tended to be overridden by higher values and, in any event, comes rather late in the history of the organization's evolution. The third world has led the way to legitimating U.N. intervention in the domestic affairs of oppressive regimes. The international community long has asserted a duty on the part of all sovereign states to take various actions—mainly economic but also military actions—which would undermine the policies and objectives of South Africa's apartheid regime.[18] Under the dictatorship of General Pinochet, Chile became a second-class citizen of the international community and its domestic system of governance was subject to intense international scrutiny.[19] Such developments correlate closely with the rise of human rights as a factor in determining a state's entitlement to the benefits of membership in the international community. Gross human rights violators find it more difficult, nowadays—as China currently demonstrates—to receive equal treatment in the terms of trade or to have equal access to loans and grants from other nations or from global lending institutions. With concern for *political democracy* entering the human rights vocabulary—as Gorbachev made clear to the Twenty-eighth Communist Party Congress—this may be the time for the law to give formal recognition to legal inequality, in the sense of different entitlement to benefits, between democratic and totalitarian regimes.

Admittedly, the implications of such a notion are both complex and far-reaching. Still, it is just possible that we have arrived at a propitious time to recognize such a change in the international normative system because, just now, so many states are rediscovering the dynamics of democratic process.

In another age, John Stuart Mill said with conviction that the moral fiber of a nation is weakened if the intervention of outsiders spares its people the trouble of liberating themselves.[20] After the recent orgies of genocide, this is a posture of insufferable insouciance. As the Supreme Court of the United States found in *Baker v. Carr,* once a political system passes a certain point of corruption, it may be unable to redress itself without help.[21] This help need not be of military kind. International lawyers have been defined as persons who will not cross a bridge even when they come to it. Be that as it may, there is no reason for lawyers now to think about military force as a remedy for governmental illegitimacy. The collective use of military force to protect the peoples' right to democracy is an extremely remote bridge which need not be crossed at present. Instead, there are more modest steps to be taken. First, there must be recognition of a defined normative *right.* Then there must be a credible process for observing whether the right is being observed. Finally, if the prescribed process is found not to have been observed, there must be available a range of collective pacific options to exert pressure on violators. These could include deprivation of privileges the community bestows on legitimate governments.

Nations may be on the verge of recognizing a *right* of all citizens of every state to participate in democratic governance and to enjoy freedom from totalitarian oppression. Evidence of this can be seen in the speed with which democracy spread through Eastern Europe during the second half of 1989, once the Solidarity government in Poland had demonstrated Moscow's repeal of the Brezhnev doctrine.[22] These developments, with their echoes in Zambia, Kenya, Mozambique, and Burma, are the latest and most powerful waves of freedom to wash over the world. But those contemporary events have their roots in an older tradition of regime legitimization, one which is central to the U.N. system. The same spirit which is evident in Eastern Europe and parts of Africa, Asia, and Latin America today was nurtured by the United Nations in the period from 1945 to 1970. It can be seen in resolutions and conventions encouraging collective action against regimes which practice colonialism, racism, or denial of self-determination.[23] That era of collective activism against illegitimate forms of domination prepared the ground for a new generation of political entitlements. Surely, the impetus that moved the world to demand collective action to liberate colonies and called on nations to come to the aid of the colonized cannot have had as its ultimate aim the mere replacement of a French or British raj with an indigenous Idi Amin. The decent instincts which clustered around the concept of "self-determination," creating a widely-accepted exception to Article 2(7)'s norm of nonintervention, is a latent but potent force for continuing the quest for meaningful participation in government as the ultimate human right.

The general nature of such a democratic entitlement is already spelled out in international instruments, in particular the Covenant on Civil and Political Rights,[24] which may now be regarded as having entered the process of becoming customary international law.[25] Article 25 purports to entitle "every citizen" to "take part in the conduct of public affairs, directly or through freely chosen representatives" and to "vote and to be elected at genuine periodic elections which shall be by universal and equal suffrage and shall be held by secret ballot...." This norm is the fundamental basis for all political rights, which the Covenant also defines. If the democratic electoral system works, if it is free and establishes open and equal access, there are reasonable prospects that the other rights of citizens will follow as a consequence.

Collective Implementation of the Democratic Entitlement

As with self-determination, however, there is a problem in applying the rule. Experience has shown that the right of colonized peoples to self-determination and of victims of racial discrimination to redress of their grievances may all too readily be turned from a generous international impulse into a license of self-promoting states to mount fishing expeditions for their own advantage. Seen in this way, a good principle may lend itself to centrifugal fragmentation and could serve as a pretext for aggression.

The international system's experiences with applying the principle of self-determination in the dramatic years 1950-75—the failures as well as the successes—have taught us that such a dynamic principle needs, first, a sound set of theoretical parameters, and second, a credibly impartial process for its case-by-case application, one capable of adapting to and shoring up the legitimacy[26] of the principle.

In practice, this means that to launch a new generation of entitlements, the international community must devise universal, credible *procedures for monitoring* compliance with the participatory right. Then, it must agree upon the range of measures which states, individually or collectively, might take to *enforce the entitlement.* Finally, it must agree upon collective *procedures for authorizing the use of a specific forceful measure* deemed necessary in a specific circumstance to secure compliance. In short, there needs to be *a standard, a system of monitoring, enforcement mechanisms*, and *procedures for their deployment.* Each of these must be seen to be legitimately conceived and applied if the nations of the world are to entrust their hard-won democratic systems to what amounts to an international system of mutual safeguards against resurgences of totalitarianism.

Such a project is bound to arouse the ire of "realists." Two points can be argued in brief reply. First, the so-called realists have been shown, in recent months, to have been remarkably unrealistic in their appraisal of prospects for systemic transformation. Second, the world already has in place several extensive systems—global[27] and regional[28]—for measuring and enforcing compliance with specific political rights. It is surely more economical, and thus more possible, to enforce the basic right of people to participate in their governance than to attempt to enforce specific governmental outcomes. Nothing about human political behavior is ever wholly predictable. Nevertheless, if the basic process for popular participation in governance can be safeguarded, respect for specific substantive rights is likely to follow as a matter of course.

The implementation of a participatory entitlement requires international monitoring of elections: not just secret and honest voting but also open campaigning free of intimidation and repression. The Covenant on Civil and Political Rights, or its customary law analogue, establishes the standard for "open elections" and commits all governments to it. What is needed, in addition, is a process for international observation and inspection of each national electoral process to ensure compliance with the existing standard. The electoral process, admittedly, is only one indicator of the viability of democracy, but it is the most fundamental, visible, and accessible one: the pressure point at which the political body's pulse most readily can be taken.

No new treaty is needed to implement monitoring. The General Assembly by resolution could authorize the Secretary-General to establish a monitoring unit able to respond to requests by governments. The resolution should urge all states, on a voluntary basis, to submit such requests at least when conducting their national elections.

For the United States to take the initiative—as it should, being the world's oldest functioning constitutional democracy—it, of course, would have to commit itself to such international inspection of its own electoral process. We have nothing to fear, and obviously, much to gain, from such a commitment. While we may believe that an open society like ours is amply monitored by a vigilant press, that is beside the point. It is simply not conceivable that a global practice of electoral monitoring could come into being if it were pressed on the "bad guys" while the "good guys" exempted themselves. Participation in monitoring should be as evidently compatible with the presumption of a high degree of democratic legitimacy as with the opposite assumption. For that reason alone, the oldest democracies must be among the first volunteers.

The international monitoring of elections may be an idea whose time has come, but it is not a new one. The United Nations has had experience in monitoring numerous elections: in trusteeship territories,[29] in some colonies just prior to independence,[30] and, more recently, in Namibia and Nicaragua.[31] The Organization of American States, similarly, has engaged in monitoring,[32] as have some international non-governmental groups.[33] Requests for electoral monitoring and technical assistance in conducting elections are becoming commonplace—from Romania[34] and Haiti,[35] for example—as a recognized means of establishing the legitimacy of outcomes. It is possible to be optimistic that there will be ample demand for the services of a global monitoring service capable of validating and legitimating national electoral process.

Technical assistance in organizing, conducting, and verifying results of elections would be provided by the proposed international monitoring agency to all requesting governments. Such help could range from non-binding advice on aspects of the actual conduct of a particular election, to more general assistance in devising electoral systems and drafting electoral laws, as well as technical assistance to improve the voting process.

As a result of its monitoring, the international agency would certify an election as being (or not) in "substantial compliance" with the normative obligation assumed by a ratifying party in agreeing to be monitored. That obligation, incorporating the terms of the Covenant on Civil and Political Rights, might simply be accepted in an exchange of letters between the Secretary-General and the requesting government.

Not every state would rush forward to avail itself of this "open elections" procedure or to embrace a new generation of participatory human rights. But the momentum of historic events surely is now on the side of a normative, institutionalized right of self-determination. Governments which are firmly established democracies would presumably see an opportunity to "lock in" self-determination in places where freedom is still fragile. Frailer democracies would see monitoring as a way to ensure and legitimate their fledgling processes of popular participation. Nations reluctant to commit themselves, would, at the very least, stand embarrassed before the world and before their own populations.

Such a system of implementation, moreover, would require no amendment to the U.N. Charter. The process of establishing election monitors and the standard to be applied by them would be by mutual consent of the Secretary-General and the monitored state. Indeed, a Secretariat memorandum has already been prepared, noting the rising demand for election monitoring from independent member states, which sets out the juridical, institutional, administrative, and fiscal parameters.[36]

It should be expected that the implementation of a normative, democratic entitlement would give rise to interpretation. Among the issues which might arise are disputes concerning the fairness of the rules governing candidacy or the apportionment of electoral districts. These are the sorts of questions which, at least initially, would be addressed by the report of the U.N. monitors, applying the norms of the Covenant on Civil and Political Rights. Nevertheless, a state being monitored reasonably might wish to have some aspects of a report's conclusions, especially if these were negative, subject to review by the International Court of Justice. Thus, the General Assembly might give a general authority to the Secretary-General to request an advisory opinion on matters pertaining to his monitoring function under Article 26(2) of the Charter, whenever this is requested by a monitored state.

Enforcement

Beyond implementation lies the murkier realm of systemic enforcement. What if the monitoring agency were to issue a negative finding on compliance after observing an election? To some extent, the process would enforce itself. This being a relatively new enterprise, it would be appropriate to applaud its small victories without dwelling unduly on its vicissitudes and shortcomings. At a minimum, the illegitimacy of any government that had been chosen in non-compliance with the normative standards would stand starkly exposed before its own people and other nations. That psychological effect should not be underestimated and, initially, might suffice to justify the enterprise.

Over time, however, other consequences might ensue by operation of new thinking about international law. Some of this might be quite radical, challenging the formidable and venerable bastion of post-Grotian international law.

As we have noted, traditional international law perceives all states and their governments as equals.[37] The U.N. Charter is based on this historic notion. The Charter nevertheless has been used to exclude "pariah" nations such as Southern Rhodesia[38] and the Bantustans of South Africa.[39] These were denied legitimation and membership because they were deemed to exist in violation of basic international norms. Increasingly, the entitlement of states to "equality"—whether in access to the resources of the World Bank and International Monetary Fund, or to preferential terms of trade under the General Agreement on Tariffs and Trade—is coming to depend on the international community's belief that those nations meet basic, normative behavioral standards. Standards of environmentalism and of human rights now commonly are weighed together with more traditional fiscal and economic ones. Respect for democracy, once tested by a credible verification process, could be added to the equation. It is to be expected that non-compliance, or an unwillingness to submit to the "open elections" process, increasingly would be taken into account in collateral relations between states and in determining eligibility for benefits accorded states by international institutions. Noncompliant governments gradually would find their "equality" undermined, and, with it, their ability to share in the benefits for full membership in the international system.

Beyond such denial of equal access to international and bilateral privileges and facilities lies the possibility of invoking economic sanctions.

The authorization of extensive sanctions has been demonstrated by the Security Council's Resolution 253 of 1968 which ordered states, in accordance with Chapter VII of the U.N. Charter, to prevent trade, investment, and other economic activity between themselves and Rhodesia as a means to end the Unilateral Declaration of Independence regime which was held to constitute a "threat to international peace and security" as a result of policies it was pursuing vis-à-vis its own population and its manifest lack of legitimacy. Such use of Chapter VII economic sanctions against a state because of its undemocratic policy towards its own population thus does have an established precedent in U.N. practice. The repeated failure of a government to submit to the free and monitored judgment of its own people, in certain egregious cases, might cause the Security Council to act again in accordance with that precedent.

There is no need to speculate about collective armed military intervention against states which violate the normative rights of their own population to self-determination. In theory, if Chapter VII of the Charter is applicable for purposes of economic measures, it is also possible to defend collective recourse to military measures. However, the situation is very unlikely to arise. First, the entitlement to free, multilaterally-supervised elections needs time to become firmly established. The more draconian the remedies, the less likely that the norm will receive rapid, widespread acceptance on the part of the states which are still jealous guardians of their sovereignty. Second, the effectiveness of lesser levels of pressure needs first to be tested before a case can be made for more serious measures. Third, the horrendous sort of undemocratic regime which might warrant implementation of collective military measures under Chapter VII—an analogue of Hitlerite Germany comes to mind—would almost certainly constitute a threat to peace sufficient to arouse the sleeping dogs of Chapter VII on far more egregious grounds than its undemocratic practices. Such regimes practice aggression, genocide, and other activities far more firmly fixed among the grounds justifying forceful intervention than the denial to their people of a still-fragile right to democratic governance.

Thus it is both morally and legally appropriate to avoid being drawn into the distraction of a discussion as to whether the world—or, the United Nations—is ready to constitute itself as a league to fight for democracy. What is now both desirable and possible, however, is to create the normative and institutional framework within which an already-evident popular proclivity will transform a fortuitous conjunction of opportunities into an irreversible universal momentum.

Notes

1. An earlier draft of parts of this essay, together with other materials, has been published: Franck, *United Nations Based Prospects for a New World Order*, 22 N.Y.U. J. INT'L L. & POL'Y 601 (1990).

2. Maynes, 78 FOREIGN POL'Y 3 (1990).

3. Fukuyama, *The End of History?*, 16 THE NATIONAL INTEREST 3 (1989).

4. Mearsheimer, *Why We Will Miss the Cold War*, THE ATLANTIC MONTHLY Aug. 1990, at 35.

5. G. Sherry, *The United Nations Reborn*, Council on Foreign Relations Critical Issues Paper, 1990.

6. D. RICHARDS, FOUNDATIONS OF AMERICAN CONSTITUTIONALISM 19-20 (1989).

7. *Id.*

8. The gift of half a century of peace, however, is at least to some extent attributable to the post-war system of which the United Nations is a part. As Dankwart A. Rustow has pointed out, it is the first time that democracy has broken out as a result of an era of peace rather than an era of war. Rustow, *Democracy: A Global Revolution?*, 69 FOREIGN AFF. 75 (1990).

9. Kant argues that "perpetual peace" could be based on a "pacific union" of "republican" states that observed categorical imperatives of ethical fairness in their pursuit of the common good. I. KANT, THE PHILOSOPHY OF KANT: IMMANUEL KANT'S MORAL AND POLITICAL WRITINGS 430-76 (C. Friedrich ed. 1949).

10. Mearsheimer, *supra* note 4, at 46.

11. T. Smith, *Democracy Resurgent,* in SEA CHANGES 153, 157 (N. Rizopoulos ed. 1990).

12. U.N. Doc. A/34/PV.14 (1979).

13. *Excerpts From Gorbachev Speech at the 28th Communist Party Congress,* N.Y. Times, July 3, 1990, at A10, col. 1.

14. THREE WORKS OF JOHN ADAMS 451 (C. Adams ed. 1969).

15. *Id.* at 453.

16. For a discussion of this *see* T. FRANCK, THE POWER OF LEGITIMACY AMONG NATIONS 153-74 (1990).

17. *Haiti Wants U.N. to Monitor Vote,* N. Y. Times, July 22, 1990, at A10, col. 6.

18. *See Legal Consequences for States of the Continued Presence of South Africa in Namibia (South West Africa) Notwithstanding Security Council Resolution 276* (1970), 1971 I.C.J. 16, 57 (Adv. op. of June 21), which found South Africa's racial policies in violation of the U.N. Charter.

19. *See, e.g.,* the report of Professor Felix Ermacora, the U.N. Human Rights Commission's expert investigating the question of the fate of missing and "disappeared" persons in Chile, which fixed responsibility on the Government of General Pinochet while still in power. U.N. Doc. E/CN.4/1987/13 at 23.

20. J.S. MILL, THREE DISSERTATIONS AND DISCUSSIONS: POLITICAL, PHILOSOPHICAL AND HISTORICAL 238-63 (1873).

21. Baker v. Carr, 369 U.S. 186, 228-31 (1962).

22. Following the 1968 Soviet invasion of Czechoslovakia, the Soviet newspaper, Pravda, in an article, *International Duties of Soviet Countries* (Sept. 25, 1968), set forth the basic tenets which were to become the Brezhnev Doctrine. *Reprinted and translated in* N. Y. Times, Sept. 27, 1968, at A3, col. 1. Later, Soviet Foreign Minister Gromyko would state that "[t]he Soviet Union and other socialist countries have on many occasions warned that those who are tempted to try to roll back the socialist commonwealth, to snatch at least one link from it, that we will neither tolerate nor allow that to happen." A. Gromyko, addressing the U.N. General Assembly, U.N. Doc. A/PV.1679 (1968), at 26, 31.

23. *Declaration of Principles of International Law Concerning Friendly Relations and Co-operation among States in Accordance with the Charter of the United Nations* (fifth principle, para. 5), G. A. Res. 2625, 25 U.N. GAOR Supp. (No. 28) at 121, U.N. Doc. A/8028 (1970). This resolution solemnly proclaims the principle of equal rights and self-determination of peoples stating:

> Every State has the duty to refrain from any forcible action which deprives peoples...of the present principle....In their actions against, and resistance to, such forcible action in pursuit of the exercise of their own right to self-determination, *such peoples are entitled to seek and to receive support* in accordance with the purposes and principles of the Charter. [Emphasis added.]

See also G. A. Res. 2708, 25 GAOR Supp (no. 28) at 7, para. 5, U.N. Doc. A/8028 (1970) ("*Reaffirms* its recognition of the legitimacy of the struggle of the colonial peoples and peoples under alien domination to exercise the right to self-determination and independence by all the necessary means at their disposal"); Definition of Aggression, G.A. Res. 3314, Art. 7, 29 U.N. GAOR Supp. (No. 31) at 142, U.N. Doc. A/9631 (1974).

24. *International Covenant on Civil and Political Rights,* Dec. 19, 1966, Art. 1 (1) and (3), 999 U.N.T.S. 171 (entered into force Mar. 23, 1976).

25. *See generally* T. MERON, HUMAN RIGHTS LAW-MAKING IN THE UNITED NATIONS 178-89 (1986). The International Law Commission has also incorporated the right of self-determination set forth in the International Covenant on Civil and Political Rights in its draft Article 19 on State responsibility:

> Art. 19 - International Crimes and International delicts....
> 3. Subject to paragraph 2, and on the basis of the rules of international law in force, an international crime may result, *inter alia,* from: ....
> (b) a serious breach of an international obligation of essential importance for safeguarding the rights on self-determination of peoples, such as that prohibiting the establishment or maintenance by force of colonial domination; and
> (c) a serious breach on a widespread scale of an international obligation of essential importance for safeguarding the human being, such as those prohibiting slavery, genocide and apartheid...

[1976] 2 Y.B. Int'l L. Comm'n 75, U.N. Doc A/CN.4/SER.4/1976/Add.1 (Part 2).

26. *See Legitimacy: A Matter of Degree* in FRANCK, THE POWER OF LEGITIMACY AMONG NATIONS (1990), which identifies four indicia conducive to "shoring up" compliance with the international principles: determinacy, symbolic validation, coherence, and adherence.

27. *See, e.g.,* the reporting and monitoring provisions of the International Covenant on Civil and Political Rights, Part IV. G.A. Res. 2200 (XXI), 21 U.N. GAOR Supp. (No. 16) at 52, U.N. Doc. A/6316 (1966). Entered into force March 23, 1976. *See also* Optional Protocol. *Id.*

28. *See, e.g.,* American Convention on Human Rights, O.A.S.T.S. No. 36 at 1, O.A.S. Off. Rec. OEA/Ser. L/V/II.23, doc. 21, rev. 2 (1975). Entered into force July 18, 1978. *See also*, European Convention for the Protection of Human Rights and Fundamental Freedoms and Five Accompanying Protocols, 213 U.N.T.S. 222. Entered into force Sept. 3, 1953; and, African [Banjul] Charter on Human and Peoples' Rights, adopted June 27, 1981, O.A.U. Doc. CAB/LEG/67/3 Rev. 5 reprinted in 21 I.L.M. 58 (1982). The European Convention establishes monitoring by a commission and a court, as also does the American Convention.

29. The United Nations has supervised or monitored numerous plebiscites in those trust territories located in Africa and the South Pacific.

In Africa, the United Nations conducted the May 9, 1956, plebiscite by which the people of British Togoland elected to unite with the independent Gold Coast. Report of the United Nations Plebiscite Commissioner for the Trust Territory of Togoland under British Administration, U.N. Doc. T/1258 and Add. 1 (1956).

The United Nations also conducted plebiscites in the British Cameroons in November of 1959 (re: Northern Cameroons) and in February of 1961 to ascertain the wishes of the residents of both the Northern and Southern Cameroons. *See* G.A. Res. 1350, 13 U.N. GAOR Supp. (No. 18A) at 2, U.N. Doc. A/4090) Add. 1 (1959) (whether the Northern Cameroons wished "to be part of the Northern Region of Nigeria when the Federation of Nigeria becomes independent"); G.A. Res. 1352, 14 U.N. GAOR Supp. (no. 16) at 26, U.N. Doc. A/4354 (1960) (whether the Southern Cameroons wished to achieve independence by "joining the independent Federation of Nigeria [or] the independent Republic of Cameroons); G.A. Res. 1473, 14 U.N. GAOR Supp. (No. 16) at 38, U.N. Doc. A/4354 (1960) (putting the questions posed in the G.A. Res. 1352 plebiscite before the Northern Cameroons); *see also Report of United Nations Plebiscite Commissioner for the Supervision of the Plebiscites in the southern and northern parts of the Trust Territory of the Cameroons under United Kingdom Administration,* U.N. Doc. T/1556 and Appendix (1961).

Following the November 1959 violence between the Hut and Tutsi movements in Ruanda-Urandi (under Belgian administration), the United Nations supervised a referendum to determine whether the institution of the Mwami should be retained in Ruanda and, if so, whether Kigeli V was to continue as the Mwami. The referendum took place in conjunction with the general legislative elections (also under U.N. supervision) on September 25, 1961. G.A. Res. 1579, 15 U.N. GAOR Supp. (No. 16) at 34, U.N. Doc. A/4684 (1961) (elections); G.A. Res. 1605, 15 U.N. GAOR Supp. (No. 16A) at 8, U.N. Doc. A/4684/Add.1 (1961) (referendum).

In the South Pacific, the United Nations aided in the May 6, 1961, plebiscites conducted in Western Samoa under the Administering Authority of New Zealand. G.A. Res. 1569, 15 U.N. GAOR Supp. (No.16) at 33, U.N. Doc. A/4684 (1961) (whether the inhabitants of the Territory accepted "the Constitution adopted by the Constitutional Convention on 28 October 1960" and endorsed "that on 1 January

1962 Western Samoa should become an independent State on the basis of that Constitution"); *see also Report of United Nations Commissioner for the Supervision of the Plebiscite in Western Samoa*, U.N. Doc. T/1564 and Add. 1 (1961).

The United Nations has also monitored various plebiscites and referendums in the United States Pacific Trust Territories. On June 17, 1975, the residents of the Northern Mariana Islands voted to accept the Covenant to Establish a Commonwealth of the Northern Mariana Islands in Political Union with the United States of America. *Report of the United Nations Visiting Mission to Observe the Plebiscite in the Northern Mariana Islands, Trust Territory of the Pacific Islands, June 1975, 43* U.N. TCOR Supp. (No. 2) at 24, U.N. Doc. T/1771 (1976).

Likewise, in the early 1980s, the United Nations supervised plebiscites whereby the other regions constituting the Pacific Trust Territories voted to enter into a Compact of Free Association with the United States of America. *See Report of the United Nations Visiting Mission to Observe the Plebiscite in the Federated States Of Micronesia, Trust Territory of the Pacific Islands, June 1983,* 51 U.N. TCOR Supp. (No. 1) at 14, U.N. Doc. T/1860 (1984) (June 21, 1983, plebiscite for the islands of Truk, Yap, Kosrae and Ponape); *Report of the United Nations Visiting Mission to Observe the Plebiscite in the Northern Mariana Islands, Trust Territory of the Pacific Islands, September 1983,* 51 U.N. TCOR Supp. (No. 2) at 26 (Annex III), U.N. Doc. T/1865 (1984) (September 7, 1983, plebiscite); *Report of the United Nations Visiting Mission to Observe Plebiscite in Palau, Trust Territory of the Pacific Islands, February 1986,* 53 U.N. TCOR Supp. (No.2) at 14 (Annex IV), U.N. Doc. T/1885 (1986) (February 21, 1986, plebiscite).

30. The United Nations has also served in a supervisory role in elections prior to their independence.

The United Nations monitored the Spanish-administered referendums in Equatorial Guinea in which the residents elected a legislature (September 22, 1968) and a president (September 23, 1968) under their 1968 constitution. *See generally* G.A. Res. 2355, 22 U.N. GAOR Supp. (No. 16) at 54, U.N. Doc. A/6716 (1968); *United Nations Mission for the Supervision of the Referendum and the Elections in Equatorial Guinea,* U.N. Doc. A/7200/Add.4, Annex V and Annex VI (1968). Independence was firmly achieved on October 12, 1968.

In the Cook Islands, the United Nations oversaw the New Zealand administration of the April 21, 1965 referendum regarding a new constitution for the islands. *See generally* G.A. Res. 2005, 19 U.N. GAOR Supp. (no. 15) at 7, U.N. Doc. A/5815 (1965); *Report of the United Nations Representatives for Supervision of Elections in the Cook Islands,* U.N. Doc. A/5962 and Corr. 1 (1965).

The United Nations was involved in monitoring the referendum in West New Guinea (West Irian) which took place from July 14 until August 2, 1969. *See generally* G.A. Res. 1752, 17 U.N. GAOR Supp. (No. 17) at 70, U.N. Doc. A/5217 (1963); *Report of the Secretary-General regarding the Act of Self-Determination in West*

Irian, U.N. Doc. A/7641 (1969).

Lastly, the United Nations oversaw the November 14, 1980, elections conducted in New Hebrides (under French and British administrations) in which the independent country of Vanuatu was created. G.A. Res. 34/10, 34 U.N. GAOR Supp. (No. 46) at 199, U.N. Doc. A/34/46; Report of the U.N. Mission to Observe the Elections in the New Hebrides, U.N. Doc. A/34/852, Annex (1990).

31. In Nicaragua, the 235-member United Nations election observation team, under Elliot L. Richardson, linked up jeep, plane, and helicopter forces by satellite communications to monitor what was "described as one of the most closely supervised elections in history." N.Y. Times, Feb. 23, 1990, p. A3, col. 4. The monitoring activities in the independent sovereign nation of Nicaragua by the United Nations represented an exceptional case. Involvement in the elections was based on three conditions: (1) the elections were part of the Central American peace process, (2) the entire process was observable—over ten months, and (3) the United Nations supervisory role was backed by the presidents of Central America and the U.N. General Assembly. Comments by Francesco Vendrell, Chief, Europe and the Americas Unit, Research and Early Warning Service, Office for Research and the Collection of Information, United Nations Study Group, N.Y.U. Center for International Studies, March 7, 1990.

In Namibia, following the timetable envisioned by the U.N. Security Council's 1978 resolution concerning Namibia's transition to independence, "the United Nations supervised new elections and monitored a South African administration, spending $700 million and using 7,000 to 8,000 military and civil personnel" prior to the November 1989 elections. N.Y. Times, Jan. 11, 1990, A3, col.1; *see also* S.C. Res. 435, 33 U.N. SCOR (Resolutions and Decisions) at 13, U.N. Doc. S/INF/34 (1978); S.C. Res. 431, 33 U.N. SCOR (Resolutions and Decisions) at 12, U.N. Doc. SD/INF/34 (1978).

Upon the request of the sovereign nations of Haiti (1956) and Costa Rica (1958), the United States provided technical assistance in these two countries' elections. According to B.G. Ramcharan, in both of these cases, only "experts" were made available to the requesting governments. As such, these experts did not serve as official representatives of the United Nations. *See* interview with B.G. Ramcharan, Chief, Drafting Service, Office for Research and the Collection of Information, United Nations, in New York (February 28, 1990).

32. The Organization of American States (O.A.S.) formed one of the three international missions (along with the U.N. task force and the Council of Freely Elected Heads of Government led by former U.S. President Jimmy Carter) to monitor about 70% of the polling sites in the February 25, 1990, elections in Nicaragua. The O.A.S. team included some 435 observers. N. Y. Times, Feb. 22, 1990, at A22, col.4.

33. In the Nicaragua elections of February 25, 1990, a third non-governmental group sponsored by the Carter Presidential Center in Atlanta, the Council of Freely Elected Heads of Government also participated in the monitoring of elections. N.Y. Times, Aug. 9, 1989, at A13, col.1.

34. Silviu Brucan, a senior member of the ruling council of National Salvation, stated that Romania intended to ask the United Nations to send a team to monitor the preparation and conduct of the elections to take place in late May of 1990. N.Y. Times, Jan. 24, 1990, at A12, col. 5. In the circumstances, the request was not granted.

35. N. Y. Times, July 22, 1990, at A10, col. 6.

36. Principles for United Nations Observance of Elections. U.N. Confidential Memorandum, June 6, 1989.

37. E. VATTEL, LE DROIT DES GENS OU PRINCIPE DE LA LOI NATURELLE, sec. 18 (Introduction) (C. Fenwick trans. 1758) reprinted in CLASSICS OF INTERNATIONAL LAW 7 (J. Scott ed. 1916):

> Since men are by nature equal, and their individual rights and obligations the same, as coming equally from nature, Nations, which are composed of men and may be regarded as so many free persons living together in a state of nature, are by nature equal and hold from nature the same obligations and the same rights. Strength or weakness, in this case, counts for nothing. A dwarf is as much a man as a giant is; a small Republic is no less a sovereign State than the most powerful Kingdom.

38. Sanctions were imposed upon Southern Rhodesia by the U.N. Security Council from 1966 until 1979. *See* S.C. Res. 232, 21 U.N. SCOR (Resolutions and Decisions) at 7, para. 2 (a-f), U.N. Doc. S/INF/35 (11966); S.C. Res. 253, 23 U.N. SCOR (Resolutions and Decisions) at 13, U.N. Doc. S/INF/35 (1979). Sanctions were withdrawn December 21, 1979, in coordination with the Lancaster House Agreement which led to the eventual creation of the independent state of Zimbabwe on April 17, 1980. *See* S.C. Res. 460, 34 U.N. SCOR (Resolutions and Decisions) at 15, U.N. Doc. S/INF/35 (1979).

39. G.A. Res. 34/93 (G), 34 U.N. GAOR Supp. (No. 46) at 29-38, U.N. Doc. A/34/46 (1979). Paragraph 1 reads:

> *The General Assembly...*
> 1. *Again denounces* the establishment of bantustans as designed to consolidate the inhuman policy of *apartheid*, to destroy the territorial integrity of the country, to perpetuate white minority domination and to deprive the African people of South Africa of their inalienable rights[.]

See also G.A. Res. 35/206, 35 U.N. GAOR Supp. (No. 48) at 29-39, U.N. Doc A/35/48 (1990) (further condemning the Bantustans, continuing prior sanctions, and imposing more comprehensive sanctions as well as an oil embargo on Southern Rhodesia).

15

Commentary on Intervention Against Illegitimate Regimes

Anne-Marie Burley

Self-determination is surely a primary—if not the primary—indicium of legitimacy. The question is to what extent other nations can intervene to help the citizens oppressed by an illegitimate regime govern themselves.

When contemplating how to promote *legitimate* regimes, we should pause for a moment to reflect on the causes of *illegitimate* regimes. Not surprisingly, they are the obverse of the conditions that universal democracy is supposed to promote. Professor Thomas Franck listed the goals of a new global system as peace, economic growth, prosperity, and prevention of the deterioration of the human, physical, and environmental conditions. Conversely, I would suggest that the leading causes of illegitimate regimes are: the establishment or maintenance of a regime by force, or the threat of force; economic and social conditions, such as poverty and illiteracy; and long-term and systematic deprivation of fundamental human rights. The latter is obviously a symptom, or an effect of illegitimate regimes, but I would argue that over the long term it is also a cause. In South Africa today it is clear that people have been denied their human rights for so long that it is very difficult to expect them suddenly to exercise civil and political rights of which they have had no first-hand experience. Global efforts to assure free elections would seem to be somewhat beside the point. As Professor Igor Lukashuk recognizes, the answer in the first instance is not intervention; rather it is to strengthen a norm of non-intervention that involves pressuring the external power to withdraw, so as to allow the people in the subject country to follow their own course.

Should this approach fail the next alternative becomes counter-intervention. Here, both Lukashuk and Franck duck the hard question: when is it appropriate to use force to help a population throw off a regime sponsored or maintained by another power? One need not look very far to find examples of uses of force, either direct or indirect, justified on just those terms: Grenada, Nicaragua, and Afghanistan. What would the United States have done and how would it have justified its actions in the Middle East if Iraq, instead of invading Kuwait, had simply sponsored the overthrow of the government of Kuwait and its replacement by a puppet regime?

With respect to the second set of causes—economic and social—there is an interesting contradiction. In Eastern Europe and the Soviet Union, economic want was a major catalyst for democratization; however, many of the newly-industrializing countries have followed a very different pattern. The experiences of Taiwan, Korea, and Singapore suggest that economic development may be more easily and quickly achieved under conditions that would not meet the standards of democracy elaborated here. On the contrary, democracy in these countries seems to follow only after a quantum of economic development has been achieved.

There is a similar paradox with respect to literacy. Saddam Hussein managed to boost Iraq's literacy rate from 11 to 80 percent. The Sandinistas boosted Nicaragua's literacy rate from 58 percent in 1977 to 87 percent in 1982.[1] These figures suggest that although literacy may be a prerequisite for the exercise of democratic rights, dictatorship may contain the seeds of its own undoing. It may not be wise, in the literal sense, to recommend intervention against regimes that are significantly raising the literacy rate of their own people.

The question in these cases is whether a global effort in some countries might be counterproductive at certain stages of their development. More generally, these examples underline at least the importance of tailoring efforts to promote democracy to different cultural traditions and stages of economic development.

The third cause of illegitimate regimes is the systematic repression and denial of human rights—both violations of human dignity and the denial of civil and political rights. There, both Lukashuk and Franck are correct. The first countermeasure they suggest is publicity and, in particular, public condemnation of another government's violation of human rights. One of the precursors of the revolutions of 1989 was Hungary's willingness to condemn Romania's violations of human rights at the United Nations in the summer of 1989. It was an important public statement that one country was willing to stand up in the United Nations and publicize the violations of human rights in another. Similarly, as Lukashuk points out, *glasnost* was an important underpinning of the changes that the world has been witnessing in the Soviet Union.

A second countermeasure is Franck's suggestion of global efforts to promote free and open elections. His notion of essentially shaming undemocratic governments, by having all democratic regimes volunteer for election monitoring, is both ingenious and very promising. However, simply presenting citizens with a taste of the forms of democracy will have little effect if they cannot also grasp its substance. Here Mill's argument has some resonance, although perhaps not exactly as Franck presents it.

The purpose of allowing people to liberate themselves, or to establish their own democratic governments, is not simply to force them to demonstrate their moral fiber. Ultimately, the people themselves must desire to govern themselves, understand what that requires, and have the means to do it.

Franck correctly notes that, particularly with the weapons available to an illegitimate regime today, it is up to the global community to help create the conditions under which democracy can occur. But monitoring elections is clearly only the first step; institutions must also be created that are designed to develop the longer-term infrastructure of democracy. This is the process underway in Eastern Europe. There efforts are being undertaken largely by private parties but also by international institutions to provide education in the party system, in popular mobilization-building techniques, and in grass-roots organization. In short, it is the inculcation of the culture and institutions of political participation.

Therefore, in mounting an effort to develop criteria for intervention against illegitimate regimes, or to promote legitimate regimes, it is worth looking at the causes of illegitimate regimes. Each of the causes listed above—external oppression, economic and social conditions, and the long-term and systematic denial of human rights—arguably calls for a different response. As to the first, there must be an effort to strengthen the norm of non-intervention and to develop criteria for counter-intervention. The second cause requires both economic aid and a global response that takes account of different cultural traditions and stages of economic development. Third, there is a need not only for mechanisms that monitor elections, but also grass-roots efforts to develop lasting institutions of democracy.

In conclusion, it is significant that Franck comments on the connection between democracy and peace: There has been empirical research in political science that has shown that democracies do not go to war with each other—although the War of 1812 is always cited as a counter-example.[2] The great paradox of this research is that Kant's argument does not seem to hold. Democracies are not inherently more pacific—they are quite willing to go to war with non-democracies. However, they do not go to war with each other. The reason is yet to be explained. Tony Smith argues that it is because those who fight, or those who pay the price of fighting, make the decision whether or not to fight.[3] Still, the deeper question is why the people are willing to pay the price to mount wars against non-democratic regimes but not against other democratic regimes. Why is it that with all the anti-Japan hysteria of our times, no one suggests going to war with Japan in the military, not economic, sense? A similar question might be raised with respect to any of the European democracies.

There are many obvious reasons, of course. But Lukashuk touched on one that is particularly important in a global effort to promote legitimate regimes. He comments on the prospective U.S. acquiescence in a Soviet intervention in Romania in 1989: "Only the significant increase in mutual trust between the USSR and the United States has made it possible for the United States to look favorably on potential humanitarian intervention by the USSR."[4] These "new conditions" are critical because they establish the bases under which the fundamental political values of the United States and the Soviet Union are finally beginning to converge.

The growth of trust between the superpowers breaks what Robert Jervis has identified as the "security dilemma," whereby every move made by one state to enhance its security automatically threatens its neighboring states, who take measures to enhance their security, which threatens the original state.[5] To the extent that the spread of democracy breeds openness and openness breeds trust, the international community must indeed make a collective effort to promote democratic regimes through a graduated series of interventionary measures.

Notes

1. THE WORLD ALMANAC AND BOOK OF FACTS 1978, 1982.

2. Doyle, *Kant, Liberal Legacies and Foreign Affairs (pts. 1-2),* 12 Philosophy and Public Affairs, Summer & Fall 1983, at 205-235, 325-353.

3. Smith, *Kant's Political Philosophy: Rechtsstaat or Council Democracy?,* 47 REV. OF POL., April 1985, at 253-80 (particularly at 261-62 and 266-67).

4. Lukashuk, *supra* ch. 13, at 145.

5. R. Jervis, *Cooperation under the Security Dilemma,* WORLD POL., Jan. 30, 1978, at 167-214.

16

Commentary on International Intervention to Promote the Legitimacy of Regimes

Ved Nanda

Professor Thomas Franck calls for multilateral action to promote the legitimacy of regimes. But what regimes are legitimate? How is legitimacy to be determined? Which of the contending regimes is to be considered legitimate, using what criteria? Who enunciates those criteria? Similar questions can be raised in the discussion on intervention and nonintervention.

Franck's proposed criterion for legitimacy is defined in light of the norms in Article 25 of the International Covenant on Civil and Political Rights, which declares a right to political participation. The first clause of that article prescribes the right "to take part in the conduct of public affairs, directly or through freely chosen representatives." The second clause prescribes the right "to vote and to be elected at genuine, periodic elections, which shall be by universal and equal suffrage, and shall be held by secret ballot." This latter right must guarantee "the free expression of the will of the electors." After examining the legislative history of the two clauses, Professor Henry Steiner has concluded that during the drafting period of both the Universal Declaration of Human Rights[1] and the Covenant, greater attention was given to the explicit election clause than to the rather abstract "take part" clause, which was not explored and elaborated by those drafting the Covenant.[2]

The recent formulation adopted at the Copenhagen meeting of the Conference on Security and Cooperation in Europe[3] specifies the necessary minimum of political participation as a prerequisite for states to meet the legitimacy requirement.[4] The constant refrain has been on non-coerced, secret elections, pluralism, and multiparty systems as elements to determine legitimacy.

Franck's concern with the election clause, and the machinery he suggests, are both necessary and commendable. But his recommendation does not go far enough, and it may not ensure and guarantee "the free expression of the will of the electors," which is required by Article 25 of the Covenant. To illustrate, there are such questions as: How significant was the electoral participation? Was there equal access of the different classes and ethnic groups in the political processes? This will necessitate asking further questions about the electoral process and access to mass media. What is the distribution of economic and political power in a society? Is there a competition of views? What is the role of the various centers of power, including elected officials, in a society?

Our inquiry should not be confined simply to non-coerced, secret elections, but to the genuineness of the elections, which are difficult to monitor given the inadequacy of the existing international fact-finding machinery. Free and open elections may not suffice to determine legitimacy; that may be only the first step. And in many circumstances, it may not guarantee the free expression of the will of the electors.

Further, international intervention to "promote the legitimacy" of regimes may require much more than simply monitoring elections and enforcing the entitlement by collective enforcement mechanisms and procedures which are primarily in the nature of economic sanctions, as suggested by Franck. There may need to be devised mechanisms for providing positive assistance in many instances. Is there an obligation to ensure that there is legitimacy in the sense that Franck recommends? Even if international intervention is confined to monitoring the elections, it will take financial resources to do so. Would an international fund be established for this purpose? Will there be efforts to provide economic aid to countries to ensure that some of the causes which are responsible for illegitimacy might be alleviated?

The situations of Fiji, Burma, and China illustrate these problems. In Fiji, military coups in 1987 led to the overthrow of its duly elected government and suspension of its constitution. Subsequently, under its newly drafted constitution all non-native racial groups have been permanently deprived of their right to participate in governing their country. In Burma, despite the resounding victory of the civilian opposition groups in the elections held under the auspices of the military regime, the military has refused to permit the duly-elected representatives to form a government. Instead, it harasses those who were elected and is bent upon crushing them. In China, the events of June 1989, when the military crackdown against the pro-democracy movement occurred, continue to resonate with little prospect of being reversed.

Franck contends that non-coercive efforts on the part of the international community, by denying non-complying governments equal access to international and bilateral privileges and facilities, probably will bring about a change in policies. As seen in the three cases mentioned above, there has not been a great deal of change in these countries' policies. The only discernible change has been in the policies of the external actors—the International Monetary Fund, the World Bank, and the major donor countries. For example, they have decided no longer to continue their sanctions in lending to China and providing assistance to it.

Perhaps if a major power were involved, it would be treated by the application of more favorable standards. On the other hand, if the country is of marginal interest, like Burma or Fiji, it is likely to fall outside the ambit of generally formulated prescriptions. The international community has been almost silent about the situations in Fiji and Burma. Perhaps in the future there will be created the kind of institutional structures and procedures which ensure that these norms can be universally applied and enforced. Franck certainly has hinted at the establishment of the necessary institutions. But in terms of institutional structures and enforcement, there is at present very little to show.

Unilateral military intervention is not a legally justified means to bring about legitimacy of the kind that Franck and Professor Igor Lukashuk mention, that is, to promote democracy and free choice. Professor Oscar Schachter has most appropriately objected to the use of an expansive interpretation of Article 2(4) to topple a repressive regime[5]. It is unacceptable to use force unilaterally to topple a repressive regime or to bring about legitimacy. Such use of force would be a violation of the plain language of the U.N. Charter. Schachter has suggested that an expansive interpretation of the Charter has not been accepted in the United Nations, and I have given similar reasons elsewhere why it ought not to be accepted as a desirable alternative in the international arena.[6]

What about collective intervention to address, for example, Iraq's invasion of Kuwait? What is an appropriate recourse for the international community? Lukashuk mentions the examples of Pol Pot and Idi Amin, which are extreme cases. Lukashuk argues that there must be collective action to address such situations, since they fall under the rubric of humanitarian intervention. In extreme cases like these, unilateral military intervention as a last resort would be a justifiable response under international law.

The nature and scope of justifiable intervention would vary and proportionality would have to be met. Furthermore, it must be prompt action of short duration, without affecting the governmental structures, and must be subject to review by the world community through its established structures at the United Nations.

The establishment of a U.N. parliamentary assembly, which Lukashuk suggests, is certainly an ingenious and innovative idea, but at present in the United Nations there would be no support for such action. The USSR and the United States would be among the first to object to the exercise of such a function by the United Nations.

Notes

1. *Universal Declaration of Human Rights*, G.A. Res 217 A (III) of 10 Dec. 1948.

2. *See* Steiner, *Political Participation as a Human Right*, 1 HARV. HUMAN RTS. YB. 77 (1988).

3. *Conference on Security and Cooperation in Europe*, 29 I.L.M. 1305 (1990).

4. 29 I.L.M. 1306 (1990).

5. *See* Schachter, *The Right of States to Use Armed Force*, 82 MICH. L. REV. 1620 (1984); Schachter, *The Legality of Pro-Democratic Invasion*, 78 AM. J. INT'L L. 645 (1984).

6. *See* Nanda, *The Validity of United States Intervention in Panama*, 84 AM. J. INT'L L. 494 (1990).

17

An Inquiry into the Legitimacy of Humanitarian Intervention

Tom J. Farer

Finding the Law: On the Importance of Where You Begin

At this extraordinary moment in history—when so many ideas, relationships, and institutions which only yesterday seemed solid, dissolve before us—at least two things endure in world politics. One is the conspicuous role of force. A second is the conspicuous disagreement among putative experts about the conditions for its legitimate use. We disagree not only or primarily about the applicability of received doctrine to stipulated facts. We disagree about the doctrine itself.

In their discourse concerning the propriety of so-called "humanitarian intervention"—by which I mean the threat or use of force by one state against another for the purpose of terminating the latter's abuse of its own nationals—Anglo-American scholars noisily parade their differences. According to Professor Anthony D'Amato, for instance, there are at least "three paradigmatic cases justifying humanitarian intervention...[They] are genocide, slavery, and widespread torture."[1] On the other hand, the British scholar, Michael Akehurst, finds no persuasive grounds for claiming that humanitarian intervention is legitimate under any circumstances.[2] The fault line of scholarly opinion is not the Atlantic Ocean. Professor Oscar Schachter has written that "governments by and large (and most jurists) would not assert a right to forcible intervention to protect the nationals of another country from atrocities carried out in that country."[3] On a separate occasion he sharply rejected Professor Michael Reisman's slightly broader claim that one state may invade another to displace tyrannical governments,[4] a claim echoed by D'Amato following the United States' occupation of Panama in 1989.[5]

These disputes over the legal status of humanitarian intervention sometimes coincide with and appear heavily influenced by the disputants' divergent approaches to the question of how to identify any international legal norm. The celebrants of what I will call the classical view display the following characteristics: while recognizing that states can establish and alter norms both through explicit agreements normally expressed in written texts and implicit agreements manifested in practice, they tend in their epistemology toward a rather strict separation of these two processes; when attempting to identify norms arising from explicit agreements they presume that the parties had an original intention which can be discovered primarily through textual analysis and which, in the absence of some unforeseen change in circumstances, must be respected until the agreement has expired according to its terms or been replaced by mutual consent; when attempting to identify norms from implicit agreement, they employ formal, cumulative categories of proof which, among other things, deemphasize the relative power of states and imply a high threshold below which alleged norms are entirely without legal character.

While the great majority of British and Continental scholars accept with varying degrees of zeal the doctrines of classicism, many of the most influential scholars in the United States are, if not votaries, at least tributaries of a jurisprudential scheme associated originally with the Yale Law School and particularly with the seminal figures of Professors Myres McDougal and Harold Lasswell.[6] At a minimum that scheme requires reversal of the tendencies I impute to the classical school. Realists, as I will call the largely American schismatics, see explicit and implicit agreements, formal texts, and state behavior as being in a condition of effervescent interaction, unceasingly creating, modifying, and replacing norms. Texts themselves are but one among a large number of means for ascertaining original intention. Moreover, realists postulate an accelerating contraction in the capacity and the authority of original intention to govern state behavior. Indeed, original intention does not govern at any point in time. For original intention has no intrinsic authority. The past is relevant only to the extent that it helps us to identify currently prevailing attitudes about the propriety of a government's acts and omissions.[7]

The schism between hard-core classicists and realists has added dimensions and implications. While the former seem to treat all states as equal participants in the process of law-making, the latter adopt a frankly hierarchical view of the process: Politically influential countries have, as it were, more votes in elections to determine the contents of the law. A differential weighting of national positions is a corollary of discrepant conceptions of the legal expert's vocation.

Classicists aspire to identify and publicize a qualitatively distinct corpus of norms for evaluating state behavior and to maintain a system of procedural norms for modification of the behavioral ones as alterations occur in the consensus among states about the requirements of international order. They imagine themselves guardians of a symbol that contributes distinctively to the maintenance of order in an anarchical system.[8] Adulterate the symbol and anarchy slides toward chaos.

Adulteration can occur in a variety of ways. One is by disparaging the capacity of language to express intention. Another is by disintegrating intention, that is, rhetorically transforming intention from a sharply conceived act of will into a complex semi-conscious hierarchy of desires and inadequately imagined means for their attainment at various points in a future dimly perceived.

But the worst form of adulteration results from the constant revision of standards to heighten their congruence with discrepant behavior. In this way acts that would otherwise appear delinquent are alchemized into harbingers of revised standards. Indeed they become instruments of revision. And thus law is transformed from a stern judge of political action into a pathetic dependent.

Classicists want to preserve law's contribution to order by protecting its autonomy from ephemeral shifts in power and interest. Realists want to save it from irrelevance.[9] D'Amato illustrates their intentions and methods by postulating two sets of rules which he calls, respectively, "X" and "Y." The X rules

> are those that governments profess and proclaim to be following when they undertake particular actions or restraints in the international arena. These governmental statements typically comport with academic versions of what international law requires [by which he presumably means the Classicist version]. On the other hand, the [Y] rules are those that actually cohere with the actions or restraints of the acting government....The reason that governments typically do not proclaim the Y theory is that the academics expect them to proclaim the X theory and would charge that the Y theory would be a governmental admission of violation of international law. But these are simply academic, or at best strategic, considerations; in fact, unbiased reasonable observers would agree that the operative theory is Y.[10]

It is from the actual behavior of states, D'Amato declares, that we can induce the considerations which inform their notions about permissible behavior. These considerations can then be expressed by scholars in a normative idiom that clarifies and facilitates discussion and understanding of the operational codes which at any given moment are the real ordering elements of international relations.

One salient methodological implication of this conception of the scholar's task is, as I have noted above, to deemphasize what governments say, however solemnly, in favor of what they do. The researcher, D'Amato writes,

> should be highly skeptical about...the briefs [governments] file in a court or arbitral tribunal, the opinions of their attorneys general or their foreign offices. The researcher should also be skeptical of protests by one government or another; the filing of a protest does not mean that the protesting government means or believes what it says. And skepticism is also a good antidote to the all too easy tendency to view General Assembly resolutions, or Security Council condemnations of state actions, as expressive of international rules of law. Sometimes a Security Council condemnation that is not followed by any forcible action on the part of the Council is another way of saying to the ostensibly offending state, "We have to condemn you verbally, but don't worry, we're not going to do anything about it." In such cases, the lack of action by the Security Council may be a more eloquent way of approving the Y set of rules than its verbal recommendation reciting the X set.[11]

In this last statement D'Amato offers a convenient hint about the practical relationship between the wars of the jurisprudes and the question of humanitarian intervention's legal status. The connection in brief is that the case for the contemporary legitimacy of humanitarian intervention is harder to make convincingly if one adheres to the classical school. The acolytes of realism have a somewhat easier time.

Weighing the Evidence

All of his school's tendencies contribute to the classicist's burden. Its doctrines concerning the interpretation and normative influence of texts and the appropriate method for deriving norms from the practice of states make the arguably relevant acts and agreements resist recruitment to the service of humanitarian intervention's claims.

One can readily grasp the weight of that burden by first employing the classical idiom to state the strongest possible case *against* legality. It rests firmly on certain language in the U.N. Charter considered in light of the overall text, the *travaux préparatoires,* and the circumstances and atmosphere surrounding and closely following the Charter's adoption. Since the arguments are familiar to most scholars in the field, I will simply sketch them for persons whose primary interests lie elsewhere.[12]

The key words are, of course, to be found in Article 2(4) of the Charter, where all member states are enjoined to "refrain in their international relations from the threat or use of force against the territorial integrity or political independence of any state or in any other manner inconsistent with the Purposes of the United Nations," and in Article 51's declaration that, "Nothing in the present Charter shall impair the inherent right of individual or collective self-defense if an armed attack occurs against a Member of the United Nations...."

During the four and one-half decades since the Charter's adoption, scholars have exposed every grain of ambiguity and contradiction embedded in these clumsily drawn directives. For instance, as Derek Bowett was quick to note,[13] the word "inherent" could conceivably refer to the totality of past occasions when a leading European state had without demurrer from its peers invoked self-defense as a justification for its use of force. On a large number of such occasions the self-justifying state was not responding to an armed attack but rather enforcing other interests. Hence if "inherent" were deemed to incorporate precedent, Article 51 was self-contradicting.

That left textual analysts with at least two alternatives. They could follow Bowett and treat the reference to "armed attack" as exemplary at best. Or they could treat "inherent" as a way of emphasizing the retained right by stating in effect that even if a state attempted to surrender the right to defend itself against attack, it would fail because that right was immanent in the idea of sovereignty.

Bowett defended his choice—unconvincingly, I think—by reference to that interpretative canon of classicism which establishes a refutable presumption that states have not consented to surrender important rights, in this case forceful self-help. However plausible in the generality of cases, it seemed inappropriate as a guide to interpreting a constitutional document purporting to define a new international order for a geopolitically transformed world. Moreover, Bowett himself appeared to concede that the founding members had intended at least to limit significantly the dimensions of self-help. Probably the most serious objection to Bowett's approach, however, is that while it was possible to find alternative utility for the word "inherent," Bowett's construction deprived the words "if an armed attack occurs" of any plausible function, a result obnoxious to the classical canons.

Article 2(4) offered greater latitude for exegetical rivalry. Those scholars eager to legitimate the use of force for ends beyond self-defense from an actual or imminent attack seized on the apparently qualifying reference to territorial integrity, political independence, and U.N.

"Purposes."

Champions of humanitarian intervention found special comfort in the reference to Purposes: The Charter Preamble explicitly lists the advancement of human rights as one of the organization's purposes; Article 55 both provides the purpose with a little body and connects it to the conditions for realizing peaceful relations among nations, a second and in the view of many the central purpose of the organization; and in Article 56 the "Members pledge themselves to take joint and separate action in co-operation with the Organization" for the achievement of higher standards of living, full employment, the universal respect for and observance of human rights and fundamental freedoms for all without distinction as to race, sex, language, or religion, and the other goals enumerated in Article 55.

An initial if slight obstacle to legitimating humanitarian intervention by wrapping it in the second part of Article 2(4) was the *travaux*. For the *travaux* appeared to evidence a belief within the drafting committee that, by virtue of its relative specificity, the referential language would reinforce rather than narrow the intended ban on force as an instrument of statecraft.[14]

A more serious objection to this well-intentioned legitimation exercise is that it ignores persuasive evidence of a distinct hierarchy of purposes in the Charter as originally conceived. Anyone who considers with some measure of objectivity the Charter's normative logic, its allocation of coercive jurisdiction, its omissions, as well as the preferences manifested by most participants in the drafting process and their immediately subsequent behavior, cannot help concluding that the promotion of human rights ranked far below the protection of national sovereignty and the maintenance of peace as organizational goals.

Note, to begin with, that despite reiterating its concern for maintaining peace, the Charter explicitly concedes a right of self-defense and sharply limits the power of the Security Council. The dominant states at the time, confident of their control of the Council, might, after all, have given it coercive authority in connection with all the principles and purposes of the organization.

The Security Council can legitimate or itself employ force only in case of a threat to the peace, a breach of the peace, or an act of aggression. Nothing in the *travaux* suggests that the parties envisioned a government's treatment of its own nationals as likely to catalyze a threat or breach. Nor had they much reason to do so. Historical examples were rare at best. And the few precedents enumerated in certain scholarly works were both susceptible to alternative classification and the product of a vanished phenomenon—a polyglot and decaying and non-Christian Empire with European subjects.[15]

Taken together with the so-called "veto" power and Article 2(7)'s explicit denial of U.N. jurisdiction with respect to matters of a primarily domestic character, these structural elements and normative arrangements imply that the ultimate shared value of the member states remained what it had been for the two previous centuries, namely national sovereignty.

That human rights had only a tenuous place among the concerns of the founding members was not simply implied. When faced with the proposal to include a bill of rights in the new Charter, a majority of states rejected it.[16] The rapid activation of a Human Rights Commission does, of course, support the view that the Charter's references to human rights were not wholly cosmetic. But the Commission's immediate denial of any right to consider the thousands of individual petitions for help that had already reached the U.N. Secretariat[17] constitutes an additional reason for the view that the founding states did not regard a state's treatment of its nationals, however egregious, as grounds for violent intervention.

The nub of the matter, then, is that if one deems the original intention of the founding states to be controlling with respect to the legitimate occasions for the use of force, then humanitarian intervention is illegal.

Of course, one may argue that with respect to the interpretation of legislative texts, intentionality has a dual and hence uncertain character. The author or authors of any such texts no doubt had a conscious intention to mitigate or resolve the problems to which they had alluded. To that end they had sketched certain strategies which appeared efficacious in the light of the world as they knew it. But even if we succeed in identifying beyond reasonable dispute what they intended to accomplish, there will remain the question of their intentions with respect to the interpretive discretion of future generations.

Often the question is translated into a query about how the founding fathers would have wanted their words construed had they envisioned the world in which the act of interpretation is occurring. Thus posed the question seems disingenuous until we achieve some form of necromancy. We can, of course, inquire into the deepest values of the founders and their most general principles. But we cannot disaggregate those values and principles from the historical conditions in which they were formed; by hypothesis those conditions have been radically altered. Given altered conditions, the same people might have had different values. This is just another way of saying that they would not be the same people. Moreover, the effort to express values in everyday life invariably involves complicated tradeoffs as, for example, between liberty and order. Trying to extrapolate from the tradeoffs they made in vastly different circumstances is an enterprise which leaves the extrapolators with a wide margin of discretion.

In effect, realism responds to the Sisyphean difficulties associated with attempting to keep original intention current by dispensing with original intention, not immediately, to be sure, but progressively. As noted earlier, the text is invoked, interpreted, ignored. The text may tell us with fair accuracy what the governing elites who adopted it wanted at that time. Study of the text's subsequent adventures is the only way to determine what elites want now. Language, structure, and *travaux* will in varying degrees influence practice; that and only that is their enduring utility or, if one prefers, their authority.

Members of the classical school concede the utility of subsequent practice to interpretation, although they are constrained to invert the temporal value of practice so that the most recent in time is least valuable, since it is least likely to register original intent. A classicist will concede as well that subsequent practice could reveal an implicit agreement to alter or replace the original text. But in order to sustain the stability of formal agreements, a principal aim of classicism, its adherents must impose a heavy burden of proof on parties claiming that such a change has occurred. *I fear that burden cannot be sustained for the purposes of legitimating humanitarian intervention under the Charter.*

I have reviewed the rather abundant instances of interstate violence since the Charter's adoption. The overlap between them and instances of unspeakable crimes committed by governments against their own nationals is modest. If, as D'Amato claims, "widespread torture" is a paradigmatic case for justified intervention,[18] a case where the international community in a sense has issued a standing invitation to well-armed Samaritans, one must say that it has rarely if ever been accepted.

The reports of Amnesty International and other highly credible organizations engaged in the defense of human rights document widespread torture in a large number of countries that appear blissfully unaware of their vulnerability to legitimate intervention. Turkey, for instance, has been repeatedly cited for the use of torture virtually as standard operating procedure in investigations of both ordinary and political crimes.[19] A recent study finds a similar pattern in the Mexican criminal justice system.[20] I mention these two countries not because I think they have particularly bad records, but rather because they are so evidently not perceived as eligible for intervention.

Even slaughters of near genocidal proportions do not consistently induce a substantial number of states to call for armed rescue, much less to attempt it themselves. The globe's governing elites have been mute in instances where the delinquent among them were comparatively powerful: One thinks of the Indonesian campaign to suppress opposition in East Timor, an *a fortiori* case since in that instance slaughter bonded with aggression against a small but unquestionably sovereign people. They have also been mute in instances, such as the massacre of the Hutu people in Burundi, where a small force from any high-technology state could have disabled the delinquent regime in a matter of hours.

I submit that there is not a single case in the entire post-war era where one state has intervened in another for the exclusive purpose of halting mass murder, much less any other gross violation of human rights. This fact obviously does not settle the issue. The question is whether states have a choice; no one claims they have a duty. Still, the absence of even a few murmured threats is not entirely without probative value.

What we do have in the post-war era are a few instances where an intervening state invoked or at least could have invoked the target government's thuggery as one among several justifications for its initiative. Neither the claiming behavior of the intervenor nor the international community's response to claims and facts lends strong support to the view that humanitarian interventions now enjoy broad tolerance.

Three cases—India in East Pakistan,[21] Tanzania in Uganda,[22] Vietnam in Cambodia[23]—appear on every scholar's list because at the time of the respective invasions the target regime's crimes were notorious. Hence, all three invaders had solid ground on which to rest a claim of legitimate humanitarian intervention. Yet they ignored the doctrine, choosing instead to claim self-defense from an armed attack, a claim not one of them could persuasively sustain. Their choice hardly suggests confidence in the exculpatory power of a humanitarian motive.

Nevertheless, these cases are not fatal to the doctrine's status. Third parties assessed each intervention differently. Although a number of states criticized Tanzania, neither the Organization of African Unity nor the United Nations took any formal action. India needed a Soviet veto to block a Security Council demand for its withdrawal prior to the defeat of Pakistani forces. A similar resolution passed the General Assembly by an enormous majority including most of the non-aligned movement. Still, India was able to persist without serious threat of widely-supported sanctions and the result of its work—an independent East Pakistan—was quickly recognized and admitted to the United Nations. Vietnam, on the other hand, after failing to comply with a demand for withdrawal, was battered by severe economic sanctions and bled by means of sanctuary for and military assistance to the murderers it had displaced.

An obvious factual difference between Vietnam's behavior and that of India and Tanzania is that the latter quickly withdrew behind their original frontiers. By remaining in Cambodia to support the government it had imposed, Vietnam appeared indictable for an ongoing violation of the country's political independence and territorial integrity. Moreover, the people it had installed were a breakaway faction of the Khmer Rouge movement. Having held important positions in the terrorist government, they were implicated in its crimes. And while they did not slaughter on the previous scale, they showed no disposition to establish a model of humanitarian order.

But despite its own tarnished record, the post-invasion regime seemed a long step up from Pol Pot. And given the geopolitical setting—intense superpower competition and Chinese-Soviet enmity, the exhausted condition of Cambodian society, and the continued coherence and zeal of Pol Pot's cadres—the Vietnamese Army may then have been the only plausible means for preventing a Khmer Rouge restoration. If those were the only two plausible options for years after the invasion, then does broad-based international rejection of Vietnam's presence signify the continuing normative primacy of sovereignty over human rights whenever the two values clash harshly?

Not necessarily. Suppose that once the Vietnamese had displaced Pol Pot and his cronies, many states concluded that a Vietnamese occupation of indefinite duration was not the only way of barring the Khmer Rouge. Suppose it was widely assumed that if Vietnam were prepared to see a neutral non-communist government in its neighbor, then Hanoi could have prevailed on Moscow to work with the West, China, and the Association of South-East Asian Nations to create such a government under the sort of transitional arrangements that are finally taking shape today. Under this hypothesis, human rights and national independence would not be competing values. Any regime acceptable to the West and established under U.N. auspices would have had to acquire an electoral mandate.

As epistemic units (to borrow Michael Reisman's useful phrase),[24] all international incidents can be minced into their singular facts so that they end up standing for nothing but themselves. Claimed examples of humanitarian intervention may be especially susceptible to this process because they neither appear nor are claimed to be driven solely by philanthropic passion. A mixture of motives and consequences undoubtedly influences the way third parties characterize and otherwise respond. The resulting adulteration of the precedent frustrates efforts to extract a generally accepted, normative meaning. It conversely encourages tendentious imputations of significance.

The U.S. interventions in Panama and in Grenada are cases in point. Neither could be characterized as a response to mass murder, slavery, or even widespread and systematized torture. Both involved the forcible replacements of de facto governments unresponsive to the human right of self-government recognized in the U.N. Covenant on Civil and Political Rights (Article 25) and the American Convention on Human Rights (Article 23). In each case the U.S. government listed humanitarian concerns among the reasons for action but in neither case did it suggest that they were a sufficient justification or a primary cause. Hence, for purposes of appraising the legal status of humanitarian intervention, authoritative denunciation—by the Organization of American States (O.A.S.) in the case of the Panamanian intervention,[25] by the U.N. General Assembly in the Grenadan case[26]—can be dismissed as irrelevant. Or one could argue that they evidence intolerance of pro-democracy interventions to end mass slaughter. Or, since no action followed denunciation and the cases have not reappeared on the agenda of either organization, one could follow D'Amato and say that when the community reaction over time is properly decoded, we discover an impressive tolerance for the use of force to displace authoritarian regimes. In other words, these precedents provide large playgrounds in which scholars may frolic.

Precisely because state practice is at best ambiguous, it provides very flimsy support for any claim that the restraints of the Charter have been superseded by a new consensus concerning the use of force to protect human rights. So adherents of the classical school eager to legitimate humanitarian intervention are driven to strained interpretations of key Charter articles or an equally problematic *rebus sic stantibus* argument that the Cold War represented so great a change in the conditions anticipated by the member states as to nullify their obligations.[27]

How liberating it is, then, to flee the straitened confines of the classical idiom and to romp in the measureless fields of realism. Now you are free from the suffocating embrace of the past with its heavy burdens of proof, free as well from the tyranny of words and majorities. From the backs of powerful states you may skip lightly over the wall between law and normative preference, between the law that was and the law that you ardently hope is to be.

Is intervention in cases of genocide, slavery, and widespread torture already sanctified by law or in the process of so becoming? "[C]ustomary law can change," D'Amato has written, "and state practice may add a fourth paradigmatic case to the list. The U.S. intervention in Grenada...and the...policy to remove the Sandinista regime in Nicaragua may be steps along the way towards a new rule of customary international law."[28] But he later writes:

> [T]he truly operative rules generated by the customary practice of states...are the rules that in reality accommodate the most deeply felt interests of the community of states. *If* concern for human rights is one of those deeply felt interests, that concern will be manifested in the *emerging* rules of custom even if those new rules are at variance with received wisdom.[29]

Realists seek "law" by foraging for it among the shifting preferences and tolerances—however inarticulate, informal, and self-characterized—of all the heterogeneous actors in world politics. Classicists, by contrast, look for law not down in the raw stuff of elite subjectivities but rather in the inherited forms that aggregate those subjectivities into normative summations. If law is the raw material itself, then of course it is very much a matter of degree, a continuum from raging dissensus to widespread but never perfect agreement. From that conception stems the loss of definition implied by D'Amato's formulation.

Certain realists concede the loss while celebrating what they see as consequential gains. In defending a transfer of emphasis from cases to "incidents"—a transfer required by realism's central notions about law and the tasks of legal specialists—Reisman concedes that "in recognizing the potential desuetude of the formal legal order, that approach may, in the short term, exacerbate" the tendency of elites to jettison the rational and deliberative elements of lawmaking. However, he adds, "insofar as it aids in diagnosis, it may be hoped that the incidents approach [to identifying the apparent normative expectations of elites] will be a positive step in restoring rational, deliberate lawmaking in the international community."[30]

Toward Consensus

Perhaps the most important first step in the direction indicated by Reisman would be initiation within the community of legal scholars of a more open and nuanced discourse. We need more candor about the element of discretion in the choice of means for determining what is lawful. We need more candor about the reasons for and consequences of the choices that are made. Without that candor, efforts to enhance the potency of legal scholars in the decision-making process may have reverse effect by heightening the perception of them as tractable beauticians for *raison d'état.*

Why do scholars of the classical school adhere to its received formulas, in the words of H.L.A. Hart, its "rules of recognition"?[31] Why in the case of agreements do they insist on the centrality of the text and the durability of original intention? Why in the case of customary law do they insist on a showing of a widespread coincident practice and evidence that the practice is motivated by a sense of legal obligation? And why do they attribute such importance to words in the face of discrepant deeds? More generally, why did they not follow the lead of contemporary political scientists who, in their explorations of the network of principles, norms, rules, and decision-making institutions which help stabilize state relationships, show little if any interest in the origins or formal normative character of the network's components?[32]

In his critique of Michael Akehurst, D'Amato declares that "[i]t is surely more difficult to do this kind of international law research [in other words, the microscopic tracking of state interactions and the induction from them of normative propositions] than to follow Akehurst and simply take governmental statements at face value."[33] D'Amato's implication that sloth may be the answer to the questions just posed is not very persuasive. A more credible explanation is that classicists respond to the demands of practical statecraft which has for centuries employed and apparently seen utility in a sharply defined distinction between formal and informal arrangements for reducing the volatility of international politics.

Classicists work to maintain the integrity of an idiom specially crafted for the communication of desire and intention to achieve an unusual degree of stability with respect to a particular set of issues. The idiom provides an economical and relatively unambiguous way for political leaders to communicate this intention not only to each other but also to their bureaucracies and polities and, of course, to third parties.

Among its other virtues, the idiom functions to precipitate debate and reflection within the concerned societies about the consistency of the proposed arrangement with national interest. The more open the society, the more extensive the consultation. If, after this deliberative exercise, the parties go forward, it follows that powerful domestic constituencies have been convinced that the proposed arrangement is desirable. That conviction will serve thereafter as a restraint on temptations at the peak of the political hierarchy to violate the expectations of other parties in order to exploit opportunities for unilateral gains arising from a new conjuncture. Restraint arises as well from identifying the new arrangement as law since it thereby acquires some of the symbolic power that term enjoys within national societies. While the process I have described is much more subtle and elongated in the case of norms arising from practice rather than from single texts, it is not qualitatively different.

Realism's appropriation of the idiom and disparagement of its conservators threatens to impair a traditional instrument of statecraft while at the same time reducing the benefits which should flow from the realist's insights and efforts. With its aspiration to universality of customary law and its associated bright-line distinction between law and mere development toward law, classicism tends to obscure significant differences among elites over the law's real content. Realism has the tools and the vocation to expose them and therefore to sharpen expectations and to clarify discord over causal assumptions and values. But if the realist, seeking to marshall support for one among several competing views of acceptable behavior, summarizes the results of his or her inquiries in the conventional idiom, real differences are obscured.

This, I submit, is what has happened in our debates over humanitarian intervention. D'Amato has conceded that the elites who drafted and approved the Charter intended to preclude invasions in defense of human rights.[34] Nor has he (nor as far as I can tell any other advocate of humanitarian intervention) claimed that, if the question were put to them frankly, a large majority of governments would declare it lawful. To be sure, the question has not been openly addressed. And opportunities for expressing a clear position—for example, when considering the definition of aggression or the Declaration on Friendly Relations—have been ignored. Nevertheless, I am confident that few if any scholars doubt that on a clear up or down vote, the majority of states would vote no. My own reading of the evidence, particularly the U.N. and O.A.S. votes on Panama, Grenada, and the bombing of Libya, detects a strong continuing preference for limiting unilateral recourse to force to the defense of territorial integrity and political independence.

But that fact, if it is a fact, should not end the normative discussion. Here I am very much a realist. Votes and declarations are only one way in which states express themselves. They are not, as D'Amato suggests, extracted by fear of the condemnatory power of scholars.[35] They are, rather, efforts to maintain the basic tilt of Charter law. But behind the broad general preference, states evidence participation in complex, highly nuanced codes of mitigation reflected in differential response to cases which, when described without reference to all contextual elements, seem equally to exceed the Charter limits on the legitimate use of force.

Even liberal democratic states have seemed reluctant openly to impute legitimacy to humanitarian intervention. The concern they share with potential objects is abuse of any conceded expansion of legitimate force beyond the imperious necessity of self-defense. As a practical result, any state or group of states prepared to defend themselves on that ground must bear a heavy burden of extenuation. Vietnam failed. India and Tanzania were more successful. If the putschists in Grenada had begun a general massacre of the population and if the United States did not at the time of its invasion seem dedicated to the elimination of all radical governments in the Western Hemisphere, and oriented in general toward unilateral rather than collective measures, Washington would have been more successful in rallying support, particularly among its allies.

The factors that will govern response to a justification grounded in concern for human rights have been enumerated in many scholarly works.[36] Obviously, they include exhaustion of alternative remedies, severity of the human rights violations, the diversity of the intervening forces, the relative prominence of the humanitarian motive, the effect on human rights in the target country, and the consequences of intervention for its political independence and territorial integrity. The last factor is particularly troubling. For usually there is a connection between the severity of violations and the irremediable character of the delinquent regime. Should any government risk the lives of its own citizens to achieve a temporary cessation of a slaughter likely to be renewed? If we believe that in certain ineffable cases the dangerous expedient of humanitarian intervention should be attempted, we should concede the probable necessity of reconstructing the political order that created the imperious necessity.

That every effort should be made to operate within multilateral frameworks when contemplating intervention and, *a fortiori*, reconstruction hardly requires saying. But for the past two decades in the Western Hemisphere and for longer elsewhere, the prospect for doing so was extremely bleak. In this respect as in many others, we see auguries of change: the message flashed to Moscow from Paris and Washington during the Romanian uprising that Soviet intervention would not be unwelcome; the joint appeal for intervention in Liberia issued by European ambassadors; the subsequent intervention in Liberia by African governments.

As D'Amato rightly says, the claims of human rights are becoming clamorous and more effective. The carapace of national sovereignty is one of the many shapes beginning to dissolve. The law, even as traditionally perceived and proved, is changing. Our task as scholars is to expedite the changes we observe without at the same time stripping international law of those distinctive qualities that have made it a useful instrument of conservative statecraft in a still anarchical world. For the order that statecraft serves is a necessary albeit insufficient condition of human dignity.

Notes

1. D'AMATO, INTERNATIONAL LAW: PROCESS AND PROSPECT 226 (1987).
2. M. Akehurst, *Humanitarian Intervention* in INTERVENTION IN WORLD POLITICS (H. Bull ed. 1984).
3. O. Schachter, *The Right of States to Use Armed Force*, 82 MICH. L. REV. 1620, 1629 (1984).
4. *See* Reisman, *Coercion and Self-Determination: Construing Charter Article 2(4)*, 74 AM. J. INT'L L. 642 (1984), and Schachter, *The Legality of Pro-Democratic Invasion*, *id.* at 645.
5. *See Agora: U.S. Forces in Panama*, 84 AM. J. INT'L L. 494 (1990).
6. Among the principal works applying and elaborating the jurisprudential views of the Yale School are the following: M. MCDOUGAL & ASSOCIATES, STUDIES IN WORLD PUBLIC ORDER (1960); M. MCDOUGAL & F. FELICIANO, LAW AND MINIMUM WORLD ORDER (1961); M. MCDOUGAL & W. BURKE, THE PUBLIC ORDER OF THE OCEANS (1962); M. MCDOUGAL & H. LASSWELL, THE INTERPRETATION OF AGREEMENTS AND WORLD PUBLIC ORDER (1967); M. MCDOUGAL & L. CHEN, HUMAN RIGHTS AND WORLD ORDER (1980); M. MCDOUGAL & W.M. REISMAN, INTERNATIONAL LAW IN CONTEMPORARY PERSPECTIVE: THE ORDER OF THE WORLD COMMUNITY (1981).
7. *Compare* Michael Reisman's remark that

> International lawyers...persist in constructing their normative universe from texts. Thus they confine their attention to sources of international law that were either merely ceremonial at their inception, or that, although animated by more normative intentions when they were created, have ceased to be congruent with expectations of authority and control held by effective elites.

INTERNATIONAL INCIDENTS 6-7 (M. Reisman & A. Willard eds. 1988) [hereinafter "Reisman"]. *See also* M. McDougal, *Agora: McDougal-Lasswell Redux*, 82 AM. J. INT'L L. 41, 55 (1988)("[Recommended intellectual procedures include the] examination of past trends in decision upon problems raising comparable policies *for whatever wisdom they may yield about options in decision and the value consequences of different options*." (emphasis added)).

8. The conception of interstate relations as an "anarchical system" was skillfully elaborated by H. Bull in THE ANARCHICAL SOCIETY (1971).

9. *See* MCDOUGAL & REISMAN, *supra* note 6, at 6:

> The reasons for the diminished relevance of international lawyers are attributable less to the system...than to the international lawyers themselves and the jurisprudential framework within which they operate. For key areas of public international law, international lawyers make themselves irrelevant by failing to identify what international law in this context is and by failing to report it to those who are responsible....The discrepancy [between international legal description and elite expectations] is so painfully obvious that, outside the small circle of international lawyers, it brings discredit upon the very notion of international law.

10. *Supra* note 1, at 227-228.

11. *Id.* at 229-231.

12. For a more extended review of the competing claims, *see* T. Farer, *Law and War*, in THE FUTURE OF THE INTERNATIONAL ORDER: CONFLICT AND MANAGEMENT 15 (C. Black & R. Falk ed. 1981).

13. D. BOWETT, SELF-DEFENSE IN INTERNATIONAL LAW 11-20 & 80-101 (1958).

14. *See* Farer, *supra* note 12, at 32-33.

15. *See, e.g.*, Pogany, *Humanitarian Intervention in International Law: The French Intervention in Syria Reexamined*, 35 INT'L & COMP. L. Q. 182 (1981).

16. P. Meyer, *The International Bill of Rights: A Brief History*, in THE INTERNATIONAL BILL OF HUMAN RIGHTS xxiii (P. Williams ed. 1981).

17. *Report of the First Session*, U.N. Doc. E/259 paras. 21, 22 (1947).

18. *See supra* note 1.

19. *See, e.g.*, TURKEY, AMNESTY INT'L REP. 238 (1990).

20. MINNESOTA LAWYERS INT'L HUMAN RIGHTS COMM., PAPER PROTECTION: VIOLATIONS AND THE MEXICAN CRIMINAL JUSTICE SYSTEM (July 1990).

21. *See, e.g.*, Franck & Rodley, *After Bangladesh: The Law of Humanitarian Intervention by Military Force*, 67 AM. J. INT'L L. 275 (1973).

22. *See, e.g.*, Hassan, *Realpolitik in International Law: After Tanzanian-Ugandan Conflict: "Humanitarian Intervention" Reexamined*, 17 WILLAMETTE L. REV. 859 (1981).

23. *See generally* F. TESON, HUMANITARIAN INTERVENTION (1988).

24. Reisman, *supra* note 7, at 8.

25. *See* OAS Boletin de Noticias, Dec. 22, 1989.

26. G.A. Res. 38/7, U.N. Doc. A/38/L.8 (1983).

27. Well before the end of World War II, important participants in the U.S. foreign policy establishment had concluded that the post-war relationship with the USSR was likely to be tense. Hence, they could not have been surprised by the

immediate lack of cooperation in the Security Council between the wartime allies. By definition, *rebus sic stantibus* is inapplicable to conditions that the parties could reasonably have foreseen. *See generally* J.L. GADDIS, STRATEGIES OF CONTAINMENT, esp. at 10-15 (1982).

28. *See supra* note 1, at 228.

29. *Id.* at 287.

30. Reisman, *supra* note 7, at 22.

31. HART, THE CONCEPT OF LAW (1961).

32. *See, e.g.,* INTERNATIONAL REGIMES (S. Krasner ed. 1983).

33. *See supra* note 1, at 231.

34. *Id.* at 54.

35. *See supra* note 1, at 227.

36. *See, e.g.,* Bazyler, *Reexamining the Doctrine of Humanitarian Intervention in Light of the Atrocities in Kampuchea and Ethiopia,* 23 STAN. J. INT'L L. 547, 597-611 (1987); Fonteyne, *The Customary International Law Doctrine of Humanitarian Intervention: Its Current Validity Under the U.N. Charter,* 4 CAL. WEST. L. J. 203, 258-268 (1974).

18

Human Rights and Humanitarian Intervention

Vladimir Kartashkin

In accordance with modern international law everyone is now entitled to certain basic human rights under U.N. conventions, regional treaties, and bilateral agreements. However, the question of the rights of individuals living abroad—so-called aliens—seems to be different. Even today their rights are restrictive.

From the time international law emerged and began to develop, relations between the state and its citizens were viewed as an internal affair of the state. At the same time a nation's unilateral use of force, including the prosecution of war, to protect the life and property of its citizens located on another state's territory was considered legitimate.

However, it was not always so. In the very earliest period of human history anyone outside of his family or tribe was regarded as one to whom the ordinary standards did not apply. As a matter of fact the alien was literally a non-person in ancient Greece and Rome. Not only was he unable to participate in political affairs, he could not marry a citizen, own property, or have access to legal machinery.

In the Middle Ages the situation became somewhat different, to a certain degree because Christianity emphasized the inherent dignity and equality before God of all human beings. The alien, therefore, was no longer a non-person in the rigid sense that he had been in ancient Greece. But, as a matter of fact, the aliens still did not enjoy rights which had been provided for nationals. In the case of loss or injury of their property they were authorized to participate in self-help activities by receiving letters of reprisals from their ruler.[1] Beginning approximately in the sixteenth century the newly emergent nation-states of Europe were becoming more involved in the diplomatic protection of their citizens abroad. The reason for this protection was based mainly on their economic interests. A loss sustained by an individual was considered a loss to the nation. States in general and the colonial powers in particular were very loath to see their citizens injured by foreigners.

With the development of international relations and legal doctrines, views have been expressed about the right of the state to protect its citizens abroad. Hugo Grotius in his book *On the Law of War and Peace,* published in 1625, justified so-called just wars waged by a state to protect both its own subjects and the nationals of other states, if the treatment they were accorded clearly violated the law.[2] Swiss jurist Emmerich de Vattel, in his classic book of 1758 on the *Law of Nations,* wrote that the state is bound to protect its citizens.

Traditional international law doctrine attributed a wrongful act (for example, arresting the alien without cause or mistreating him) to the state in which the alien resided or did business. The doctrine proceeded from the position that the respondent state must first have been given an opportunity to redress the injury. The state could exercise a right to resort to remedies on the international plane, including use of force, when local ones had proved futile. History is full of examples of the use of military force on a massive scale to redress alleged wrongs, even quite minor ones.[3] It was used as a pretext for economic and political objectives. The most notorious such case is known as the *Don Pacifico* incident. Don Pacifico was a British subject living in Athens whose house had been plundered by a mob in 1847, as a consequence of which the British blockaded the Greek coast and captured a number of Greek vessels. It might also be recalled that one of the reasons which the United States officially gave for declaring war on Mexico in 1846 was to redress grievances allegedly inflicted by Mexico on United States nationals. It was generally recognized by that time that any state could use force for protection of its nationals, even for recovering debts owed to its nationals by other states. At the same time, many jurists attacked the doctrine. The most famous among them was the Argentine jurist Carlos Calvo. He believed that whenever an alien suffers an alleged injury his only remedies are local ones.

At the Hague Peace Conference of 1907 the Argentine minister Drago proposed prohibiting of the use of force to collect debts. But his proposal was rejected. Only a few scholars of that time, such as Professor A. Gefter, held that if a state violates fundamental human rights and freedom then "all relations must be severed with it," but the force of arms must not be used to interfere in its internal affairs.[4]

Some proponents of the theory of humanitarian intervention believed that such intervention is justified only with regard to "uncivilized" states. Fedor Fedorovich Martens wrote that the enlightened powers' intervention is legitimate in principle in the case where the Christian population of lands in uncivilized states is subjected to barbaric persecution and extermination. In these cases an intervention is justified by common interests and humane considerations, such as natural law principles that on the whole govern the relations between enlightened and unenlightened peoples.[5] The view that intervention on a humanitarian basis is justified only in relation to "uncivilized" peoples was advanced by Russian scholar N. A. Zakharov as well.[6]

Supporting the legitimacy of intervention in the name of "humanism," quite a few scholars held that the right to "humanitarian" intervention emerges as the result of the decision of a group of states rather than on a unilateral basis. Franz von Liszt argued that it is impossible to agree that the right to intervene exists where one state has the opinion, however well-founded, that intervention is required to safeguard mankind's common interests. He believed that the right to intervene may be granted to several states (the so-called right of collective intervention).[7]

Humanitarian intervention involving the use of force in the internal affairs of other peoples in the name of "humane" purposes was extensively employed in international relations in the eighteenth and nineteenth centuries. The doctrine was one of numerous theories that served to "justify" the enslavement of "uncivilized" peoples. European powers, in the name of "humane" ends and under the pretext of "protecting" ethnic and religious minorities, fought to divide and redivide the already divided world. The right of intervention was officially reflected in many international agreements and treaties of that period. For instance, the Act of the 1878 Berlin Congress granted the great powers of the time the right to monitor Turkey's fulfillment of its obligations to improve the well being of the Armenians and to defend them from the Circassians and Kurds (Article 61). This provision served as the formal ground for England's interference in the internal affairs of Turkey.

Professor Ian Brownlie of Oxford University, in analyzing the foreign policy practices of states during the nineteenth century, concluded that in fact no intervention was undertaken for humane purposes with the exception, perhaps, of the occupation of Syria in 1860-1861.[8]

After World War I and the creation of the League of Nations, special limitations were imposed on the right of states to resort to intervention. The U.N. Charter completely prohibited the unilateral first use of force by states. Nevertheless, even today many scholars hold that humanitarian intervention is legitimate, while others still employ it as a pretext and use armed force for the purpose of "protecting" and saving the lives of citizens.

The United States has used force in its international relations on numerous occasions by referring to the necessity of "saving" its citizens' lives. This justification was furnished when U.S. troops invaded Grenada on October 25, 1983. The United Nations regarded that invasion as an act of aggression, as a gross violation of international law, and as an encroachment on Grenada's independence and sovereignty. One hundred and eight member states voted for the resolution of the General Assembly that condemned the aggression and demanded an immediate withdrawal of foreign troops from Grenada.[9] Many prominent international jurists, including American ones, considered U.S. actions against Grenada as an armed aggression that threatened universal peace. Such eminent American jurists as Francis Boyle, Abram Chayes, C. Clyde Ferguson, Richard Falk, and others observed that U.S. military actions clearly demonstrated to the entire world community that in the view of the U.S. government, traditional rules that limit the use of force are no longer applied in resolving numerous international disputes. Such policies may lead to international tensions, chaos, and anarchy in their consequence.[10]

However, U.S. President George Bush did not heed the American jurists' warning. On December 20, 1989, following Bush's decision, U.S. troops invaded Panama. One of the causes of the invasion, according to Bush, was the need to "protect" U.S. citizens in Panama.

The issue of the legitimacy of so-called humanitarian intervention and its limits is vigorously debated at various international fora. The problem has been discussed in several conferences of the International Law Association (I.L.A.). The report submitted by the Sub-Committee on Human Rights at the Fifty-fourth Conference of the I.L.A., held in 1970, stated that the "humanitarian" intervention doctrine is well-founded, and it is not its existence but its limits that may constitute the subject matter of debates.[11] However, many members of the Association, such as Voitto Saario of Finland, Syed Sharifuddin Pirzada of Pakistan, M. Miloyevich of Yugoslavia, and others opposed the "humanitarian" intervention doctrine on the grounds that it runs counter to the U.N. Charter, and its application in practice may only exacerbate relations among states.[12]

Despite the negative attitude of many international jurists to the "humanitarian" intervention doctrine, the second report submitted in 1972 by the Sub-Committee on Human Rights to the Fifty-fifth Conference of the I.L.A. stated that the doctrine deserves to be treated most favorably.[13] The proponents of this theory, as the third report of the Sub-Committee indicates, believe that intervention for "humane" purposes is legitimate only in cases where gross violations are "inevitable" or "unavoidable." "Humanitarian" intervention, they claim, may be undertaken both by the United Nations and by an individual state.[14] This report, submitted to the Fifty-sixth Conference of the I.L.A. held in December 1974-January 1975, marked a change of approach to the nature of the issue of legitimacy of "humanitarian" intervention, recognizing it as "disputable."[15]

What are the arguments given by those in favor of the "humanitarian" intervention doctrine to prove its legitimacy? For this purpose many scholars refer to customary law which exists alongside the U.N. Charter. They hold that "humanitarian" intervention does not run counter to customary rules of international law. Professor Sri Ram Sharma writes: "If the world organization does not act, individual initiative is the alternative and it is not unlawful if it is necessary and proportionate."[16]

Professor Richard Lillich also supports the thesis of humanitarian intervention on the basis of proportionality and of its limited duration in time.[17] In his opinion such intervention is legitimate not only when human rights are being violated, but also in the presence of a clear danger of such human rights violations.[18] Professor Tom Farer elaborates in greater detail on the preconditions of legitimate humanitarian intervention, stating:

> [A]lmost every member of a group representing a considerable position of the U.S. foreign policy spectrum *agreed* on the desirability of humanitarian intervention to prevent large-scale abuse, on the appropriateness of exhausting multilateral remedies whenever time allowed, on the need to calculate the damage to the target society as well as to the imminent victims, and on the inadmissibility of interventions designed to safeguard commercial property or ideologically congenial regimes.[19]

However, to prove its legitimacy, most proponents of the humanitarian intervention doctrine refer to the U.N. Charter and generally recognized principles of international law rather than to customary law.

Professors Michael Reisman and Myres McDougal hold that the U.N. Charter not only confirmed the legitimacy of humanitarian intervention, but also "strengthened" it.[20] Citing the Preamble and Article I of the U.N. Charter, they state that this fundamental international treaty confirmed the legitimacy of the use of force for such common interests as self-defense and humanitarian intervention.[21] Article 2(4) of the U.N. Charter, according to Reisman and McDougal, prohibits the use of force only for "illegitimate purposes" such as encroachments upon territorial integrity or political independence of states. Humanitarian intervention, in their opinion, does not violate the purposes of the Charter but rather corresponds fully to the mandatory provisions of the U.N. Charter.[22] Certainly, Reisman and McDougal admit, it is preferable that the decision on humanitarian intervention should be taken by the Security Council or regional organizations, or by the General Assembly according to Article 13 of the U.N. Charter. In case of their inaction, however, the decision to use force for humane purposes may be either by several states or one state.[23]

Supporting the arguments put forward by Reisman and McDougal, Jean-Pierre Fonteyne wrote that the prohibition on the use of force reflected in the U.N. Charter does not cover humanitarian intervention and implementation of the self-determination principle, while Article 2(7) of the U.N. Charter prohibits the United Nations, not states, from interfering in the internal affairs of its members.[24]

Conclusions of this kind are at variance with the U.N. Charter and universally-recognized international customary and codified law. The U.N.

Charter prohibits not only the use of force, but also the threat thereof. As is provided for in Article 2(4), states must refrain "in their international relations from the threat or use of force against the territorial integrity or political independence of any state, or in any other manner inconsistent with the Purposes of the United Nations." According to this provision any use of force which is inconsistent with the purposes of the United Nations is illegitimate. The U.N. Charter allows use of force only in the exercise of the right of self-defense of a state (Article 51). As to the U.N. authority with respect to threats to the peace, breaches of peace, or acts of aggression, only the Security Council on the basis of Article 42 of the U.N. Charter may decide to use U.N. armed forces to restore international peace and security.

Does this mean that human rights and freedoms are not protected by contemporary international law? What measures can a state take to safeguard the rights of the individual? Contemporary international law generally differentiates between two categories of international legal delicts, such as international crimes and international offenses. The categorization of a number of international delicts as international crimes is reflected in numerous international documents. According to these documents the concept of "international crimes" includes crimes against "humanity" and crimes against "international law." They consist of violations by states of international obligations that are fundamental for safeguarding peace, protection of the individual and vital interests of the world community as a whole. Article 6 of the Statute of the International Military Tribunal created to try war criminals following World War II included three kinds of crimes: crimes against peace, war crimes, and crimes against humanity.

The 1948 Convention on the Prevention and the Punishment of the Crime of Genocide lists genocide among international crimes, which, under Article 1 of the Convention, is a crime violating "rules of international law." The 1968 Convention on the Non-Applicability of Statutory Limitations to War Crimes and Crimes Against Humanity treats as international crimes war crimes, crimes against humanity, "eviction by armed attack or occupation and inhuman acts resulting from the policy of apartheid, and the crime of genocide." (Article 1).

The 1973 International Convention on the Suppression and Punishment of the Crime of Apartheid also classifies apartheid as a crime "violating the principles of international law." The Convention classifies as criminal the policy and practice of racial segregation and discrimination, policies which are similar to apartheid. (Articles 1 and 2).

The U.N. International Law Commission, in its draft providing for responsibility of states, listed as international crimes such grave violations of international obligations as aggression, the establishment or maintenance by force of colonial rule, as well as slavery, genocide, apartheid, and ecocide (Article 19(3)).

All of these criminal actions of states lead to flagrant violations of fundamental human rights and freedoms and endanger international peace and security.

Therefore, the United Nations, under Chapter VII of its Charter, is obliged to take measures to stop such violations. It should be specifically noted that measures involving the use of armed force may be taken only on behalf of the United Nations on the basis of the decision of the Security Council and not at the individual initiative of some state. Any U.N. member state may request the Security Council to take appropriate measures with a view toward redressing a situation endangering peace and international security (Article 35(1) of the U.N. Charter). Article VIII of the Convention on the Prevention and Punishment of the Crime of Genocide specifically provides that "any Contracting Party may call upon the competent organs of the United Nations to take such action under the Charter of the United Nations as they consider appropriate for the prevention and suppression of the act of genocide...." The action implied may be economic sanctions, the severance of diplomatic relations, or the use of U.N. armed forces.

Decisions of the Security Council to apply sanctions to stop criminal human rights violations are binding on all member states. Article VI of the International Convention on the Suppression and Punishment of the Crime of Apartheid explicitly emphasizes the obligations of states to carry out the Security Council's decisions aimed at eliminating apartheid.

Regional organizations are able to and must play a more active role in suppressing mass human rights violations. However, under the U.N. Charter no enforcement action may be taken by regional organizations without proper authorization of the Security Council (Article 53(1)).

Human rights violations may occur on a massive scale or in isolated incidents. States must respond to both types of violations. A number of international agreements provide for the creation of special bodies that monitor the compliance of states with commitments they undertake, such as the Committee on Human Rights, the Committee on Racial Discrimination, and the Committee Against Torture. These bodies are authorized to monitor the compliance of states with their commitments and have no powers to coerce or apply sanctions. In fact all major and many auxiliary U.N. organs whose functions are extremely diverse deal with human rights.

Finally, the states participating in the Conference on Security and Cooperation in Europe (CSCE), in conformance with the Vienna Final Document, hold bilateral and multilateral meetings to examine and redress concrete violations of the rights of the individual.

Thus, the response of the world community to violations of basic human rights and freedoms may manifest itself in various forms. However, it should be taken into account that measures employed must completely exclude humanitarian intervention involving the use of armed force if it is not appropriately authorized by the Security Council.

The fact must be recognized that the existing system of measures of international production of individual rights and freedoms is not always effective. In many instances, such as the cases of Uganda, Cambodia, and Liberia, states and the United Nations have taken no action even when mass human rights violations, cruel murders, and encroachments upon the life and health of the individual occur. Therefore, the world community still faces the task of looking for more effective ways of safeguarding human rights and protecting the lives of the individual. It can be accomplished by the revision of the U.N. Charter and inclusion in that fundamental international treaty of a special chapter on human rights. This task also can be fulfilled by drafting and concluding a special international convention on the protection of the rights of the human being. Such a convention should provide for the creation of an international criminal court to try persons guilty of mass human rights violations, murders and destroyed human lives. When the international community leaves such crimes unpunished, it usually winds up hostage of one criminal or another.

However, until all these measures are considered and decided upon, it is essential that the United Nations and especially the Security Council without any further delay become much more active in taking appropriate action to stop mass and flagrant violations of human rights. The provisions of the U.N. Charter must be fully invoked. Under the Charter, member states "shall hold immediately available national air-force contingents....The strength and degree of readiness...and plans for their combined action shall be determined...by the Security Council with the assistance of the Military Staff Committee" set up to assist the Security Council on all the questions relating to the employment of forces (Articles 45, 46, and 47). To date these provisions have not been activated, but once the Security Council has such forces available, it should use them without any delay to stop mass human rights violations and to punish the culprits.

The Cold War hampered the implementation of a number of U.N. Charter provisions. U.N. armed forces for enforcement action were never created. Only peacekeeping forces with entirely different functions were established. Now that the Cold War is over, there exists a very real opportunity to implement fully the provisions of the U.N. Charter aimed at maintaining international peace and protecting the individual.

What should be done to accomplish it? An agreement must be urgently concluded between the U.N. member states and the Security Council, making available to the latter certain contingents of armed forces. A new impetus also should be given to the activities of the Military Staff Committee which at present meets once or twice a month just for a few minutes to endorse the protocols of the preceding session and to decide on the time a new session is to be held. The potential of the United

Nations must be used fully. This is the most realistic, the swiftest, and the most effective way of ensuring peace and safeguarding fundamental human rights and freedoms.

Notes

1. R. LILLICH, THE HUMAN RIGHTS OF ALIENS IN CONTEMPORARY INTERNATIONAL LAW 5-8 (1984).
2. H. GROTIUS, ON THE LAW OF WAR AND PEACE 562-63 (3 vols. 1956, in Russian).
3. E. DE VATTEL, LAW OF NATIONS 161 (L. Chitty ed. 1833).
4. A. GEFTER, EUROPEAN INTERNATIONAL LAW 99 (1880, in Russian).
5. F. MARTENS, CONTEMPORARY INTERNATIONAL LAW OF CIVILIZED PEOPLES 297-298 vol. I (1882, in Russian).
6. N. ZAKHAROV, A HANDBOOK OF GENERAL INTERNATIONAL LAW 134 (1917, in Russian).
7. F. LISZT, INTERNATIONAL LAW IN A SYSTEMATIC EXPOSITION 87 (1917, in Russian).
8. I. BROWNLIE, INTERNATIONAL LAW AND THE USE OF FORCE BY STATES 339-340 (1963).
9. *U.S. Allies Join in Lopsided Vote Condemning Invasion of Grenada,* Wash. Post, Nov. 3, 1983, at A1, col. 1.
10. 78 AM. J. INT'L L. 133 (1984).
11. The International Law Association. Report of the Fifty-Fourth Conference. London, 1972, at 633-641.
12. *Id.*, at 602-624.
13. The International Law Association. Report of the Fifty-Fifth Conference. London, 1974, at 608-624.
14. The International Law Association. Third Interim Report of the Sub-Committee. New-Delhi Conference 1974-1975, at 15-19.
15. *Id.*, at 15-19.
16. Report of the Fifty-Fifth Conference, New York, 1974, at 617.
17. HUMANITARIAN INTERVENTION AND THE UNITED NATIONS 130 (R. Lillich ed. 1973).
18. *Id.*, at 130.
19. T. Farer, *Humanitarian Intervention: The View from Charlottesville*, in HUMANITARIAN INTERVENTION AND THE UNITED NATIONS 164 (R. Lillich ed. 1973).
20. M. Reisman & M. McDougal, *Humanitarian Intervention to Protect the Ibos,* in HUMANITARIAN INTERVENTION AND THE UNITED NATIONS 167-195 (R. Lillich ed. 1973).
21. *Id.*, at 172.
22. *Id.*, at 175.
23. *Id.*, at 188.

24. Fonteyne, *Forcible Self-Help by States to Protect Human Rights: Recent Views from the United Nations,* in HUMANITARIAN INTERVENTION AND THE UNITED NATIONS 197-221 (R. Lillich ed. 1973).

19

Commentary on Humanitarian Intervention

Theodor Meron

Professors Vladimir Kartashkin and Tom Farer appear to agree on the *lex lata,* that humanitarian intervention by one state in favor of citizens of another state cannot be reconciled with the U.N. Charter and is unlawful. They differ, however, in their vision of the desirable law. Kartashkin is content with the present prohibition of humanitarian intervention; Farer seeks ways to make at least some humanitarian interventions possible.

To better protect individuals from atrocities, Kartashkin proposes to revise the Charter by including in it a chapter on human rights, not an easy task, and adopting a treaty providing for the establishment of an international criminal court to try persons guilty of mass human rights violations. With respect to the latter, the laborious but inconclusive work done by the International Law Commission in elaborating the draft code of crimes against the peace and security of mankind reflects the difficulties inherent in the subject.

Kartashkin draws attention to the growing corpus of international criminal law and to the sanctions that it contains. One should add to his catalogue additional instruments, such as the Geneva Conventions for the Protection of Victims of War, with their provisions for universal criminal jurisdiction. One should also mention in this context the possibility of resorting to countermeasures falling short of use of force in the vindication of *erga omnes* human rights. In other words, it should not be assumed that humanitarian intervention is the only means for the protection of third state citizens from massive violations.

Kartashkin supports the right of the U.N. Security Council to authorize resort to force for the protection of human rights as a substitute for unilateral humanitarian intervention. The protection of human rights is, of course, one of the purposes of the United Nations, but the powers of the Security Council under Article 39 are not co-extensive with these purposes. Those powers are limited to cases of threats to the peace, breaches of the peace, and acts of aggression. The question arises whether the Security Council can authorize forcible action to protect human rights in situations which do not present threats to the peace, breaches of the peace, and acts of aggression. Another issue is the legality of a collective humanitarian intervention by several neighboring states that, in the first instance, has not been authorized by a regional organization, and in the second instance, has been authorized by a regional organization under Article 53 of the Charter, but without additional Security Council approval.

As always, Farer stimulates us to question the law as it is and to search for the law as it ought to be. He discusses humanitarian intervention in terms of the doctrinal controversy between what he calls the classical school and the realist school. This is a worthwhile intellectual exercise. But we must not lose sight of the *Nicaragua* judgment of the International Court of Justice. That judgment provides, as Professor Louis Henkin recently wrote, an authoritative construction of the law.[1] The Court determined in that case that the only exception to Article 2(4) is Article 51.

Farer does not like the classical school's conclusion that outlaws humanitarian intervention, but he agrees that the basic components applied to the analysis of the legality of humanitarian intervention lead to that conclusion. Those components include the text of the Charter and its interpretation by states, the original intent, hierarchy of Charter norms, the behavior and statements by states, their *opinio juris,* and subsequent practice of states. Farer recognizes the potentially abusive character of use of force justified on grounds of humanitarian intervention.

A British Foreign Policy Document points out that to establish any semblance of legality of humanitarian intervention it would be necessary to demonstrate that Article 2(4) does not apply to violations of human rights. This study concludes:

> But overwhelming majority of contemporary legal opinion comes down against the existence of a right of humanitarian intervention, for three main reasons: First, the U.N. Charter and the corpus of modern international law do not seem specifically to incorporate such a right; secondly, state practice in the past two centuries, and especially since 1945, at best provides only a handful of genuine cases of humanitarian intervention, and, on most assessments, none at all; and finally, on prudential grounds, that the scope for abusing such a right argues strongly against its creation.[2]

Professors Yoram Dinstein, Henkin, Schachter, and others persuasively argue that humanitarian intervention in favor of persons who are not citizens of the intervening country can be reconciled with neither Article

2(4) of the Charter nor with the practice and *opinio juris* of most states. Nevertheless, there is a basis for resorting to humanitarian intervention in truly exceptional circumstances where there is a real international consensus. But this policy should be implemented without necessarily redrafting the existing norms.

Already the sixteenth-century classical writers on international law considered armed action by a state to protect its citizens abroad as an aspect of the necessary defense, or self-defense of that state. Some international practice and many scholars including Judge Humphrey Waldock and Professor Schachter accept the continuing legality of humanitarian intervention on behalf of citizens abroad under the rubric of self-defense. To reach that conclusion they had to stretch the Charter text somewhat, especially by giving a broad reading to Article 51, without creating exceptions to Article 2(4) unrelated to self-defense. But they remained within the tradition of international law. To a certain extent their position is sustained by the subsequent interpretative practice of states in the application of the Charter.

One of the most difficult issues remains the relevance and the applicability of international law rules prohibiting humanitarian intervention in states where the *de jure* government has lost control and no effective government has taken over because of civil war.

As Farer points out, the case for the contemporary legitimacy of humanitarian intervention would be easier to make if one adheres to the realist school. His interesting inquiry is worth pursuing.

Notes

1. L. Henkin, *The Use of Force: Law and U.S. Policy*, in RIGHT V. MIGHT: INTERNATIONAL LAW AND THE USE OF FORCE 49 (1989).

2. Foreign and Commonwealth Office, Foreign Policy Document No. 148, *reprinted in* 57 BRIT. Y.B. INT'L L. 614 (1986).

20

Commentary on Collective Military Intervention to Enforce Human Rights

Lori Fisler Damrosch

Even under the most optimistic predictions for world order after the Cold War, it will not be easy to reach consensus about the legitimacy of attempting to terminate serious human rights violations through forcible means. My conviction is that unilateral military action for humanitarian purposes violates the prohibition on use of force under Article 2(4) of the U.N. Charter. I do not intend to review here the arguments on the law of the Charter, which have been set forth by other contributors to this volume and in a large literature.[1] Suffice it to say that although the proponents of use of force to promote human rights have argued that their position can be reconciled with the Charter, I find their legal argumentation both fallacious and dangerous, at least as regards human rights violations that do not entail massive loss of life. If the issue were confined to the legitimacy of using force against outrages of genocidal proportions, I would find the legal arguments closer. But typically the proponents of humanitarian intervention advance claims concerning worthiness of purpose that are then pressed into service to try to legitimize forcible action against a much broader range of conduct in violation of human rights, including denial of self-determination or rights of democracy. I find these claims unacceptable under the law of the Charter.

It is fair to ask whether the law that has governed the world community since 1945 is ripe for change, and if so, what sorts of changes might be acceptable. I will address one issue relevant to the calls for change: Should the international community move toward the development of collective mechanisms for authorizing forcible interventions in support of human rights?

Many international lawyers who agree that existing law does not permit unilateral uses of force for "humanitarian" purposes would find multilaterally authorized uses of force more acceptable, or at least less objectionable. The proposals for internationalization of force seem to present an attractive alternative to accepting the contentions of those who would shake off the Charter's constraints or who would engage in far-fetched feats of "interpretation" to defend unilateral intervention. The requirement of approval through a collective organ such as the U.N. Security Council could be a safeguard against pretextual claims of humanitarian concern and would ensure full consideration of all relevant community policies. Most important, the proposals hold out the possibility of bringing to an end the kinds of egregious violations of human rights that have long cried out for effective remedies.

Yet despite the attractions of the proposals, there are many dangers. Multilateral approval, even Security Council authorization, does not necessarily provide the touchstone of legitimacy. Moreover there are serious risks to the very institutions we would seek to strengthen. I will survey some of these problems and suggest some of the reasons why I remain skeptical of proposals for collective intervention to enforce human rights.

Some preliminary words are in order concerning forms that collective humanitarian intervention might take. Professor Kartashkin has made a proposal according to which the Security Council would be empowered to use armed forces under its command to stop mass violations of human rights. Professor Kartashkin believes that the legal framework for such a system is already available under Chapter VII of the U.N. Charter and that all that is necessary is to invigorate mechanisms that exist on paper but have never been put to use. Activation of these mechanisms could in his view take place immediately, without awaiting broader Charter reforms which he also recommends for the more effective promotion of human rights. In favor of the proposal, it could be said that the diversity of interests within the Security Council and especially among the permanent members would ensure that such intervention would not be undertaken lightly but only in cases where the entire world community decisively condemns the ongoing human rights violations. Thus the very features that produced stalemate in the Cold War could be turned to advantage as a safeguard in the post-Cold War era.

The Kartashkin proposal is but one of various possibilities that share the common ingredient of multilateral approval for use of force as a remedy against abuses of human rights. As the Security Council is not now in fact in a position to command its own forces, a more likely possibility is that the Security Council could be asked to authorize use of force by other actors, including by states that might otherwise be inclined to act unilaterally. Another possibility is that force might be used under the auspices of a regional organization, either with or without the imprimatur of the Security Council. Loosely linked to these possibilities are uses of force by *ad hoc* groupings of states, in which the fact of multilateral action is emphasized to lend political if not necessarily legal legitimacy. Thus in the case of the 1983 intervention in Grenada, the U.S. government endeavored to portray the operation as a multilateral one to prevent bloodshed and promote human rights, and pointed to a decision taken by the Organization of Eastern Caribbean States and the participation of military forces from several Caribbean countries along with those of the United States.[2] In 1990 and 1991, a multinational force of African countries has been attempting to keep peace in Liberia following a period of severe human rights violations and a disintegration of civil order; the force is drawn from five neighbors of Liberia with the sponsorship of the Economic Community of West African States.[3]

Collective Humanitarian Intervention Under the U.N. Charter

Certain of these mechanisms would not require new law, but others arguably might. Professor Meron has drawn our attention to the consideration that the powers of the Security Council to employ or authorize force are delineated by Charter provisions that are formulated more narrowly than the clauses enunciating purposes and principles for the organization in the field of human rights. While the Council may investigate any dispute or situation in order to determine whether it is "likely to endanger the maintenance of international peace and security" (Article 34; see also Article 24 on the Council's primary responsibility for the maintenance of peace and security), the Council's enforcement powers are defined in terms of threats to the peace, breaches of the peace, and acts of aggression (Article 39 and Chapter VII generally). These conditions may exist in the case of certain serious human rights violations, but not necessarily so.

When human rights violations do pose a threat to international peace, then the Security Council has authority to deal with them under its Chapter VII enforcement powers, which include the power to adopt binding economic or diplomatic sanctions as well as the power to decide upon forcible measures. During the years of the Cold War, despite many instances in which serious violations of human rights were closely linked to breaches of international peace and security, the Council rarely acted in its enforcement capacity to adopt measures of any kind. The two precedents most relevant to the present issue are the Council's resolutions concerning Southern Rhodesia and South Africa, which in both instances included a determination by the Council that international peace and security were threatened as the predicate for the decisions to impose binding economic sanctions under the Council's enforcement authority.[4] Although the United Nations as an organization did not attempt to put together a military force to act in these cases, the Security Council's characterization of the situations as threats to the peace is nonetheless pertinent: the foundation was laid for the application of coercive measures, which could legitimately have included forcible action if the Council had been willing to go that far. In the case of Southern Rhodesia the resolutions called upon the United Kingdom to quell the rebellion of the racist minority regime, using all "appropriate measures which would prove effective."[5] This language (which is similar to the "necessary means" language of Resolution 678 concerning the Persian Gulf) can be read as an authorization running from the Security Council to a state to use force to bring serious human rights violations to an end.

Among the cases that are typically cited as instances of "humanitarian intervention" in the sense that the intervening state acted to terminate violations of human rights entailing massive loss of life, several would quite likely have qualified as posing threats to the peace or actual breaches of the peace sufficient to warrant the involvement of the Security Council. Thus it is no coincidence that most such cases of intervention have entailed a claim by the intervening state that it acted in self-defense against attacks emanating from the territory of the state where gross human rights violations were occurring. Scholars studying the problem of humanitarian intervention (including Professor Farer in this volume) have noted this fact but drawn divergent conclusions from it. For present purposes these cases illustrate an advantage to involving the Security Council, not necessarily by way of directing the use of force as Professor Kartashkin suggests, but rather as an organ for authoritative ascertainment of the facts and application of community policies. As an example, the Security Council might appropriately have become more involved in appraising the situation in Uganda in the 1970s, which was surely one that threatened international peace and security. The Council might have taken decisions aimed at preserving the peace by sanctioning Uganda for its endemic lawlessness, and among other things it might have approved the course of action that Tanzania ultimately took unilaterally to remove Idi Amin from power.

Involvement of the Security Council along these lines could entail authorization to states to act as military enforcers of international human rights law in circumstances when states would not have a valid claim of self-defense. Because the Security Council may anticipate and respond to "threats to the peace" as well as actual breaches and aggression, it has broader authority than states acting in reliance on a right of self-defense, which in accordance with Article 51 of the Charter is permissible in cases of "armed attack" rather than more remote threats. Thus the Security Council may be able to authorize prophylactic military action aimed at preventing a deterioration of a human rights situation from a threatened to an actual breach of the peace.

But violations of human rights, even when massive and pervasive, do not necessarily entail threats to peace and security, and where those elements are absent the analysis of the powers of U.N. organs must proceed in a different fashion. Undoubtedly the United Nations has a variety of techniques available to it for enforcement of human rights even when peace and security are not threatened. The international community has long recognized the legitimacy of international concern over human rights violations even of a purely "internal" character, and has rejected the position that a state's treatment of its own nationals is a matter of "domestic jurisdiction" beyond the reach of the United Nations.[6] It is beyond question that the United Nations should keep the human rights performance of states under continuous scrutiny and that the organization indeed is obliged to take measures to promote universal observance of human rights.[7] Economic sanctions and other nonforcible measures are quite acceptable methods for enforcement of the full range of international human rights law, whether or not the human rights violations in question endanger international security. States may adopt such nonforcible measures on their own or through collective mechanisms, including those sponsored by the United Nations as well as by regional organizations.[8] But there is no clear authority to be found in the U.N. Charter for transboundary *uses of force* against violations that do not themselves pose a transboundary threat to peace and security.

To be sure, plausible arguments could be developed in support of the proposition that either the Security Council or the General Assembly has legal authority to decide in favor of military action in enforcement of human rights standards, even in the absence of threats to international security. I find these arguments far more acceptable than the ones put forward in purported justification of humanitarian intervention by states acting on their own, but even so they are not free from doubt. In the case of the Security Council, the argument would run that the explicit conferral of coercive powers with respect to threats to the peace, breaches of the peace and acts of aggression does not necessarily preclude exercise of analogous powers in a wider range of circumstances linked to the purposes and principles of the organization, including those in the area of human rights. This would be a form of teleological interpretation of the Charter that would allow the Council to carry out expanded functions as the international community matures. In the case of the General Assembly the argument might be based on the power under Articles 10-14 of the Charter to make recommendations to the organization or to member states; such recommendations could arguably include measures approving military action to enforce human rights, either under U.N. flag or by national military forces acting singly or collectively.[9]

Some Cautions

My concern about using the Security Council or the General Assembly in the kinds of situations under discussion relates not so much to the constitutional law of the U.N. Charter as to the wisdom of starting down this road. I have serious doubts about authorizing forcible measures against human rights violations that are confined in their actual and threatened impact to the territory of the violating state. Introducing transboundary force in such circumstances runs the risk of escalating rather than confining the violence. Even if an international police force were feasible for the near future, which hardly seems likely, it could not be injected into the territory of the violator without drawing in other states as well. As a practical matter, implementation of any collective action would require the cooperation and most likely the active involvement of other states in the region. Adjacent states and regional powers that might participate in an international military operation could hardly be confined to altruistic motivations of promoting human rights; rather they would follow self-interest. International law would ironically be transformed from a system of restraints on transboundary projections of military power into a system of affirmative approval for achieving political objectives through forcible means.

My concerns are not materially allayed by the assurance that the multiplicity of interests represented on the Security Council would guarantee the predominance of community policies as opposed to the self-interest of states that might otherwise unilaterally choose to intervene. Indeed, it is even possible that the Security Council's involvement could result in a global (extra-regional) internationalization of a conflict that would otherwise have been confined not only to a particular region but by definition to the territory of a single state. (Recall that we are speaking here of human rights violations that do not themselves have a transboundary impact.) The end of the Cold War may have reduced the risk of a local conflict metamorphosing into a U.S.-Soviet one, but it does not remove the risk that violence might metastasize elsewhere, such as through terrorism against targets associated with the collective military action.

On the practical level, it is doubtful that military force can be an effective instrument against most kinds of human rights violations. The ability of the international community to deploy military means toward the achievement of such laudable objectives is quite limited today. The problem of mass intrastate human rights violations may be inherently more intractable, or at least less amenable to military solution, than the cases when U.N. organs have authorized military operations in the past. U.N. peacekeeping, for example, typically entails interposition of a buffer force between two factions that can be territorially separated along an international boundary or a ceasefire line. It is simply not possible for a U.N. force, or any external force, to serve this kind of buffering function in most human rights situations. Indeed, when (as is all too frequently the case) the perpetrators of human rights violations are members of the indigenous military establishment, injection of an international military element could be counterproductive if it resulted in an upsurge of support for the military regime, which would surely portray itself as defending the country from foreign interference.

Regional Intervention

These cautions about the wisdom of collective humanitarian intervention apply not only to U.N.-sponsored actions but, in general, to regional efforts as well. There are some special considerations concerning regional operations that may either increase or decrease their acceptability. On the positive side, regional actions may be able to achieve the objectives of humanitarian intervention with less risk of escalation and greater tolerability to the international community than when global superpowers mount the operation. On the negative side, however, regional organizations have more than once been manipulated by the superpowers in the service of less than purely humanitarian motivations. The enlistment of the Organization of American States in aid of U.S. intervention in the Dominican Republic and of the Organization of Eastern Caribbean States in Grenada did not add much if anything in the way of legitimacy to these questionable operations; on the contrary, the transparency of the "fig leaves" seemed to compound cynicism about these organizations and about multilateralism and international law more generally.[10] Furthermore, regional organizations have been seen as acting contrary to or at least outside of their own charters when they have aided military interventions of this kind.

As for regional intervention through *ad hoc* groupings of states, their legal status at the present time is no different from that of unilateral intervention. The General Assembly declarations on the problem of intervention, which do not authorize humanitarian intervention, make clear that actions by groups of states stand on no better footing than interventions of a single state.[11] While it is true that the international community has been relatively tolerant of some *ad hoc* regional approaches (such as the current one in Liberia), it would be imprudent to assume that whatever works is lawful. In particular, we should not ignore the potential risks to world order from excessive reliance on military actions taken outside the framework of any organization authorized to engage in enforcement activities.

In short, I do not see that the objectives of international order would be better served by asking an external military force, whether approved by the United Nations or at the regional level, to step in as *deus ex machina* to try to terminate human rights violations. Concerted diplomatic and economic pressure is by far the better route.

To those who argued as recently as the mid-1980s that international law should recognize the legitimacy of force to promote democracy, I reply that the revolutions of 1989 proved them wrong. The waves of freedom that swept across Europe came about by force of ideas, political pressure, and economic influence—but not by forcible intervention. The same is largely true of the pattern in the 1980s of replacement of repressive dictatorships in Latin America and elsewhere with elected governments. If these breathtaking transformations could come about without the need for unilateral force, then surely we do not need multilaterally authorized force either.

Notes

1. In addition to the Farer and Kartashkin essays above and the works cited therein, *see generally* F. TESON, HUMANITARIAN INTERVENTION: AN INQUIRY INTO LAW AND MORALITY (1988); HUMANITARIAN INTERVENTION AND THE UNITED NATIONS (R. Lillich ed. 1973). Both of the cited books contain valuable bibliographies.

2. Scholars have disagreed on the persuasiveness of the U.S. government's argumentation. *Compare* Moore, *Grenada and the International Double Standard,* 78 AM. J. INT'L L. 145, 154-59 (1984) *with* Joyner, *Reflections on the Lawfulness of Invasion*, 78 AM. J. INT'L L. 131, 135-37, 142 (1984).

3. *See Liberians Agree to Form a Government,* N. Y. Times, Feb. 15, 1991, at A3, col. 4.

4. Concerning Southern Rhodesia, *see* S.C. RES/216 & 217/1965, S.C. RES/232/1966, S.C. RES/253/1968. Concerning South Africa, *see* S.C. RES/181/1963 and S.C. RES/282/1970.

5. *See* S.C. RES/217/1965, at para. 5; *see also* S.C. RES/221/1966, discussed in Chayes, *supra* ch. 1.

6. Thus Article 2(7) of the Charter presents no barrier to action by U.N. organs in aid of human rights.

7. *See, e.g.,* U.N. CHARTER arts. 55, 56.

8. *See generally* Damrosch, *Politics Across Borders: Nonintervention and Nonforcible Influence Over Domestic Affairs*, 83 AM. J. INT'L L. 1, 28-34, 45-47 (1989).

9. The possibility of such recommendations by the General Assembly has been aptly dubbed "Uniting-Against-Genocide," by analogy to the Assembly's Uniting for Peace Resolution. *See* discussion in Lillich, *supra* note 1, at 123-32.

10. Lillich, *supra* note 1, at 78-86, 100-01.

11. *Declaration on the Inadmissibility of Intervention in the Domestic Affairs of States and the Protection of Their Independence and Sovereignty*, G.A. Res. 2131 (XX) (Dec. 21, 1965) (term "States" defined to cover "both individual States and groups of States"); *Declaration on Principles of International Law Concerning Friendly Relations and Co-Operation Among States in Accordance with the Charter of the United Nations,* G.A. Res. 2625 (XXV) (Oct. 24, (1970) ("No State, *or group of States*, has the right to intervene, directly or indirectly, for any reason whatever, in the internal or external affairs of any other State." (emphasis added)); *Declaration on the Inadmissibility of Intervention and Interference in the Internal Affairs of States,* G.A. Res. 36/103 (Dec. 9, 1981) (similar language on this point).

INTERVENTION AGAINST CRIMINAL ACTIVITY

21

Intervention to Combat Terrorism and Drug Trafficking

Geoffrey M. Levitt

Terrorism and drug trafficking are, in a way, mirror images of one another. To oversimplify somewhat, international terrorism is a political challenge expressed through criminal activity, while international drug trafficking is criminal activity that has risen to the level of political challenge. Thus, despite their differing origins and motivations, terrorism and drug trafficking share an inherent duality as both criminal and political threats. This duality makes them relatively difficult to handle both from a legal as well as from an operational point of view. In particular, it makes for an uncomfortable fit with the traditional model of self-defense and armed intervention. And if this model can be made to fit (albeit with some fairly substantial alterations) in the case of terrorism, in the case of drug trafficking there is serious question whether we are left with anything of the original model at all.

To turn first to terrorism, the historical development is not hard to trace. After two decades of treating terrorism as essentially a matter of political criminality, the U.S. government with the advent of the Reagan administration began to frame the issue much more broadly. As the 1980s opened, senior officials spoke of terrorism in almost apocalyptic terms, signalling its central place in their concerns about the international order. As former Secretary of State Alexander Haig put it, with his unique syntax: "International terrorism will take the place of human rights, our concern, because it is the ultimate abuse of human rights."[1]

Within a relatively short time, however, concerns about terrorism shifted dramatically from the abstract to the all-too-real. Terrorist bombings took a fearful toll of lives and property in the Middle East, particularly beginning in 1983 with the attacks on embassies and military installations, and more spectacularly with the Marine barracks bombing in October of that year. In growing frustration, officials began to speak of the terrorist threat in openly military terms. The Department of Defense report on the Marine barracks bombing spoke of terrorism as "warfare 'on the cheap'," and noted that terrorism "permits small countries to attack U.S. interests in a manner which, if done openly, would constitute acts of war and justify a direct U.S. military response."[2] Civilian authorities picked up the torch with enthusiasm. In a 1984 speech that received wide attention, Secretary of State George Shultz flatly said, "We now recognize that terrorism is being used by our adversaries as a modern tool of warfare...To combat it, we must be willing to use military force."[3]

The concept of terrorism as an act of war, meriting a military response, underwent further elaboration in the "low-intensity warfare" concept. Implicitly acknowledging the multi-dimensional nature of terrorism, with its combination of political, criminal, and security threats, low-intensity warfare theory was aimed at cutting through these so-called "ambiguities" and making the case for force against terrorism as starkly as possible. The leading enunciation of this theory was again given by Shultz in a January 1986 speech at the National Defense University: "We do not have the luxury of waiting until all the ambiguities have disappeared...Our intellectual challenge is especially to understand the need for prudent, limited, proportionate uses of our military power...." Shultz then addressed the issue of the legality of such responses, as he put it, "head-on." His speech offered an explicit and authoritative statement of the argument in support of armed intervention against terrorism:

> ...[T]he [U.N.] Charter's restrictions on the use or threat of force in international relations include a specific exception for the right of self-defense....A nation attacked by terrorists is permitted to use force to prevent or preempt future attacks, to seize terrorists, or to rescue its citizens, when no other means is available. The law requires that such actions be necessary and proportionate. But this nation has consistently affirmed the right of states to use force in exercise of their right of individual or collective self-defense....

And further:

> There is substantial legal authority for the view that a state which supports terrorist or subversive attacks against another state, or which supports or encourages terrorist planning and other activities within its own territory, is responsible for such attacks. Such conduct can amount to ongoing armed aggression against the other state under international law.

Shultz concluded with flourish adapted from a famous U.S. constitutional case. "The U.N. Charter," he said, "is not a suicide pact."[4]

In order to take on any practical meaning, however, the theory in support of the use of force against terrorism had to acquire one key ingredient: a target. It hardly made sense to deploy military forces against suicide bombers who were destroyed along with their victims, or against airplane saboteurs whose very identities never came to light. Terrorism had to have, as former President Ronald Reagan once put it, an address—or in the language of counter-terrorism, a state sponsor. And indeed, throughout the early 1980s, the pattern of state support for acts of international terrorism seemed to become more and more evident.

One country in particular attracted the attention of U.S. officials: Muammar Qadhafi's Libya. A series of terrorist incidents linked to Tripoli, against a background of overt military confrontation between the United States and Libya, finally came to a head in April 1986, when the United States mounted a substantial air raid against various targets in that country. The catalyst was a bombing in West Berlin in which two persons were killed and scores injured. The U.S. Government put forth apparently hard evidence that Libya was responsible.

The day after the U.S. attack, the U.S. representative to the United Nations made a report to the Security Council, in accordance with Article 51 of the Charter. "[T]he United States forces," he stated in a letter to the President of the Security Council, "have exercised the United States right of self-defense by responding to an ongoing pattern of attacks by the Government of Libya....The Libyan policy of threats and use of force is in clear violation of Article 2(4) of the U.N. Charter. It has given rise to the entirely justifiable response by the U.S."[5] The United States also took pains to note that it had exhausted all other means of response before resorting to armed force.[6] The President and the Secretary of State also made clear that the action had a preemptive and deterrent goal—to prevent future terrorist attacks—and that the targets had been selected on the basis of their "full terrorist connection."[7]

In a capsule view, then, we now have the theory and the practice of armed intervention against terrorism, and we are in a position to sketch its elements. Its basis, of course, is the characterization of terrorism as an "armed attack," within the meaning of Article 51 of the Charter, as the predicate for the right to take measures of self-defense. Terrorist incidents, however, rarely if ever fit the conventional paradigm of an armed attack, such as a land invasion or an attack by one country's naval or air forces against another country's military forces, where the necessity of a response is obvious and overwhelming, and its timing and location clear. Rather, terrorist incidents have a disturbing tendency to be over almost before they begin. A state clearly cannot respond directly to them in the exercise of self-defense the way it can to a conventional military attack.

To circumvent this problem, proponents of the use of force against terrorism deploy two basic variations of the classical theme. The first variation is the idea of a pattern of incidents which, taken as a whole, amounts to an ongoing armed aggression. That is, the periods between actual terrorist incidents are viewed as analogous to pauses between successive waves of a military offensive, rather than as a termination of that offensive. Such pauses do not mean that the attack is over, or that the necessity for self-defense has disappeared. On the contrary, they merely present the most opportune time, from a tactical point of view, to respond. The second variation, which is closely related to this, is the notion of preemption. The doctrine of preemptive self-defense, which has a long and controversial history, has perhaps come to full flowering in counter-terrorism theory. As evidenced in the Libya case, its application to terrorism is quite straightforward. The target country has demonstrated, by a consistent set of actions, that it has the intention and the capability to carry out further attacks. We therefore act to remove the capability before it can be used again. Both the "ongoing pattern" and the "preemption" rationales have, of course, the same purpose in legal terms: to distinguish the use of force against terrorism as sharply as possible from illegal retaliation, which it might otherwise be thought to resemble. As Shultz put it after the Libya raid: "It's not a question of settling scores. It's a question of acting against terrorism."[8]

Rounding out the picture are the two major legal restraints on the use of force in self-defense: necessity and proportionality. Thus, U.S. justifications for the Libya raid carefully noted that a series of non-violent means to respond to the terrorist threat had previously been tried in vain, leaving no alternative but the use of force. And of course, the restriction of the attack to targets "with a full terrorist connection" and the attempt to avoid collateral damage—at least in planning, if not in execution—was a prominent feature in Washington's explanations of the attack.

But if the classical self-defense paradigm required re-sculpting in order to be fashioned into a justification for a forcible response to terrorism, practically an entire new foundation seemed to be needed in the context of drug trafficking. The background here is not dissimilar from what we saw with international terrorism: a growing frustration at the seeming inability of other means to address the problem, followed by an increasing characterization of the problem in military terms, and finally, actual resort to military action. As with terrorism, the beginning of this process seemed to coincide with the advent of the Reagan administration, although in the case of drug trafficking the Congress played a more active role in shaping the terms of reference.

In particular, in December of 1981, Congress enacted a law that established a broad framework for involvement of the armed forces in anti-drug efforts, including equipment loans, training, and radar coverage of major drug trafficking routes; the law also provided for several restrictions on military participation in drug enforcement.[9] The increasing role of the military in drug enforcement efforts over the next several years was complemented by a growing tendency toward public discussion of the drug problem in military terms. Senior officials linked the drug problem directly to more traditional threats to U.S. security, citing the role of Cuba and Nicaragua in narcotics trafficking.[10] By 1986, the flow of drugs into the United States was being explicitly compared to an armed attack on this country. As one Senator put it: "If the drug boats and planes were carrying bombs across our borders, our Defense Department would be mobilized to stop them."[11] In the same year the U.S. government officially identified the drug trade as a national security threat to the United States; a presidential directive authorized the use of the U.S. military to fight drugs in other countries.[12] Later in the year U.S. troops and aircraft were sent to Bolivia to assist Bolivian authorities in suppression of the drug trade.[13] Although this "Operation Blast Furnace" did not, of course, constitute a case of intervention, it illustrated that the U.S. government was prepared to back up its militant rhetoric with the use of military forces.

A specific sub-theme that began to emerge in this connection was the right of intervention to apprehend accused drug traffickers in foreign countries. This issue, which had received much attention in the terrorism context,[14] was brought to the forefront by the Legal Adviser of the State Department before a congressional committee. The Legal Adviser said in particular that "[w]e are reaching the point...at which the activities and threats of some drug traffickers may be so serious and damaging as to give rise to the right to resort to self-defense."[15]

As with counter-terrorism, however, in order to be translated into practice, the notion that drug trafficking could be an appropriate subject of armed intervention needed a convenient target. And once again, an arrogant foreign dictator provided just such a target. In December 1989, after months of confrontations, harassments, and violent and near-violent incidents between Panamanian and U.S. personnel, U.S. forces invaded Panama, ousted the government of General Manuel Noriega, and arrested Noriega for trial in the United States on narcotics charges. Although a number of justifications were cited, including the protection of the Panama

Canal and the restoration of a democracy, one of the primary rationales for the invasion was the arrest of Noriega, and implicitly, the elimination of Panama as a regional center for the drug trade.[16]

The elements of the theory and practice of armed intervention against drug trafficking are considerably less articulated than those we examined in the terrorism context, although there are certain resemblances. In particular, in both cases the core concept is the characterization of the underlying problem as a threat to national security of a type warranting an armed response. And although the explanation may take a bit more effort, presumably some notion of responding to an ongoing pattern of "attacks" in such a manner as to preempt or prevent their continuation would also be used in the drug area. The state of counter-narcotics theory is, however, altogether stunted when compared with that of counter-terrorism theory; it is not even clear, for example, whether the national security threat in question is expressed primarily through the shipment of drugs itself, or whether some degree of actual armed violence in connection with such shipment is required as a trigger for the right of self-defense. I do not mean to suggest that the U.S. intervention in Panama was wholly without colorable support in international law; the government did articulate its non-drug-related legal justifications adequately, if somewhat perfunctorily.[17] But insofar as the action was predicated upon the Noriega regime's role in drug trafficking and the status of Noriega himself as an indicted felon under U.S. law, we are left largely to fill in the theoretical gaps for ourselves.

In any event, having briefly examined these recent applications of the law of self-defense to terrorism and drug trafficking, we should consider some of their broader implications. They are clearly extensions, and substantial ones, of the traditional concept of the legitimate use of force in international law. Such an extension can be sustained, as we have seen, by some strenuous conceptual footwork in the case of terrorism; in the case of drug trafficking, the connection is strained to the breaking point—many would say past it.

So it is not surprising that the actions taken by the United States in these areas, and the justifications advanced for them, have proven quite controversial. For example, the United States came under virtual siege in the United Nations after the Libya raid, although a negative Security Council resolution was blocked by the U.S. veto, as well as the vetoes of Britain and France. The U.S. permanent representative was driven to ask rhetorically: "If the inherent right of self-defense, specifically recognized in Article 51 of the Charter, does not include the right to protect one's nationals and one's ships, what does it protect?"[18] Similarly, the drug-related rationale for the Panama invasion, although not aired in any significant way in international fora—which tended to concentrate on debating the more traditional explanations for the action—has come under withering criticism from scholars. Professor Ved Nanda wrote, for example, about this aspect of the invasion: "[I]t is unclear which international law principle the United States was invoking in its attempt to justify its action...Since a state has no authority to violate the territorial integrity of another state in order to apprehend an alleged criminal, the U.S. claim cannot be sustained."[19]

The reluctance on the part of most of the international political and scholarly community to countenance such expanded force in the name of self-defense has a quite logical basis. As Professor Oscar Schachter noted in his article on *Self-Defense and the Rule of Law,* there is "a widespread perception that widening the scope of self-defense will erode the basic rule against unilateral recourse to force."[20] Applying this thought specifically to the argument for the use of force against drug trafficking, Professor Tom Farer has noted that the Panama precedent "is not easily contained;" "Noriega's [government]," he points out, "is neither the first nor likely to be the last...to become involved in the narcotics trade;" moreover, "pollutants including toxic wastes are other deeply injurious substances that can be pushed across frontiers."[21]

In response, proponents of the expansion of the use of force into these areas tend to speak of "new dangers for civilized peoples," and of the need for the "continued development of legal rules that enable states to deal effectively with new forms of aggression."[22] While such "development" might seem a bit precipitous to many, the fact remains that certainly terrorism, and probably drug trafficking, are not only "dangers for civilized peoples," but in some sense offenses against the international order itself. They not only subvert international commerce and transportation, but undermine the very fabric of international relations in an insidious way.[23]

Therefore, it is simply not enough to conclude that the law of self-defense stops short of these problems, and leave it at that. If intervention against international terrorism or drug trafficking is a somewhat novel and possibly disturbing expansion of traditional concepts, it is perhaps because terrorism and drug trafficking are themselves somewhat novel and disturbing threats to the international community. Certainly there are other means available to deal with these threats. But—leaving aside the question of whether the use of force was justified in the specific cases I have discussed here—does it really make sense to say that the law of self-defense does not cover terrorism or drug trafficking?

Professor Thomas Franck has noted that the superficial determinacy or clarity of the Charter rules on the use of force masks a truly radical indeterminacy that can lead to the lack of essential legitimacy.[24] If the strict application of those rules in certain situations leads to results that seem absurd, as it certainly can, then those rules will lose their credibility in those situations, and perhaps more broadly as well. International law can and must set strict limitations on the use of force. But to interpret international law to flatly prohibit such use in all cases that do not meet the classic paradigm—to tell a government confronted with international terrorism that it cannot under any circumstances respond with force because terrorism is not really an "armed attack"—is to undermine the legitimacy and credibility of the legal restraints on the use of force themselves. Clearly, the circumstances in which force may be used legally against terrorism are most extreme ones, and must be narrowly defined. But those circumstances are nonetheless possible. In the case of drug trafficking, such circumstances are perhaps much harder to envision, particularly when we are talking about armed intervention to arrest drug traffickers who also happen to be heads of state. But new challenges demand new responses. The manner in which those response are framed can help determine whether the international legal restraints on the use of force will come to be perceived as a meaningful basis for efforts to uphold international law, or as an anachronistic and irrelevant obstacle to such efforts.

Notes

1. DEPARTMENT OF STATE, AMERICAN FOREIGN POLICY: CURRENT DOCUMENTS, 1981 at 395 (1984).
2. *Quoted in* DEPARTMENT OF STATE, AMERICAN FOREIGN POLICY: CURRENT DOCUMENTS, 1983 at 349 (1985).
3. *Quoted in* DEPARTMENT OF STATE, AMERICAN FOREIGN POLICY: CURRENT DOCUMENTS, 1984 at 314-15 (1986). *See also* Address by the Director of the Central Intelligence Agency (Casey) before the Fletcher School of Law and Diplomacy, Medford, Mass. Apr. 17, 1985, quoted in AMERICAN FOREIGN POLICY: CURRENT DOCUMENTS, 1983 at 279 ("We cannot and will not abstain from forcible action to prevent, preempt, or respond to terrorist acts where the conditions justify...the use of force").
4. *Low-Intensity Warfare: The Challenge of Ambiguity,* Remarks by the Honorable George P. Shultz, Secretary of State, before the Low-Intensity Warfare Conference, National Defense University, Washington, D.C. Jan. 25, 1986, at 7, 11-12.
5. Letter from Ambassador Herbert S. Okun, Acting U.S. Permanent Representative, to the President of the U.N. Security Council, April 14, 1986, *quoted in* 80 AM. J. INT'L L. 632 (1986).
6. Statement of U.S. Permanent Representative Vernon Walters before the U.N. Security Council, Apr. 15, 1986, *quoted in id.* at 633.
7. 86 DEPT. ST. BULL. 2, 4 (1986).
8. *Id.*

9. *See* GENERAL ACCOUNTING OFFICE, DRUG LAW ENFORCEMENT: MILITARY ASSISTANCE FOR DRUG ENFORCEMENT AGENCIES 4 (1988).

10. *See, e.g.*, address by Secretary of State of Shultz before the East-West Center and the Pacific and Asian Affairs Council, Honolulu, Hawaii, Jul. 17, 1985, *reprinted in* 85 DEPT. ST. BULL. 35 (1985).

11. Morrison, *The Pentagon's Drug Wars*, NATIONAL JOURNAL 2104 (1986) *quoting* Senator Alfonse D'Amato (R-NY).

12. COLLETT, THE COCAINE CONNECTION: DRUG TRAFFICKING AND INTER-AMERICAN RELATIONS, 33-34 (1989); *see also* Note, *Drug Diplomacy and the Supply-Side Strategy: A Survey of the United States Practice*, 43 VAND. L. REV. 1259, 1283-84 (1990).

13. COLLETT, *supra* note 12, at 34; Note, *supra* note 12, at 1283-84.

14. *See, e.g.*, Rogers, *Prosecuting Terrorists: When Does Apprehension in Violation of International Law Preclude Trial?*, 42 UNIV. OF MIAMI L. REV. 447 (1987).

15. Statement of State Department Legal Adviser Abraham D. Sofaer Before the House Judiciary Committee Subcommittee on Civil and Constitutional Rights, Nov. 8, 1989, *reprinted in* 84 AM. J. INT'L L. 735, 727 (1990).

16. *See* Note, *supra* note 12, at 1287.

17. *See* the statements reprinted in 84 AM. J. INT'L L. 545-549 (1990).

18. Quoted in 86 DEPT. ST. BULL. No. 2111, at 21 (1986).

19. Agora, *U.S. Forces in Panama*, 84 AM. J. INT'L L. 494, 502 (1990).

20. 83 AM. J. INT'L L. 259, 272 (1989).

21. Agora, *U.S. Forces in Panama*, *supra* note 19, at 509.

22. Sofaer, *supra* note 15, at 726-727.

23. *See* the discussion of this point, as to terrorism, in Randall, *Universal Jurisdiction Under International Law*, 66 TEX. L. REV. 785, 815 (1988).

24. Franck, *Legitimacy in the International System*, 82 AM. J. INT'L L. 705, 721 (1988).

22

Limiting the Use of Force: Self-Defense, Terrorism, and Drug Trafficking

Yuri M. Kolosov

Historians claim that humanity has survived about 14,000 wars. Progressive philosophers and politicians dream about non-violent worlds.[1] Pragmatic lawyers discuss the problem of legitimate and illegitimate uses of force.

Modern international law legitimizes the use of armed force in two cases—to counter aggression (the right of self-defense) and to counter grave violations of certain norms of international law (collective sanctions by decisions of the U.N. Security Council). International law doctrines undertake to justify some other cases of the use of armed force. One such case is intervention to combat terrorism and drug trafficking.

The principle of international law which prohibits the use of force in international relations is vital for contemporary world order. Article 2(4) of the U.N. Charter provides as follows: "All Members shall refrain in their international relations from the threat or use of force against the territorial integrity or political independence of any state, or in any other manner inconsistent with the Purposes of the United Nations." Yet there exists no guarantee that any legal rule may not be violated. Therefore, the Charter reflects the right of self-defense in Article 51: "Nothing in the present Charter shall impair the inherent right of individual or collective self-defense if an armed attack occurs against a Member of the United Nations, until the Security Council has taken measures necessary to maintain international peace and security."

During the second half of the twentieth century Article 51 was implemented far too often. In too many cases both sides in an armed conflict justified the use of force by invoking the right of self-defense. In 1974, the U.N. General Assembly adopted the Resolution on the Definition of Aggression.[2] Article 1 of the Definition states: "Aggression is the use of armed force by a State against the sovereignty, territorial integrity or political independence of another State, or in any other manner inconsistent with the Charter of the United Nations...." Article 2 of the Definition says: "The first use of armed force by a State in contravention of the Charter shall constitute *prima facie* evidence of an act of aggression." Thus, the only lawful way to use armed force against another State is grounded on the provisions of the U.N. Charter. Involvement of a State in organizing terrorist acts or drug trafficking cannot justify intervention.

In every case of an armed conflict the problem of the interpretation of respected legal norms arises. Their universal interpretation is vital for international peace and security. In my view the five permanent members of the Security Council should undertake an effort to reach this consensus in a joint restatement of the right of self-defense. One may say that this is a utopian idea, but I believe it is a necessary and plausible proposal.

Let us try to outline the elements which unite and divide American and Soviet doctrines of international law with regard to the right of self-defense. These doctrines may be divided into narrow and broad concepts of the notion of self-defense. Both doctrines recognize legality of one state's assistance to another in case of external armed attack. There is no agreement about such a right in case of a *threat* of an external armed attack. The latter case should be excluded from the list of lawful uses of armed force unless such a threat violates the political and territorial integrity of the victim state.

There is a rule that no state may take sides in a civil war by means of use of armed force, although ideological support is permitted. There is no agreement on whether internal insurgency or revolution constitutes a lawful basis for armed assistance. It might be wise to agree that cases of internal insurgency or revolutions belong to the category of civil wars.

Humanitarian intervention should not be regarded as self-defense, even if it is justified by the need to counter terrorism or drug trafficking. This understanding is shared by many outstanding lawyers. For example, Eduardo Jiménez de Aréchaga, in his book *El Derecho Internacional Contemporáneo,* claims that humanitarian considerations do not make intervention a lawful act.[3] If and when the international community agrees to recognize the legality of humanitarian intervention it should be defined as one more case of lawful use of armed force, in addition to self-defense and collective sanctions.

The legitimacy of preemptive self-defense is doubtful in the light of the definition of aggression. Humanitarian intervention as an act of preemptive self-defense normally would be qualified as an act of aggression. Is it realistic to bridge the opposing views on the problems of humanitarian and preemptive self-defense? Such an attempt deserves some consideration. The way to reach agreement on these outstanding issues is to negotiate a new international treaty dealing with the legitimate use of armed force on the basis of the broad notion of self-defense.

I share the opinion of Professor Louis Henkin that the principal conclusions of the International Court of Justice (I.C.J.) in *Nicaragua v. the United States of America* will be accepted by states generally and by the large majority of the legal community both in the United States and elsewhere.[4] Among his principal conclusions Henkin reaffirms the view that the only exception in Article 2(4) of the Charter is Article 51. The I.C.J.'s findings, summarized by Henkin, may be a good basis for a future international treaty on the right of self-defense. They could constitute draft articles of such a treaty. They include:

1. The use of armed force against another state may be justified only pursuant to the right of self-defense;
2. The exercise of the right of collective self-defense is subject to the state concerned having been the victim of an armed attack;
3. There is no general right of intervention in support of an opposition within another state; and
4. The use of armed force is not the appropriate method to ensure respect for human rights.[5]

Where there is an imminent danger of an armed attack, a right of self-defense could be recognized, but not in the form of an armed attack. The same attitude should be applicable to situations when the problem of "protecting rights" arises. In other words, there may exist methods of self-defense other than the use of armed force.

To avoid arbitrariness in the use of the right of self-defense, the international community might establish a special body to assist the Security Council. Such a body could perform fact-finding functions and submit to the Security Council preliminary conclusions and recommendations. The deliberations of such a body could be guided by special rules of procedure and by a special international treaty that establishes a universal interpretation of the right of self-defense.

There exist certain relationships between the right of self-defense and so-called military defense doctrines of states. The contents of a military defense doctrine may essentially depend on the contents of the notion of self-defense. A narrow interpretation of the latter may be the only realistic foundation for international negotiations on establishing states' military defense doctrines. The broad approach would justify military offensive doctrines and prevent any substantial progress on arms limitations.

On the other hand, if nuclear arms are not banned it is meaningless to make attempts to agree on military defense doctrines. Indeed, nuclear weapons may be used only as an instrument of armed attack. If the international community agrees to adopt the broad interpretation of the right of self-defense, then it will be impossible to reach an agreement on military defense doctrines.

International terrorism sponsored by states represents an imminent danger for world peace and security. This is also true with regard to drug trafficking beyond national boundaries. The international community has two choices: either to recognize the right of self-defense against states which support terrorism or drug trafficking; or to recognize the competence of the Security Council to undertake collective sanctions against such states. The second approach seems to be more promising since it enables the international community to avoid those cases where armed force would be used as a pretext to combat terrorism or drug trafficking.

Notes

1. A recent example is the 1986 Soviet-India Declaration about Non-Violent and De-Nuclearized World.

2. G.A. Res. 3314 (XXIX) (1974).

3. JIMÉNEZ DE ARÉCHAGA, EL DERECHO INTERNACIONAL CONTEMPORANEO 143 (1983, Russian ed.).

4. L. Henkin, *Use of Force: Law and U.S. Policy,* RIGHT V. MIGHT: INTERNATIONAL LAW AND THE USE OF FORCE 49 (1989).

5. *Id.* at 48-49.

23

Commentary on the Use of Force Against Terrorism and Drug Trafficking

Jane E. Stromseth

Professor Yuri Kolosov and Geoffrey Levitt present two distinct positions regarding how international law should address the threats to international security posed by terrorism and drug trafficking. Kolosov suggests that neither terrorism nor drug trafficking can give rise to a right to use force unilaterally in self-defense. He would limit legitimate responses to collective sanctions imposed by the Security Council.

Levitt, on the other hand, does not reject the applicability of the doctrine of self-defense to the threats of terrorism and drug trafficking. He concludes that at least with respect to terrorism, and possibly with respect to drug trafficking, a flat prohibition on the unilateral use of force would undermine the legitimacy and credibility of the legal restraints on the use of force themselves.

I agree with Levitt that it is too categorical to conclude that force can never legitimately be used unilaterally in self-defense in combatting terrorism. Granted, such cases may be exceedingly rare, and collective sanctions rather than unilateral action may be preferable for reasons of policy as well as of international law. But it is at least possible to envision a series of violent attacks against a state originating from a terrorist training camp in another state that may arguably constitute an "armed attack" giving rise to a right of self-defense.

When it comes to drug trafficking, however, I am skeptical that international law should evolve to permit unilateral action under the umbrella of self-defense. It is hard for me to envision any plausible scenario that could fairly be characterized as an "armed attack" against the territorial integrity of another state giving rise to a right of self-defense. To characterize the shipment of drugs across borders as an "armed attack" justifying the unilateral use of force against drug traffickers in another state broadens the concept of self-defense to such a degree that unilateral action would become the norm, not the exception, in law enforcement efforts to combat drug trafficking.

Levitt draws an analogy between terrorism and drug trafficking in discussing modifications in traditional models of self-defense to take account of these threats. As a matter of intellectual history, I think he is right that thinking in the U.S. government about use of force against drug trafficking has rested, implicitly as well as explicitly, on an analogy to use of force against terrorism: combatting drug trafficking has increasingly been characterized in military terms and the issue of forcible abduction of suspects in foreign countries has been a common theme in both cases. For example, in testimony given before the U.S. Congress in November 1989, both the Legal Adviser of the State Department, Abraham Sofaer, and the Assistant Attorney General for the Office of Legal Counsel, William Barr, drew an analogy between terrorism and drug trafficking in discussing the issue of arrests on foreign territory without host country consent. Specifically, Sofaer noted that some drug traffickers have been trained in terrorist tactics, and that the activities and threats of these drug traffickers "may be so serious and damaging as to give rise to the right to resort to self-defense."[1]

However, to modify a thought of philosopher Alfred North Whitehead: One must first make analogies, then distrust them. Drug trafficking encompasses a quite diverse set of activities, ranging from processing, to smuggling, distribution, and the laundering of ill-gotten profits. There is also, regrettably, a considerable demand for drugs on the part of consumers. Violence is certainly a by-product of the process; but unlike terrorism it is not its specific goal or its only means. Moreover, the role of the state as sponsor is often remote or non-existent. Indeed, in the overwhelming majority of cases, host country leaders actively cooperate in apprehending and prosecuting drug traffickers. Because such arrests involve host country consent, the issue of self-defense never arises.

Given these differences, one must be careful in speaking of drug trafficking as a seamless web of activity, all of whose parts can be treated equally under international law. Those aspects of the drug trade that take on the trappings of terrorist activity may need to be subjected to a different test from others that are more commercial in nature.

The U.S. intervention in Panama in 1989 should not be viewed as a paradigmatic case of intervention to combat drug trafficking. The apprehension and prosecution of General Manuel Noriega on drug trafficking charges was one of the four goals articulated by the Bush administration when the invasion began,[2] but it was conspicuously absent in subsequent efforts to explain and justify the action in national and international fora. Instead, the administration argued that it was defending U.S. nationals, defending rights under the Panama Canal Treaty, and acting with the consent of the lawfully-elected leader of Panama, President Guillermo Endara.[3] No argument was advanced that Noriega's drug trafficking activities gave rise to a right of self-defense, perhaps because it was recognized that such a claim would be a novel and controversial extension of international law.

The *Alvarez* case[4] better illustrates the thorny issues that commonly arise in efforts to combat drug trafficking by means of forcible abduction on foreign territory. The Mexican government's reaction to the abduction of Humberto Alvarez Machain strongly suggests that extraterritorial arrests without the clear consent of the host country will undermine efforts to achieve cooperative solutions, both bilateral and multilateral, to the problem of drug trafficking.[5]

It is important to be sensitive to the reciprocal implications of constructing a norm that justifies unilateral use of force in extraterritorial apprehensions, whether for drug trafficking or for other criminal activity. In October 1989, for example, a flurry of international criticism greeted press reports that the U.S. Department of Justice had issued an opinion concluding that the U.S. government had the domestic legal authority to abduct suspects on foreign territory without the consent of the host state.[6] Iran quickly passed a law authorizing the extraterritorial arrest of U.S. citizens who had committed offenses under Iranian law.[7] Some Iranian commentators suggested that the new policy should first be applied to the former commander of the U.S.S. Vincennes.[8]

In short, it is ill-advised to construct an expansive notion of self-defense to justify forcible seizure of drug traffickers on foreign territory without the host country's consent. Such a move would encourage the unilateral use of force and would undermine the political consensus needed to fashion effective multilateral solutions to the problem of drug trafficking.

Notes

1. Statement of Abraham D. Sofaer, Legal Adviser of the U.S. Department of State, before the Subcommittee on Civil and Constitutional Rights of the Committee on the Judiciary, U.S. House of Representatives, 101st Congress, 1st Session, November 8, 1989, *reprinted in* 84 AM. J. INT'L L. 725, 727 (1990). *See also* the Statement of William P. Barr, Assistant Attorney General, U.S. Department of Justice, before the same subcommittee.

2. Address to the Nation Announcing United States Military Action in Panama, 25 WEEKLY COMP. PRES. DOC. 1974 (Dec. 20, 1989). *See also* President's Memorandum Directing the Apprehension of General Manual Noriega and Others in Panama Indicted in the United States for Drug Related Offenses, *id.* at 1976; Remarks by Secretary of State James A. Baker, III, in State Department Press Release No. 250, Dec. 20, 1989, at 2.

3. *See, e.g.*, Government's Memorandum of Law in Response to Defendant Del Cid's Request for an Evidentiary Hearing to Demonstrate that the Government Acted Illegally in Effectuating His Arrest, filed February 16, 1990, in United States v. Manuel Antonio Noriega, et al., Case No. 88-0079-Cr., U.S. District Court for the Southern District of Florida, at 17-25.

4. United States v. Rafael Caro-Quintero, et al., Case No. CR 87-422, U.S. District Court for the Central District of California.

5. *See Mexico Asks U.S. to Seize 2 Men Accused in Abduction of Doctor*, N.Y. Times, July 21, 1990, at A10, col. 5; *see also Defendant was Abducted in DEA Case, Judge Says*, Wash. Post, Aug. 11, 1990, at A3, col. 5.

6. *See, e.g., FBI Seizure Policy Slammed*, Daily Telegraph (Australia), Oct. 16, 1989, at 2. Press reports of the U.S. Department of Justice opinion appeared in *FBI Gets O.K. for Overseas Arrests*, L.A. Times, Oct. 13, 1989, at A1, col. 5; *U.S. Cites Rights to Seize Fugitives Abroad,* N.Y. Times, Oct. 14, 1989, at A6, col. 4; and *FBI Told It Can Seize Fugitives Abroad,* Wash. Post, Oct. 14, 1989, at A15, col. 1.

7. *See Tehran Enables Arrest Abroad of Americans Harming Iran*, Wash. Post, Nov. 2, 1989, at A51, col. 1.

8. *Id.*

24

Commentary on Intervention to Combat Terrorism and Drug Trafficking

John F. Murphy

The kind of "intervention" to combat terrorism and drug trafficking that is our primary concern is limited to intervention involving the use of armed force. Accordingly, I will not examine various other possible forms of intervention, such as the use of agents to apprehend an alleged terrorist or drug trafficker. Moreover, the use of armed force to assist law enforcement officials of another country, at their request, to combat terrorism or drug trafficking does not constitute intervention and is therefore outside the scope of our subject.

I strongly share Professor Yuri Kolosov's traditional view that the only exceptions to the constraints that Article 2(4) of the U.N. Charter places on the use of armed force by states are the right of individual and collective self-defense as set forth in Article 51 of the Charter and the Security Council's authority, under Chapter VII of the Charter, to authorize the use of force by member states. Like Kolosov, I reject the thesis that a state may interfere on the basis of humanitarian considerations.

Under the doctrine of self-defense a state may resort to the use of armed force only in response to an "armed attack" (or, perhaps, the threat of an "imminent" armed attack). As Geoffrey Levitt notes, state sponsorship of terrorism and, especially, of drug trafficking does not fit easily into the classical paradigm of attack. I would go further and state categorically that state sponsorship of drug trafficking can never constitute an armed attack and that therefore the use of armed force against state sponsorship of drug trafficking would constitute a violation of Article 2(4), at least if sponsorship were the only justification advanced in support of the military action.

It is worth noting that the United States did not cite General Manuel

Noriega's alleged involvement in drug trafficking as a legal justification under Article 51 for its invasion of Panama in 1989. Rather, the Department of State cited Article 51 and the right of self-defense as entitling the United States "to take necessary measures to defend U.S. military personnel, U.S. nationals and U.S. installations."[1] Similarly, President George Bush, in his notification to Congress of the U.S. military action in Panama, contended that the "deployment of U.S. Forces is an exercise of the right of self-defense recognized in Article 51 of the United Nations Charter and was necessary to protect American lives in imminent danger...."[2] The seizure and arrest of Noriega as "an indicted drug trafficker" was cited by the Department of State as an "objective" of the U.S. invasion, but not as a legal justification.[3]

Geoffrey Levitt suggests that, with respect to state sponsorship of terrorism and drug trafficking, "new challenges demand new responses." An appropriate response to state sponsorship of drug trafficking might be that suggested by Kolosov: economic sanctions authorized by the Security Council. State sponsorship of drug trafficking clearly constitutes a threat to the peace justifying action by the Council under Chapter VII of the Charter.

Use of armed force by states to combat terrorism raises more complex issues of law and policy, and Levitt explores these in a sophisticated and nuanced fashion. He concludes that "the circumstances in which force may be used legally against terrorism are most extreme ones, and must be very narrowly defined." By contrast, Kolosov appears to rule out the right of self-defense as justification for the use of force to combat state sponsorship of terrorism and would rely instead upon the competence of the Security Council to impose collective sanctions against such states. I share Levitt's view on this issue, but would stress that armed force may be used only in the most extreme cases and normally after all peaceful means have been exhausted, including resort to the Security Council. The United States is disingenuous when it claims that it exhausted all peaceful means before resorting to the use of armed force against Libya in 1986. The backdrop to the attack included deliberatively provocative action by the U.S. fleet in the Gulf of Sidra, when a simple protest would have been sufficient as a response to Libya's claim, which enjoys no support, that the Gulf constitutes its internal waters. Moreover, the United States failed to submit either the Gulf of Sidra dispute or the dispute over Libya's support of terrorism to the Security Council before taking military action, despite Article 37(1)'s requirement that the parties to any dispute, the continuance of which is likely to endanger the maintenance of international peace and security, *shall,* if they fail to settle it by the means indicated in Article 33 (negotiations, enquiry, mediation, conciliation, arbitration, etc.), refer it to the Security Council.[4]

More generally, greater and more creative use should be made of measures other than the use of armed force to combat state-sponsored terrorism. Such measures might include, for example, quiet diplomacy and public protest, international and transnational claims, and economic sanctions. Creative use of such measures might make resort to armed force unnecessary.[5]

Notes

1. 84 AM. J. INT'L L. 545, 547-48 (1990).
2. 25 WEEKLY COMP. PRES. DOC. 1974-47 (Dec. 25, 1989), quoted in *id.* at 546-47.
3. 84 AM. J. INT'L L. 547
4. For further consideration of this issue, *see* J.F. MURPHY, STATE SUPPORT OF INTERNATIONAL TERRORISM 102-109 (1989).
5. For further consideration of such measures, see the report of the American Society of International Law's Committee on Response to State-Sponsored Terrorism, dated September 1990. The report is scheduled for publication as part of the Society's series, Studies in Transnational Legal Policy, in early 1991.

PART FOUR

Arms Control Agreements

25

Limitations and Safeguards in Arms Control Agreements

John B. Rhinelander

The U.N. Charter was signed in June 1945, one month before the explosion of the first atomic bomb at Alamagordo, New Mexico. In August of that year the only two nuclear weapons used in war destroyed Hiroshima and Nagasaki. John Foster Dulles, then Secretary of State, said in 1953:

> The United Nations Charter now reflects serious inadequacies....When we were in San Francisco in the Spring of 1945, none of us knew of the atomic bomb....The Charter is thus a pre-atomic age Charter. In this sense it was obsolete before it actually came into force. As one who was at San Francisco, I can say with confidence that if the delegates there had known that the mysterious and immeasurable power of the atom would be available as a means of destruction, the provisions of the Charter dealing with disarmament and the regulation of armaments would have been far more emphatic and realistic.[1]

We will never know what might have been, but a heavy dose of skepticism is in order as to what changes to the Charter would have been achievable, and "far more emphatic and realistic," during the Cold War. Now that the Cold War has run its course, we should ask what is currently feasible—whether in the form of amendments to the Charter or radically new arms control agreements.

A description of the present circumstances in the forty-fifth year of the nuclear age is necessary before exploring the future.

An Overview

Nuclear-Weapon States

There are now nine nuclear-weapon states which either have, or could at any time shortly have, nuclear weapons. The United States and the USSR are the only nuclear superpowers, each having between 20,000 and 30,000 nuclear weapons, of which about 10,000 are strategic weapons. Modern fusion weapons are small and light compared to the first atom bombs. Recent changes in declared intent and posture have not significantly reduced the nuclear capabilities of either.

China, France, and the United Kingdom each have acknowledged and deployed hundreds of nuclear weapons. While the numbers are few compared to the United States and the USSR, they are very potent indeed in terms of weapons ever used in war. The United States, after all, had emptied its inventory with the bomb dropped on Nagasaki, and the yield of that weapon was small and the weapon itself primitive by today's standards, yet awesomely destructive.[2]

Israel, India, Pakistan, and South Africa are nuclear-capable. Israel has the largest inventory, but has not conducted a confirmed test. India exploded one device in 1974. South Africa, which may have been party to a clandestine Israeli test over the South Atlantic in 1979, dismantled an above-ground test stand without detonating a nuclear device. Pakistan's nuclear program is now a major political issue before Congress under United States domestic law.

There are many countries which have the capability to become nuclear-weapon states in a relatively short period of time if the political decision were taken to do so. They include Canada, Germany, Japan, Sweden, and Switzerland. Others, of greater political concern, would take longer. They include Argentina and Brazil, Iraq, North and South Korea, and Taiwan.

The nuclear age has seen the advent of various new means of delivering nuclear weapons. The Hiroshima and Nagasaki atomic bombs were dropped by B-29s, which were slow propeller-driven planes. Land-based intercontinental ballistic missiles (ICBMs) and submarine-based ballistic missiles (SLBMs) have changed the nature of the threat, at the high-technology end of the spectrum, because of their potential accuracy (within hundreds of feet of the intended target for U.S. strategic ballistic missiles) and short flight time (less than thirty minutes) even at strategic range. The theoretical threat of a bolt out of the blue will always remain less than an hour away. In addition, nuclear weapons can be delivered by aircraft and, if small and sophisticated, by cruise missile, artillery shell, torpedo, depth charge, or an emplaced land mine.

Defensive systems—whether Anti-Ballistic Missiles (ABMs) or Anti-Tactical Ballistic Missiles (ATBMs), or Surface-to-Air Defense Missiles (SAMs) against aircraft—are now, and will remain under foreseeable circumstances, ineffective against a sophisticated or concerted attack. Further, there are no defenses against many types of simple or terrorist threats other than foreknowledge and prevention.

Arms Control Agreements to Date in the Nuclear Age[3]

For purposes of analysis, it is useful to divide the nuclear past into three eras: (1) 1945-1960, (2) 1961-1980, and (3) 1981-88.

The first period (1945-1960) saw a single agreement—the Antarctica Convention of 1959. This era was dominated under President Truman by the failure of the Baruch Plan, the start of the Cold War, and the Western response based on containment. Following Stalin's death, President Eisenhower later sought to begin the arms control process, but stated in 1955 that the nuclear genie was out of the bottle forever. He was right.

The second period (1961-1980) brought as many failures as achievements, but the latter were significant under the circumstances. Most noteworthy were:

1. the Limited Test Ban Treaty (1963), which prohibited all nuclear explosions except underground;
2. the Nuclear Non-Proliferation Treaty (1968), which placed restrictions on the five acknowledged nuclear weapons states (only three of which have become parties) not to transfer, and on all other states not to receive, manufacture or develop, "nuclear weapons or any other nuclear weapons device," and included full-scope safeguards in Article III;
3. the initial Strategic Arms Limitation Talks (SALT) agreements (1972), including the Anti-Ballistic Missile (ABM) Treaty which limits deployment to a single ABM site in the United States and USSR and prohibits development, testing, and deployment of all space-based ABM components; and
4. the SALT II Treaty (1979), which was never ratified.

The third period (1981-1988) first brought the abortive Star Wars escape from nuclear reality. It was followed by the precedent-breaking 1987 Treaty between the United States of America and the Union of Soviet Socialist Republics on the Elimination of Their Intermediate-Range and Shorter-Range Missles (INF)[4] which requires destruction of all missiles of specified range and, for the first time, provides for intrusive on-site inspection (OSI) on top of very detailed data exchanges. However, the weapon-grade materials from INF missiles have been transferred to the United States and USSR stockpiles, respectively; only the delivery systems are being destroyed.

The Limited Test Ban Treaty (LTBT) and the Nuclear Non-Proliferation Treaty (NPT) are multilateral agreements although the Soviet Union, the United Kingdom, and the United States took the negotiating lead. However, some key states are still not parties, including two permanent members of the U.N. Security Council.

The SALT and INF Treaties are bilateral. They were made possible by the acceptance of the United States in the late 1960s of verification by national technical means (NTM) and by Soviet acceptance in the late 1980s of intrusive on-site inspection. Verification is, was, and will be a critical limiting function for the United States of any arms control agreement over important weapons systems. Trust will not suffice, nor will promises contained in international agreements.

The pre-nuclear age saw the Geneva Protocol of 1925 which, as ratified, prohibits the first use of chemical and biological weapons. The Geneva Protocol is now accepted as reflecting customary international law, but was, of course, violated in the Iran-Iraq war. The nuclear age has not yet produced a similar no-first use agreement on nuclear weapons. To the contrary, NATO has maintained the right to use nuclear weapons first because of the doctrine of extended deterrence and the Warsaw Pact's conventional superiority.[5]

While international organizations and consultative fora have been created under current agreements in force, including the International Atomic Energy Agency (IAEA) and the Standing Consultative Commission (SCC) under the ABM Treaty, third-party adjudication has had no role under any arms control agreement.

An explicit right of withdrawal, upon giving notice of three or six months, is the norm of the nuclear-age agreements. Treaties, not customary international law, are the means of law development and each treaty contains the right of each party to withdraw. In addition, each agreement implicitly recognizes the right under international law to suspend or terminate in the case of a material breach.[6] Of course, treaties are binding only on parties and even a treaty with more than 140 parties may not include all that are critical. An example is the NPT—the non-parties include China, France, India, Israel, Pakistan, and South Africa. Notwithstanding the NPT, American and Soviet interests, while parallel, have not been particularly noteworthy to date in achieving effective and universal non-proliferation policies.

The Immediate Future

November 19, 1990, witnessed the signing in Paris of the Treaty on Conventional Armed Forces in Europe (CFE) requiring severely asymmetrical reductions in European-based conventional forces (for example, tanks, armored personnel carriers, artillery, helicopters, and aircraft). This agreement was made possible by a series of remarkable decisions by Soviet President Mikhail Gorbachev and a changed strategic landscape. The conventional imbalance in Central Europe will be a concern of the past. The Warsaw Pact is, for practical purposes, no more. The European Community, a reunified Germany, a reborn but stricken Central and Eastern Europe, and a changing, inward looking, and perhaps fragmenting USSR are parts of the central landscape of the new Europe.

The Strategic Arms Reduction Treaty (START), which should be signed in 1991, will reduce the strategic offense delivery systems of the United States and the USSR. The reductions, while less than the advertised 50 percent (except in the case of the heavy Soviet ICBMs), are nonetheless significant. In addition, a bilateral chemical weapons treaty also may be completed in the near future.

The year 1991 may be the year of ratification of important arms control agreements, with the focus initially on the U.S. Senate. The review by the Supreme Soviet could, for the first time, be interesting. The year 1991 will also see debate on the first defense budget in the United States prepared after the end of the Cold War.

Further, if favorable East-West trends continue (despite the Persian Gulf War), 1991 and the following year could see the formulation and beginning of negotiations on the most far-reaching and comprehensive arms control proposals since the late 1950s and early 1960s, when the efforts were in large measure rhetorical and without realistic expectation of success.[7]

Of course, the future need not lead toward utopia. China, but particularly the USSR, might descend into partition, anarchy, or chaos. These were not concerns in the earlier, simpler days of the Cold War. The world has never had to deal with nuclear weapons in a disintegrating state. More immediately, the use of ballistic missiles by Iraq against Israel and Saudi Arabia in the Gulf region in early 1991 raises ominous warnings about the control of ballistic missile technology in the future. Further, if India and Pakistan were to go to war over Kashmir, this would be the first instance of war between nuclear-weapon capable states.

Glasnost, perestroika, and *demokratizatsia* are truly remarkable developments that American and Soviet international lawyers should applaud and help nurture. Notwithstanding this, it is unfortunately true that the 1990s could see the first use of nuclear weapons since 1945.

Keys to the Past and Clues to the Present

Returning to John Foster Dulles, what "far more emphatic and realistic" courses are now open to the United States and USSR?

In any contemporary examination of international law and the authorized use of force, the contrast will be drawn between the right of self-defense under Article 51 of the U.N. Charter and collective security and enforcement measures under Chapter VII of the Charter.

Implicitly, these issues deal with the use, or non-use, of conventional weapons. While many times more destructive than those generally used during World War II, conventional weapons are still orders of magnitude different from "weapons of mass destruction"—nuclear, chemical, biological, and radiological. Further, we must recognize that as the proliferation of nuclear and chemical weapons continues, individual states will address the question whether, in a retaliatory role, to use chemical weapons in war or even to use nuclear weapons.

It is difficult to imagine a U.N. collective security decision that authorizes even the retaliatory use of nuclear, chemical, or biological weapons. Further, while the Clark-Sohn draft disarmament treaty of the 1960s envisioned that the U.N. peace force alone would control dispersed, residual nuclear weapons,[8] it is inconceivable to imagine a future world in which all nuclear-weapon capability is transferred from nation-states to the United Nations.

The rejection of the Baruch Plan, which undoubtedly was dead on arrival in 1946, saw the birth of the age of national control of nuclear weapons. The most achieved to date, and the most that can be expected in the future, is international regulation of nuclear-weapons capabilities. Actual nuclear weapons will assuredly remain under national control.

The essence of the international regulation of nuclear weapons to date includes:

1. National control by nuclear-weapon capable states of weapon-grade materials and delivery systems, subject only to limits by explicit or implicit international agreement;
2. Verification by "full scope safeguards" of peaceful uses under the NPT by IAEA inspectors, and verification of nuclear weapons of the United States and the USSR by means of non-intrusive NTM and by highly intrusive OSI;
3. The explicit right of withdrawal from any agreement upon giving of notice; and
4. The unilateral right of a nuclear-weapon state to decide whether or not to use nuclear weapons.

Compliance with agreements in force has not been perfect, but Soviet conduct has not been as bad, and American conduct not as perfect, as the U.S. government has suggested. The Krasnoyarsk radar was a clear violation of the ABM Treaty, a fact which the USSR has belatedly admitted, and now that radar is being dismantled. Other compliance issues involving the USSR are more ambiguous.[9] None equal the audacity of the United States in 1985 seeking to re-interpret, unilaterally, the ABM Treaty, a step subsequently rejected by congressional use of the purse strings and the Senate's adoption of the Byrd-Biden Resolution attached to the INF Treaty on shared understanding between the Executive and Congress of the meaning of treaties.[10] Moreover, this step backwards by the U.S. Executive may be legally cured by a binding condition attached to the ratification of the START Treaty, thereby restoring the meaning of the ABM Treaty to the *status quo ante*.[11]

Compliance measures (including both NTM and OSI) are expensive. This issue will certainly be discussed during the ratification hearings of the CFE and START Treaties. OSI measures are also very intrusive, and all nations of the world may not be willing to accept them. A first broad test could be the multilateral Chemical Weapons Convention still under negotiation, whose prohibitions include efforts to develop, produce, stockpile, or otherwise acquire or retain chemical weapons. Verification of its provisions will raise new legal issues, including the protection of trade secrets and proprietary technology of industrial concerns.

Arms control has not, and surely will not, include limits on research. Research bans would be non-verifiable, even if desirable. The focus will remain on possession, manufacturing, development, testing, and deployment with the type of verification appropriate to the particular legal constraints.

International controls will, in some instances, require intensive national implementation. By way of example, there is a need for stringent national export controls if non-proliferation efforts are to be truly effective. To date, such efforts have been spotty at best.

There are proposals from time to time for radical new approaches to arms control, akin to fundamental amendments to the United States Constitution, such as changing from a separation of powers approach to a parliamentary system. The likelihood of that occurring is remote or less, as is the likelihood of a fundamental change to the U.N. Charter, John Foster Dulles notwithstanding.

The likelihood of near-term, fundamental changes to a central arms control treaty, such as the NPT, is poor. While that treaty is imperfect, the near-term primary objective, which may or may not be achieved, will simply be agreement in 1995 to extend the term of the NPT for an unlimited term. The failure to do so would be a major step backwards.

Arms control treaties that deal with changing technology require adaptation over time. Unfortunately, even this relatively modest need has been difficult or impossible in the past.[12] Further, in the glow of the post-Cold War era, it will be as important to deal with the relatively mundane—the operational details of current treaties in force—as with possible new agreements. However, the latter task certainly requires the attention of international lawyers.

Challenges of the Future

The results of arms control negotiations to date may be meager, or even unsatisfactory, in the eyes of some, but the negotiation process and dialogue itself helped persuade the Soviet leadership that United States security interests were defensive. This acceptance made possible the kinds of unilateral decisions and the proposals for agreement made by Gorbachev starting in 1987.

The future of arms control could, and should, involve a combination of agreements, parallel actions, and unilateral decisions of the type discussed by George Bunn, the first General Counsel of the Arms Control and Disarmament Agency (ACDA), in 1969.[13] New agreements, however, will remain an essential element, particularly as barriers against reversals of political decisions and as the legal basis for OSI. Verification standing alone from substantive provisions—such as an open skies agreement—is almost certainly a non-starter.

CFE should lead to a CFE II, assuming the diplomatic process can keep up with unilateral reductions, and to a separate agreement on zero short-range, tactical U.S. and USSR nuclear weapons in Europe. A bilateral U.S.-USSR chemical weapons agreement will probably lead to agreement on zero chemical weapons forward-based in Europe. More important, though, will be the nature of the new security arrangements for an evolving Europe.[14] The Conference on Security and Cooperation in Europe (CSCE) experience, and its future evolution, may be the key. Transparency through regular exchanges of information and intrusive OSI will be critical confidence building measures.

CFE and the CSCE are multilateral processes, but START (and SALT before it) have been bilateral. START II will have to deal with multiple independently targetable re-entry vehicles (MIRVs) and other qualitative issues and eventually the concept of minimum deterrence, which may be a process rather than a finite number. At some point, reductions will have to lead to fundamental re-examinations of targeting policies, a highly classified subject even within the U.S. government.

If not at START II then at START III, China, France, and the United Kingdom will have to become involved and their nuclear weapons systems explicitly or implicitly limited if the United States and USSR are to continue to reduce theirs. The five permanent members of the Security

Council have never concluded an arms control agreement among themselves. Even if they do in the future, there are then the infinitely more complex and perhaps intractable problems involving the nuclear-weapon capable states in the Indian subcontinent and the Middle East. A comprehensive approach to the latter would probably have to involve the Arab states, Iran, and Israel. The hope that there may, one day, be a world without any nuclear weapons is almost surely to be frustrated and never to occur.

There will, however, be future arms control limitations, particularly multilateral agreements. Two possibilities are worth noting.

The first is a comprehensive test ban treaty (CTBT) first sought in the late 1950s. Mexico and other non-aligned countries insisted upon a CTBT at the 1990 NPT Review Conference as a condition to extension of the NPT in 1995. Will the United States accept a CTBT by that date? Will France accept the NPT, and if so only at the price of rejecting a CTBT? While a CTBT is important, it would not necessarily prevent a nation from going nuclear. Even at the beginning of the nuclear age, the United States never tested the type of bomb dropped on Hiroshima.

The second type of new international agreement is the cutoff of production of weapon-grade fissionable materials and the conversion of excess inventories to peaceful means. The former was discussed in U.S.-USSR negotiations in the 1960s to no effect. The latter has not yet been addressed internationally.[15] These initiatives could serve twin purposes: reinforcing deep cuts of delivery systems and reducing proliferation concerns.

Conclusion

U.S. Senator Sam Nunn has observed that our task remains awesome in that "we must reverse the record of history."[16] Is there reason to believe that present or future generations will do so, and thus overcome the failures of John Foster Dulles' generation before the public dawn of the nuclear age?

International lawyers are interested in process and in issues such as the non-use of force and the application of third-party dispute resolution mechanisms to arms control agreements.[17] However, there are even more fundamental questions. Will the Soviet Union as we presently know it remain a single nation-state on the world scene and will it keep secure all its thousands of nuclear weapons? What can be done internationally to meet this latter and newly emerging concern?

Notes

1. Address before the American Bar Association in Boston, Mass. (August 26, 1953), *reprinted in* STATE DEPT. PRESS REL. 458, at 6.

2. *See* THE COMMITTEE FOR THE COMPILATION OF MATERIALS ON DAMAGE CAUSED BY THE ATOMIC BOMBS IN HIROSHIMA AND NAGASAKI, HIROSHIMA AND NAGASAKI: THE PHYSICAL, MEDICAL AND SOCIAL EFFECTS OF THE ATOMIC BOMBINGS (1981).

3. The best and most current compilation of post-World War II agreements is UNITED STATES ARMS CONTROL AND DISARMAMENT AGENCY, ARMS CONTROL AND DISARMAMENT AGREEMENTS: TEXTS AND HISTORIES OF THE NEGOTIATIONS (ACDA, 1990 ed.).

4. 27 I.L.M. 84 (1988).

5. International law experts have not been at the center of the debate on no-first use by NATO. One of the better known articles urging a change of U.S. policy was written by the "Gang of Four". See Bundy, Kennan, McNamara & Smith, *Nuclear Weapons and the Atlantic Alliance*, FOREIGN AFFAIRS (Spring 1982).

6. *See* Earle & Rhinelander, *The Krasnoyarsk Radar - "A Material Breach" of the ABM Treaty?*, ARMS CONTROL TODAY 9 (Sept. 1988).

7. *See generally*, Bunn and Rhinelander, Deep Cuts in a Peaceful World: Steps Toward a Minimum Deterrent After START (Lawyers Alliance for Nuclear Arms Control, 1990).

8. *See* CLARK & SOHN, WORLD PEACE THROUGH WORLD LAW (3rd ed. 1966).

9. The discovery of SS-23 missiles in Eastern Europe countries after the entry into force of the INF Treaty raises disturbing problems of lack of candor by Soviet officials. Unfortunately, it brings to mind similar Soviet negotiating conduct during SALT I with respect to an undisclosed, but later claimed, second ABM test range.

10. *See* Biden & Ritch, *The End of the Sofaer Doctrine: A Victory of Arms Control and the Constitution*, ARMS CONTROL TODAY 3 (Sept. 1988).

11. *See* Rhinelander, *The ABM Treaty Regime in the 1990s* (American Association for the Advancement of Science, Occasional Paper, 1990), at 6-8.

12. Adaptation is the focus of Chayes and Doty (editors), DEFENDING DETERRENCE: MANAGING THE ABM TREATY REGIME INTO THE 21ST CENTURY (1989).

13. Bunn, *Missile Limitation: By Treaty or Otherwise?*, 70 COLUM. L. REV. 1 (1970).

14. *See* an excellent recent article including a draft treaty, in Flynn and Scheffer, *Limited Collective Security*, 80 FOREIGN POLICY 56 (Fall 1990).

15. Leonard S. Spector, a preeminent authority on non-proliferation matters, recently noted that in his *Atoms for Peace* speech of December 1953, President Eisenhower proposed that the U.S. and USSR contribute a small portion of their nuclear weapons material to the IAEA for denaturing. Nothing came of that idea. *See* Spector, *START Needs Ike's Atoms for Peace*, CHRISTIAN SCIENCE MONITOR, Oct. 31, 1990.

16. *See* Nunn, *Arms Control in the Last Year of the Reagan Administration*, ARMS CONTROL TODAY 7 (March 1988).

17. *See* Trimble, *Beyond Verification: The Next Step in Arms Control*, 102 HARV. L. REV. 885 (1989).

26

Commentary on Dispute Resolution Mechanisms in Arms Control Agreements

John H. McNeill

There are multiple negotiations on important arms control goals currently underway, and some of the most significant of these may soon result in binding agreements. While political developments in Europe somewhat outpaced negotiations to reduce conventional weapons in Europe and other arms talks, the opportunity may now exist for the establishment, in part through the technique of arms control agreements, of a solid foundation for more stable relations in the future between the United States and the USSR. This is both a qualitative and quantitative change. Previously, mutual arms control efforts were undertaken to achieve crucially important but still essentially limited goals such as the enhancement of strategic stability. As such, arms control became an integral part of the strategic culture of both sides, and was criticized by many—including Alva Myrdal in her book *The Game of Disarmament*[1] —as merely a cynical extension of what she and others saw as the continuation of the arms race between the United States and the USSR through diplomatic means.

Members of the international legal community should reflect upon the role of international law in the arms control process and how it can contribute further to progress in that field. Arms control agreements are, after all, only one of a number of techniques available to international law for conflict management. Yet another highly developed and flexible legal technique in the field of conflict management—procedures for the peaceful settlement of disputes—has not yet been widely employed in arms control arrangements.

One of the more negative occurrences in this field in recent years was the fact that the Geneva Protocol of 1925 was repeatedly violated with impunity during the Iran-Iraq war. This fact is frequently invoked as evidence that international law is no more than an aspiration or mere admonition.[2] It is also cited for the proposition that arms control commitments are essentially unenforceable. The correctness of this conclusion to date has been difficult to challenge.

Simple prudence dictates that no party to an arms control agreement could take the national security risk of assuming compliance by other parties, especially in the absence of on-site verification. Therefore, the maintenance of a significant hedge against breakout always has been necessary. But is a dispute resolution process, tailored to the security needs of the parties, necessarily compatible with a prudent approach, especially now when it appears intensive monitoring procedures will soon become commonplace?

In the absence of a procedure for dealing with disputes, problems of compliance and achievement of the fundamental goals of arms control—be they the reduction of the risk of an outbreak of war or the enhancement of strategic abilities—will depend upon the transparency and the predictability of relationships, including legal arrangements. But the stability of legal relationships depends in large measure on the availability of an effective dispute resolution process.

In 1789, Jeremy Bentham published his well-known arms control proposals (as we would term them today), which formed one of the first plans to place major emphasis on disarmament as a prerequisite for attaining peace. His plan called for the pacification of Europe, to be implemented through general and perpetual treaties limiting the number of troops to be maintained by individual nations. His proposal also called for the establishment of a common court of judicature for the resolution of differences—including those relating to treaty compliance—"although," as he cautioned in words mirrored in a concern still relevant today, "such a court was not to be armed with any coercive powers."[3]

The decades of the 1920s and 1930s saw the successful conclusion of several arms control agreements, such as the Washington and London Naval Treaties, which did not contain specific measures for dispute settlement, relying implicitly on mechanisms such as the Permanent Court of International Justice to accomplish this task. Later, interest in general and complete disarmament focused attention on the need for a dispute resolution mechanism tailored to the specific requirements of an arms control regime. An interesting example of this approach is found in a 1928 proposal for immediate, general, and complete disarmament and for the establishment of a permanent International Commission of Control to enforce the treaty. The body was to be empowered to settle all the disputes under the new treaty, and also would have been able to carry out investigations of any activities which, in its view, "give rise to doubts concerning the observance of the undertakings solemnly entered into...."[4] The author of this rather visionary proposal was the Union of Soviet

Socialist Republics.

A generation later, the United States proposed something similar in its well-known and carefully-elaborated *Outline of Basic Provisions on a Treaty on General and Complete Disarmament in a Peaceful World,* issued on April 18, 1962. This proposal, which sought to implement the McCloy-Zorin principles agreed to by the United States and the USSR during the first year of the Kennedy administration, contained a provision stating that all disputes concerning the interpretation or application of the treaty which were not settled by negotiation or by the International Disarmament Organization (similar to what the Soviets in 1928 termed the Permanent International Commission of Control) "would be subject to referral by any party to the dispute to the International Court of Justice...."[5] Not long after the United States made this proposal, the British delegate to the Eighteen-Nation Disarmament Committee, Sir Michael Wright, observed in support that, in thinking about a treaty for general disarmament, "...we should realize that there are three legs to the stool—disarmament, verification, and strengthened peace-keeping machinery" (in which he included dispute resolution). "The stool cannot rest on one leg or on two legs only, it must rest on all three," he said.[6] Although today this image might initially bring to mind the strategic triad instead, it is certainly true that from that time—the beginning of the modern arms control era—considerably more detailed attention has been paid to dispute resolution. But the results during the Cold War were rather mixed at best, and there were many disappointments. In that political context such an outcome was probably inevitable.

For example, the 1963 Treaty Banning Nuclear Weapon Tests in the Atmosphere, in Outer Space, and Under Water contained no procedures for dispute resolution. Instead, it was the first to employ the now famous "national sovereignty" withdrawal clause. The treaty endures, albeit with a history of less than perfect compliance. Other treaties, such as the Nuclear Non-Proliferation Treaty of 1968, have similar withdrawal clauses. The 1972 Biological Weapons Convention contains such a withdrawal clause, but combines it with a compliance investigation and review procedure using the U.N. Security Council as the engaged forum.[7] If the limitations of this device were not obvious at the outset, the 1979 Sverdlovsk incident in the Soviet Union made them all too clear.

The Interim Agreement on Strategic Offensive Arms and the Anti-Ballistic Missile Treaty, while containing national sovereignty withdrawal clauses, also provided for the consideration of compliance questions and related ambiguous situations by a specially established U.S.-USSR Standing Consultative Commission. This body, a bilateral forum which is essentially diplomatic rather than judicial in nature, continues to entertain important questions. A similar body, the U.S.-USSR Standing Verification Commission, has been established under the Treaty between the United

States of America and the Union of Soviet Socialist Republics on the Elimination of Their Intermediate-Range and Shorter-Range Missiles and has been extremely busy with implementation concerns since that treaty entered into force in 1988. Important new arms control agreements, likely to be unprecedented in both scope and complexity, are nearing completion.

What does our experience suggest regarding the prospects for successful dispute resolution in the future? Should we not consider the more traditional techniques available in international law to increase our options for dealing with compliance questions? A regularized system for dispute settlement in this area could be highly productive in the new era following the Cold War. After all, the Statute of the International Court of Justice (Article 36(2)) defines as a legal dispute the existence of any fact which, if established, would constitute a breach of an international obligation. This suggests the possibility of an important role for the judicial process in determining the existence of violations of ever more complex arms control agreements.[8] A number of the many means available for doing so, whether dispositive or advisory, whether based on compulsory jurisdiction or not, and indeed, whether strictly judicial or not, were recently described in Professor Phillip Trimble's stimulating article in the *Harvard Law Review*.[9]

In this way, the proven techniques available as part of the international legal process could be made available more fully in this new era for the enhancement of the effectiveness of limitations and safeguards in arms control agreements.[10]

Notes

1. A. MYRDAL, THE GAME OF DISARMAMENT 106 (1976).
2. *See, e.g., The Perils of "Legality,"* Newsweek, Sept. 10, 1990, at 66.
3. *Quoted in* A DOCUMENTARY HISTORY OF ARMS CONTROL AND DISARMAMENT 29 (T. Dupuy and G. Hammerman ed. 1973).
4. *Id.* at 153 (Art. 55).
5. *Id.* at 506 (Sec. H.3.b).
6. As quoted in A. Martin, *Legal Aspects of Disarmament*, INT'L. & COMP. L. Q. Supp. No. 7, at 39 (1963).
7. 26 U.S.T. 583; T.I.A.S. 8062; 1015 U.N.T.S. 163 (Art. 6).
8. As noted in A. GOTLIEB, DISARMAMENT AND INTERNATIONAL LAW 151 (1965).
9. Trimble, *Beyond Verification: The Next Step in Arms Control*, 102 HARV. L. REV. 885 (1989).
10. The above comments are based in part on remarks made by the author as moderator of a panel at the Annual Meeting of the American Society of International Law, March 31, 1990.

27

Commentary on Arms Control Agreements and Dynamic Obligations

Edwin Smith

Arms control limitations in the context of international law and the use of force evoke several observations. While many legal scholars outline circumstances authorizing or limiting the use of force, those concerned with arms control focus on mechanisms that constrain access to the most dangerous weapons. While other scholars review the legal rules applicable to states involved in international or internal conflicts, analysts of arms control agreements will benefit very little from traditional notions of legal obligation. From many perspectives, arms control agreements seem to fall beyond the realm of international legal arrangements.

My contention that arms control agreements do not fit traditional legal analysis is not heretical. In fact, the critical importance of extra-legal considerations to the analysis of arms control agreements should not be surprising. A decade ago, Professor Richard Bilder wrote a very perceptive book that alerted us to the importance of structural, non-legal considerations to the functioning of many types of international agreements.[1] Arms control agreements fall into a special group of international commitments. These agreements hinge upon the nature of the relationship between the parties, the structure of incentives and risks generated by the agreement, and the context within which the agreement operates. In another context, I have written that arms control agreements create "dynamic obligations."[2] This complex interweaving of rules, structures, relationships, incentives, and risks probably characterizes many types of agreements, international and domestic, public and private.

A state party to an arms control agreement may ignore potential legal claims if the relationship established under an evolving arms control agreement preserves that state's substantive interests. In this respect, arms control agreements may resemble long-term or relational contracts which have been examined by scholars of domestic law.[3] Phillip Trimble notes that inaction is one course that a state may take when confronted with the violation of an arms control agreement.[4] I am less troubled at this prospect than Trimble to the extent that inaction reflects a judgment that no material breach has occurred. In fact, the presence of a formal tribunal may lead to political pursuit of claims of non-compliance even though the claims may have little practical relevance to strategic reality.

John Rhinelander correctly notes that President Mikhail Gorbachev's *glasnost, perestroika,* and *demokratizatzia* cannot be overemphasized: These new attitudes have generated a sea-change in the possibilities for reducing the risks of war. In the particular arena of arms control, this sea-change has special meaning. The nature of the relationship between the United States and the USSR plays a critical role in the viability of future arms control agreements. In fact, the radical shift in Eastern Europe has allowed the execution of a new conventional arms control agreement.[5] Equally important but less often noted, the new atmosphere changes the calculus of risks that undergirds the attitudes of committed states toward their obligations. Attitudes toward the importance of verification provide a revealing example.

One recent incident demonstrates this shift. On March 6, 1990, *The Washington Times* reported that U.S. military observers had discovered two dozen SS-23 missiles in eastern Germany.[6] In total, more than forty SS-23s were discovered in Germany, Czechoslovakia, and Hungary.[7] Since the Treaty Between the United States and the USSR on the Elimination of Their Intermediate-Range and Shorter-Range Missiles[8] required that all Soviet SS-23s were to have been destroyed, the discovery was remarkable. On the face of it, the mere existence of the SS-23s appeared to be a violation of the Treaty. At the very least, the presence of the weapons violated the "spirit" of the treaty.

Instead of the storm of protest that might have been expected, the U.S. response was surprisingly mild. Senator Richard Lugar, a Republican member of the Foreign Relations Committee, suggested that "sometimes there are disagreements."[9] Defense Department officials, noting that the discovery could be "very serious" and a "potential violation," said that they would consider the matter.[10] The entire matter, never very prominent in the American press, faded almost completely from the public eye.

As Rhinelander notes, third-party dispute resolution mechanisms may never be viable for arms control agreements. The consequences of material non-compliance will jeopardize the fundamental national interests of the complying state.[11] Third-party determination of legal rights and responsibilities provides little assurance that the non-complying party will give up a known strategic advantage resulting from that non-compliance. These treaties generally contain provisions permitting termination of all obligations upon notice to the other party.[12] The parties see the invocation of the termination provision as the ultimate sanction for non-compliance.

From most traditional perspectives, arms control agreements are essentially unenforceable through traditional legal means.

Because of these risks, American officials have always maintained that adequate verification provides the sole means for managing the risks of arms control agreements. Consequently, U.S.-Soviet arms control agreements invariably contain "verification" provisions that assist each party in evaluation of the compliance of the other party.[13] The decision that a given level of verifiability is adequate constitutes a political determination that a certain level of risk of undiscovered noncompliance is politically acceptable. The presence of the SS-23s pointed out the operational limitations of American national technical means. The implications of those limitations rested on a political judgment. While a "legal" violation of the agreement may have occurred, the import of that violation vanishes if the risks prove to be politically acceptable.

The discoveries of SS-23s might have generated a series of questions about the efficacy of the compliance and enforcement mechanisms upon which the United States relies. The astounding changes generated by Gorbachev prevented the SS-23 incident from generating a firestorm of controversy and accusations. The reaction to the discovery of the missiles indicates that American officials will now accept a higher level of risk of undiscovered non-compliance with U.S.-Soviet arms control agreements than was true in the past. The new relationship between the superpowers combines with a fair history of compliance with previous agreements, whether formally "binding" or not, to create a regime within which new strategic and conventional agreements are likely to prosper.[14]

Rhinelander makes an additional point that merits emphasizing. He participated in a project led by Antonia Chayes and Paul Doty which evaluated the Anti-Ballistic Missile Treaty (ABM) regime.[15] The authors of that study make a central point that should be of interest to lawyers, particularly those that might be characterized as positivists. They note that arms control treaties must adapt over time to changes in technology and the strategic context.[16] At the same time, Rhinelander shares with those authors a firm belief in the value of the ABM regime and the obligations that it creates.[17]

Those responsible for constructing agreements that are both predictably constraining and adaptable over time face some interesting problems. Solving these problems requires more than artful crafting of legal language. Innovative structures must be established within the relationship created under the agreement. The parties to such an agreement must have sufficient mutual confidence to rely upon such structures. That confidence may flow from rational calculations of self-interest as well as from a history of cooperation. These agreements force legal scholars to develop new perspectives on formalized international commitments. My own effort to work out the concept of dynamic obligations is an attempt to expand the available approaches. Traditional jurisprudence cannot adequately meet the demands posed by agreements which create such dynamic obligations.

One point is clear. The new U.S.-Soviet relationship enhances the prospect for increasing confidence and cooperation in this critically important era. Unfortunately, the reverse is equally true: Any failure of the program of *glasnost, perestroika,* or *demokratizatzia* will pose serious risks for all of us. Consequently, the United States and the Soviet Union should move as quickly as possible toward a broader regime of bilateral arms control.

Notes

1. R. BILDER, MANAGING THE RISKS OF INTERNATIONAL AGREEMENTS 1980.

2. I have defined "dynamic obligations" as those resulting from agreements structured to allow consensual adaptation of their obligations to permit fulfillment of the object of the agreement under conditions of uncertainty. Smith, Understanding International Obligation: The Case of Arms Control (unpublished manuscript).

3. *See generally* I. MACNEIL, THE NEW SOCIAL CONTRACT (1980); Scott, *Conflict and Cooperation in Long-Term Contracts*, 75 CAL. L. REV. 2005 (1987); MacNeil, *Relational Contracts: What We Do and Do Not Know*, 1985 WIS. L. REV. 461; Macauley, *An Empirical View of Contract*, 1985 WIS. L. REV. 465.

4. Trimble, *Beyond Verification: The Next Step in Arms Control*, 102 HARV. L. REV. 885, 891 (1989).

5. *See The Ice Finally Melts; But Formal End to Cold War Competes for Attention with Mideast Threat*, L.A. Times, Nov. 20, 1990, at B6.

6. Gertz, *Soviet Missiles in East Germany May Violate Treaty*, Wash. Times, Mar. 6, 1990, at A3.

7. Gertz, *Congress Told Soviets May Be Violating INF*, Wash. Times, May 4, 1990, at A6.

8. Treaty Between the United States of America and the Union of Soviet Socialist Republics on the Elimination of Their Intermediate-Range and Short-Range Missiles, done at Washington, D.C., December 8, 1987, entered into force, June 1, 1988, 27 I.L.M. 84 (1988) (the "INF Treaty").

9. Garrett, *Lugar Doubts Arms Accord Ready for Summit*, Wash. Times, Mar. 16, 1990, at A3.

10. Department of Defense Press Briefing, March 6, 1990.

11. Haass, *Verification and Compliance,* in A. CARNESALE AND R. HAASS, SUPERPOWER ARMS CONTROL: SETTING THE RECORD STRAIGHT 303-28 (1987).

12. *See, e.g.*, INF Treaty, art. XV, para. 2, *supra* note 8.

13. *See* Article V, *Interim Agreement Between the United States and the Union of Soviet Socialist Republics on Certain Measures with Respect to the Limitation of Strategic Offensive Arms, done at Moscow, May 26, 1972*, 23 U.S.T. 3462, T.I.A.S. No. 7504, 11 I.L.M. 791 (1972); Article XIII, *Treaty Between the United States and the Union of Socialist Republics on the Limitation of Anti-Ballistic Missile Systems, done at Moscow, May 26, 1972*, 23 U.S.T. 3435, T.I.A.S. No. 7503, 11 I.L.M. 784; INF Treaty, arts. XI-XIII, *supra* note 8.

14. Senator Lugar noted the good compliance record in Garrett, *supra* note 9.

15. A. CHAYES AND P. DOTY, DEFENDING DETERRENCE: MANAGING THE ABM TREATY REGIME INTO THE 21ST CENTURY (1989).

16. *See* Chayes and Chayes, *Living Under a Treaty Regime: Compliance, Interpretation, and Adaption, in* CHAYES AND DOTY, *id.*

17. *See* Rhinelander and Goodman, *The Legal Environment,* in CHAYES AND DOTY, *supra* note 15.

PART FIVE

Judicial Procedures

28

Judicial Procedures Relating to the Use of Force

Richard B. Bilder

Few people believe that states are likely soon to agree to settle all of their armed conflicts by referring them to international courts. But there may be more scope for the effective use of judicial techniques than is presently assumed, particularly in a post-Cold War and Persian Gulf crisis era.

This issue has current relevance for several reasons. First, in view of the danger and cost the use of force poses for all in the international community, it is important to explore and imaginatively develop every conceivable means of preventing or resolving potential or actual international conflicts; certainly, judicial procedures are among the most salient of these possible techniques.

Second, the concept of legal regulation of the use of force necessarily presupposes the possibility of assessment and appraisal by the international community of use-of-force issues, particularly claims of self-defense; courts have traditionally formed at least one authoritative means of providing such objective appraisal.

Third, the United States government, both in and since the *Nicaragua* case,[1] has taken the position that it is at least inappropriate, perhaps *ultra vires*, and in any case inherently beyond the capability of the International Court of Justice (I.C.J. or the Court), for that tribunal to deal with a case involving the ongoing use of force—at least absent very clear consent by all the parties. While this position was most emphatically stated during the Reagan administration,[2] the Bush administration apparently continues to maintain this stance.[3] In view of the influence of U.S. attitudes on the development of international law and institutions, including the I.C.J., it seems important to examine the basis, scope, and validity of its position in this respect.

Finally, the U.S. and Soviet governments, together with the other permanent members of the U.N. Security Council, are currently discussing the possible conclusion of an agreement providing for the compulsory reference of certain categories of disputes to the Court.[4] This agreement would presumably provide an alternative to, or perhaps in practice supplant, the Court's compulsory jurisdiction under Article 36(2) of its Statute—and, indeed, perhaps even provisions for the Court's compulsory jurisdiction under compromissory clauses in other agreements. Current reports indicate that it is contemplated that any such agreement would provide an opportunity to exclude a broad range of cases involving national security and the use of force. In view of the possible consequences of any such agreement on state practice and the future work of the Court, it again seems useful to reexamine the basis for and reasonableness of any such exclusion.

I have thought it most useful to structure this discussion in terms of certain questions which seem to me particularly relevant to appraising the usefulness of courts—and especially the I.C.J.—in dealing with situations involving the use of force. Some of these questions have been well-discussed elsewhere—particularly in Professor Oscar Schachter's recent article on this subject[5] and in Professor Thomas Franck's recent monograph on the Court.[6] As appropriate, I will draw on their conclusions here, permitting me to focus this paper on additional issues.

While discussion concerning the role of judicial procedures in use-of-force cases has focused primarily on the Court and similar judicial or arbitral tribunals, brief mention should be made of the potential role of international criminal tribunals, such as the Nuremberg and Tokyo tribunals which were established to try certain war crimes, crimes against the peace, and other crimes after World War II.[7] Despite early, continuing, and current interest and study, to date little progress has been made towards the actual establishment of any permanent international criminal tribunal.[8] It is significant, however, that growing concern regarding international terrorism and the international drug trade, as well as the Iraq-Kuwait crisis, have given rise to renewed interest in the possible establishment of a permanent tribunal capable of imposing criminal responsibility for, *inter alia,* certain types of war-related international crimes.[9]

What Are "Situations or Disputes Involving the Use of Force"?

The position of the U.S. government during and since the *Nicaragua* case has been that situations or disputes involving the use of force are different from other kinds of international controversies or disputes as regards their suitability for settlement through resort to judicial procedures.

However, as Schachter points out, it is not easy to say precisely what we mean by "situations involving the use of force," or exactly how and why they are different from other disputes.[10]

The concept of "use of force" presumably describes some type of use by a state of armed force or organized military power to coerce another state. Of course, one or another party to a dispute, whatever the subject matter, may threaten or use coercive force in an attempt to prevail. In this sense, any dispute may potentially become "a situation involving the use of force." Certainly, for the purpose of this analysis, the most relevant use-of-force situations will be those where the use of force is in itself central to the dispute, and an issue which any judicial tribunal, should it become involved, will presumably need to address. However, we should not, in my opinion, exclude from our analysis and discussion those situations in which a use of force, while not central to an international dispute, is nevertheless a significant factor capable of affecting its development or eventual resolution.

Some reasons why situations involving the "use of force" arguably might differ from those which do not are that "use-of-force" situations may (i) implicate particularly significant U.N. Charter norms and procedures regarding the use of force, such as Articles 2(4) and 51, and Chapter VII; (ii) be regarded as particularly important and politically sensitive by officials in that they may involve issues of national sovereignty, integrity, independence, or "honor;" (iii) relate to military situations which are rapidly changing, difficult to "undo," and involve complex and hard to determine facts and sensitive intelligence information; and (iv) threaten to involve or cause collateral harm to other states or the international community.

Since situations and disputes involving the use of force may differ from one another, it may be useful to suggest a rough typology of such situations:

1. What type of force is being used? Is coercion occurring through the use of active military forces, such as an armed attack by troops, ships, or planes; through a naval or air blockade; through the use of irregular or "proxy" forces; or through seizure of diplomats or nationals or property?
2. What is the temporal dimension of the use of force? Is the use of force only threatened, currently occurring, or "ongoing", or already past? If the use of force is only threatened, what is the probability that it will be employed, and how imminently? If the use of force is continuing, how long has it been going on?
3. What is the scale and significance of the use of force involved? Is the situation involving the use of force one of generalized conflict and war, limited but recurrent border skirmishes, or other

incidents, or only one or a few isolated incidents, such as the downing of an aircraft or sinking of a single vessel?

4. Which states are involved, what is their relative power, and what has been their prior relationship and dispute-settlement experience? Factors such as these may bear on the seriousness of the dispute and its likelihood of escalating, the negotiating positions of the parties, and their willingness to accept judicial or other types of third-party settlement procedures.
5. How do the states involved perceive the situation? Do one or both believe that their national security, "vital interests," or "national honor" are involved? Could a compromise or adverse judicial decision be politically acceptable to both or all parties?
6. What is the controversy or dispute really about, and how central to the principal dispute is the use of force involved? Is the issue primarily the alleged illegal use of force itself, as, for example, in the shooting down of a commercial aircraft which has somehow strayed across an accepted border? Or is the use of force marginal or incidental to a dispute primarily about some other matter, which is the real focus of the controversy, as, for example, with maritime incidents arising out of disputed maritime claims?
7. What are the attitudes and interests of third states or the international community? Is the situation involving the use of force likely to escalate or more generally threaten or otherwise affect third states or international peace or security? Or are other states largely indifferent to the continuation or outcome of the situation, or perhaps even have an interest in its continuing?[11]

To What Extent Have States Used Judicial Procedures to Resolve Cases Involving the Use of Force?

There have been relatively few cases in which the Court or other tribunals have been called on to deal with situations in which the threat or use of force was, even to some limited extent, involved.

Reviewing recent experience in this respect, Schachter comments that: "When we consider the number of such disputes since 1945 (surely in the hundreds), it is striking that there have been only thirteen cases brought to the Court which could be said to have involved the use of armed force."[12] He notes that, of these, eight were brought by the United States against unwilling respondents (the six *Aerial Incident* cases brought by the United States against the Soviet Union, Hungary, and Czechoslovakia,[13] the *El Al* case against Bulgaria[14] and the *Tehran Hostages* case against Iran);[15] three were brought by the United Kingdom (the *Corfu Channel* case against Albania,[16] the *El Al* case against Bulgaria,[17] and the *Fisheries Jurisdiction* case against Iceland)[18] and one was brought by Israel (the *El*

Al case against Bulgaria.)[19] Only one case—the *Nicaragua* case brought by Nicaragua against the United States—involved an ongoing use of armed force on a significant scale.[20] There might be added to Schachter's list the late 1950s frontier dispute between Honduras and Nicaragua involving the *Arbitral Award Made by the King of Spain* in 1906,[21] the 1975 *Advisory Opinion on the Status of the Western Sahara*,[22] and several more recent cases including Iran's case against the United States concerning the downing of Iran Air 655,[23] the *Burkina Faso-Mali* territorial dispute, and the recently filed *Libya-Chad* territorial dispute.[24]

If one looks beyond the Court to cases before arbitral tribunals, there are a number of other instances in which states have submitted disputes involving the use of force to arbitration. These include the *Alabama Claims (United States v. U.K.)*,[25] *I'm Alone (U.K. for Canada v. United States)*,[26] *Naulilaa* incident *(Portugal v. Germany)*[27] and *Rann of Kutch (Pakistan v. India)*[28] arbitrations. In addition, there have been some important instances in which disputes involving the use of force have been submitted to international fact-finding or conciliation processes.[29] These include the *Dogger Bank* inquiry *(U.K. v. Russia)*,[30] the *Tavignano* inquiry *(France v. Italy)*,[31] the *Tiger* inquiry *(Norway v. Germany)*,[32] the *Tubantia* inquiry *(Netherlands v. Germany)*[33] and the more recent 1961 *Red Crusader* inquiry *(U.K. v. Denmark)*.[34]

It is apparent from this listing that, as the United States asserted in the *Nicaragua* case, there is little precedent for the use of judicial tribunals to resolve large-scale on-going armed conflicts. On the other hand, there appears to be considerable precedent for resort to judicial procedures to resolve disputes relating to limited and already terminated incidents involving the use of force, or those in which the threat of force is largely peripheral or ancillary to the principal issues involved.

Does International Law Require States to Submit Disputes Involving the Use of Force for Settlement by Judicial Procedures?

The answer appears to be "No."[35]

The prevailing view is that, in the absence of special agreement, states are under no international legal obligation to settle, or even to try to settle, their disputes. It is well established in particular that, absent special agreement, a state has no international legal obligation to submit a dispute with another state to impartial arbitral or judicial settlement.[36] This would appear to apply to disputes involving the use of force as well as other types of disputes.

Of course, if a state does consent to arbitration or judicial settlement of a dispute with another state, either by special *ad hoc* agreement or by agreement in advance through a compromissory provision in a treaty or otherwise, it is legally bound by that decision and the appropriate tribunal may exercise jurisdiction in accordance with the terms of that consent. This principle is reflected in Article 36 of the Court's Statute, and would appear, prima facie, to apply to disputes involving the use of force as well as other types of disputes—absent, at least, some reservation or other evidence clearly establishing that a state intended to exclude some or all of such use-of-force disputes from its consent.

However, member states of the United Nations (now including virtually all states) have assumed at least certain broad treaty obligations under the U.N. Charter regarding dispute settlement, which are relevant in this respect.[37] While Article 2(3) of the Charter establishes an essentially negative obligation—that member nations not settle disputes by means that might endanger international peace—Article 33 affirmatively requires that member nations actively seek to settle by peaceful means any dispute the continuance of which is likely to endanger international peace. However, it is well established that Article 33 does not purport to establish an exclusive list of such peaceful means or any particular order in which they should be used.

Chapter VI (Articles 33-37) of the Charter, entitled "Pacific Settlement of Disputes," establishes further obligations of U.N. members as well as various dispute settlement powers of the Security Council.[38] Other articles of the Charter authorize the General Assembly and Secretary-General to make recommendations or take certain action with respect to disputes, and encourage the development of pacific settlement through regional arrangements.

It is apparent that the U.N. Charter establishes international obligations of the parties and interventionary powers of the Organization principally with respect to a particular category of disputes—those whose continuation "is likely to endanger the maintenance of international peace and security." It is less clear whether member states are also under an obligation to seek to settle all disputes—even those which are not likely to threaten international peace and security. Article 38 makes clear that, absent consent of all parties to the dispute, the Organization has no general authority to intervene to bring about a settlement of international disputes which do not involve either coercion or a threat to international peace and security. Presumably, while a dispute involving the use of force might well be considered by the Security Council to constitute a "dispute the continuance of which is likely to endanger the maintenance of international peace and security" within the language of the Charter, the Council need not necessarily do so.

The obligation that any settlement of disputes must be accomplished peacefully is, of course, buttressed by the prohibition on the use of force contained in Article 2(4) of the Charter and by the authority of the Security Council under Chapter VII of the Charter to intervene when it determines that any situation or dispute involves a "threat to the peace, breach of the peace, or act of aggression." It is an interesting question whether the Security Council's authority to "decide what measures shall be taken in accordance with Articles 41 and 42, to maintain or restore international peace and security" (which "decisions" are binding on all members under Article 25 of the Charter) could include a "decision" requiring the parties to a dispute to adopt particular peaceful settlement procedures. Arguably, such authority might be included by implication in the Council's far more drastic authority to employ economic or even military coercion, under Articles 41 and 42. On the other hand, judicial settlement would normally be considered within the scope of Chapter VI of the Charter, which does not provide any such mandatory Security Council powers.

The characterization of the dispute, and thus the potential application of these obligations, is presumably a matter upon which the Security Council may appropriately reach its own judgment, rather than one solely within the judgment of one or all of the disputing states themselves. Thus, Article 34 expressly authorizes the Council to investigate any dispute, or any situation which might lead to international friction or give rise to a dispute, in order to determine whether the continuance of the dispute or situation is likely to endanger the maintenance of international peace and security. The obligations of Articles 2(3) and 33 to seek to settle disputes peacefully, at least if their continuance is likely to threaten international peace and security, is probably now customary international law. This has generally been accepted as the case with respect to the analogous obligations of Article 2(4) of the Charter.

In summary, this discussion suggests that nothing in the Charter requires a state that has not otherwise agreed to do so to submit a dispute involving the use of force specifically to the Court or other judicial procedures. However, the Charter does appear to impose broad obligations on states to actively seek to settle, by some means, disputes "the continuance of which is likely to endanger international peace and security," which in at least some cases are likely to embrace disputes involving the use of force. Moreover, the Charter would appear, in Article 36 and otherwise, to provide a basis for the Security Council or General Assembly to recommend that the parties submit such disputes to judicial settlement. Indeed in the *Corfu Channel* case between the U.K. and Albania, the Security Council made such a recommendation, which was in fact accepted by the parties. As indicated, it is arguable that the Security Council, acting under Chapter VII, has some broader powers to compel particular actions by states to seek to resolve or de-escalate use-of-force disputes. It seems unlikely, however, at least in the present state of the law, that the U.N. Charter, I.C.J. Statute, or international law could be interpreted as permitting the Security Council either to require parties to submit such cases to judicial settlement, or in itself to confer such jurisdiction on the Court or another judicial tribunal.

Are There Inherent Legal Barriers to Adjudication of Use-of-Force Cases?

In the *Nicaragua* case, the United States argued that the Court should reject Nicaragua's suit, not only because the Court lacked jurisdiction, but because the dispute, involving as it did the right of self-defense and an ongoing use of armed force, was inherently beyond the Court's appropriate competence and inadmissible.[39] Prior to the *Nicaragua* case, it was apparently never suggested, either by the Court, by any government, or by any scholar, that a dispute involving the use of force was inherently inadmissible.

There is some uncertainty, as the Court noted in its opinion in the *Nicaragua* case,[40] whether the United States was claiming that there was an inherent legal bar to the adjudication of such use-of-force cases, or rather only that the Court should reject them as an exercise of prudential discretion in order to protect the integrity of its judicial function—or perhaps both. However, more recently, spokesmen for the U.S. Government appear to have taken the somewhat narrower position that the Court cannot (or perhaps should not) accept such cases without express consent by the states concerned. This qualification implies that the Court is not barred from dealing with such use-of-force cases if the parties make very clear their wish that the Court do so.[41]

The suggestion that use-of-force cases may be inherently nonjusticiable by the Court, or perhaps more broadly by any judicial tribunal, raises important and interesting questions of obvious relevance for this inquiry. They have been discussed extensively, however, both by the Court in its *Nicaragua* opinion rejecting United States arguments to this effect,[42] and by a number of scholars, including Schachter in his recent thorough and persuasive study of these particular issues.[43] Since I substantially agree with Schachter's analysis, here I will simply note the principal questions raised and Schachter's conclusions, referring the reader to Schachter's article and to the Court's judgment for a fuller discussion.

1. Is a dispute involving the use of force "non-legal" or "political," and thus for some reason inherently outside the competence of the Court and other judicial tribunals?

As noted in the recent revision of the *Restatement of the Foreign Relations Law of the United States,*[44] while the jurisdiction of the Court over cases brought pursuant to declarations under Article 36(2) of the Court's Statute is expressly limited to "legal disputes", the framers of the Statute rejected a proposal to impose that limitation also on cases submitted by the parties *ad hoc* pursuant to Article 36(1), which provides that the jurisdiction of the Court comprises "all cases" which the parties refer to it and "all matters" specially provided for in the U.N. Charter or other treaties. While in the *Northern Cameroons* case the Court recognized that "there are inherent limitations on the exercise of the judicial function which the Court, as a court of justice, can never ignore,"[45] the Court has as yet never rejected a case on the ground that it involved non-legal issues. Thus, in the *Tehran Hostages* case the Court refused to accept the view that, "because a dispute is only one aspect of a political dispute, the Court should decline to resolve for the parties the legal question at issue between them", or to impose such "a far-reaching and unwarranted restriction upon the role of the Court in the peaceful solution of international disputes."[46] In the *Nicaragua* case, the Court rejected a similar broad objection, although the United States in that case apparently never took the position that the dispute was not a "legal dispute" within the meaning of Article 36(2).[47]

With respect to the question of whether use-of-force issues, in particular, are somehow inherently "non-legal," Schachter concludes:

> ...whether the use of force has violated a legal obligation and given rise to international responsibility is on its face a legal question. Nothing in the U.N. Charter or the Statute of the Court suggests a contrary conclusion.[48]

2. *Would the Court's judicial consideration of armed conflicts be fundamentally inconsistent with the primary responsibility of the U.N. Security Council for international peace and security?*

In the *Nicaragua* case, the United States contended that use-of-force claims of the sort made by Nicaragua were intended by the Charter exclusively for resolution by political mechanisms, in particular the Security Council, and that consequently the Court should not intrude into such matters.[49] But the Court in that case again rejected the U.S. argument. The Court's communiqué on the judgment summarized its position on this issue as follows:

> The second ground of inadmissibility (paras. 89-90) relied on by the United States is that Nicaragua is, in effect, requesting that the Court in this case determine the existence of a threat to peace, a matter falling essentially within the competence of the Security Council because it is connected with Nicaragua's complaint involving the use of force. The Court examines this ground of inadmissibility at the same time as the third ground (paras. 91-98) based on the position of the Court within the United Nations system, including the impact of proceedings before the Court on the exercise of the inherent right of individual or collective

> self-defense under Article 51 of the Charter. The Court is of the opinion that the fact that a matter is before the Security Council should not prevent it from being dealt with by the Court and that both proceedings could be pursued pari passu. The Council has functions of a political nature assigned to it, whereas the Court exercises purely judicial functions. Both organs can therefore perform their separate but complementary functions with respect to the same events. In the present case, the complaint of Nicaragua is not about an ongoing war of armed conflict between it and the United States, but about a situation demanding the peaceful settlement of disputes, a matter which is covered by Chapter VI of the Charter. Hence, it is properly brought before the principal judicial organ of the United Nations for peaceful settlement. This is not a case which can only be dealt with by the Security Council in accordance with the provisions of Chapter VII of the Charter.[50]

On this question, Schachter concludes that, while it is theoretically conceivable that problems may arise in this respect:

> It is difficult to see why a judicial finding should be regarded as inimical to the Council's deliberations...
> ...the possibility that the Court and Council may impose conflicting requirements on a State does not appear to be a significant problem.[51]

3. *Does the U.N. Charter preclude the Court from adjudicating the legality of claims of self-defense?*

The United States argued that claims to the exercise of the inherent right of individual and collective self-defense were excluded by Article 51 of the Charter from review by the Court.

In the *Nicaragua* case, the Court again rejected the American argument and found that, "the inherent right of self-defense referred to in the Charter is a 'right indicative of a legal dimension'."[52] Schachter concludes: "The International Court rejected the argument that it was precluded from passing on a state's claim to self-defense because of the Security Council's primary responsibility for maintaining international peace and security. It noted that nothing in the Charter or the Statute of the Court suggests such a limitation."[53]

4. *Is the Court incapable of dealing with cases involving the use of force due to inherent limits on its fact-finding capabilities in such cases?*

The United States has suggested on numerous occasions that the Court faces enormous difficulties in determining the facts in a situation of ongoing armed conflict.[54] However, Schachter writes:

> ...one cannot conclude as an *a priori* matter that limits on the fact-finding capabilities of the Court preclude adjudication in cases involving the use of force.[55]....It cannot be said that they [current military operations on a substantial scale] are *a priori* intractable to judicial procedures because they relate to conflicts or because one party is uncooperative.[56]

The conclusion of the Court, of Schachter, and of others, as well as my own judgment, is that there are no inherent legal barriers to the adjudication of cases involving the use of force, either by the Court or by other judicial tribunals.[57]

Are Judicial Procedures Likely to be a Useful Way to Resolve Situations Involving the Use of Force?

To conclude that the Court or other international tribunals can legally decide use-of-force cases does not mean that they are necessarily a good way of handling such problems.

Obviously, adjudication is only one of many possible ways of dealing with international disputes. The most usual, and in most cases the best, way of doing so is through direct negotiation between or among the parties; consequently, it is not surprising that states will normally prefer negotiation to any other dispute settlement method, particularly those involving third parties. But if the parties are at an impasse, or for some other reason wish to try other ways of trying to resolve their differences, there are, of course, a spectrum of other methods available. These include, as described in Article 33 of the Charter, inquiry, mediation, conciliation, and various non-binding third-party techniques, as well as judicial techniques such as arbitration and resort to the Court.

Thus, in deciding whether to resort to adjudication of a dispute, rather than to use some other method, the parties generally will weigh the advantages and disadvantages of adjudication against those of various other techniques, choosing that method or combination of methods which seems on balance to offer the best prospect of success with the least amount of risk. In a recent effort to understand better how states might approach these decisions, Professor Thomas Franck and I,[58] among others, have tried to suggest some of the possible advantages[59] and disadvantages[60] of adjudication, as compared with other techniques. This comparison may suggest why states are often reluctant to turn to adjudication for the settlement of their disputes—especially those which they view as involving their "vital interests."

While this analysis was primarily directed at developing the pros and cons of adjudication generally, it also would seem relevant to decisions by foreign office officials regarding the use of judicial procedures to deal with cases of a particular character, such as use-of-force cases. Consequently, it may be useful, drawing on this previous work, to note certain features of adjudication which may particularly influence decision-making, one way or the other, as to the submission of use-of-force cases to the Court or other international tribunals.

Some Possible Advantages

Some reasons why a state might be particularly interested in considering the use of judicial procedures as a way of trying to resolve a dispute involving the use of force might include the following:

1. Adjudication may be able peacefully to resolve the problem. If the risks or costs of armed conflict are very great, and the parties are at impasse and there is no hope for negotiated settlement, even a state generally reluctant to accept judicial procedures may prefer them to the alternative of war. For example, in the Iraq-Kuwait crisis, either the United States, Iraq, or both, conceivably could have referred some or all of the issues concerned to the Court as a way of escaping armed conflict.
2. Adjudication may make compromise or concession politically possible. Situations involving the actual or threatened use of force are often seen by the public as involving "national honor," raise strong public emotions, and thus are politically sensitive. Even if government officials privately consider compromise reasonable and desirable, they may as a practical matter be politically unable to do so. As often pointed out, adjudication may offer a way of escaping from this dilemma by "passing the buck" to a court, and letting it take the responsibility for any compromise or concession. Indeed, where one or both states have agreed in advance to the compulsory jurisdiction of the Court or another tribunal, there will be a presumption in favor of permitting the dispute to be resolved through judicial procedures rather than resort to force, at least somewhat insulating officials from political attack for doing so.
3. Adjudication may be preferable to the use of force for a state which believes that it will probably or certainly lose a test of force. Settling disputes through the use of force may be a good way for great powers or militarily stronger states, but it is obviously not a very good way for smaller and weaker states. In contrast, for weaker states, adjudication is likely to provide more of a "level playing field" in which they can present their case on a plane of

equality, without the outcome being preordained by superior military, political, and economic power. Indeed, even if a weaker state thinks it has a poor legal case, it may still be better off going to court than going to war.

4. Adjudication may provide a "cooling-off" period in which the parties can negotiate or where the situation may de-escalate. If reference of the dispute to a Court has the effect of forestalling or restraining the use of force, this may be useful to one or both parties by providing time in which violence or threats can de-escalate, emotions cool, and negotiated solutions be explored. This may be the case even if the parties later decide not to pursue their legal claim to final judgment.
5. Adjudication can help one state by at least delaying the use of force. Even if one state is not serious about seeking a judicial settlement, or believes that the other state will not accept a final judicial settlement, any delay may still be useful in allowing it time to ready its defenses, secure allies, or otherwise position itself more favorably for an eventual conflict.
6. A willingness to accept adjudication may lend legitimacy to a state's position and help it gain internal and international support. By indicating that it is prepared to go to court, a state can demonstrate not only that it is willing to settle the matter peacefully but that it believes in the justice of its cause. This may strengthen internal and external support for its position, even if conflict subsequently occurs.
7. Adjudication can strengthen international law regarding the use of force and the peaceful settlement of disputes, as well as the international institutions supporting them. Every state has a stake in supporting U.N. Charter and other rules designed to prevent aggression and conflict, as well as the continued viability of international institutions such as the Court. A willingness to submit use-of-force cases to the Court or other judicial procedures will both demonstrate and implement this interest and commitment.

Some Possible Disadvantages

Some of the reasons why a state might be averse to considering judicial procedures as a way of trying to resolve a dispute involving the use of force include the following:

1. Adjudication may result in decisions which are politically unacceptable in that they are perceived to threaten a state's

national security or other vital interests. As indicated, disputes involving the use of force may sometimes involve issues of national security, national honor or self-defense which officials are unwilling to entrust to third parties or to risk losing. If officials lack confidence in the Court or in the impartiality of its judges, they will be particularly reluctant to take such risks.

2. Adjudication may prevent or inhibit a state from protecting its interests through the use of force, or at least delay its doing so. What is usually an advantage to a weaker state—the fact that reference to a court makes outcomes less dependent on military or political power—may, of course, often be a disadvantage to a militarily or politically more powerful state. However, it is worth noting that a proposal to refer a dispute to adjudication may conceivably be used by an aggressive state as a tactic to forestall or obstruct its victim or other countries from taking effective self-defensive or retaliatory measures, or at least to delay such coercive reactions while it strengthens its own military or political position. For example, where a state has used force to occupy territory, it might hope that reference of the matter to the Court would work to its advantage by freezing the status quo in its favor.
3. An international tribunal may have particular difficulty in dealing with disputes involving the use of force, due to the rapidly changing nature of such situations, the difficulty of securing evidence in chaotic situations of conflict, and the confidential or sensitive nature of relevant evidence based on intelligence. While, as indicated, such evidentiary problems may not be present in all cases, they are likely to occur in at least some situations, particularly those involving a continuing and large-scale use of force.
4. Disputes involving the use of force may often be only a symptom of deeper, highly political and more complex conflicts or differences, which adjudication cannot effectively resolve. As Franck and others have pointed out, courts are inherently conservative, looking primarily to the past and deciding who wins and who loses strictly according to law rather than the practical and ongoing needs of the parties and situation. But use-of-force situations may require, for their appropriate disposition, more sophisticated and crafted types of compromise solutions, capable of continual adjustment and fine-tuning as the situation is dealt with.

Some Hypotheses and Suggestions

Despite the complexity of the interests involved, there are some specific points to make on the usefulness of adjudication in use-of-force cases:

1. There are at least some cases involving the use of force in which adjudication is likely to be useful and acceptable to the parties as a way of resolving such disputes.

While adjudication has not been widely used, there have been a number of cases in which it has proved helpful in resolving disputes in which at least some use of force was involved—for example, the *Corfu Channel* and *Fisheries Jurisdiction* cases and the *Alabama Claims, Naulilaa* and *I'm Alone* arbitrations. Some would argue that it was also helpful in the *Nicaragua, Tehran Hostages* and (thus far) the *Iran Air 655* cases. Consequently, it seems very important that we not automatically rule out, *a priori*, the use of courts as a way of trying to deal with use-of-force disputes, but instead keep the adjudicative option open and readily available.

2. The attitude of states towards adjudication of cases involving the use of force will depend largely on their perception as to whether the use of force, on the one hand, or adjudication, on the other, is more likely to advance their immediate interests.

Normally, relatively more powerful states should be expected to be more reluctant to submit use-of-force cases to adjudication than less powerful states. Thus, in the *Nicaragua* case, the United States apparently regarded Nicaragua's reference of the case to the Court as obstructing its efforts to employ more coercive means of achieving its objective of ousting the Sandinista regime, while the Sandinista government apparently saw bringing the case as a way of counterbalancing United States power and achieving a "more level playing field."[61]

However, military or political power cannot be judged simply in the abstract, but rather only, first, as compared with that of an actual or anticipated adversary and, second, as effectively deployed at the time and place of confrontation. Thus, in the *Fisheries Jurisdiction* case, it was the United Kingdom, unable to deal effectively with Icelandic harassment and port closings, that decided to take the matter to the Court, and Iceland which refused to accept the Court's jurisdiction. Again, in the *Tehran Hostages* case, the United States found it preferable to take Iran to court rather than to try to use its superior military power, since it was unwilling to risk a major military confrontation with Iran which might in any event result in the loss rather than the saving of the hostages.

3. There is probably no category of use-of-force disputes which can *a priori* be said so inherently to involve national security or "vital interests" that a state would never consider submitting such cases to adjudication.

As indicated, it is evident that states will not normally wish to entrust matters affecting their national security to the uncertain decisions of third party tribunals. This will be the case particularly where they believe they are in a position to protect their interests best through the unilateral use of force or other coercive individual or collective pressures. However, if the alternative is sufficiently grim, a nation might conceivably be willing to put even the question of its national survival before a court. For example, in the Iraq-Kuwait crisis, absent effective help by the United States or the United Nations, Kuwait presumably would have been willing to submit the question of its right to independence to the Court, rather than face the certainty of continued Iraqi occupation and annexation. And, indeed, in retrospect Iraq might have reasonably preferred to submit its claims against Kuwait to adjudication rather than to face continued blockade and the devastating war that ultimately was visited upon both countries.

4. Adjudication is likely to be most useful in cases in which the use of force is restricted to a small-scale and already-completed incident.

In the case of disputes arising out of a single incident or small-scale use of force, the advantages of adjudication seem most likely to outweigh its disadvantages. Thus, in most cases, all of the parties will wish the dispute quickly settled, the situation involved does not pose a serious or continuing threat, and adjudication will permit officials to shift responsibility for settlement to a third party tribunal. The various Court and arbitration cases just mentioned are principally of this kind and again tend to support this hypothesis.[62]

Similarly, Professor Andreas Lowenfeld argued persuasively for the usefulness, to both the United States and Iran, of letting the Court decide the dispute between them concerning the downing of Iran Air 655.[63] It is of interest in this respect that the United States itself has brought a number of cases involving such aerial incidents,[64] that it has consistently distinguished its position in the *Nicaragua* case from the situation in the *Corfu Channel* case, and that the United States apparently has indicated in the *Iran Air 655* case that it will dispute only the Court's exercise of jurisdiction over the matter.

5. In view of the special risks and complexity of decisions concerning adjudication of use-of-force cases, states anticipating disputes involving the use of force will be reluctant to agree in advance to their adjudication.

This is likely to be true in particular of relatively powerful states, which may wish to retain maximum flexibility to employ their power to protect their interest and achieve their policy. They may consider that, even if adjudication might in some cases be a useful option, any such choice should best be left to *ad hoc* decision, based on the particular facts and circumstances at the time. It is likely to be less true of states which are either relatively weaker than their potential enemies, believe that they are very unlikely to be involved in disputes involving the use of force, or have an especially strong commitment to the principle of international law and adjudication and wish to encourage support for such judicial procedures.

6. It may be possible to devise arrangements and procedures which increase the willingness of states to resort to judicial procedures as a way of dealing with use-of-force cases.

If we wish to encourage states to be more willing to use judicial procedures to deal with cases involving the use of force, we can try to find ways of meeting their special concerns regarding the risks of using adjudication in such cases.

Some possibilities might include the following:

- permit states to agree only to nonbinding or advisory opinions in use-of-force cases;
- make greater use of the U.N. General Assembly's and Security Council's authority under Article 95 of the Charter to request the Court to give an advisory opinion on legal questions relevant to their consideration of situations involving the use of force;
- authorize the U.N. Secretary-General to request advisory opinions of the Court when legal questions arise within the scope of the Secretary-General's activities in dealing with matters which may threaten the maintenance of international peace and security;[65]
- more carefully define the circumstances and conditions under which the Court may issue interim orders of protection in use-of-force cases, or make it clear that they will not be regarded as mandatory;
- facilitate the parties "tailoring" the scope of the Court's jurisdiction, and hence its judgment, to their particular needs and wishes—for example, by agreements limiting the Court's judgments to a declaration of generally applicable principles regarding eventual settlement, to findings only on particular factual issues, or to rulings only on certain legal issues;
- continue to make available and improve procedures for special chambers, limited to judges mutually acceptable to the parties;
- make available an expedited procedure to facilitate the rapid reference of use-of-force cases to the Court;
- alternatively, develop arrangements for expedited arbitration of such issues by special arbitration procedures, outside the framework of the Court;
- develop special procedures for dealing, as necessary, with any special evidentiary issues relevant to the handling of use-of-force cases, including the problem of providing protection for confidential information;
- develop arrangements for coordinating, as necessary, the judicial consideration of use-of-force cases with other types of peaceful settlement procedures, either in the U.N. Security Council or

elsewhere; and
develop more flexible procedures regarding agreement in advance to adjudication (or "compromissory" arrangements) respecting use-of-force cases, which permit states some freedom to "opt out" of such arrangements in particularly compelling circumstances.

The Relevance of Current United States-Soviet Discussions Concerning the Court

In 1987, Soviet President Mikhail Gorbachev proposed a variety of measures to strengthen the role of international law and institutions in maintaining international peace and security, including agreements among the states which are permanent members of the Security Council to expand the Court's compulsory jurisdiction.[66] The United States responded to this initiative and, since July 1989, the two governments have been conducting discussions concerning possible cooperation between them to extend the Court's jurisdiction. The Soviet Union subsequently demonstrated its seriousness regarding the Court by agreeing to subject itself to the compulsory jurisdiction of the Court with respect to disputes involving six human rights treaties to which it is party.[67]

On September 23, 1989, as one of the outcomes of talks between the U.S. Secretary of State and the Soviet Foreign Minister, a joint statement was issued indicating that the two governments had agreed that it is desirable to enhance the role of the Court in the resolution of international disputes in a manner consistent with national security and other interests, that they had jointly developed proposals for this purpose, and that they agreed that the permanent members of the U.N. Security Council should lead the way in seeking to carry out this policy.[68] According to the statement, the proposals, which would involve agreement in advance to the Court's compulsory jurisdiction over certain types of disputes, incorporate three principal ideas:

(1) relying on existing treaties to identify disputes to be covered;
(2) providing the opportunity to select a chamber chosen from among the members of the full court to adjudicate the dispute; and
(3) excluding from the jurisdiction of the Court certain categories of issues that are widely recognized to be highly sensitive to states and inappropriate for resolution by judicial action in the absence of express consent of the states involved.

The United States and the Soviet Union have reportedly initiated consultations regarding these ideas with the other permanent members of the Security Council (China, France, and the United Kingdom), with a view to developing a common approach to the jurisdiction of the Court among the five that can be embodied in an agreement which would then be opened to all other countries. Several meetings among the five permanent members on this subject have been held. The Chinese and French governments, traditionally averse to the concept of compulsory Court jurisdiction, have agreed to continue these discussions.

The discussions have remained confidential and their exact content and status are not public knowledge. It is understood, however, that the discussions contemplate a framework agreement, based on Article 36(1) rather than 36(2) of the Court's Statute, with an Annex separately listing those specific agreements, or possibly categories of disputes, which the parties consent to make subject to the Court's jurisdiction. Reportedly, it is contemplated that the agreement would initially provide for the Court's jurisdiction over disputes involving certain agreements relating to terrorism and to the control of narcotics.[69]

The conclusion of such an agreement among the permanent members, particularly if joined in by other nations, could significantly affect international dispute settlement and the work of the Court in the near future. In particular, if such an agreement is in fact concluded, and if, as seems probable, the United States insists that any such agreement broadly exclude use-of-force cases, the Court might play an even less significant role in the resolution of use-of-force disputes in the future than it has in the past.

Conclusion

There is broad agreement that judicial procedures are likely to have only a limited role in resolving cases involving the use of force.[70] Indeed, Schachter concludes that "[a] future acceptance of compulsory jurisdiction by the United States might reasonably include a carefully drafted reservation excluding disputes relating to ongoing large-scale hostilities."[71] And Franck proposes a quite far-reaching United States reservation of this nature.[72]

I agree with this assessment that judicial procedures are unlikely, at least in the near future, to play a major part in international dispute resolution, either generally or in relation, more particularly, to disputes involving the use of force. Indeed, in other writings I have emphasized my belief that adjudication has distinct limitations as a dispute settlement technique, and that other dispute settlement methods, such as negotiation and conciliation, are often preferable and more effective.[73]

Nevertheless, judicial procedures can serve a useful function in at least some significant disputes involving the use of force and, consequently, it is important, both to the United States and to other nations, that this possibility not be foreclosed.[74]

For this reason, I am concerned about the potential breadth of the U.S. position in this respect, both as expressed in and since the *Nicaragua* case and, more particularly, in the current U.S.-Soviet and related discussions concerning a possible agreement among the permanent members of the Security Council regarding the compulsory jurisdiction of the Court. I have elsewhere raised various questions concerning the usefulness of this current initiative, particularly in its apparently deliberate bypassing of the accepted Article 36(2) procedure, its stress on the use of special chambers rather than the full Court, its suggestion of broad and self-judging exclusions from any jurisdiction, and its consequent potential, in my opinion, for damaging the Court and the concept of international adjudication.[75] I will confine my comments here, however, solely to the issue of the scope of any use-of-force exclusion.

While the discussions are confidential, it seems likely that the United States will seek to couch such exclusions in very broad terms, and that it will expect its views in this respect to be shared, or in any event accepted, by the Soviet Union and the other permanent members. Moreover, while it is true that any such agreement among the permanent five (and possibly other countries) need not preclude any or all of them from also accepting the Court's compulsory jurisdiction under other additional arrangements, such as the "optional clause" of Article 36(2) of the Court's Statute or specific compromissory provisions in particular treaties, it seems likely that it will in practice have such an effect, at least for the United States. Consequently, given these potentially far-reaching consequences, the United States should take such a position only after the most careful governmental consideration and with full opportunity for congressional and public comment. Moreover, if there is to be an exclusion of some type for use-of-force situations, it should be as narrow as possible.

Indeed, the fact that any such agreement on compulsory jurisdiction between the United States and Soviet Union, or among the permanent members, includes some type of reservation respecting use-of-force cases may, in practice, be less important than the attitudes which states have towards any such exclusion, and the procedures they provide regarding its waiver. As indicated, it seems evident that the United States, and probably at least some other states, are likely to insist on some such use-of-force exclusion as a "last ditch" protection against what is perceived as the "Nicaragua experience." But the parties might nevertheless expressly recognize in their agreement that all use-of-force cases are not necessarily inappropriate for judicial settlement, and that states should normally give "good faith" consideration to the submission of such cases to the Court wherever practicable. The agreement also should provide procedures facilitating the waiver of any "use-of-force" exclusion in cases where states are in fact prepared to accept adjudication.

Any such review by the United States of its position in this respect should, in particular, take into consideration the following:

1. The fact that judicial procedures may prove very useful in dealing with some, if not many, kinds of use-of-force situations, and that it is important that such use not be either legally or politically discouraged;
2. The fact that the U.S. position in this respect has developed largely as an outgrowth of a single unique situation and experience—the *Nicaragua* case—and is undoubtedly strongly influenced by the peculiar history and politics of that case. With the passage of time, of the officials particularly connected with the *Nicaragua* case, and of the political context in which that case arose and has been viewed, it may be time to reconsider, from a more detached perspective, its significance and implications;
3. The fact that U.S.-Soviet relations are at a particular cusp of history in which the prospects of their cooperation have opened unique and previously undreamed-of possibilities for the development of international law and institutions and the collective promotion of international peace and security. There are indications that the Soviet Union might be prepared to take the risk of accepting broad Court jurisdiction concerning at least some types of disputes, even those which might involve use-of-force issues;[76] if so, it would be very regrettable for the United States to be the one to obstruct such a development; and
4. The fact that, in the course of the Iraq-Kuwait crisis, the United States, and indeed most of the international community, evidenced and acknowledged a heightened appreciation of the importance of international law and institutions, and a renewed commitment to their development.[77] Moreover, it became apparent from the crisis, as it was implicit in the *Tehran Hostage* crisis, that the United States and other permanent members may be increasingly not the chief instigators, but rather among the victims and those seriously affected by the use of force by other countries, and that they may consequently have a renewed interest in subjecting the use of force to more effective legal control.

We would do well to recall the words of Andrew Carnegie in his letter of December 14, 1910, establishing the Carnegie Peace Fund. The purpose of his gift, Andrew Carnegie wrote, was:

> ...to hasten the abolition of international war, the foulest blot upon our civilisation. Altho [sic] we no longer eat our fellow men nor torture prisoners nor sack cities killing their inhabitants, we still kill each other in war like barbarians....The nation is criminal

which refuses arbitration and drives its adversary to a tribunal which knows nothing of righteous judgment.[78]

We owe it to our own and future generations to encourage and leave the door open to judicial settlement of international disputes in use-of-force as well as other cases.

Notes

1. *Case Concerning Military and Paramilitary Activities In and Against Nicaragua (Nic. v. U.S.)*, 1984 I.C.J. 392 (Judgment of Nov. 26, 1984 on Jurisdiction and Admissibility), *reprinted in* 23 I.L.M. 468 (1984)[hereinafter *Nicaragua (Juris.)*]; 1986 I.C.J. 14 (Judgment of June 27, 1986 on Merits), *reprinted in* 25 I.L.M. 1023 (1986) [hereinafter *Nicaragua*].

2. *See, e.g.*, Statement of U.S. Department of State concerning "U.S. Withdrawal From the Proceedings Initiated by Nicaragua in the International Court of Justice," Jan. 18, 1985, *reprinted in* 24 I.L.M. 246 (1985); U.S. Department of State Statement of October 7, 1985, and Legal Adviser Sofaer's Statement of December 4, 1985, Concerning U.S. Termination of its Declaration Submitting to the Compulsory Jurisdiction of the International Court of Justice, *both reprinted in* 24 I.L.M. 1742 (1985).

3. *See, e.g.,* Sofaer, *Adjudication in the International Court of Justice: Progress Through Realism*, 44 Record of the Assoc. of the Bar of the City of New York 462 (1989)[hereinafter "Sofaer"].

4. *See* Department of State Fact Sheet: "International Court of Justice," Sept. 23, 1989. *See also U.S. and the Russians Agree to Bigger World Court Role,* N.Y. Times, Aug. 7, 1989, at A5, col. 1; *see generally* Sofaer, *supra* note 3.

5. Schachter, *Disputes Involving the Use of Force* [hereinafter "Schachter"], in THE INTERNATIONAL COURT OF JUSTICE AT A CROSSROADS 223 (L. Damrosch ed. 1987) [hereinafter "Damrosch"]. *See also* Schachter, *Self-Defense and the Rule of Law*, 83 AM. J. INT'L L. 259 (1989)[hereinafter "Schachter, Self-Defense"].

6. T.M. FRANCK, JUDGING THE WORLD COURT (1987)[hereinafter "FRANCK"].

7. *See* Agreement for the Prosecution and Punishment of Major War Criminals of the European Axis (London Agreement), signed at London, Aug. 1945, 82 U.N.T.S. 279, with Annexed Charter of the International Military Tribunal (Nuremberg); International Military Tribunal for the Far East Proclaimed at Tokyo, 19 Jan. 1946 and amended 26 Apr. 1946, T.I.A.S. No. 1589, with Charter of the International Military Tribunal for the Far East. *See, e.g.*, A. TUSA & J. TUSA, THE NUREMBERG TRIAL (1989).

8. For a historical review, discussion, and various U.N. and other proposals

see, e.g., FERENCZ, AN INTERNATIONAL CRIMINAL COURT (1980); Pella, *Towards an International Criminal Court*, 44 AM. J. INT'L L. 37 (1980); M. Bassiouni, *Introduction to the History of Establishing an International Criminal Court*, in III INTERNATIONAL CRIMINAL LAW 181-85 (M. Bassiouni ed. 1987); M. BASSIOUNI, A DRAFT INTERNATIONAL CRIMINAL CODE AND DRAFT STATUTE FOR AN INTERNATIONAL CRIMINAL TRIBUNAL (1987); Draft Statute of the International Criminal Tribunal, prepared by the International Institute of Higher Studies in Criminal Sciences, *Eighth U.N. Congress on the Prevention of Crime and the Treatment of Offenders, Havana, Cuba (27 Aug. to 7 Sept. 1990)*, U.N. Doc. A/CONF.144/NGO ISISC (1990).

For earlier proposals by the International Law Commission, *see Draft Statute for an International Criminal Court* (Annex to the *Report of the Committee on International Criminal Jurisdiction, August 31, 1951)*, 7 GAOR (No. 11) at 23, U.N. Doc. A/2136 (1952); and *Revised Draft Statute for an International Criminal Court* (Annex to the *Report of the Committee on International Criminal Jurisdiction*, August 20, 1955), 9 U.N. GAOR Supp. (No. 12) at 21, U.N. Doc. A/2645 (1954).

In the most recent session of the International Law Commission, the concept of an international criminal court was examined at the request of the General Assembly of the United Nations. In July 1990, the International Law Commission reported its agreement in principle on the desirability of establishing a permanent international criminal court to be brought into relationship with the U.N. System. *See Report of the International Law Commission on the Work of its Forty-Second Session, Chapter II*, 45 U.N. GAOR Supp. (No. 10) at 36-54, U.N. Doc. A/45/10 (1990). For discussion, see, e.g., McCaffrey, *The Forty-Second Session of the International Law Commission*, 84 AM. J. INT'L L. 930 (1990).

9. *See, e.g., Foreign Minister Shevardnadze's Address to the U.N. General Assembly, Sept. 25, 1990*, U.N. Doc. A/45/PV6 (Sept. 28, 1990) at 41, excerpted in N.Y. Times, Sept. 26, 1990, at A10, col. 1. For an earlier proposal for an international court to investigate acts of international terrorism, see M. Gorbachev, *The Realities and Guarantees of a Secure World*, Pravda, Sept. 17, 1987; USSR Mission to the U.N., Press Release No. 119 (Sept. 17, 1987).

See also the recent request of the General Assembly that the International Law Commission report to it on this question, *supra* note 8.

In October 1990, the U.S. Congress adopted legislation stating the sense of the Congress as to the need to explore the establishment of an international criminal court. The President was requested to report to the Congress by October 1, 1991, on the results of his efforts in that regard and the Judicial Conference of the United States was requested to report to the Congress on the feasibility of and the relationship to the federal judiciary of such a court. *See* H. Con. Res. 66, 101st Cong., 1st Sess. (1989), revised and adopted by Congress as a result of amendment 3068 proposed by Senator Arlen Specter to the Foreign Operations Appropriation Bill for the 1991 fiscal year, 142 CONG. REC. 516216 (daily ed. Oct. 19, 1990) (Statement of Sen. Specter) and Supp. Statement of Senator Arlen Specter for the Congressional Record Regarding the Need for an International Criminal Court (Oct. 27, 1990).

10. Schachter writes:

> Cases involving the use of force extend over a wide variety of situations. The issues of law and fact raised by these different situations are almost endlessly diverse. Moreover, the political contexts vary widely. Obviously, one cannot easily generalize about the suitability of judicial settlement for such cases or foresee the national interests in using or avoiding judicial procedures in particular situations.

Schachter, *supra* note 5, at 223.

11. For example, it has been suggested that some third states believed that their interests were furthered by a continuation, rather than solution, of the Iran-Iraq conflict, and may have similar interests in prolonging or exacerbating the current Persian Gulf crisis.

12. Schachter, *supra* note 5, at 223. For a brief description of the relevant cases, *see* Schachter, *supra* note 5; *see also*, S. ROSENNE, THE WORLD COURT: WHAT IT IS AND HOW IT WORKS ch. 6 (4th rev. ed. 1989).

13. 1954 I.C.J. 99 and 103; 1956 I.C.J. 6 and 9; 1958 I.C.J. 158; 1959 I.C.J. 276.

14. 1960 I.C.J. 146.

15. 1980 I.C.J. 3.

16. 1949 I.C.J. 4 and 244.

17. 1959 I.C.J. 264.

18. 1974 I.C.J. 3.

19. 1959 I.C.J. 127.

20. *See Nicaragua, supra* note 1, and Schachter, *supra* note 5, at 223-4.

21. 1960 I.C.J. 192.

22. 1975 I.C.J. 12.

23. *Aerial Incident of 3 July 1988 (Iran v. U.S.)*, brought before the I.C.J. by Iran on May 17, 1989.

24. *Territorial Dispute (Libya v. Chad),* Order of 26 Oct. 1990, 1990 I.C.J. 149.

25. PAPERS RELATING TO THE TREATY OF WASHINGTON 49 (1872); MOORE, I HISTORY AND DIGEST OF THE INTERNATIONAL ARBITRATIONS TO WHICH THE UNITED STATES HAS BEEN A PARTY 653 (1898); WETTER, THE INTERNATIONAL ARBITRAL PROCESS PUBLIC AND PRIVATE 27-173 (1979).

26. *I'm Alone (Can. v. U.S.)*, 3 R. INT'L ARB. AWARDS 1609 (1935).

27. *Naulilaa Incident Arbitration,* 2 R. INT'L ARB. AWARDS 1012 (1928).

28. *Indo-Pakistan Western Boundary (Rann of Kutch) (India v. Pak.)*, 50 I.L.R. 2 (1968).

29. For discussion of these inquiries, see, e.g., J.G. MERRILLS INTERNATIONAL DISPUTE SETTLEMENT ch. 3 (1984).

30. SCOTT, HAGUE COURT REPORTS 410 (1916).

31. *Id.* at 413.

32. BAR-YAACOV, THE HANDLING OF INTERNATIONAL DISPUTES BY MEANS OF INQUIRY 156-171 (1974).

33. SCOTT, HAGUE COURT REPORTS 135 (1932).

34. I.L.R. 485 (1962) and Appendix A.

35. I have previously discussed certain aspects of this question in Bilder, *An*

Overview of International Dispute Settlement, 1 EMORY J. INT'L DISPUTE RES. 1, 7-11 (1986)[hereinafter "Bilder"].

36. *See* RESTATEMENT (THIRD) OF THE FOREIGN RELATIONS LAW OF THE UNITED STATES sec. 902 (Comment (e) and Reporters' Note 3).

37. *See* U.N. CHARTER art. 1, para. 1, art. 2, para. 3, art. 33.

38. *See* U.N. CHARTER arts. 35-38. Under Article 35, any state may bring any dispute to the attention of the Security Council or General Assembly. Under Article 36, the Security Council may, at any stage of a dispute the continuance of which is likely to endanger the maintenance of international peace or security, recommend appropriate procedures or methods of adjustment; in doing so, the Council should take into consideration that legal disputes should as a general rule be referred by the parties to the International Court of Justice. Article 37 provides that, should the parties to a dispute of the nature referred to in Article 33 fail to settle it by the means indicated in Article 33, they shall refer it to the Security Council which, if it deems that the continuance of the dispute is in fact likely to endanger the maintenance of international peace and security, shall decide whether to take action under Article 36 or to recommend such terms of settlement as it may consider appropriate. Article 38 provides: "Without prejudice to the provisions of Article 33 to 37, the Security Council may, if all the parties to any dispute so request, make recommendations to the parties with a view to a pacific settlement of the dispute."

39. Thus, in its statement explaining the United States withdrawal from the case, the Department of State said:

> The conflict in Central America...is not a narrow legal dispute; it is an inherently political problem that is not appropriate for judicial resolution. The conflict will be solved only by political diplomatic means--not through a judicial tribunal. The International Court of Justice was never intended to resolve issues of collective security and self-defense and is patently unsuited to such a role....The Court's decision raises a basic issue of sovereignty. The right of a state to defend itself or to participate in collective self-defense against aggression is an inherent sovereign right that cannot be compromised by inappropriate proceedings before the world court.... We are profoundly concerned about the long-term implications for the Court itself. The decision of November 26 represents an overreaching of the Court's limits, a departure from its tradition of judicial restraint, and a risky venture into treacherous political waters.... cases of this nature are not proper for adjudication by the Court.

See Statement on the U.S. Withdrawal from the Proceedings Initiated by Nicaragua in the International Court of Justice, Jan. 18, 1985, 24 I.L.M. 246 (1985).

40. *See Nicaragua, supra* note 1, at para. 84.

41. In a recent speech and article, then State Department Legal Adviser Abraham Sofaer noted:

> The United States considered its objection to the admissibility (subject matter jurisdiction) of the Nicaragua application to be fundamental. It goes to the relative allocation of authority to the Security Council, the Court, and to nations which exercise their right to individual and collective self-defense. The United States

> argued, and continues to believe, that the framers of the Charter intended to exclude the Court from these functions, absent consent by all interested parties.

See Sofaer, *supra* note 3, at 491, n. 87.

42. *See Nicaragua (Juris.), supra* note 1, at para. 84-103, and *Nicaragua, supra* note 1, at para. 32-35.

43. *See* Schachter, *supra* note 5.

44. RESTATEMENT (THIRD) OF THE FOREIGN RELATIONS LAW OF THE UNITED STATES sec. 903 (Reporters' Note 7).

45. 1963 I.C.J. 15, 29.

46. 1980 I.C.J. 19-20.

47. *See Nicaragua, supra* note 1, at para. 32. *See also* Gordon, *Legal Disputes Under Article 36(2)*, in Damrosch, *supra* note 5, at 183.

48. Schachter, *supra* note 5, at 228.

49. *See, e.g.*, Statement of Legal Adviser Sofaer to Senate Foreign Relations Committee, Dec. 4, 1985. *See also* Acevedo, *Disputes Under Consideration by the U.N. Security Council or Regional Bodies,* in Damrosch, *supra* note 5, at 242.

50. I.C.J. Communiqué No. 84/39, Nov. 26, 1984, at 10.

51. Schachter, *supra* note 5, at 232.

52. I.C.J. Communiqué No. 84/39, 26 Nov. 1984, at 9.

53. *See* Schachter, *supra* note 5, at 233. Schachter continues:

> These judicial decisions [the Nicaragua, Nuremberg and Hostages judgments] are consistent with the firm proposition that there are legal limits on the use of force and with its corollary that it cannot be left solely to the discretion of a state to determine whether, how far, and how long it may use force in its self defense.

54. *See, e.g.,* FRANCK, *supra* note 6, at 43-47, *citing, e.g.*, Rashkow, *Fact Finding by the World Court*, 148 WORLD AFF. 50 (1985).

55. Schachter, *supra* note 5, at 236.

56. *Id.* at 240.

57. Several years ago I wrote in a broader context:

> A distinction is sometimes drawn between so-called "legal" or "justiciable" disputes, and "political," "non-legal", or "non-justiciable disputes". . . . It is true that nations may typically be less willing to agree to adjudication of some kinds of disputes than others; . . . It is also probably true that judicial settlement is not necessarily the "best" or most useful technique for dealing with certain kinds of disputes. However, . . . it is difficult to argue that particular types of disputes are inherently beyond the jurisdiction or capacity of a Court or arbitral tribunal to decide, even if the parties desire and have given their consent to the Court doing so. . . . Consequently, if Iran and Iraq [during their conflict] both decided they wished to submit their consent to the International Court for settlement . . . I do not believe that the Court either would or could appropriately decline jurisdiction. Thus, at least in theory, all international disputes seem to be "justiciable. . . .

Bilder, *supra* note 35, at 15-17.

58. *See Franck, supra* note 6, and Bilder, *International Dispute Settlement and the Role of Adjudication*, 1 EMORY J. INT'L DISPUTE RES. 339 (1987) and in Damrosch, *supra* note 5, at 155; Bilder, *International Third Party Dispute Settlement*, 17 DENVER J. INT'L L. & POL'Y 471 (1989); BILDER, MANAGING THE RISKS OF INTERNATIONAL AGREEMENT 56-61 (1981).

59. For example, the suggested advantages of adjudication listed in the articles in note 58 *supra*, include: (i) it is dispositive, ideally, at least, putting an end to the dispute; (ii) it is impersonal, permitting the parties to pass responsibility for unfavorable outcomes to the tribunal; (iii) it is principled and impartial, ostensibly deciding the matter by neutral principle rather than power, bias or whim; (iv) it is serious and demonstrates that the state instituting suit really believes in its claim; (v) it is orderly and can be useful in resolving complex factual and technical disputes; (vi) it can sometimes "depoliticize" a dispute, reducing tensions or buying time; (vii) it can provide rules socially useful for guiding conduct and resolving disputes more broadly; (viii) it can reflect, and educate the community as to, social values and interests of the international community more broadly, apart from those of the parties alone; and (ix) it can be system-reinforcing, supporting respect for and the development of international law.

60. Suggested disadvantages of adjudication listed in the articles in note 58 *supra*, include: (i) it involves the possibility of losing; (ii) adjudicative settlement may be illusory or superficial, deciding the "legal" but not the "real" issues in dispute; (iii) it can be inflexible, resulting in a "win-lose" rather than a compromise decision; (iv) it can be judgmental, labeling one party as a "lawbreaker," rather than providing for a shared acceptance of responsibility as a face-saving way out of a conflictual situation; (v) it looks primarily to the past rather than to the future, possibly jeopardizing the maintenance of a useful ongoing relationship; (vi) it is conservative; (vii) its results are unpredictable; (viii) it may not be impartial; (ix) an adjudicative settlement is imposed on the parties; (x) it is adversarial and may escalate the dispute or conflict; (xi) it may freeze the parties' options and discourage settlement; (xii) it can be complex and costly; and (xiii) there is no assurance that an adjudicative decision will be enforceable.

61. *See, e.g.*, Gill, *Litigation Strategy in the Nicaragua Case at the International Court*, INTERNATIONAL LAW AT A TIME OF PERPLEXITY 197 (Y. Dinstein ed. 1989).

62. Schachter comments on this question:

> Having these cases in mind, it hardly seems perilous for a state to agree to adjudicate cases involving acts of force such as shooting incidents or isolated attacks under reciprocally binding acceptances of compulsory jurisdiction.

Schachter, Self-Defense, *supra* note 5, at 276.

63. Lowenfeld, *Looking Backward and Looking Ahead* in *Agora: The Downing of Iran Air Flight 655*, 83 AM. J. INT'L L. 336 (1989).

64. *See supra* note 13.

65. *See Report of the Secretary-General on the Work of the Organization*, 45 U.N. GAOR Supp. (No. 1), U.N. Doc. A/45/1 (1990); *see also* Schwebel, *Widening the Advisory Jurisdiction of the International Court of Justice Without Amending Its Statute*, 33 CATH. U. L. REV. 355 (1984).

66. *See* Mikhail Gorbachev, *The Realities and Guarantees of a Secure World,* Pravda, Sept. 17, 1987; USSR Mission to the UN, Press Release No. 119 (Sept. 17, 1987), *supra* note 9.

67. *See Soviets to Accept World Court Role in "Human Rights"*, N.Y. Times, Aug. 7, 1989, at A5, col. 1. The Soviet Union did so by withdrawing reservations it had previously entered to the articles of these agreements providing for such compulsory jurisdiction.

68. *See supra* note 4.

69. Discussions reportedly have recently "run into difficulties, with Britain and other critics contending that the initiative might reduce the role of international law rather than enhancing it." It is reported that under the proposal

> ... any country could exclude any dispute it deems to touch upon national security, self-defense, internal affairs or territorial integrity. Critics call these standards so broad that they could be invoked to exclude almost any case. Moreover, the United States could use the new settlement mechanism to escape from its obligation to accept the jurisdiction of the full court in disputes over treaties of commerce and navigation with about 60 countries.

World Court Plan Meets Difficulties, N.Y. Times, June 24, 1990, at A9, col. 1.

70. *See, e.g.*, Schachter, Self-Defense, *supra* note 5, at 276-77; I.L. CLAUDE, JR., SWORDS INTO PLOWSHARES 234-35 (4th ed. 1971).

71. Schachter, *supra* note 5, at 241.

72. Franck, *supra* note 5, at 111. The reservation would provide:

> The acceptance...shall apply to all disputes, subject to the foregoing reservation, other than disputes relating to or connected with facts or situations of hostilities, armed conflicts, individual or collective actions taken in self-defense, resistance to aggression, fulfillment of obligations imposed by international bodies, and other similar or related acts, measures or situations in which the United States is, has been, or may in the future, be involved.

73. *See* references in *supra* notes 35 and 58.

74. As Professor John Murphy pointed out in discussing this issue some years ago:

> None of the foregoing cases, of course, indicates that the Court has played or is likely to play a major role in maintaining peace. The Court's contribution in the area has been much less than was originally expected...This situation is unlikely to change. What should be avoided, however, is a conclusion that the Court has no meaningful role to play in the control of international violence. As we have seen above in the Fisheries Jurisdiction, Nuclear Tests and Iran Hostages cases, the Court may be able to make a contribution to the control of international violence even where the defendant state refuses to acknowledges the Court's jurisdiction. At

a minimum, the Court remains one of the means of peaceful settlement that states may turn to as an alternative to the use of armed force.

J.F. MURPHY, THE UNITED NATIONS AND THE CONTROL OF VIOLENCE 121 (1982).

75. Presentation at Panel on "The International Court of Justice," Annual Meeting of the American Branch of the International Law Association, Nov. 3, 1989, New York City.

76. *See, e.g., USSR Memorandum on Enhancing the Role of International Law,* U.N. Doc. GA/A/44/585 (Oct. 2, 1989); *Soviets Urge Stronger Role for World Court*, N.Y. Times, Oct. 8, 1989, at A4, col. 1.

77. President's Address Before a Joint Session of the Congress on the Persian Gulf Crisis and the Federal Budget Deficit, 26 WEEKLY COMP. PRES. DOC. 1358 (Sept. 11, 1990); President's Address Before the 45th Session of the United Nations General Assembly in New York City, 26 WEEKLY COMP. PRES. DOC. 1496 (Oct. 1, 1990); Foreign Minister Shevardnadze's Address to the U.N. General Assembly, Sept. 25, 1990, *supra* note 9.

78. Original letter on display at the Carnegie Endowment for International Peace, Washington, D.C.

29

Indirect Aggression in the International Court

Stephen M. Schwebel

We are living through dramatic days of the direct use of force by one state against another across an internationally recognized frontier. Today's issue is not one of indirect aggression but of direct conquest. Apart from the failed but bloody and destructive attempt to conquer the Republic of Korea in the early 1950s, this use of force is largely without parallel in the 45 years in which the U.N. Charter has been in force. As has been widely appreciated, current events rather evoke events of the 1930s.

Equally unparalleled is the unity and trenchancy of the resultant resolutions of the Security Council. Those resolutions are replete with invocations of international law and the authority of the Security Council to bind states—to bind both the object of the sanctions and the states enjoined to apply sanctions. Current concerns thus focus on a direct use of force which the Security Council has authoritatively condemned and is seeking vigorously to deal with by applying the panoply of powers accorded it by the terms of the Charter.

I cannot speculate on whether the International Court of Justice may play a part in these portentous proceedings, nor can I address events bearing on cases pending before the Court; I am obliged to confine my remarks to the substance of what I have earlier expressed in Court opinions. Within those confines, I do wish to make some observations on what part the Court can play in dealing with the legal aspects of the use of force in international relations, and what role it has played.

In a recent case of exceptional notoriety, the Court rejected the contention that it was only for the Security Council and not for the Court to adjudge an allegation of the continuing use of force internationally. The permanent member of the Security Council which was respondent in that case, the United States, argued that the scheme of the Charter and the Statute of the Court was one in which it fell to the Security Council to adjudge and deal with ongoing uses of international force, whereas the Court's authority fell, so to speak, not under Chapter VII of the Charter but under Chapter VI. Article 36 of Chapter VI provides that the Security Council should take into consideration that legal disputes as a general rule should be referred by the parties to the International Court of Justice. Chapter VII makes no reference to the Court at all. It entrusts to the Security Council alone the determination of a threat to the peace, breach of the peace, or an act of aggression. It was argued that it made little sense to read the Charter and the Statute as empowering the permanent members of the Security Council to veto such a determination in the Council while permitting the Court to make precisely that determination by a veto-free decision in the very same case and on the very same facts.

The Court as a whole did not accept this argument, nor did I, though I found it more plausible than did most of my colleagues. A difficulty with the argument, in my view, is that it requires reading the provisions of the Charter and the Statute as implicitly withholding from the Court the authority to render judgment respecting allegations of acts of aggression, while nothing explicit in the Charter or the Statute so prescribes. On the contrary, the language of the Statute cuts the other way. The Statute provides that the jurisdiction of the Court comprises "all cases" which the parties refer to it and "all matters" specially provided for in treaties in force,[1] and it further provides that the States parties to the Statute may recognize the compulsory jurisdiction of the Court "in all legal disputes" concerning the interpretation of a treaty, any question of international law, the existence of any fact which, if established, would constitute a breach of an international obligation, and the nature or extent of the reparation to be made for such breach.[2] These are capacious terms, which may embrace disputes over the use of force in international relations, whether that use be past, present, or threatened. Cases before the Court in which issues of the current use of force have been posed have been rare, but it does not follow that such a case is beyond the authority of the Court, if jurisdiction in the particular case has been accorded to it. The relevant practice of the Court and the argumentation of parties before it, while not extensive, support this conclusion.

In addition to the argument of admissibility, a prudential argument of justiciability was made, namely that the Court was not in a position to find the facts of the ongoing use of force, where the situation was inherently fluid and where the facts at issue were in controversy and were indeed covertly rather than overtly treated. While I was not impressed with the argument of fluidity, I must say that the judgment of the Court was to impress—and depress—me with the inability which the Court then displayed to get at facts which were concealed rather than acknowledged.

I believe that it is increasingly recognized, as it should have been recognized at the time, that while the Court was essentially correct in finding the facts of the actions of the respondent state—the United States—it was essentially incorrect in its fact-finding in respect to the applicant state, Nicaragua. That miscarriage of justice was not to be attributed to the Court alone, since the applicant state purposefully and emphatically misled the Court about the truth of its actions while the respondent state was not present to refute those misrepresentations. The result was that the Court's judgment turned essential facts on their head, and found that no responsibility could be attributed to Nicaragua for acts in blatant violation of international law for which it indubitably was responsible.

A second divisive issue was not factual but legal. Even if Nicaragua had done what was charged, were such acts tantamount to an armed attack in response to which action in individual and collective self-defense could lawfully be undertaken? Here the Court moved from its inadequacies of fact-finding to innovations of legal doctrine, which, in my view, do not correspond to customary international law or the law of the Charter as they were before the Court's judgment and as they are today.

The United States charged that it was Nicaragua which was the aggressor, because, before (and after) the United States responded, Nicaragua had extended material support to an insurgency in a neighboring state, El Salvador, which was tantamount to an armed attack, consisting as it did of the provision of arms, a command-and-control apparatus for the continuing direction of the insurgency, sanctuary, and training for the insurgents, and ceaseless transit of the leadership of the insurgency between the territory of Nicaragua and the territory of El Salvador. The Court dealt with these allegations in two ways. It ignored critical elements of them, essentially reducing the multiple charges to the single charge of whether "the provision of arms to the opposition in another State constitutes an armed attack on that State."[3] Then, while refusing to attribute responsibility to the government of Nicaragua for the undeniable and undenied transfer of arms through its territory to the Salvadoran insurgents, it held that in any event the provision of arms could not be tantamount to an armed attack. Since there was no armed attack, there could be no self-defense, individual or collective.

I found difficulties with this disposition and still do. In the first place, customary international law, reflected on this issue by the Definition of Aggression adopted by the General Assembly of the United Nations after half a century of intense though intermittent negotiation, treats as an act of aggression the "substantial involvement" of a state in the sending of armed bands, groups, irregulars, or mercenaries which carry out acts of armed force against another state of such gravity as to amount to an actual armed attack conducted by regular forces.[4] There was in this case compelling evidence of such substantial involvement of Nicaragua (acting together with Cuba), since the flow of insurgents trained and armed by it, and of the leadership of those insurgents, from its territory to that of El Salvador was very substantial indeed and since those insurgents carried out armed attacks in the course of their insurgency equivalent to the armed attacks of regular forces. Such substantial involvement, as Professor Julius Stone put it in his critical analysis of the Definition of Aggression, gave rise "like any other direct aggression to response by self-defense under general international law and under Article 51 of the Charter."[5] While the Court for its part held that the Definition of the Aggression reflects customary international law, in effect it dismissed the import of the Definition on this paramount point by failing to deal seriously with Nicaragua's "substantial involvement." It addressed only the question of the provision of arms and on this question arrived at an answer at odds with the weight of the evidence before it.

In the second place, not only is the Court's judgment inconsistent with customary international law as expressed in the Definition of Aggression, it is also inconsistent with the law applied by the inter-American system in the very area at issue. The Organization of American States had earlier interpreted and applied the Inter-American Treaty of Reciprocal Assistance, the Rio Treaty, precisely to characterize acts very similar to those at issue in this case as "acts that possess characteristics of aggression and intervention" which could justify the essential rights of member states to "the use of self-defense in either individual or collective form, which could go so far as resort to armed force...."[6] The Court ignored this precedent.

In the third place, the Court's interpretation of the meaning of armed attack was inconsistent with the shared interpretation of the applicant and the respondent states in the case. They did not essentially differ on the law of self-defense but on the facts. Nicaragua admitted and indeed expounded the very law pleaded by the United States. Nicaragua set out in its pleading the extensive practice of the United Nations and the considerable commentaries of scholars which tend to equate acts of direct and indirect aggression. But Nicaragua maintained that the armed bands at issue in the case were organized and provisioned only by the United States and not by Nicaragua. The problem with the Nicaraguan argument on the facts was that it was untrue. But it remains remarkable that the Court should have arrived at conclusions of law so hard to reconcile with the shared interpretation of the parties.

Finally, there is the question that if the Court's construction of what is armed attack is not consistent with customary international law, the Definition of Aggression, the practice of the United Nations and the Organization of American States, and the shared interpretation of the parties to the case, is it nevertheless a sound view of the law *de lege ferenda?*

The argument for the Court's position is that a narrow construction of the meaning of "armed attack" produces a narrow ambit for the use of measures of self-defense, individual and collective. In the Charter era, states resorting to the use of force characteristically invoke self-defense, whether justifiably or not. If states cannot be heard to invoke measures of self-defense in response to actions by other states which, summarily speaking, constitute indirect rather than direct aggression, then there will be a desirable constraint on what in some cases will be unjustified resort to allegedly defensive measures.

In my view, this argument is superficially appealing but unpersuasive. The Court's judgment demonstrates just how unpersuasive it is.

Assuming for the sake of argument the charges against Nicaragua to be true (at any rate in the provision of arms to the Salvadoran insurgents), the Court treated its actions not as tantamount to armed attack but as acts of intervention. It then held that, while an armed attack would give rise to an entitlement to collective self-defense, a use of force of a lesser degree of gravity cannot produce any entitlement to take collective counter-measures involving the use of force. The acts of which the applicant state was accused, "even assuming them to have been established and imputable to the state," could only have justified proportionate counter-measures on the part of the state which had been the victim of these acts. "They could not justify counter-measures taken by a third State...and particularly could not justify intervention involving the use of force."[7]

One wonders from what source the Court derived this construction. It provides no foundation whatsoever for it in treaty law, customary international law, state practice, general principles of law, judicial decisions, or the writings of scholars. Presumably, it did not derive this construction from the provisions of the U.N. Charter, since it maintained that it was debarred from applying the Charter by reason of the invocation by the United States of the "Vandenberg" reservation; and the Charter does not require such a construction in any event. But quite apart from these infirmities and the obvious infirmities of application of this theory to the facts of the case then before it, let us consider the worrisome questions of principle which this innovative *dictum* imports.

Let us suppose that State A's support of the armed subversion of State B, while serious and effective enough to place the independence of State B in jeopardy, does not amount to an armed attack upon State B as the Court narrowly defines armed attack. Let us further suppose that State A acts against State B not only on its own behalf but together with a Great Power and with other significant international actors. If the Court's *obiter dictum* were to be treated as the law to which states deferred, other Great Powers and other states would be or could be essentially powerless to intervene effectively to preserve the independence of State B and other similarly situated states, most of which will be small. According to the Court, State B could take counter-measures against State A, but whether they would include measures of force is not said. What is said is that third states could not use force, whether or not the preservation of the territorial integrity or political independence of State B depended on the exertion of such measures. In short, the Court appears to offer, quite gratuitously, a prescription for the overthrow of weaker governments while denying potential victims what in some cases may be their only hope for survival.

There is more which is no less critical which could be said about the judgment of the Court in question—a judgment which in my view must remain just that, very much in question. While in principle the Court is a judicial organ which may adjudicate cases turning upon the continuing use of force, in practice the record to date is not wholly reassuring. What that may suggest for the future, however, is difficult to say.

Notes

1. Statute of the International Court of Justice, art. 36, para. 1.
2. *Id.* at art. 36, para. 2.
3. *Case Concerning Military and Paramilitary Activities In and Against Nicaragua (Nic. v. U.S.),* 1986 I.C.J. 14, at 119.
4. G.A. Res. 3314 (XXIX), Appendix, *quoted id.* at 103, 343.
5. J. STONE, CONFLICT THROUGH CONSENSUS 75 (1977), *quoted in* 1986 I.C.J. 14, at 343.
6. *Quoted in* 1986 I.C.J. 14, at 360.
7. *Id.* at 127.

30

Commentary on Judicial Procedures Relating to the Use of Force

Gennady Danilenko

Judicial procedures traditionally have not played a major role in the resolution of cases involving the use of force. From a purely legal point of view, there may be no inherent limitations or legal barriers to the adjudication of cases involving the use of force. States are generally unwilling, however, to submit cases to international adjudication. As the International Court of Justice (I.C.J.) stressed in the *Corfu Channel* case,[1] a policy of force is reserved for the most powerful states. They are now the permanent members of the Security Council, which under the Charter enjoy the legal right to remain judges in their own cases involving the use of force. Practice shows they actively use their right of veto for their own political purposes.

The argumentation of the United States in the *Nicaragua* case[2], which aimed at shifting the issue to the Security Council, dramatically illustrates the desire to avoid third-party assessment of the legality of the use of force. The Security Council's right of veto was the decisive factor for the United States in that case, and not technical considerations relating to judicial procedure as such. If the permanent members of the Security Council had the right of veto in the I.C.J., the United States probably would have taken a different position in the jurisdictional phase of the *Nicaragua* case.

Professor Richard Bilder has done an admirable job of articulating the pros and cons of judicial process. Unfortunately, in reality, this probably will not bring us too much comfort because there will always be pros on one side, and there will be cons on the other side. If there were pros for Kuwait, for example, at the same time there would be strong cons on the part of Iraq. One might, of course, believe that if Saddam Hussein had been a wise leader, he would have understood that judicial procedures would have been a convenient way to escape the imbroglio in which he entangled himself. In practice, however, such beliefs rarely take hold.

The bottom line is, of course, the absence of political will, especially on the part of major powers, to submit cases involving use of force to international adjudication. One can only hope that recent political changes will result in a reassessment of the prevailing policies of governments. In particular, one can only hope that there will be a new attitude toward compulsory jurisdiction in this matter. One of the main official reasons for the U.S. withdrawal from the compulsory jurisdiction of the I.C.J. was the fact that the United States was not able effectively to curtail Soviet expansionism, which was described as not bound by any legal provisions relating to compulsory jurisdiction. This political rationale now has largely disappeared. From the American perspective, the time has come for a more sober and technical reconsideration of the compulsory jurisdiction of the I.C.J., an exercise which hopefully would be free from particular considerations relating to the *Nicaragua* case.

The Soviet Union, for its part, proposed measures to strengthen the I.C.J. So far the results are not sensational. The Soviet Union has withdrawn reservations relating to a number of human rights treaties; it has been engaged in discussions with a number of permanent members of the Security Council relating to possible recognition of the compulsory jurisdiction of the I.C.J. on mutually-agreed terms. Whatever the outcome of these negotiations, however, nothing prevents the Soviet Union from accepting compulsory jurisdiction unilaterally, in accordance with Article 36(2) of the I.C.J. Statute, including in cases involving the use of force. If the Soviet Union is really serious about its commitment to the rule of law, and thus prepared to abandon former policies to use force to promote national interest, then it also should be willing to submit its actions to scrutiny by the I.C.J., which represents the main legal systems of the world and the main forms of civilization.

For international lawyers in both countries committed to the rule of law, the only way to accomplish this objective appears to be to work within their respective communities, encouraging both governments to join the compulsory jurisdiction system. If the Soviet Union and the United States were to join the system, it would provide the most persuasive evidence of their true commitment to the rule of law. Such a step also would provide an excellent example for others to follow.

I join Bilder in his concerns that current negotiations between the five permanent members appear to have excluded the use of force from the compulsory jurisdiction of the Court. I also support his suggestion that the issue should be fully debated within the relevant communities and parliaments. I think there is still a chance that a broad public debate may result in narrowing the proposed exclusion of use of force situations from the jurisdiction of the Court.

At the same time I think it would be a mistake to focus entirely on the current negotiations. In this connection, with all respect, I do not agree with the assessment of the proposed agreement on compulsory jurisdiction given by Bilder. He argues that the envisaged agreement would "presumably provide an alternative to, or perhaps in practice supplant, the Court's compulsory jurisdiction under Article 36(2) of its Statute; and indeed, perhaps even provisions for the Court's compulsory jurisdiction under compromissory clauses in other agreements."[3] Would the agreement really supplant Article 36(2), or would it just be a legal means to bring it into operation? Will the parties to it still have an opportunity to commit themselves unilaterally to wider obligations which were not achieved, or were not achievable within this particular arrangement? I think they will have such an opportunity, and therefore, the issues of the individual country's attitude towards the Court in general, of compulsory jurisdiction in particular, and more narrowly, of compulsory jurisdiction relating to use of force cases are still on the agenda.

In view of the new political situation in the international community in general and in the Security Council in particular, there may be new opportunities for adopting recommendations to submit cases involving use of force to international judicial settlement. In this, I agree with Bilder. One may also keep in mind that the prospects for enforcing the judgments may also be brighter. In addition, there may be more opportunity for advisory opinions of the Court. While, obviously, the advisory opinions are not binding, they may clarify legal issues involved, and therefore contribute to the resolution of particular disputes.

Advisory opinions are likely to have a wider role, namely the development and clarification of the applicable law. It appears that uncertainty about the applicable law relating to the use of force is one of the main factors explaining the unwillingness of governments to submit cases to judicial settlement. As a result, clarification of the applicable law is of great importance for the future of dispute settlements in this area.

Dissatisfaction with the existing law may, of course, be another factor. One may assume that, for instance, strict limitation of the use of force upheld by the *Nicaragua* decision may be one of the factors which will influence the U.S. attitude towards the compulsory system involving the use of force. Here, of course, we deal with the broader issue of stability and change in law, which should be both clarified and developed in order to reflect broader community consensus.

Wider exposure of states to compulsory jurisdiction in broader matters of law also will contribute to greater control over violence in the international community. If states are drawn into many specific legal relationships leading to compulsory judicial settlement, the use of force may be indirectly curtailed as well. There also are situations when technical disputes are used for demonstrations of force. The Gulf of Sidra incident obviously involved the policy of force, presented as a technical dispute over maritime spaces.[4] Taking this into account, one can probably argue that the availability of compulsory jurisdiction over technical issues will make it more difficult to resort openly to force. Therefore, there is every reason to press governments to recognize compulsory jurisdiction generally, not only in the area of non-use of force, but in many other areas of law too.

The characteristics of the international legal system are important. This is a system which has started to incorporate some innovative notions, like the notion of *jus cogens* and the concept of crimes of states. At the same time, this very system refuses to make any progress towards adoption of implementing mechanisms in areas of law affecting the vital interests of the international community. A student of international law may find it interesting how much energy and time have been spent in order to loosen the consent requirements in the area of international law-making. The time may have come to channel that kind of creative energy into finding the ways which would compel states to submit disputes involving the interpretation and implementation of basic community rules of behavior, in particular the rules involving the use of force to community judgments. The principle of non-use of force, which was recognized by the I.C.J. in the *Nicaragua* case as belonging to the corpus of *jus cogens*[5], is a norm which obviously affects the vital interests of the international community. From a broad community perspective, it is clear that no state should be immune from community judgment of its behavior in this vital area of law.

Notes

1. 1949 I.C.J. 4, 244.
2. *Case Concerning Military and Paramilitary Activities In and Against Nicaragua (Nic. v. U.S.)*, 1984 I.C.J. 392 (Jurisdiction and Admissibility), *reprinted in* 24 I.L.M. 59 (1985).
3. *See* Bilder, *supra* ch. 28, at 270.
4. *U.S., Citing Libyan Fire, Reports Attacking a Missile Site and Setting 2 Ships Ablaze*, N.Y. Times, March 25, 1986, at A1, col. 6; *see also, Libya's Gulf Claim: 13 Year Dispute with U.S.*, N.Y. Times, March 25, 1986, at A11, col. 1.
5. 1986 I.C.J. 100.

31

Commentary on Formal Dispute Mechanisms Other than the International Court of Justice

Barry Carter

Professor Richard Bilder presents a balanced, thorough analysis of the issues. I share his general views. Here I will focus on one issue and try to push a little beyond where Bilder ends.

When considering disputes involving the use of force, the United States and other countries ought to focus more on the possibilities for using formal dispute mechanisms other than the International Court of Justice (I.C.J.). We should especially consider arbitration. I propose this even though I have a great deal of respect for the I.C.J.

There is an important role for mechanisms other than the I.C.J. in the future. Too often today, when people (especially public international law experts) begin talking about resolving major disputes among states, they initially refer to the I.C.J. For example, *The New York Times* suggested that maybe the I.C.J should be brought into the Iraq-Kuwait border dispute. My answer is: why not arbitration or some other method?

Arbitration admittedly has had somewhat of a mixed history in the past. It is like an empty vessel that the parties can shape and control. Arbitration provides the parties much more flexibility and discretion than the I.C.J., whose structure and rules have already been largely determined by the international community.

The goal is to encourage states to accept the use of formal dispute mechanisms when those states have hesitated to use such institutions often in the past. It will often be going to the other extreme to ask the states to swallow entirely the whole I.C.J. with its community-imposed rules, or even the I.C.J. chambers approach which gives the parties only a little more say.

Arbitration allows each state to select one arbitrator (assuming there are three or more arbitrators). The party can select an expert on the issues involved and, frankly, someone who appreciates the state's views. The state can negotiate with the other disputing party or parties as to what substantive rules and which procedural rules apply, including the question of confidentiality.

An important advantage of arbitration can be enforceability. Most arbitral awards for money damages would be enforceable under the New York Convention on the Recognition and Enforcement of Foreign Arbitral Awards, which has been ratified by over eighty states, including all the major industrialized countries. Recently, a U.S. court of appeals ruled that a decision against a U.S. company by the Iran-U.S. Claims Tribunal was enforceable in the United States under the New York Convention.[1] Further, since arbitration is largely a vehicle of the parties' design, they can add specific wrinkles to reflect a party's needs or the special circumstances.

Alternatively, the parties might try other methods to resolve their disputes. For example, one potentially helpful procedure is that followed by the dispute panels of the General Agreement on Tariffs and Trade. The panel initially provides its report and conclusions privately to the parties, and allows the parties to comment and even take steps in accord with the panel's views. Only later is the panel's report made available to non-parties. Other helpful institutions and approaches can be found in the European regional courts, both the Court of Justice for the European Communities and the European Court of Human Rights.

The relative usefulness of the various international dispute resolution institutions is suggested in part by the frequency with which they are resorted to, even though these institutions might be handling different kinds of cases among different types of parties. Arbitration is a growth stock industry. The International Chamber of Commerce has over 300 new arbitration cases a year, 20 percent of which involve a governmental entity. The American Arbitration Association has over 130 international arbitration cases a year. The Canada-U.S. Free Trade Agreement has already had at least fifteen requests for arbitration panels, even though the Agreement only became effective in 1989.

The European regional courts are also very active. The European Community's Court of Justice had 385 cases brought to it in 1989. Its own court of first instance, or trial court, had to be organized in September 1989 to meet the press of the Court's business. The European Court on Human Rights has received about thirty new cases each year for the past several years.

Compare all this activity to the I.C.J. In its forty-five years, it has had a total of about eighty-two cases, or an average of less than two per year. There were eight pending in the fall of 1990, but some have been there for years and even this number of cases—and the cases themselves—is not particularly impressive.

Why is there this apparent reluctance to use the I.C.J.? First, its judgments are often unenforced. Recalcitrant states have on occasion refused to comply voluntarily with the court's judgment, and the Security Council has yet to back any enforcement measures in those situations.[2] Even with the success of the Security Council in forging a consensus on U.N. resolutions in the Iraq-Kuwait matter, the veto still remains as a potential obstacle to future enforcement of I.C.J. decisions.

The Court also has been burdened by the reactions to some of its early decisions, by its relatively rigid procedures, and by lack of confidentiality. A state that wants prompt resolution of a dispute finds this cumbersome body uninviting. The 15 judges usually only ask what the Chief Judge has cleared in advance. Also, the procedures are not well-designed for fact-finding, and a long time usually passes before the Court renders a decision, even with its light caseload.

The 1978 revised rules of the Court have made it easier for a state to bring cases before a three or five-judge "chamber" (or panel), in which each country could have one of its nationals as judge and a voice regarding the selection of other judges (besides the national for the other party). This begins to look a little like arbitration, but it still lacks flexibility. The parties have much less control over the procedures and norms. Moreover, a national judge might have been selected for the I.C.J. pursuant to the international procedure before the present government came into power. As a result, he or she might not be as sensitive to the government's views as would be a newly designated arbitrator. The I.C.J. chambers approach also still has the potentially serious problem of judgments not being effectively enforced.

In sum, the I.C.J. should clearly exist and steps to improve and strengthen it should be encouraged. At the same time, however, the United States and other countries should not overlook—indeed, they should actively consider—international arbitration, regional courts, and other methods of dispute resolution when it comes to questions about the use of force.

Notes

1. *Ministry of Defense of the Islamic Republic of Iran v. Gould, Inc.*, 887 F. 2d 1357 (9th Cir. 1989), *cert. denied,* 110 S. Ct. 1319 (1990).

2. Besides the recent, much publicized refusal by the United States to abide by the Court's judgment in the *Nicaragua* case, let me recall the I.C.J.'s first decision in a contentious case—the *Corfu Channel* case. In 1949 the I.C.J. determined that Albania should pay monetary damages to the United Kingdom for damages to British naval ships. Over forty years later, Albania has yet to do so.

About the Book and Editors

Momentous events of recent years have shown the tremendous potential for developing and applying international law, even in the area that has always presented the greatest challenge to the rule of law—the use of force. The collaborative response by the United States, the Soviet Union, and other major powers to the Iraqi army's invasion and occupation of Kuwait showed unprecedented unity on the relevance of international law, its rules, and its enforceability through decisions of the UN Security Council. What explains this historic convergence of views? What differences remain about the legality of using armed force in the new international order that is emerging with the end of the Cold War?

Law and Force in the New International Order offers a timely and comprehensive inquiry into the growing number of situations where the temptation or necessity to use military force confronts the tenets of international law. Distinguished American and Soviet legal scholars and practitioners explore the idea of the primacy of law over politics, the notion held by some that U.S. military force may be applied for the sake of democracy at a time when Moscow has rejected the Brezhnev Doctrine, the tension between collective security and collective self-defense during the Iraq-Kuwait crisis, and the prospects for the use of force being authorized by the United Nations and regional organizations. The contributors also examine the vexing legal issues raised by interventions to protect human rights, to overthrow "illegitimate" regimes, and to combat international terrorism and drug trafficking; the restraints on the use of force promised by new arms control agreements; and the future role of the World Court and other tribunals in preventing or settling disputes involving the threat or use of force.

Lori Fisler Damrosch is professor of law at Columbia University. **David J. Scheffer** is senior associate at the Carnegie Endowment for International Peace.

Index*

* *Page number occasionally refers to information located in the text of a footnote cited on the referenced page.*

www.ingramcontent.com/pod-product-compliance
Lightning Source LLC
LaVergne TN
LVHW011111300926
849160LV00008B/346
9780367154257